L.A.
Job Market
Handbook

Every effort has been made to obtain the most accurate, up-to-the-minute information possible for this book. However, the job market changes rapidly and so do titles, addresses, and phone numbers. Consequently, we cannot guarantee the currency of every item presented. We regret if any discrepancies have worked their way in since the time of printing. Any updates, corrections, or suggestions should be sent to the publisher.

How to Order:

Quantity discounts are available from the publisher, Prima Publishing & Communications, P.O. Box 1260EB, Rocklin, CA 95677; telephone (916) 624-5718. On your letterhead include information concerning the intended use of the books and the number of books you wish to purchase.

U.S. Bookstores and Libraries: Please submit all orders to St. Martin's Press, 175 Fifth Avenue, New York, NY 10010; telephone (212) 674-5151.

E. PAGE BUCY

L.A.
Job Market
Handbook

This book is printed on recycled paper.

Prima Publishing & Communications
P.O. Box 1260EB
Rocklin, CA 95677
(916) 624-5718

Typography by Col D'var Graphics
Production by Carol Dondrea, Bookman Productions
Copyediting by Anne Montague
Interior Design by Renee Deprey
Jacket design by The Dunlavey Studio

Prima Publishing & Communications

Library of Congress Cataloging-in-Publication Data

Bucy, E. Page, 1963–
    L.A. job market handbook / by E. Page Bucy.
        p.   cm.
    Includes bibliographical references and index.
    ISBN 1-55958-046-1
    1. Job hunting—California—Los Angeles Metropolitan Area—Handbooks, manuals, etc. I. Title.
HF5382. 75. U62L72   1990   90-8676
650 . 14 ' 09794 ' 94—dc20   CIP

90 91 92 93 RRD 10 9 8 7 6 5 4 3 2 1

Printed in the United States of America

To my friends and colleagues
displaced by the unfortunate closure
of the Los Angeles Herald Examiner.

CONTENTS

Rumors had been circulating for months. But when the axe fell, it fell suddenly. With a brief announcement by Hearst Corp. Vice President Robert Danzig that began with the words, "It is with great regret that we have made this decision to close the *Los Angeles Herald Examiner* . . . ," some 775 dedicated employees of the city's second-largest metropolitan daily newspaper were instantly out of work. I was one of them.

More and more, career change is entirely unpredicted and unplanned. An unexpected offer may come over the telephone. A company may implement a restructuring or downsizing plan that results in mass layoffs, even of valued, veteran employees. Or, in the case of those who lost their jobs the day the *Herald Examiner* printed its final edition (Nov. 2, 1989), unemployment may come abruptly and without warning.

The paper's demise had been a long time in coming and everyone knew it was perhaps inevitable—a decade-long strike dating back some 20 years had doomed any hope of a turnaround. But when it finally happened, the shock over losing your job was still real, the confusion over what to do disorienting. Some of the area's finest journalists, and an even larger contingent of support staff, were thrown out of work. It's hard to fathom just what a plant closing means until you experience one.

First, there is this sort of weird hysteria that winds into a strange celebration party at the end of the day, although no one's quite sure what they're celebrating—the relief of not having to work with an axe over your head any longer, or the liberation from responsibility. The evening is filled with reminiscences of good, and not so good, times past. You rejoice in the fact that you'll never have to answer to your boss again. You're glad for having remained diplomatic through it all.

The cold, gray reality of loss begins to hit you when, on the day after, you perform the solemn ritual of cleaning out your desk and packing your belongings in the dead quiet of your now-former office. You take your belongings home, only there's no place for them there. They belong at work. You store them somewhere temporarily, just as you have to temporarily store your professional aspirations. Your career has been derailed.

Then come the postmortem gatherings. Finally, after you attend enough wake parties, and your vague sense of relief turns into a very real feeling of apprehension about your immediate future, you start to realize that you're neither mourning nor socializing any longer, only postponing the inevitable: getting on with your life.

The apprehension that sets in after a job loss isn't limited to people involved in plant closings, downsizings, or restructuring efforts; it applies to anyone unhappy with his or her current position, company, or career. If you're thinking about changing careers, you're not alone. The U.S. Department of Labor reports that the average American entering the workforce today will change careers—not just jobs, but careers—three times. Some private experts call that estimate conservative.

The search for meaningful employment isn't easy. Indeed, it probably ranks as one of the most difficult journeys in life. For some, job satisfaction equals the amount of money earned. Others define it as a process: the intellectual chase, or the art of the deal. Still others view career gratification in terms of psychic income—the intangible rewards derived from making the world a better place to live. However you perceive job satisfaction, the longer you avoid the issue, the longer it will take to achieve happiness. And after all, isn't that what the search for meaningful employment is all about?

Regardless of career field, there is a vast difference between holding a job you are capable of doing and pursuing a career you truly delight in and identify with. Job satisfaction begins when you enjoy the unavoidable day-to-day tasks of your job. "Do what you love, the money will follow." There's some truth to that statement, worn out as it is.

Another cliché worth mentioning is that success doesn't always come easy. By and large, the most successful are those who have persisted in an idea, purpose, or task despite the obstacles confronting them. In a word, they have persevered. In my interviews with over 400 working professionals and industry experts across a broad spectrum of career fields, perseverance would come up time and again as a quality necessary to succeed.

Although I started writing this book before the *Herald Examiner* closed, its potential importance didn't really hit me until I personally was out of a job. Rather than rush back into another reporting position and give the book only half my attention, I decided to take some time off and write it the way it ought to be written—with all the energy, information, and relevance of a front-page news story. I felt the reader deserved at least this much, for I now know firsthand how trying it is to experience a job loss, and how frustrating the ensuing job search can be.

The *L.A. Job Market Handbook* highlights the fastest-growing, best-paying, and most promising career fields in Los Angeles and Orange counties and describes how to gain employment in them. To help the job seeker or career changer make informed life decisions, I have incorporated employment projections and addressed emerging job trends in my chapters on individual careers. The book also features insights and advice from working professionals—*real* people in *real* jobs.

At the end of each chapter you will find up-to-date reference lists providing the addresses of key employers and, where relevant, professional organizations, publications, directories, and recommended reading lists for further research. Where possible, I have included tables illustrating salary schedules and career ladders. The final section covers the basic aspects of a job search.

The Southern California region is changing rapidly both structurally and demographically. The last 10 years have witnessed dramatic change. The next 10 will see even more. Inasmuch as the L.A. job market is a frontier for the future, there are issues emerging here that are likely to spread throughout the workforce and workplace in other parts of the country in the years ahead, if they haven't already.

In specially designated "Career Trends" chapters, I have addressed the issues associated with such cutting-edge topics as telecommuting, job sharing, job stress, working for a foreign employer, job loss, relocation, and new office technologies. In addition, the book includes advice-oriented chapters for athletes making the transition from the playing field to the job market and for job seekers contemplating vocational training.

Each year, people spend thousands of dollars on career training they might not need or that doesn't adequately prepare them for a career. The Career Trends chapter on how to choose a vocational school lays out the argument for and against private programs, including how much some of them cost, while describing the benefits and drawbacks to public community colleges. Finally, it lists the agencies to check with if you are unsure about the reputation of a particular school.

The Los Angeles area, expected to generate some 3 million new employment opportunities over the next 20 years, is the premier job market in the country. But it is not self-explanatory;

it comes with no set of instructions. There isn't even a comprehensive business directory. There are plenty of frivolous books on the market that either perpetuate L.A.'s myths or merely list addresses. Precious few provide any substantive and really useful information. The *L.A. Job Market Handbook* promises to fill that void.

As of this writing, some six months after the *Herald Examiner's* closure, many former staff members are still looking for a new career that suits them. Some, unfortunately, are floundering. Many, however, have used the opportunity as a springboard for advancement and are working for larger newspapers, or have found meaningful self-employment as freelancers (or authors). Still others have retired early or have left the field of journalism altogether.

What happened at the *Herald Examiner* is happening all over the country. People are losing their jobs en masse, frequently through no fault of their own, and are left to deal with the consequences. An important thing to remember during these tumultuous times is that individual jobs may come and go, but the skills you learn and the experience you gain remain. Indeed, skills from one career are often directly, or indirectly, transferable to another.

This book, while not intended to serve as a substitute for professional career counseling, nevertheless provides a solid foundation for career exploration—of the job market in general and the Los Angeles area in particular. I have endeavored to make it as relevant and helpful as possible for the graduating student and seasoned professional alike. My hope is that a broad range of job seekers and career changers will find this book useful in their search for meaningful employment and the ongoing quest to improve the quality of their working lives.

E. Page Bucy

Los Angeles, CA
April 1990

ACKNOWLEDGMENTS

I would like to thank the following people, without whom this book project would not have been possible. From the editorial department of the late, great *Los Angeles Herald Examiner*, editor-in-chief Max McCrohon, managing editor John Oppedahl, and city editor Larry Burrough, for calling on me to write a careers column. From the Money section of the paper, Kathleen Ingley and Don Nicoson for their guidance and editing skill, Henry Unger for his business insights, Pamela Yip for her general helpfulness, and Darcelle Infante for her watchful and critical eye.

From the *Herald Examiner's* former library staff, David Cappoli, Jamil "Jimmy Boy" Rizvi, Ann Sausedo, and Kathy Smith, for providing facts and reference materials when I needed them. To all of the newspaper's former staff, you have my utmost respect and admiration. Good luck in your future endeavors.

From the USC School of Journalism, a special thank you to professor A. J. "Jack" Langguth, for his inspiration and example, professor Jonathan Kotler for his assistance, and Ester Ramirez of the career advisement office for her graciousness and, well, for being Ester. My graduate journalism experience was instrumental in this book's formation. To all of my journalism compadres newly thrust into the job market, this book's also for you.

My undying gratitude goes out to Jack Kyser of the Los Angeles Area Chamber of Commerce for his extraordinary helpfulness, insight, and commentary, not to mention vast repertoire of bad jokes.

It takes many people to make a project of this scope happen. Chief among these are my sources. I wish to extend my heartfelt thanks to the over 400 working professionals who willingly offered their valuable insights in sometimes time-consuming interviews that are the basis for this book. Their names are too numerous to mention here, but you will get to know them in the pages ahead.

For facilitating several of my interviews, a personal thank-you to public relations specialists John Watson and Beth Hill of UCLA Extension, Gregory Elliott of Toyota Motor Sales USA, Todd Cooley of Fleishman-Hillard, James Hart of the Northrop

xvi L.A. JOB MARKET HANDBOOK

Corp., John Booth of TRW, and Allen Buis of Rockwell International.

I also wish to thank my dear friends Christopher Cagle and Diane Radich, for sharing my enthusiasm and offering advice on any number of subjects. My deepest appreciation, however, is reserved for Renee Sanchez, for supporting me through this arduous time and encouraging me to press on when I needed to hear it most.

The following people all contributed their expertise in one way or another, mostly for background, but sometimes providing nothing more than a friendly pat on the back or steer in the right direction: David R. Alexander, Dimitri Andritsakis, Katherine Arbolida, Roger Bartley, Geoff Baum, Scott Benjamin, Mike Brozda, Michael J. Filas, Deanna Hodgin, Roy M. Hughes Jr., Neil and Bert Jayasekera, Len Lipton, A. J. Matel, Dev Mazumdar, Alan Nakamura, Shaun O'Sullivan, Edgar Regalado, Andrew Reichwald, Mark Roberson, George Ruiz, Steven P. Wheeler, and Jake Wirtschafter.

I also wish to thank my parents for their encouragement and steadfast support. Throughout the years, they have allowed me the freedom to cultivate my own potential.

Many thanks also to the myriad membership organizations and local, state, and federal agencies that provided me with useful information: the California Department of Education, Department of Finance, Employment Development Department, Los Angeles Area Chamber of Commerce, City and County of Los Angeles, City of Torrance Library, International Trade Commission, U.S. Customs, U.S. Department of Labor, the CIA, DEA, FBI, IRS, NASA, RTD, LACTC, CHP, LAPD, LAFD, and the Los Angeles County Sheriff's Department and Marshal's Department, just to name a few.

Lastly, I would like to thank my publisher, Ben Dominitz, for having faith in my idea, and my agent, Michael Hamilburg, who was especially helpful in the book's early stages. Hats off also to the able staff at Prima Publishing, especially Laura Glassover and Jennifer Basye, for whom no detail was too small, no concern too trivial. Thanks also to Carol Dondrea of Bookman Productions for seeing the project through to completion, to Renee Deprey for her superb design work, and to Anne Montague, copy editor extraordinaire.

INTRODUCTION

The "Big Orange"

*Understanding the Los Angeles
five-county area.*

By Jack Kyser, chief economist
Los Angeles Area Chamber of Commerce

So it's time to find a job in the "Big Orange"—our affectionate
nickname for Los Angeles, Orange, Riverside, San Bernardino,
and Ventura counties. It's a big, fast-changing region whose size
and diversity often daunt newcomers. Almost everything about
the five-county area seems larger than life, including both the
opportunities and the challenges.

The dynamic Big Orange will be setting the pace for the rest
of the nation as we head into the 21st century. But landing a
job, or finding a new one, does take a little bit of effort. As
a job seeker or career changer, one of the first frustrations you
may encounter in your search is that there is no complete business
directory available for any of the five counties.

Why not, you ask? Because the Big Orange is so vast. With
over 14.4 million residents, the greater Los Angeles area is larger
in population than all but the states of California, New York,
and Texas. During the 1980s, the Big Orange added 2.9 million
residents and 1.3 million jobs. At last count, there were over
335,000 business firms in the area employing some 6.3 million
people. In the decade ahead, the five-county area should create
another 1.1 million jobs, with the biggest gains coming in retail
trade, business services, and state and local government (including
education).

Another interesting measure of size—and opportunity—is gross
product. The Big Orange produces over $360 billion in goods
and services each year (nearly half of the state of California's

annual output of $740 billion), which would rank the regional economy about 10th among the nations of the world, given the value of the U.S. dollar on the day you do your comparison. Viewed independently, the greater Los Angeles economy outperforms the countries of Brazil, Spain, India, the Netherlands, and Australia. Not a bad showing for an area some people still refer to as "La-La Land."

There are many myths about the Big Orange. One holds that the Los Angeles area is driven by only a "three-cylinder" economy: aerospace, motion picture and television production, and tourism. Not true. Currently, there are seven basic industries— eight if you count higher education. Basic industries offer a good or service that people from outside the area want to buy. This economic diversity developed during the 1980s, and was sparked in part by the economic and trade boom in the Pacific Rim, the defense buildup of the Reagan administration, and the unexpected surge in population.

The seven basic industries of the Los Angeles area, ranked by employment size, are as follows:

- **Business and financial services.** This includes banks, both domestic and foreign, savings and loans, brokerage firms and investment banks, accounting firms, law firms, and architectural and engineering firms. In the 1990s, business and financial services will continue to grow as Los Angeles builds as the financial center of the West Coast. Banks and especially savings and loans are currently experiencing some turmoil, but should settle down by mid-decade. Architects and engineers should do quite well in the decade ahead, given the massive need for infrastructure improvement locally, nationally, and internationally. Over 760,000 people are at work in these industries.

- **Tourism.** As more and more foreign tourists flock to Los Angeles, knowing a second language is becoming increasingly important to work in this industry. The Walt Disney Co. has announced plans for a major expansion of its facilities in either Anaheim or Long Beach, and other theme parks are expected to wage a competitive response. Convention centers in the cities of Anaheim, Long Beach, and Los Angeles are also being expanded, and many new hotels and resorts are on the drawing boards, so the 1990s should be a decade of strong growth for this industry. Some 500,000 people now work in tourism.

- **Aerospace/high tech.** Yes, the defense budget is being cut back, and there have been layoffs at local aerospace firms. However, the outlook for commercial aircraft production and rebuilding—a significant component of the aerospace industry—as well as for space exploration, is very bright. Moreover, the aerospace workforce is aging, and there are shortfalls in some specialized engineering skills, such as composite materials applications. There definitely will be job opportunity in this industry in the years ahead. About 420,000 people are employed in aerospace and high tech.

- **Wholesale trade/distribution.** A frequently overlooked fact about Los Angeles is its position as the second-largest wholesale trade and distribution center in the United States. Major product categories include motor vehicles—that's the Japanese influence—electronics, furniture, jewelry, toys, apparel, and food products. Look for slow, steady growth here in the 1990s, adding to the current base of over 400,000 workers.

- **Health services.** Given a population that is both growing and aging, and the ongoing challenge presented by AIDS and other diseases, the health care industry in the Los Angeles area will continue to boom in the 1990s. And the Big Orange has an impressive educational infrastructure that will keep it on the cutting edge in health care, including four medical schools, two dental schools, and a host of specialized medical centers such as the Estelle Doheny and Jules Stein eye clinics, the House Ear Institute, and the City of Hope. More than 370,000 people are employed in health services in the five-county area.

- **Direct international trade.** Import/export activity has had an enormous impact on the Los Angeles–area economy. In a historically significant development, the twin ports of Long Beach and Los Angeles recently surpassed New York as the nation's busiest commercial gateways in terms of shipping tonnage. And Los Angeles ranks a close second after New York in value of two-way trade handled—$101 billion in 1989. The prospects for the 1990s are bright, as the economies of the Los Angeles area's Pacific Rim trading partners continue to grow. Moreover, Los Angeles has strong, albeit unrecognized, trade ties with Western Europe. International investment is another major force in Los Angeles, and you could well find yourself working for an Asian- or European-owned firm. Regionally, some 260,000 people are directly involved in international trade activities.

- **The creative industries.** This is a broad category that includes everything from apparel and furniture design and manufacturing to motion picture and television production. While furniture and home decoration item design should thrive in the 1990s, the actual manufacturing process is expected to decline due to air quality constraints. The local apparel industry will also continue to expand, but the real growth star of the creative industries will be the movies. Deregulation of foreign television markets combined with increased foreign investment and new methods of delivering the product, namely, by cable and videocassettes, should make the 1990s a golden decade for Hollywood. And while you may think in terms of the fabled big studios, be aware that the bulk of the jobs are at smaller firms. Nearly 240,000 people work in the creative industries.

This diversified economic base sustains and cushions the five-county area's economy. It will be a rare time indeed when all seven basic industries are in the dumps. When one employment sector enters a leveling-off period, other areas of job opportunity are usually going great guns. For example, the slowdown in defense activity in the 1990s will be offset by strong gains in international trade and a resurgence in both motion picture/TV production and tourism.

In peeling the Big Orange, we must be frank and admit that the five-county area, for all its advantages, does have its problems: principally, traffic congestion, declining air quality, a precarious water supply, a troubled K-12 educational system, and crime. To listen to the news media, you would get the impression that these problems are getting worse, and that nothing is being done to solve them. This is another myth about Los Angeles. But aggressive action is being taken on several of these fronts, and the effort to find solutions will actually create new job opportunities in the years ahead.

For example, Los Angeles is the most active region in the nation in terms of mass transit development. One light rail line (Long Beach to Los Angeles) is up and running, work is under way on additional lines, a subway is being built, and area planners are looking at starting a traditional rail commuter service. Building and running this extensive transit network will create thousands more jobs, as will maintaining our famed freeway system.

On the air quality front, the South Coast Air Quality Management District (AQMD) has implemented an air quality management plan that calls for major changes in the way we live and do business. One of the key elements of this plan, Regulation 15, requires companies that employ 100 or more people to hire an employee transportation coordinator and prepare an annual trip reduction plan. The jury is still out on the socioeconomic impact of this plan, but again, some new types of jobs will be created. Waste management is another area of environmental concern, and some new agencies will be formed to handle this problem.

In the educational arena, the main challenge for the area's school districts is accommodating a growing multicultural enrollment in elementary and secondary schools while maintaining, if not improving, the quality of education. New schools are currently being built, and there is a need for more teachers. The business community, no longer a distant critic, is taking a more active role in solving this problem, sponsoring programs like the Los Angeles Educational Partnership, which has raised $10 million since 1984 for innovative educational programs, and First Break, which offers high school students summer jobs.

On the crime front, local leaders grappling with this issue are increasingly realizing that one answer, especially in the inner city, may be an aggressive economic development program. The idea here is that more and better jobs for the poor and disadvantaged will take away some of the allure of gangs for their children. In the 1990s, there will be many opportunities for those who want to work in the public and social service sector.

I am that rare bird, a native Angeleno. If you are moving to Los Angeles from out of the area, my advice is not to put down roots too firmly. Concentrations of industries are scattered throughout the 34,000-square-mile five-county area. For banking and finance, downtown Los Angeles is where the action is. The entertainment industry, on the other hand, reaches from West Los Angeles/Culver City, to Hollywood (of course), to Universal City/Burbank. If it's aerospace you're interested in, there are industry concentrations in El Segundo/Redondo Beach, the West San Fernando Valley, Palmdale/Lancaster, and in Long Beach/Huntington Beach.

Once you get a job, you can determine which area appeals

to you in terms of lifestyle, versus how much time you want to spend commuting to work, which can be a major consideration. The diversity of lifestyles that can be found here is one of the attractions of the Los Angeles area. You can pursue almost any way of life you want, from beachfront casual to Westside chic, Midwestern-style quiet to rustic retreats in canyons and foothills.

The Big Orange has offered and will continue to offer many and diverse job opportunities, as you will see by reading this book. But many people claim that the sprawling five-county area is too big and impersonal for them. Perhaps the best way to overcome this feeling is to find a civic or professional association and get involved. Not only will you make some new friends, but you may well be able to help the Los Angeles area solve some of its problems.

Good luck job hunting!

Los Angeles, CA
April 1990

SECTION 1

Careers in Finance and World Trade

CHAPTER 1

Banking

Deregulation has fueled turmoil, opportunity at L.A. area financial institutions.

Changes are being made in the financial community, and we're not talking small changes. Careers in banking will be anything but traditional over the next few years, according to industry analysts and bank personnel officers. Financial institutions, responding to increased competition brought on by deregulation, are undergoing rapid transformation. This has created opportunities for a new breed of bankers who are more sales-savvy and service-oriented than their staid predecessors.

"People who have been in banking for years and years are saying this is not what it used to be," said Paula Deslatte, career planning coordinator at First Interstate Bank's corporate headquarters in downtown Los Angeles. "What used to be a very stable environment is no longer. Banking is going through a period of total change."

Like other service industries, banks are now concerned about putting the needs of the customer first. Consequently, the business is becoming more complicated and consumer-driven.

To compete with banks, solvent savings and loan associations have expanded their range of products. Leading California S&Ls that are financially sound include Great Western, Home Savings, California Federal, and Glendale Federal, said Jack Kyser, chief economist for the Los Angeles Area Chamber of Commerce.

Banks have introduced a wider array of services than ever before, such as 24-hour customer service lines, banking by telephone, and longer hours. Thanks to the recent passing of Proposition 103, banks in California will also be able to sell insurance, allowing them to compete with insurance companies in a lucrative market that was virtually monopolized before.

"The industry used to move at a glacial pace. Now it is very fast-moving," Kyser said. "Everybody used to joke about 'bankers hours' and being out on the golf course. That's no more. It's just a hell of a competitive market out there."

It will be even more competitive in 1991, when the California market will open to out-of-state banks. Deregulation is expected to result in the first nationwide banking system and cause further upheaval in the way financial institutions do business.

In this imminent financial free-for-all, there are early rumblings that savings and loans, which have traditionally focused on the home lending market, may become passé. Some experts, including Carl Reichart, chairman of Wells Fargo Bank, have predicted that the troubled savings and loan industry will be obsolete in as little as five years. What impact will this transitional period have on the job market? "It's going to mean more turmoil than employment," Kyser said. "I think the number of jobs is going to increase, but very, very slowly."

Inevitably, as Los Angeles builds as the financial center of the West Coast, the number of finance-related jobs will gradually rise. In L.A. County, the number of people employed in commercial, mortgage, and investment banks as well as S&Ls and brokerage firms reached 138,200 in 1987. By 1992, the number of finance jobs is expected to increase to 155,800, according to Employment Development Department projections. To this, add another 36,525 openings projected for Orange County.

Even so, the last few years have witnessed the trimming of several thousand finance-related jobs, especially in banking. Some 64,517 people were employed by L.A.-area banks in 1986, compared to 66,291 in 1980, Kyser said. (An estimated 72,300 jobs are projected for 1992.) "It's a scary time in banking," said Deslatte of First Interstate, "but there are a lot of good, solid areas for people to start in and make some moves."

Over the next few years, the greatest opportunities in banking are less likely to be at corporate headquarters than at the branch level, where the small but crucial individual battles for consumer loyalty are taking place. "A branch position can be a good foundation for anywhere you want to go," Deslatte said.

"Branch operations offers the most opportunity for upward mobility," affirmed Jerry Airheart, personnel officer for

Community Bank in Pasadena, the ninth-largest bank based in L.A. County. "It's the mainstay of our entire bank."

Community Bank, which requires applicants to have previous banking experience on top of formal training in banking procedures, also looks for employees who have well-developed customer service skills, Airheart said. Being able to market financial services is now central to a career in banking.

The largest number of entry-level positions are for tellers, or what Coast Savings and Loan—the sixth-largest S&L with headquarters in the county—now calls savings representatives. Tellers perform a variety of duties. They take deposits and cash checks, update accounts calculating interest, accept loan payments, and sell travelers' checks and money orders. With additional experience, they may open new accounts and eventually be promoted into supervisory positions.

In evaluating applicants for teller positions, financial institutions look for previous experience in sales, cash handling, and dealing with the public. Basic computer skills and the ability to use a keyboard as well as a 10-by-touch adding machine are also required. Being detail-oriented and having a math or accounting background are definite pluses.

"A bank may want an applicant who knows the difference between a credit and a debit, but they also want someone who has worked with people," said Tracy Bolleter, a placement counselor for the Banking Institute, a private vocational school in Los Angeles that offers bank operations and lender training. "If you get someone with both of those skills, they're gold."

At First Interstate Bank, prospective tellers and customer service representatives are evaulated on the basis of their people skills, sales ability, and technical proficiency, Deslatte said. "We're looking for someone who has done more than what he or she needs to do just to get by, someone who doesn't expect to work a 9 to 5 job. Regular hours for banking aren't what they used to be. Officers at First Interstate probably work a 10-hour day."

Usually the primary customer contacts for any company, customer service reps handle inquiries of all kinds by phone and in person, taking action on customer requests, fielding complaints, providing information on prices and services and, increasingly, marketing additional bank services.

Like tellers, customer service reps are expected to have some experience in dealing with the public, a positive attitude, and familiarity with what the bank has to offer. First and foremost, they must enjoy people contact. "You have to have a real enthusiasm for working with others and the ability not to get rattled," said Janice Wainright, vice president and manager of First Interstate Bank's downtown Los Angeles branch. "You do have customers who get upset."

Customer service reps may be promoted to the position of supervisor and then customer service manager, the second-highest post at most of First Interstate's branch offices, Wainright said. (For more information on customer service, see Chapter 25.)

As financial institutions have moved to extend their hours and open their doors on Saturday, they've been hiring part-time tellers to fill in the gaps. In fact, there is a trend toward replacing full-time tellers with part-time employees, since they save the company money. Full-time tellers make $950 to $1,250 a month to start; part-timers earn about $7.50 an hour.

While certain basic skills are required as a foundation for employment in financial services, most larger institutions provide their own training for those just entering the field. A college degree isn't mandatory to rise in the ranks of financial institutions, but many banks offer officer development trainee programs for degree holders.

These programs, which typically entail a year's worth of intensive on-the-job and classroom training after graduation from a university, place trainees on direct career paths into management. After being exposed to a variety of departments and work situations, they are usually get junior officer positions at branch offices.

Private vocational schools also provide training for selected positions. The Banking Institute, for instance, offers a four-month certificate program in bank operations and lending for $3,500 that incorporates classes in teller training, banking office skills, new accounts, and consumer lending, Bolleter said.

A teller who performs well on the job may become a new accounts person making $1,200 to $1,800 a month after a year's time. From there, it is possible to move into a higher-level position as, say, an assistant loan or operations officer making $2,500 to $3,000 a month.

Operations officers plan, coordinate, and control a bank's work flow, updating systems and streamlining the amount of paperwork that travels between departments. Assistant loan officers are prime candidates for loan officer positions that open up. Loan officers decide whom the bank lends money to, basing their decisions on the customer's credit rating, financial statement, and overall ability to repay the loan. Loan officers typically specialize in either consumer loans for individuals or commercial loans for business.

Regardless of the department in which bank officers work, their primary responsibilities involve promoting and managing the financial services offered by the institution. With 8 to 10 years' experience, officers can work into either a vice president or branch manager position—or both concurrently—bringing in a salary of around $60,000 a year, Airheart said.

When considering employment in the financial services industry, it's important to think about the type of work environment and corporate culture you are comfortable in. "Working downtown is going to be hara-kiri all day long," Bolleter said. "But a little branch in Glendale is not going to be so bad. Some banks will even request people with a soft touch."

L.A.'s Largest Banks*

Bank	Assets (Countywide)	No. of Employees/ Branches
1. Security Pacific	$85.18 billion	42,000/1,500
2. First Interstate	$58.36 billion	6,500/106
3. City National	$ 4.29 billion	2,030/19
4. Imperial Bancorp	$ 2.57 billion	750/5
5. Mitsui Manufacturers Bank	$ 1.38 billion	918/12
6. Community Bank	$ 1.37 billion	380/7
7. Farmers & Merchants Bank of Long Beach	$ 1.19 billion	480/16
8. Tokai Bank of Califoria	$ 1.02 billion	492/11
9. First Los Angeles Bank	$865.5 million	310/11
10. Metrobank	$834.9 million	216/3
11. Santa Monica Bank	$656.7 million	372/8

* The largest banks with headquarters in Los Angeles County. Ranked according to assets as of June 30, 1989.

SOURCE: Los Angeles Area Chamber of Commerce.

A Sampling of Banking Salaries

Position	Salary
Part-time teller	$7.50/hr.
Teller	$ 950–$1,200/mo.
New accounts person	$1,000–$1,200/mo.
Operations specialist	$1,200–$1,800/mo.
Utility specialist	$1,300–$1,900/mo.
Assistant operations officer	$1,900–$2,800/mo.
Operations officer	$2,000–$3,000/mo.
Assistant loan officer	$2,000–$3,000/mo.
Loan officer	$2,400–$3,600/mo.
Senior loan officer	$2,800–$4,300/mo.
Branch manager	$3,500–$5,000/mo.

SOURCE: Community Bank of Pasadena, Banking Institute.

KEY EMPLOYERS IN THE BANKING INDUSTRY

Bank of America
555 S. Flower Street
Los Angeles, CA 90071
213/228-3716

City National Corp.
400 N. Roxbury Drive
Beverly Hills, CA 90210
213/550-5400

**Coast Savings and Loan
  Association**
855 S. Hill Street
Los Angeles, CA 90014
213/624-3055

Community Bank
100 E. Corson Street
Pasadena, CA 91103
818/577-1700

First Interstate Bancorp
707 Wilshire Boulevard
Los Angeles, CA 90017
213/614-3001

First Los Angeles Bank
2049 Century Park East
Los Angeles, CA 90067
213/557-1211

Glendale Federal
700 N. Brand Boulevard
Glendale, CA 92103
818/500-2000

Great Western Financial Corp.
8484 Wilshire Boulevard
Beverly Hills, CA 90211
213/852-3951

Home Federal Savings
275 W. Broadway
Glendale, CA 91204
818/240-9333

Imperial Bancorp
9920 S. La Cienega Boulevard
Inglewood, CA 90301
213/417-5600

Mitsubishi Bank of California
800 Wilshire Boulevard
Los Angeles, CA 90017
213/621-1200

Mitsui Manufacturers Bank
133 E. Ninth Street
Los Angeles, CA 90015
213/4898-6200

Santa Monica Bank
1237 Fourth Street
Santa Monica, CA 90401
213/394-9611

Sanwa Bank
612 S. Flower Street
Los Angeles, CA 90017
213/613-3811

Security Pacific National Bank
333 S. Beaudry Boulevard
Los Angeles, CA 90071
213/345-3721

Tokai Bank of California
314 S. First Street
Alhambra, CA 91801
213/972-0266

Union Bancorp
445 S. Figueroa Street
Los Angeles, CA 90071
213/236-5000

Wells Fargo Bank
444 S. Flower Street
Los Angeles, CA 90071
213/253-7313

PROFESSIONAL ORGANIZATIONS

American Bankers Association
1120 Connecticut Avenue, NW
Washington, DC 20036
202/663-5000

California Bankers Association
650 California Street
San Francisco, CA 94108
415/433-1894

**California League of Savings &
Loan Institutions**
9800 S. Sepulveda Boulevard
Suite 500
Los Angeles, CA 90045
213/670-6300

**National Association of Bank Loan
and Credit Officers**
c/o Robert Morris Associates
One Liberty Place
1650 Market Street
Suite 2300
Philadelphia, PA 19103
215/851-9100

National Bankers Association
122 C Street, NW
Suite 580
Washington, DC 20001
202/783-3200

PROFESSIONAL PUBLICATIONS

American Banker (New York, NY)
Bank Administration (Rolling Meadows, IL)
Bank Marketing Magazine (Chicago, IL)
Bankers Magazine (New York, NY)
Bankers Monthly (New York, NY)

California Banking Newsletter (Brea, CA)
Savings Institutions (Chicago, IL)

DIRECTORIES

American Banker's Guide to the First 5,000 U.S. Banks (American Banker, New York, NY)

Bankers School Directory (American Bankers Association, Waldorf, MD)

Findley Reports on California Savings and Loans (Findley Reports, Brea, CA)

Western Bank Directory (Western Banker Publications, San Francisco, CA)

CHAPTER 2

Accounting

The jobs start adding up at tax time.

Business, like the weather, can be seasonal, even in the temperate Southland. So as the retail industry winds down every year after its holiday peak, scores of auditors, accountants, and tax preparers in turn gear up for their busiest period of the year: tax time.

"If you have accounting skills, you can make money. The first of the year is crunch time. It's a very good time to have those skills. Tax season is when companies need staffing," said David Lewis, vice president of temporary services for the Accountants Overload Group in Westwood.

The accounting profession in Southern California has been growing at a healthy pace since the early 1980s, mainly because of accelerated economic activity, increased international trade, and a population explosion, said Jack Kyser, chief economist for the Los Angeles Area Chamber of Commerce. "It's definitely a growth industry, tax season or not."

According to the Employment Development Department, the accounting occupations, including accountants, auditors, budget analysts, tax preparers, and related workers, grew 30.1 percent in the Los Angeles area over the last decade, from 37,390 in 1980 to an estimated 48,630 in 1990. By 1992, there will be room for 54,630 accountants and auditors in Los Angeles and Orange counties, according to state projections.

Candidates for jobs at a large public accounting firm are expected to have a four-year degree and be working toward their public accounting certification, or CPA designation, which entails passing a series of tests administered by the state and accumulating at least two years' experience in public accounting.

Although the "Big Six" (it used to be "Big Eight") accounting firms generally do not hire temporary employees for the tax season, they do start many of their new hires on an extensive training program in January to become staff accountants, said Bruce Ferguson, director of recruiting for Arthur Andersen & Co., one of the remaining Big Six firms.

"Our tax people get involved in far more than tax returns," Ferguson said. "They might play a role in international trade agreements, mergers, acquisitions, valuation and appraisals, and the internal tax compliance work of a particular client company."

Beginning staff accountants at Arthur Andersen, which employs about 1,400 people in Los Angeles County (475 CPAs), earn a starting salary of around $27,000 plus overtime, Ferguson said. Within a few years' time, accountants at major accounting firms can earn $30,000 to $40,000. The salary, status, and responsibilities grow steadily with each passing year.

So do the hours. "People are working here seven days a week," Ferguson said. "Many of our employees are here until late at night and even some early mornings. When you're trying to provide the highest-quality service, time is of the essence."

After proving themselves to be competent, reliable professionals, staff accountants may achieve senior or supervisory status and, with further experience, become manager of a project and then a department. When they get to the partner level, which can be achieved in 10 to 12 years, they can start making $100,000 to $200,000 a year.

CPAs typically specialize in auditing, or examining a client's financial records and attesting to them. Increasingly, accounting firms are taking on management-advisory roles, acting as consultants and offering advice to businesses on ways to improve their operations and control costs.

In large corporations, accountants may specialize in taxation, budgeting, costs, investments, or internal auditing. Accountants and financial officers have become so important to a firm's survival and financial health that many times they take a leading role in corporate decision making.

During tax season—January through mid-April—literally thousands of temporary as well as permanent jobs open up each year in accounting, bookkeeping, general office work, and, of course, tax preparation, providing wide-ranging employment opportunities in the accounting field.

"In addition to tax preparation, a lot of opportunities come from companies doing their year-end close," said Lynn Sweeney, branch manager for Accountants On Call in downtown Los Angeles. "Large CPA firms need people to input tax returns or just help with filing. We receive orders for anything from CPAs to typists. The first quarter of the year is always very strong."

H&R Block, the nation's largest tax preparation firm with over 8,400 offices nationwide, hires some 2,500 tax preparers each tax season to staff its 235 seasonal offices in Southern California, said Nelson Manare, H&R Block's regional director.

To become licensed and qualified to prepare individual tax returns in the state of California, a tax preparer must have a high school diploma or equivalent and at least 60 hours of basic tax instruction plus 20 hours of continuing education through a program like that offered by H&R Block's Income Tax School.

The H&R Block program, considered to be the industry standard by most accounting professionals interviewed, consists of a 75-hour basic tax course with 16 hours of tax updating and about 20 hours of client interviewing and office procedures training, Manare said. The fee for the course, which does not require any previous training, is $275.

"Our course starts off assuming that they know nothing," said Darrell Gydesen, H&R Block's Los Angeles–West assistant district manager. "It covers everything they need to know about individual tax returns and sole proprietorships. It's a good course. We even train our competition." H&R Block also offers advanced classes that cover corporate and partnership returns.

Graduates of the Block program can go straight to work for any Block office, earning a 20 percent commission on each tax return they complete their first year and up to 30 percent in subsequent years. This salary schedule can easily translate to $20 or more an hour, Manare said.

After a year of experience at H&R Block, tax preparers can go in many different directions. For instance, either they can return next year—tax preparation is done by many on a part-time, moonlighting basis—or they can work for a small, independent accounting or tax preparation office.

"What we look for is someone who has had a good H&R Block class and who has maybe worked for a year," said George Simpson, CPA, president of GWS Professional Tax Services in Saugus. "If they're personable and have the ability to get along with clients, they're going to do real well right from the beginning."

As with other owners of small independent offices, Simpson each year hires a few extra part-time preparers to assist with tax season overflow. "If a tax preparer has a good season, there's a possibility he or she will be employed full-time at that office," he said, adding his office completes nearly 3,000 returns between the first of the year and mid-April, when tax returns are due.

Tax preparation is not a field for those who have difficulty coping with a stressful work environment. During tax season, tax preparers and accountants work long hours at a hectic pace for several months on end.

"It's a high-pressure job," Simpson said. "You need to be able to hear customers' criticisms and work fast and be courteous and smile and have a positive attitude. It's not for everybody. But I've come to enjoy it, knowing that I'm helping so many people in such a short period of time. You're part counselor, part confidant. Tax preparers have access to information that people don't share with their closest friends."

The money is good and can offset some of the drawbacks. "A good second or third person in a busy office can make anywhere from $12,000 to $20,000 in a three-month period," Simpson said. "My No. 2 man, who files between 500 and 700 returns a year, makes at least $30,000."

Competent preparers who have saved some investment capital also have the option of opening their own office, working on a freelance basis out of their home, or becoming affiliated with a tax preparation network like H&R Block or Triple Check Income Tax Service, based in Burbank.

They can also seek employment through a temporary employment service. The pay scales offered through specialized accounting services are competitive with permanent salaries. A clerk sent out by Accountants On Call, for instance, can earn $8 to $11 an hour, while an experienced accountant may command $30 to $40.

Accountants Overload, an employment service that specializes in providing accounting, bookkeeping, and data processing professionals to industry on a temporary basis, places about 5,000 to 6,000 job candidates yearly, according to Lewis.

Temporary employment opportunities during the tax season are also available at firms like CCH Computax, a computerized tax processing service based in Torrance, which hires upward of 1,000 seasonal programmers, computer operators, and office clerks, according to John Laughon, Computax's technical recruiter.

Tax Preparation: What the Jobs Pay
Private Industry

Job Description	Salary Range	Average Pay
Tax manager	$50,000–$110,000	$65,000
Accounting manager	$31,000–$53,000	$42,000
Tax accountant	$30,000–$50,000	$40,000
Staff internal auditor	$28,000–$50,000	$38,000
Financial analyst	$30,000–$44,000	$37,000
Senior accountant	$27,000–$43,000	$35,000
Full charge bookkeeper	$24,000–$34,000	$29,000
Staff accountant	$22,000–$34,000	$28,000
Assistant bookkeeper	$19,000–$26,000	$22,500
Accounting clerk	$16,000–$24,000	$20,000

Public Sector

Job Description	Salary Range	Average Pay
Supervisor	$37,000–$43,000	$40,000
Senior accountant	$31,000–$37,000	$34,000
Staff accountant	$22,000–$32,000	$27,000

SOURCE: The Accountants Overload Group.

Career Paths in the Accounting Industry

Typically, an accountant's career at a major
accounting firm would follow this path:

Position	Years on the Job
Assistant Accountant	8–12 months
Staff Accountant	16–24 months
Senior Accountant	2–3 years
Supervisor	2–3 years
Manager	2–3 years
Partner	Balance of career

SOURCE: Pannell Kerr Forster.

KEY EMPLOYERS IN THE ACCOUNTING INDUSTRY

Arthur Andersen & Co.
911 Wilshire Boulevard
Los Angeles, CA 90017
213/614-6500

BDO Seidman
9100 Wilshire Boulevard
Suite 500
Beverly Hills, CA 90212
213/273-2782

Coopers & Lybrand
1000 W. Sixth Street
Los Angeles, CA 90017
213/481-1000

Deloitte & Touche
333 S. Grand Avenue
Suite 2800
Los Angeles, CA 90071
213/253-4600

Ernst & Young
515 S. Flower Street
Los Angeles, CA 90071
213/621-1666

Grant Thornton
1000 Wilshire Boulevard
Suite 700
Los Angeles, CA 90017
213/627-1717

Gumbiner, Savett, Friedman & Rose
1723 Cloverfield Boulevard
Santa Monica, CA 90404
213/828-9798

KMPG Peat Marwick
725 S. Figueroa Street
Los Angeles, CA 90017
213/972-4000

Laventhol & Horwath
3699 Wilshire Boulevard
Los Angeles, CA 90010
213/381-5393

Kenneth Leventhall & Co.
2049 Century Park East
Los Angeles, CA 90067
213/277-0880

Levine, Cooper, Spiegel & Co.
11835 W. Olympic Boulevard
Suite 1000
Los Angeles, CA 90064
213/477-7111

Pannell Kerr Forster
624 S. Grand Avenue
Suite 1800
Los Angeles, CA 90017
213/680-0900

Parks, Palmer, Turner & Yemenidjian
1990 S. Bundy Drive
Suite 500
Los Angeles, CA 90025
213/207-2777

Price Waterhouse
400 S. Hope Street
Los Angeles, CA 90071
213/236-3000

Windes & McClaughry
444 W. Ocean Boulevard
Long Beach, CA 90801
213/435-1191

Arthur Young & Co.
515 S. Flower Street
Los Angeles, CA 90071
213/977-3200

PROFESSIONAL ORGANIZATIONS

**American Institute of Certified
Public Accountants**
1121 Avenue of the Americas
New York, NY 10036
212/575-6200

**American Society of Women
Accountants**
35 E. Wacker Drive
Suite 2250
Chicago, IL 60601
312/726-9030

**California Society of Certified
Public Accountants**
100 W. Broadway
Glendale, CA 91210
818/246-6000

**National Association of
Accountants**
10 Paragon Drive
Montvale, NJ 07645
201/573-9000

**National Society of Public
Accountants**
1010 N. Fairfax Street
Alexandria, VA 22314
703/549-6400

Society of California Accountants
2131 Capitol Avenue
Suite 305
Sacramento, CA 95816
916/443-2057

PROFESSIONAL PUBLICATIONS

The CPA Journal (New York, NY)
Journal of Accountancy (New York, NY)
Management Accounting (Montvale, NJ)
National Public Accountant (Alexandria, VA)

DIRECTORIES

Accountants Directory (American Business Information Inc., Omaha, NE)
Accounting Firms and Practitioners (American Institute of Certified Public
Accounts, New York, NY)
Roster (American Women's Society of Certified Public Accountants, Chicago, IL)
Who Audits America (Data Financial Press, Menlo Park, CA)

CHAPTER 3

Insurance

The industry is large and diverse, leaving
room for advancement and independence.

When appraising the job scene, consider taking out a career policy in insurance. Chances are, with the right qualifications, you won't be turned down, particularly in the rapidly growing Southland. Pressing health care needs, mandatory automobile insurance for Southern California's 9 million or so drivers, a growing number of residents, and a heightened state of readiness for natural disasters have spelled boom times for the local insurance industry.

In 1985, 70,800 people were working in the insurance industry in Los Angeles County. Only three years later, their ranks had swelled to 81,800. The greater Los Angeles area currently employs more than 25 percent of the approximately 300,000 insurance industry professionals statewide, said Marcella Marks, assistant chief of the California Insurance Licensing Bureau in Sacramento.

With more people, cars, and earthquakes than any other state in the union, California ranks as the most lucrative insurance market in the country, accounting for 15 percent of all insurance policies written in the United States, according to the Western Insurance Information Service, an industry trade association.

Given that the industry is so large and diverse, it offers a lot of potential for advancement and room for independence. In insurance you have the option of working for a company or for yourself as an agent or broker. You can choose a desk job, say, as an actuary, or spend most of the day out visiting clients as an adjuster.

The industry is basically divided into two branches: life and casualty/property. Companies typically specialize in one area or the other, but may write policies in both. As with other service industries, insurance has been significantly affected by technological developments, pressure from competitors, and a more demanding and discriminating buying public.

A degree in business, accounting, or finance provides a strong footing for eventual promotion into management. The heads of companies tend to be college-educated. But the lack of a degree doesn't close the door. In fact, the Farmers Insurance Group, which spokesman Jerry Clemans said spends $1 million a year on in-house education, has a training program that allows non-degreed employees to become agents.

The highly regulated insurance industry places great emphasis on continuing education mainly because of all the changes it is subject to from state lawmakers and voters.

Despite uncertainty over the ultimate impact of the recent consumer revolt embodied by Proposition 103, including the rollback of rates and possible workforce reductions in certain areas, the prospects for employment in insurance remain fairly bright, Clemans said. But job seekers need to be selective.

The trick, then, is to isolate pockets of continued growth. Occupations that remain good bets include underwriter, claims representative, insurance agent, broker, and the highly rated job of actuary, according to insurance industry professionals.

Actuaries, known in the industry as the numbers crunchers, use statistics to determine the amount of risk their company must assume by insuring a client. They generate reports that describe the probability of loss by calculating the likelihood of such variables as death, sickness, injury, disability, unemployment, retirement, and property loss for a given policyholder. They reach their figures by studying trends and applying statistical formulas to predict likely outcomes.

The job of actuary was recently rated as the best occupation in the nation by the *Jobs Rated Almanac*, which takes into account such occupational components as income, stress, physical demands, work environment, long-term outlook, and job security to determine overall job quality. Nationwide, actuaries work an average of 45 hours a week and earn an annual average salary of $45,780, according to the *Almanac's* 1988 edition. They usually start at around $30,000 a year and can earn $60,000 or more.

While actuaries are highly rated, they also must be highly educated. Entry into the field rarely comes with anything less than a bachelor's degree in math or statistics. "It's a very specialized area," Clemans said. "We look for people who are graduates of university actuarial training programs." The number of actuaries is expected to grow 51 percent by the mid-1990s.

Underwriters are responsible for deciding whether to accept or reject a client's insurance application. They evaluate information from applications, medical reports, and actuarial studies to determine whether their company will write a given policy. If it's accepted, they determine the appropriate rates and terms.

Like bank loan officers, underwriters perform a balancing act each time they decide on an application. If, on the one hand, they appraise risks too conservatively and price policies too high, their company may lose business to competitors. If, on the other, they are too lenient and wind up approving too many high-risk policies, their company may end up paying additional claims.

Nationwide, underwriting is ranked as one of the top dozen job prospects for new business and technical college graduates, according to the *Jobs Rated Almanac*. Underwriters, who work an average of 45.6 hours a week, make an average salary of $28,340. According to the Insurance Information Institute, no other job in the industry offers more potential for growth and advancement. Indeed, in the competitive insurance industry, much of a company's success depends on the decisions of its underwriters.

At Industrial Indemnity, the sixth-largest insurer in the state, underwriters are placed on a swift career path that leads into either management or senior status, said Kitt Bennett, senior human resources representative for the company. Excluding the executive ranks, the salary schedules are the same for managers and senior technical staff.

Claims representatives respond to claims made by policyholders, acting as the insurance industry's first line of defense against faulty and inflated claims while settling valid claims promptly and fairly. During the course of their work, they check on the veracity of claims, negotiate settlements with policyholders, and authorize payments. Within claims, the two main occupations are claims adjuster and claims examiner. Adjusters work for casualty insurance companies, while examiners are employed by life and health insurance companies.

Adjusters are the front-line troops of the insurance industry. Most of their work is done fairly independently in the field. They are frequently called to the scene of an accident, burglary, or natural disaster to assess the damage firsthand and authorize benefit payments as quickly as possible. Like other aspects of insurance, claims requires a certain amount of training, and there is a professional designation for a graduate in claims administration.

Claims examiners, who work in life and health insurance companies, also investigate questionable claims or those exceeding a specified amount. But examiners rarely leave the office. They gather information primarly by mail and by phone. They may interview medical specialists, consult policy files to verify information, and calculate benefit payments.

The entry-level salary range for underwriters and claims reps is $21,000 to $25,000, Bennett said.

Insurance agents and brokers are the sales reps of the insurance industry. They are in the business of selling protection. To this end, they make sure their clients have the financial resources they need to cope with the loss of life, health, or property. Agents may sell different lines of insurance but represent a single company, typically working out of a branch office. Brokers are independent business owners and can sell the policies of a number of different insurance companies.

"It's the kind of career where you can have a great deal of autonomy," said Ken Hovespian, a State Farm insurance agent with an office in Lomita. "The opportunity is based upon how much effort you want to put into it. I like that. I've always been a self-starter. I prefer being the captain of my own ship."

Agents and brokers must be state-licensed. Increasingly, they are entering the field with a college education. Computer literacy is important, too. Depending on their sales volume, agents and brokers, who usually work on a commission basis, can make from $30,000 to over $100,000 a year.

While the insurance industry is in the midst of a 5- to 10-year competitive shakeout from which not all companies will emerge, the long-term employment outlook is still rosy. "We're going to be here because insurance is a necessity. It's an industry that's going to be here forever, so it's a good career," Bennett said.

KEY EMPLOYERS IN THE INSURANCE INDUSTRY

Aetna Life & Casualty
101 W. Broadway Tower
Glendale, CA 91210
818/502-9292

Allstate Insurance
801 N. Brand Avenue
Glendale, CA 91209
818/507-1181

Equitable Life Assurance
3435 Wilshire Boulevard
Los Angeles, CA 90010
213/387-4470

Farmers Insurance Group
4680 Wilshire Boulevard
Los Angeles, CA 90010
213/932-3200

Fireman's Fund
3223 W. Sixth Street
Los Angeles, CA 90020
213/387-5566

John Hancock
9100 Wilshire Boulevard
Beverly Hills, CA 90212
213/278-8444

Hartford Insurance Group, ITT
3435 Wilshire Boulevard
Los Angeles, CA 90010
213/487-5051

Industrial Indemnity
3530 Wilshire Boulevard
Los Angeles, CA 90010
213/678-4129

Kemper Group
17800 Castleton Street
Industry, CA 91748
818/369-7700

Liberty Mutual
6006 Wilshire Boulevard
Los Angeles, CA 90036
213/938-2282

New York Life
4000 W. Alameda Avenue
Burbank, CA 91505
818/842-7173

Pacific Mutual Life
700 Newport Center Drive
Newport Beach, CA 92660
714/640-3011

Prudential Insurance Co.
5800 Canoga Avenue
Woodland Hills, CA 91367
818/992-2000

State Farm Insurance Companies
15315 Magnolia Boulevard
Sherman Oaks, CA 91403
213/872-0482

Transamerica Occidental Life
1150 S. Olive Street
Los Angeles, CA 90015
213/742-2111

Travelers Insurance Co.
145 S. State College Boulevard
Brea, CA 92621
714/671-8000

Wausau Insurance
74 N. Pasadena Avenue
Suite 1400
Pasadena, CA 91103
818/440-0444

PROFESSIONAL ORGANIZATIONS

American Insurance Association
1130 Connecticut Avenue, NW
Washington, DC 20036
202/828-7100

**Independent Insurance Agents &
Brokers of Los Angeles**
1541 Wilshire Boulevard
Suite 106
Los Angeles, CA 90017
213/483-3981

**Life Underwriters Association of
Los Angeles**
740 W. Olympic Boulevard
Los Angeles, CA 90015
213/742-0756

**Professional Insurance Agents of
California**
14114 Victory Boulevard
Van Nuys, CA 91401
818/988-9500

Society of Actuaries
475 N. Martingale Road
Schaumburg, IL 60173
312/706-3500

**Western Insurance Information
Service**
3530 Wilshire Boulevard
Suite 1465
Los Angeles, CA 90010
213/738-5333

PROFESSIONAL PUBLICATIONS

The Actuary (Schaumburg, IL)
Business Insurance (Detroit, MI)
California Broker (Burbank, CA)
Independent Agent (New York, NY)
Insurance Review (New York, NY)
National Underwriter (Cincinnati, OH)
Professional Agent (Alexandria, VA)

DIRECTORIES

Best's Insurance Reports (A.M. Best Co., Oldwick, NJ)
Insurance Almanac (Underwriter Publishing Co., Englewood, NY)
Kirschner's Insurance Directory (Kirschner's Publishing Co., Santa Cruz,
    CA)
Southern California Insurance Directory (Underwriters Report, San Fran-
    cisco, CA)

CHAPTER 4

Import/Export

Bountiful trade opportunities
flood the Southland.

Throughout history, cities with major trading ports have enjoyed untold opportunity and economic prosperity. In modern-day Los Angeles, international trade is helping catapult the Southern California region onto center stage of the emerging global economy. "It's one of the most exciting and dynamic markets in the United States, if not the world," said Jack Kyser, chief economist for the Los Angeles Area Chamber of Commerce.

Mainly due to the impact of trade with Pacific Rim countries, the 1980s witnessed incredible growth in foreign trade opportunities. From 1980 to 1988, the number of jobs directly tied to international trade in the Los Angeles area grew by almost 70 percent, from 174,700 in 1980 to 257,500 in 1988. When the transportation industry is factored in, there are over half a million career positions in international trade in Southern California. This number is growing all the time.

According to a report by the Los Angeles 2000 Committee entitled "L.A. 2000: A City for the Future," 1 in 10 Los Angeles–area jobs was supported by world trade in 1988. By 1995, an estimated 1 in 6 jobs will be import/export-related. Reflecting this growth in trade, the Los Angeles Customs District recently surpassed New York as the nation's busiest commercial gateway. Aggressive development of the twin ports of Long Beach and Los Angeles as well as Los Angeles International Airport will provide a framework for even further expansion.

Entry-level trade opportunities in foreign trade are divided between private enterprise (including importers, exporters, customs houses, and freight forwarders) and U.S. Customs. Most careers in foreign trade require a working knowledge of customs regulations, if not a direct working relationship with the Customs District—the eyes, ears, and hands of the federal government where trade matters are concerned. Here are four typical entry-level positions:

Documentation clerks, needed in every field of the industry (including the trafficking departments of such large manufacturers as carmakers), help coordinate shipments between the importer or exporter and customs, making sure the necessary papers are in order. All shipments must clear customs and have duties assessed before entering or exiting the country. Like many foreign trade positions, the clerk's job is paperwork-intensive.

Freight forwarders book cargo space for shipments on ships and airlines, arrange for pier deliveries and clearance through customs, prepare bills of lading (receipts listing goods shipped), obtain cargo insurance for clients, advise importers and exporters on packing arrangements, and trace and consolidate shipments—all without ever leaving the home office.

"For ocean freight, they have to know when the ship is leaving port, what its stops are in between, and make sure all of the other procedures are followed to the letter, including having the shipment brought into customs and inspected," said Tammy Bechard, placement officer for the Travel and Trade Career Institute in Long Beach. "Otherwise, it can go right back to the manufacturer."

Customs inspectors and agents work for the federal government enforcing tariff and trade laws. They are stationed at airports, seaports, and border-crossing points, where they inspect and weigh commercial cargos shipped into and out of the country to determine the amount of tax that needs to be levied.

A large part of an inspector's job is to check that shipments match their description on paper, and to seize them and impose fines if they don't. To this end, they ensure that all merchandise, including what's inside the personal baggage of a traveler returning from abroad, is properly declared and taxed accordingly.

Becoming a customs inspector entails a full background investigation, a panel interview before selection, and a nine-week training program in Glynco, Georgia. According to Maryanne Noonan, public affairs officer for U.S. Customs in Los Angeles, one drawback to the position of customs inspector is that inspectors are required to work overtime. This is mainly due to the irregular scheduling of arriving and departing flights.

Jobs in International Trade*

Position	Salary
Freight forwarder	$14,400
Documentation clerk	$14,400–$18,000
Assistant equipment control clerk	$18,000–$21,600
Import specialist	$15,738–$28,852
Customs inspector	$15,738–$23,846
Customs agent/Customs investigator	$15,738–$34,580
Senior customs inspector	$28,852–$41,121

* Salaries do not include overtime, which is common in international trade.
SOURCE: Travel and Trade Career Institute, U.S. Customs.

While the above positions don't pay that much to start, around $16,000 a year, entry-level openings are plentiful, pay raises are regular, and promotions can happen quickly. Within five years, it's easily possible to make $30,000 a year.

"I have more openings than I have recent graduates," said Bechard of the Travel and Trade Career Institute, a private vocational school that offers a comprehensive international trade program. "This industry doesn't advertise, especially for entry-level openings, but it does network. I get calls from employers every day. There's a good turnover rate. People advance quickly."

Licensed brokers deal with various government agencies and act as signatories for importers and exporters. Essentially, they handle other people's money and merchandise. Being licensed allows you to open your own customs house, employ other people, and solicit business.

Some foreign trade specialists maintain that an introduction to the industry through a school that offers a trade program or exposure from related experience is virtually essential to finding a job. But others say they would consider hiring someone without any previous training. As a bare minimum, applicants should know some math, be able to type, and have a basic understanding of business.

"In order to get things done, it's good to have a background in the forwarding industry. But it's almost easier to teach someone from scratch," said Al Mazzarella, president of West Coast Forwarding in Los Angeles. But, Bechard added: "It's a difficult industry to break into with no experience. There is no room for error in this industry. Every error results in a fine, and with every error the fine escalates."

Recent economic trends have been particularly advantageous to the exporting field, making it a good time to work your way into the industry, said Dan Young, Los Angeles district director for the U.S. Department of Commerce's International Trade Administration. "The conditions are right because the dollar is down. People overseas are buying 'Made in the USA.'"

Exports out of the Los Angeles Customs District were up 35 percent from 1987 to 1988, said Kyser of the Los Angeles Area Chamber of Commerce. "That tells you where the action is." Imports, by contrast, rose only 4 percent in 1988, but the volume of imports into Los Angeles is still significantly higher than exports, creating a local trade deficit similar in dynamics to the national trade deficit.

Japan is far and away the Southland's biggest trading partner, with Taiwan running a distant second. With smaller trading partners, such as Australia and the United Kingdom, the local trade balance favors exports. These latter countries buy more U.S. goods than we import of theirs.

"If you can sell to Paris, Texas, you can sell to Paris, France," Young said, especially if you're exporting a California lifestyle product. "The image of California, for virtually everything,

L.A.'s Trading Partners

Major Trading Partners of the L.A. Customs District

Countries	Foreign Imports	U.S. Exports	Total
1. Japan	$23.58 billion	$7.91 billion	$31.49 billion
2. Taiwan	$ 8.11 billion	$2.52 billion	$10.63 billion
3. Korea	$ 6.52 billion	$3.66 billion	$10.18 billion
4. Hong Kong	$ 2.48 billion	$1.44 billion	$ 3.92 billion
5. Singapore	$ 2.08 billion	$1.41 billion	$ 3.49 billion
6. W. Germany	$ 2.21 billion	$1.26 billion	$ 3.47 billion
7. Australia	$ 56 million	$2.61 billion	$ 3.17 billion
8. People's Republic of China (PRC)	$ 2.39 billion	$ 65 million	$ 3.04 billion
9. UK	$ 1.03 billion	$1.51 billion	$ 2.54 billion
10. Italy	$ 1.02 billion	$ 80 million	$ 1.82 billion

SOURCE: Los Angeles Area Chamber of Commerce. 1988 figures.

including computers, is a selling point. 'Made in California' has a nice ring to it. You can glamorize almost anything made here."

The local International Trade Administration office in West Los Angeles offers various support services and trade publications to help exporters and potential sellers overseas. For more information, call (213) 209-6707.

If you are interested in exporting to Japan, the Japanese External Trade Organization (JETRO) in downtown Los Angeles stocks various trade directories and reference materials all about doing business in Japan. "We try to link people together in the area they're trying to do business in," said Patti Yirahara, public relations agent for JETRO. "It's a good time for the Japanese consumer to buy, so it's a good market to consider."

Yirahara said consulting and business services, especially bilingual communications specialists who can assist Japanese businesses in becoming familiar with American culture, are particularly needed in Japan. "If you have a service people are looking for, it's wide open. The market is closed only if you didn't do your homework first. Make sure what you want to do can fit." JETRO's phone number is (213) 624-8855.

KEY EMPLOYERS IN IMPORT/EXPORT

Private Sector

George S. Bush Co.
1031 W. Manchester Boulevard
Suite 5
Inglewood, CA 90301
213/670-8953

W. J. Byrnes & Co. of Los Angeles
5758 W. Century Boulevard
Los Angeles, CA 90045
213/776-1638

Castelazo & Associates
5420 W. 104th Street
Los Angeles, CA 90045
213/649-3210

C. F. Export/Import
110 Ocean Boulevard
Long Beach, CA 90802
213/436-4779

L. E. Coppersmith
704 Isis Avenue
Inglewood, CA 90301
213/641-4751

H. H. Elder & Co.
233 S. Beaudry Avenue
Los Angeles, CA 90012
213/250-7250

Arthur J. Fritz & Co.
9800 La Cienega Boulevard
Inglewood, CA 90301
213/410-6400

Honolulu Freight Service
2425 Porter Street
Los Angeles, CA 90021
213/627-5193

J. F. Moran Co.
10804 La Cienega Boulevard
Lennox, CA 90304
213/649-6204

Porter International Inc.
5758 W. Century Boulevard
Los Angeles, CA 90045
213/646-4803

Karl Schroff & Associates
1700 E. Holly Avenue
El Segundo, CA 90245
213/772-7523

Seino America Inc.
8645 Aviation Boulevard
Inglewood, CA 90301
213/215-0500

West Coast Forwarding
3545 Wilshire Boulevard
Los Angeles, CA 90010
213/385-9935

Worldwide Freight Forwarders
611 S. Catalina
Suite 309
Los Angeles, CA 90005
213/739-2092

Public Sector

Federal Trade Commission
Los Angeles Regional Office
11000 Wilshire Boulevard
Suite 13209
Los Angeles, CA 90024
213/209-7890

**International Trade
Administration**
Los Angeles District Office
11777 San Vicente Boulevard
Suite 800
Los Angeles, CA 90049
213/209-6700

United States Customs Service
Regional Headquarters
300 N. Los Angeles Street
Los Angeles, CA 90012
213/894-5900

World Trade Commission
Export Finance Office
107 S. Broadway
Los Angeles, CA 90012
213/620-2433

PROFESSIONAL ORGANIZATIONS

**American Association of Exporters
and Importers**
11 W. 42nd Street
New York, NY 10036
212/944-2230

**Export Managers Association of
California**
14549 Victory Boulevard
Van Nuys, CA 91411
818/782-3350

**Foreign Trade Association of
Southern California**
350 S. Figueroa Street
Los Angeles, CA 90071
213/627-0634

**National Customs Brokers and
Forwarders Association of
America**
One World Trade Center
Suite 1153
New York, NY 10048
212/432-0050

PROFESSIONAL PUBLICATIONS

Export Report (Portland, OR)
Export Today (Washington, DC)
The Exporter (New York, NY)
Pacific Rim Business Digest (Santa Monica, CA)
Pacific Traffic (Long Beach, CA)
Showcase USA: The Magazine of American Export (Redondo Beach, CA)
Weekly Commercial News (Lynwood, CA)

DIRECTORIES

American Export Register (Thomas International Publishing Co., New York, NY)

Directory of Freight Forwarders and Custom House Brokers (IWS Inc., Rockville Centre, NY)

Membership Directory (American Association of Exporters and Importers, New York, NY)

U.S. Importers and Exporters Directory (Journal of Commerce, Phillipsburg, NJ)

Working with the Japanese

Opportunities at foreign-owned firms are on the rise,
but approaches toward work vary considerably.

In many ways, Los Angeles at the end of the 20th century is a lot like New York at the end of the 18th century: the city reflects the Pacific Rim and Asia the way New York reflected Europe 200 years ago. While the gateway to the United States used to be Ellis Island, it is now Los Angeles International Airport. At least 84 languages are spoken by children in L.A. public schools. Urban villages like Chinatown, Koreatown, Little Saigon, and Little Tokyo dot the cultural landscape.

California's strategic location and close ties to the Pacific Rim are having a significant impact on the corporate landscape as well, especially in Los Angeles and Orange counties, where an estimated 1,500 Asian subsidiary companies employing some 50,000 people are now doing business.

The activities of these foreign employers cut across a range of industries, from advertising, banking, and real estate investment to construction, automobile, and electronics manufacturing, said Jack Kyser, chief economist for the Los Angeles Area Chamber of Commerce.

The growing Asian business presence, of the Japanese and Koreans especially, is complemented by a growing Asian population base. The greater Los Angeles area, for instance, has the largest concentration of Koreans outside Korea. The local Korean-American community has grown to 350,000 from just 60,000 in 1980. Currently, there are over 100 Korean-owned companies in the Southland, employing close to 2,000 workers.

In terms of employment and economic influence, Japan, of

course, wields the most clout of any Pacific Rim country. Forty-six percent of all the buildings in downtown L.A. are Japanese-owned. Statewide, some 83,400 Californians were employed by Japanese-owned companies in 1987, according to the Japan Business Association of Southern California. Nationwide, over 300,000 Americans work for Japanese subsidiaries. By contrast, an estimated 100,000 Japanese work for American ventures in Japan.

With no real slowdown in sight of the factors driving Japanese investment in the United States, namely, the strong yen, the deep pockets of Japanese investors, a high rate of return on investment, and voracious American consumerism, the opportunities created by Japanese companies are expected to grow considerably in the 1990s. Tokyo's Ministry of International Trade and Industry predicts that Japanese investment will generate some 840,000 new jobs in the United States, if not more, by the year 2000.

As more and more Americans go to work for Japanese employers, it is becoming increasingly important to recognize—and appreciate—the vast, fundamental differences between the Japanese and American approaches toward work.

"Anthropologists who have researched the matter find that the Asian mind and the American mind have the biggest cultural gap among advanced countries," said Jack Whitehouse, a Los Angeles–based consultant with over 30 years' experience helping Japanese officials and businessmen adapt to American culture. "To an American, the substance of an idea is the most important part. To the Japanese, the form of an idea is the most important part."

This form versus substance conflict plays out in the way Americans and Japanese communicate. Americans, in general, speak their minds freely and like to arrive at decisions independently. The Japanese, by and large, are consensus builders who work in an environment that prizes gradual decision making. They discuss alternatives as a group and abide by the final decision of the boss.

"The Japanese are very circumspect and take a circuitous route to an idea," Whitehouse said. "Although I do know some Japanese who are very direct, their normal practice is to talk around a point rather than going straight to it. They expect Americans to be direct and they try to roll with that. But the direct American may not get a direct answer.

"The most common example of that is the Japanese 'no.' It's

very difficult for a Japanese [manager] to say no. If you ask, 'Will you sign this authorization?' he may study it and say, 'Oh, that's very difficult.' An American takes that to mean maybe or that he needs to think about it. But it means no. That's as close as many Japanese ever get to saying, 'No, I will not sign it.' "

When an American goes to work for a Japanese company, the first and most obvious difference is the language barrier, especially in a company's executive ranks. "It's not so much of a problem at the lower levels. It's a serious problem in the upper management levels," Whitehouse said. "It's one of the reasons many Americans feel it's kind of a dead end for them."

Although many Japanese have a working knowledge of English and will use it to issue directives and casually converse, it is not the language they're comfortable with and it is not the language used to communicate with the home office some 5,400 miles away in Japan, Whitehouse said. Most large companies have bilingual executive liaisons in key departments who act as coordinators between American employees and Japanese executives.

"It's frustrating when you're dealing with a group of Japanese because, as an American who doesn't know how to speak their language, they'll start talking in their native tongue and I'll have absolutely no idea what they're saying," said Gregory Elliott, public relations administrator for Toyota Motor Sales USA in Torrance. "You've got to make some compromises and you've got to work a little harder because you don't understand the language."

When working in a foreign cultural environment, things that are wrongly perceived or otherwise miscommunicated can lead to gross misunderstandings, said Bill Whitney, executive director of the international search firm Russell Reynolds Associates. "We don't understand what they in Asia refer to as losing face," said Whitney, who has overseas experience. "We have to be sensitive to those things so we don't insult people unintentionally."

Sometimes, even seemingly minor mistakes, such as typographical errors in company newsletters, can cause major waves. At Toyota, Elliott said, a Japanese executive's name was once inadvertently omitted from the company's in-house executive guide, bringing repercussions from above.

"This was something that really angered him. He thought it was sloppy. The secretary wasn't being thorough," Elliott said.

"An American executive might have said, 'Oh, these things happen—just make sure you get it in next time.' But for the Japanese, it was considered a shame and a disgrace and a failure."

Short of learning Japanese, perhaps the most important first step to take when considering employment with a Japanese-owned company is to abandon stereotypes and inflated expectations of what the Japanese are like. Skewed perceptions can only hinder mutual understanding.

"In Japan, they view America as a drug-ridden, debaucherous, weakening nation, and we view them as a homogenous group of robots," Elliott said. "Maybe there's a little bit of truth to those perceptions, but they're certainly not accurate."

Contrary to the glowing image perpetuated in business mythology, not all Japanese-owned companies emphasize teamwork, stress close worker-management relations, or promise total job security, although they often demand company loyalty and group cooperation.

"In school, all you hear about are quality circles, the teamwork type approach to work, and this sort of thing. I didn't see that at all," said Roy Hughes, who left his job as an accountant and general administration manager at JVC of America in Compton after two years despite a higher salary offer, to become a chiropractor.

According to experts, past and present employees of Japanese companies, Americans should be aware of several unwritten rules when seeking employment with a Japanese firm.

- When you accept a job with a Japanese company, it is assumed you will become a long-term (i.e., lifetime) employee. If you work for a while and quit, don't expect to be rehired, even if there are extenuating circumstances. "When I went in for my interview, my boss was very impressed because he noticed on my résumé that my father had worked for his company for over 30 years," Hughes said. "He just thought that was tremendous."
- If you want to get ahead, you need to be flexible. This can translate into working long hours (the Japanese are famous for their 12-hour workdays) and being available for after-work dinners and even weekend entertaining. Much of the substantive consensus building and alliance forming that occur at a Japanese company takes place after hours in the informal setting of a restaurant or on the fairways of a golf course.

"The Japanese try to respect the American tradition of home life, but there is some socializing after work," Whitehouse said. "The only sacrifice really is in having flexibility. A guy is more likely to be successful if he doesn't have a rigid regimen of rolling out the door at 5 p.m. We have a joke that the Americans are out the door at 5 o'clock so the Japanese can get their work done."

- You'll probably have less autonomy and input than you're normally used to having. "The frustration level reached by not being able to make decisions that affect the company can be discouraging," Whitney said. "It sometimes leads to a lack of motivation. A client of mine at one Japanese company said there was a clear lack of motivation, a listlessness on behalf of all the American employees. It was permeating the organization."

- When communicating, nonverbal cues are equally as important as, if not more important than, spoken words. "There's a great deal of nonverbal communication that Americans have to be aware of if they're going to communicate at all on a substantial basis," Whitehouse said. "It's important to realize the gap exists and that misunderstandings are likely to happen. There's plenty of reading to be done and awareness to be had."

    For insight into the Japanese mindset, Whitehouse recommends reading *The Japanese Mind That Goliath Explained* by Robert C. Christopher (Linden Press, 1983).

- Unless you are fluent in Japanese, understand the Japanese way of thinking, and appreciate Japanese culture, your chances for advancement to a senior-level position with real decision-making authority aren't that great.

    "In most foreign companies, especially in Japanese companies, it is unusual for an American to ascend up the corporate ladder much beyond a U.S. job," Whitney said. "Normally, the type of individual who appreciates positions with foreign companies is one whose career goals are not to reach the top of the ladder. Where people get into trouble is when they take a job with a foreign company just because they need a job."

There are some signs that American influence is rising. Robert McCurry, a senior vice president at Toyota, was recently named to that company's U.S. board of directors. Michael Kaye, the chief executive of Secomerica and its protective service subsidiary, Westec Security, is American. (Not surprisingly, Kaye speaks fluent Japanese.) Nissan has named Americans to important senior management positions as well.

Many prominent Japanese-owned companies like Nissan and Toyota are undertaking aggressive "Americanization" campaigns to blend more harmoniously into the U.S. corporate landscape, improve their public image, and foster better relationships between Japanese executives and their American co-workers.

Nevertheless, many American employees of Japanese firms feel completely left out of the decision-making process and denied any real opportunity for advancement. Employees bringing lawsuits charging wrongful termination and discriminatory practices against women, minorities, and older workers have settled against several prominent Japanese companies, including Sumitomo Corp. of America, Honda Motor Co., and Nissan Motor Corp. in USA.

A recent survey by the U.S.-based Japan External Trade Organization revealed that labor and personnel affairs are among the most troublesome issues facing Japanese managers working in the United States. "Japanese management has had trouble getting a feeling for equal employment opportunities," Whitehouse said. "But where they have had a look from the federal Equal Employment Opportunities Commission, they comply."

If your employment options include a position with a foreign employer—Japanese or otherwise—investigate how committed the company is to an Americanization theme, Elliott advised. One way of doing this is checking to see how many Americans— and not just white males—are in management positions throughout the company.

As Japanese companies become more entrenched in the United States, the so-called glass ceiling preventing many Americans from holding top positions at Japanese-owned companies should eventually shatter, said Jack Kyser of the Los Angeles Area Chamber of Commerce. "To really tap into the market, they're going to have to start using Americans," he said.

SELECTED JAPANESE EMPLOYERS

Brother International Corp.
20 Goodyear
Irvine, CA 92718
714/859-9700

Canon USA
123 Paularino Avenue
Costa Mesa, CA 92626
714/979-6000

Casio Computers
11893 Valley View Street
Garden Grove, CA 92645
714/891-7793

Citizen America Corp.
2425 Colorado Avenue
Santa Monica, CA 90404
213/453-0614

Epson America
2780 Lomita Boulevard
Torrance, CA 90505
213/539-9140

Fuji Photo Film USA Inc.
1211 E. Artesia Boulevard
Carson, CA 90746
213/639-8556

Fujitsu America Inc.
15303 Ventura Boulevard
Sherman Oaks, CA 91403
818/905-1985

Hitachi Sales Corp. of America
401 W. Artesia Boulevard
Compton, CA 90220
213/537-8383

JVC America Inc.
1111 W. Artesia Boulevard
Compton, CA 90220
213/537-6020

Mitsubishi Heavy Industries America
333 S. Hope Street
Los Angeles, CA 90071
213/687-0607

Mitsui & Co. USA Inc.
611 W. Sixth Street
Los Angeles, CA 90017
213/972-2500

NEC America Inc.
1411 W. 190th Street
Gardena, CA 90248
213/719-2400

Pharmavite Corp.
12801 Wentworth Street
Arleta, CA 91333
818/983-0814

Pioneer Electronics Technology Inc.
1801 Highland Avenue
Duarte, CA 91010
818/359-9271

Ricoh Electronics Inc.
2300 Red Hill Avenue
Santa Ana, CA 92705
213/583-4525

Sharp Electronics
20600 S. Alameda Street
Carson, CA 90810
213/637-9488

Sony Corp. of America
2820 W. Olive Avenue
Burbank, CA 91505
818/841-8711

Toshiba America Inc.
19500 S. Vermont Avenue
Torrance, CA 90502
213/532-0785

Also see Chapter 8 on automotive marketing and sales for a listing of Japanese car companies, and Chapter 1 for a partial list of Japanese banks based in Southern California.

SECTION
2

Retail and Sales-Oriented Careers

CHAPTER 5

The Retail Industry

Job shopping? Try retail. A start in sales can lead to the top of the ladder.

Employment opportunities in the expanding retail industry are as plentiful as the industry is competitive. The retail trade is the single largest employment sector in Southern California. In 1987, there were 835,000 people working in retail in Los Angeles and Orange counties, according to the Employment Development Department. By the year 2000, an estimated 175,000 more retail jobs will be added in Los Angeles County alone.

Fueling this tremendous expansion are ever-increasing sales figures spurred by tourism and avid consumerism. In 1988, Los Angeles retailers rang up $59.3 billion in sales, surpassing New York by more than $13 billion. Analysts expect L.A. retail sales to exceed $60 billion a year in 1990 and possibly reach $85 billion by the turn of the century. Los Angeles County accounts for roughly 30 percent of all retail sales in California.

"The retail industry is going through a period of tremendous growth and change," said Jack Kyser, chief economist for the Los Angeles Area Chamber of Commerce. "Retailing will continue to grow significantly in Los Angeles through the year 2000. New types of retail concepts are constantly entering the market. Stores are jockeying for position. What you have is a return to the concept of service in retailing."

In past years, service played a weak supporting role to the bottom line, Kyser said. But with fierce competition for the consumer dollar, intensified by cable shopping networks, wholesale discount clubs, and international competition, retailers are reviving the old axiom that the customer is king.

"Customer satisfaction is our top priority at the retail level. It's our key to moving forward," said Robert Dourian, executive vice president in charge of personnel for The Broadway–Southern California, which employs some 13,500 people. "We are looking for people who are interested in selling in a customer-oriented environment."

Retail operations fall into three basic categories: department stores, which offer a range of consumer items; discount stores, which emphasize low prices and high volume; and specialty stores, which concentrate on one type of product. (Auto dealerships, restaurants, and food stores are also in the retail trade, but the focus here is on department and chain stores.)

Within department and chain store retailing, merchandising is the largest segment, with the most job opportunities. Merchandising has two main branches: buying and, you guessed it, selling. Most people start their retail careers in the selling-related functions.

In the large department stores, salespeople work on a 6 to 7 percent commission. On a good day they can bring in $3,000 to $4,000 in sales and take home about $250. A top seller over the course of a year can make $500,000 in sales and earn an annual income of around $30,000, said Duane Johnson, senior vice president of human resources for Bullock's Department Stores. Bullock's, along with I. Magnin and Bullock's Wilshire, is a part of the R. H. Macy chain, which has some 10,200 employees in Southern California.

Working in retail sales involves certain tradeoffs. The working environment is somewhat formal, and the hours are long. Sales associates and floor managers typically work a combination of two shifts: from 9 a.m. to 6 p.m. and from 12:30 p.m. to 9:30 p.m. Weekend hours are customary, and store employees are usually required to come in an hour early to open and stay an hour late to close. Stamina and sales ability are key. And since pay is based on performance, added pressure is placed on sales staff.

But the work can be stimulating and the prospects for those who take to retailing brighten soon. What's more, a college education, though increasingly important for management jobs, is not required at the entry level. Once salespeople have acquired a few years of solid selling experience, they can advance in one of two directions: buying or management.

In general, buying is considered to be the fast track for advancement in department store retailing, while store management promises more upward mobility in specialty and other chain stores. Beginning buyers work as assistants to head buyers and start in the low $20,000 range. Full buyers can make $35,000 to $60,000 a year or more depending on their experience and how well their product lines sell, Johnson said.

"You really need training to become a buyer," said Joseph Siegel, vice president of merchandising for the National Retail Merchants Association in New York. "You're a person to whom the store gives a great deal of money and puts its faith on the line with what you do. We're in a highly competitive business, so what you want to do is not only be first, but be right. Your judgment is really key."

Senior buyers may be promoted to merchandising managers, overseeing a department staff of 6 to 20 buyers, Siegel said. Merchandising managers help buyers plan their purchases and select appropriate suppliers while coordinating inventories between other departments and divisions.

On the selling end, a salesperson can advance to the position of assistant or department manager, earning $25,000 to $40,000 a year. Eventually, a competent department head can be promoted to store manager, commanding $50,000 to $100,000. "The first promotion opportunity would be to sales leader, then to an area sales manager and department manager," said Dourian of The Broadway. "From there, based on your contribution, productivity, and performance, you can rise up through the ranks."

The retail industry continues to improve on its reputation as an equal opportunity employer. Women used to top out at the senior buyer, store manager, or fashion director level, but they now are making inroads into the higher echelons of senior management. Both the vice president and general manager of Nordstrom's Southern California region, as well as the president of The Limited Store Group, are women, Kyser said.

Indeed, some of the most upscale department stores, including Neiman-Marcus and Saks Fifth Avenue (each of which has Beverly Hills locations), employ more women than men. Both of these high-flyers have a workforce that is more than 70 percent female, according to *The Best Companies for Women* by Baila Zeitz and Lorraine Dusky (New York: Simon and Schuster, 1988). Together, they employ over 1,300 people in Southern California.

Retail employees in the large department stores receive attractive benefits. In addition to a discount on store merchandise, employees at Nordstrom receive full medical and dental benefits, along with automatic enrollment in a life insurance policy. Employees of The Broadway are also entitled to a personal disability program and a profit-sharing plan.

People in the retail industry cite opportunities for promotion and the ever-changing nature of the business as the two main reasons they have chosen it as a career. But they warn that opportunities at the entry level are largely performance-oriented and employees who don't produce by bringing in sales may soon find themselves out of a job. Managers also must do everything they can to make sure sales happen. Managers who can adapt to continuing innovations in retail management and foresee opportunities for their company in a changing world will be highly valued in the 1990s, Kyser said.

One way to get a head start in retailing is to go through an executive training program offered by the large department stores. Bullock's brings in 100 to 200 new hires a year to participate in its training program, according to Johnson of the store's human resources department. Area sales managers at the Broadway are trained in a 12-week executive development program that provides on-the-job training in different store departments as well as classroom instruction.

Like most other aspects of the retail industry, entry into these coveted training programs is highly competitive. Neiman-Marcus, for example, receives over 1,000 applications each year for its

Southern California's Largest Department Store Chains

Chain	No. of Employees
May Department Stores (May Co.–California; Robinsons)	29,800
Dayton Hudson (Target; Mervyns)	14,175
Sears, Roebuck and Co.	14,055
The Broadway–Southern California	13,500
R. H. Macy (Bullock's; Bullock's Wilshire; I. Magnin)	10,200
JC Penney	8,200
Nordstrom	7,200
Buffum's	2,500
Neiman-Marcus Group (includes Contempo Casuals)	1,400

SOURCE: Los Angeles Area Chamber of Commerce.

executive training program. Only 60 are accepted. Department store employers say they look for a combination of strong interpersonal skills, a basic grasp of general business practices, and previous retail experience in potential trainees.

Many executive training programs do not require a college degree. (It never hurts, however.) Half of those who are accepted at The Broadway, for example, come up through the store's own sales ranks, Dourian said. Ninety percent of all promotions at Bullock's are internal, Johnson said, adding that most of company's top decision makers have worked on the sales floor at one time or another.

Another route into retailing is through smaller, independently owned specialty stores whose only hiring requirement for appli- cants might be a positive attitude and good people skills. Many of these stores start their employees at minimum wage, but promotions can come quickly. And the pressure to sell isn't as furious.

Said Tracy Matthews-Holbert, shift manager at Aahs Cards & Gifts in Westwood Village, "Mainly, if they're outgoing and can work with people, we'll hire them. We start at minimum wage, but there are promotions and raises."

For job seekers who aren't interested in merchandising but would still like to work in the retail industry, numerous behind- the-scenes jobs are available at the major department stores, including positions in customer service, credit, finance, personnel, stocking, warehousing, and distributing. However, the vast majority of opportunities in retailing are in merchandising and store management—the buying- and selling-related activities.

Although a flurry of department store mergers and acquisitions has caused streamlining and cutbacks in some areas, local buying patterns ensure a strong overall retail outlook. "We are a society that consumes at a tremendous rate," said Richard Green, president of Westfield Inc., owners of the swanky Westside Pavilion mall in West Los Angeles. "Those consumption needs require goods and services. Therefore, there's always new trends coming in and a need for additional help. No one's really sure what the saturation point is."

Jobs in retailing are likely to remain a consistent staple of the Southern California economy for another reason as well: tourism, which accounts for a large percentage of the retail dollars spent here. In fact, a recent survey found that shopping is one of the L.A. area's main attractions, aside from the beach and

Disneyland. "Many tourists stop here on their way home from somewhere else just to shop," Kyser said.

KEY EMPLOYERS IN THE RETAIL INDUSTRY

Boston Stores
1010 E. Sandhill Avenue
Carson, CA 90746
213/774-3310

Big 5 Sporting Goods Stores
14440 Ocean Gate Avenue
Hawthorne, CA 90250
213/772-2772

The Broadway–Southern California
General Offices
3880 N. Mission Road
Los Angeles, CA 90031
213/227-2142

Buffum's
Corporate Offices
301 Long Beach Boulevard
Long Beach, CA 90802
213/775-6451

Carter Hawley Hale Stores
550 S. Flower Street
Los Angeles, CA 90071
213/620-0150

Fedco
9300 Santa Fe Springs Road
Santa Fe Springs, CA 90670
213/946-2511

Federated Group
(Federated Electronics Stores)
5655 E. Union Pacific Avenue
Commerce, CA 90022
213/728-5100

JC Penney
Buying Office
6131 Orangethrope
Buena Park, CA 90624
714/670-2500

May Department Stores
(May Co. & Robinsons)
6160 Laurel Canyon Boulevard
N. Hollywood, CA 91606
818/508-5226

Neiman-Marcus Group
(Neiman-Marcus & Contempo Casuals)
280 Fashion Valley Road
San Diego, CA 92108
619/692-9100

Nordstrom
Southern California Headquarters
3120 W. Lake Center Drive
Santa Ana, CA 92704
714/546-9500

R. H. Macy
(Bullock's, Bullock's Wilshire, I. Magnin)
Corporate Buying Office
723 N. Fairfax Avenue
Los Angeles, CA 90046
213/653-6729

Saks Fifth Avenue
9600 Wilshire Boulevard
Beverly Hills, CA 90212
213/275-4211

Sears Roebuck and Co.
13330 E. Telegraph Road
Santa Fe Springs, CA 90670
213/903-2220

Sportmart Inc.
1401 Hawthorne Boulevard
Redondo Beach, CA 90278
213/542-6908

Target Stores
District Offices
3635 Thousand Oaks Boulevard
Westlake Village, CA 91361
805/379-1933

PROFESSIONAL ORGANIZATIONS

California Retailers Association
11th Street and L Building
Sacramento, CA 95814
916/443-1975

General Merchandise Distributors Council
1275 Lake Plaza Drive
Colorado Springs, CO 80906
719/576-4260

National Retail Merchants Association
100 W. 31st Street
New York, NY 10001
212/244-8780

Purchasing Management Association of Los Angeles
11222 La Cienega Boulevard
Lennox, CA 90304
213/645-7621

PROFESSIONAL PUBLICATIONS

California Apparel News (Los Angeles, CA)
Chain Merchandising Magazine (Piedmont, CA)
Chain Store Age (New York, NY)
College Store Executive (Westbury, NY)
Daily News Record (New York, NY)
General Merchandise News (South Pasadena, CA)
Journal of Retailing (New York, NY)
Stores (New York, NY)

DIRECTORIES

Directory of General Merchandise/Variety Chains and Specialty Stores (Chain Store Guide Information Services, New York, NY)
Fairchild's Financial Manual of Retail Stores (Fairchild Books, New York, NY)
Nationwide Directory: Major Mass Market Merchandisers (Salesman's Guides, New York, NY)
Sheldon's Retail Stores (PS&H Inc., New York, NY)

CHAPTER 6

Fashion Design

L.A.'s apparel industry has arrived, in style.

The Los Angeles area's fashion industry is no longer fledgling. The rise of surfwear, children's wear, and Southern California-inspired sportswear lines has helped place L.A. on the fashion map, while world-renowned designers like Nolan Miller ("Dynasty"), Bob Mackie (Cher), and Jimmy Galanos (Nancy Reagan) have earned their rightful place among a select company of international couturiers from New York, Milan, and Paris.

"We do almost everything, from swimsuits to high-fashion gowns," said Jack Kyser, chief economist for the Los Angeles Area Chamber of Commerce. "The industry tends to specialize in middle price points with a fairly high fashion content, but you can find almost anything in this market you want. It's viewed as being a must-stop for retailers around the nation."

On the wholesale and production level, Los Angeles is the second-largest fashion center in the country, smaller only than New York. "People may talk about Dallas and Chicago, but they don't hold a candle to L.A.," Kyser said.

Anchored by three major wholesale marketing facilities that serve as meccas for buyers—the California Mart, the 127 Building, both on Ninth Street, and the Eastern-Columbia Building on Broadway—the local fashion trade has evolved into a dynamic, trend-setting industry with far-reaching influence.

"The world is looking to L.A. for inspiration," said Sharon House, spokeswoman for the California Mart, "and we're providing it. We're no longer just into swimwear and sportswear. There's haute couture and kiddie couture. We've finally grown up. More and more, people are realizing that if you're going to be in fashion, you might as well be in Los Angeles."

45

The industry's stature isn't the only thing growing; so is the number of jobs. As of January 1990, 93,000 people were at work in apparel manufacturing in Los Angeles County—1,800 more than the previous year, Kyser said. All told, over 100,000 people are employed under the fashion umbrella (encompassing apparel, textiles, and jewelry making) in Los Angeles and Orange counties.

Fashion is an exciting, fast-paced industry that constantly changes. It demands people who are flexible, aggressive, and attuned to the fluctuating moods of the consumer. In women's clothing, new lines are introduced five times a year: January (for summer); March (for fall 1); June (for fall 2); August (for the holiday season); and October or November (for spring).

Several highly rated design programs make the L.A. area an attractive place to launch a career in fashion. These include, most notably, those offered by the Fashion Institute of Design and Merchandising (FIDM), UCLA Extension, the American College for the Applied Arts, and the Otis Art Institute of Parsons School of Design, all of which are based in Los Angeles.

An education in fashion is becoming crucial. Even small employers are skittish when it comes to hiring potential designers without some kind of a fashion background. As House notes, "The business is more competitive than in the past. Even if you have that passion for fashion, you need to be well prepared."

When considering a school, look for one that enjoys strong industry support and maintains close ties to the professional world. Ideally, try to find a program whose instructors are professionals who can provide you with an entry into the field. "You want a program strong enough to propel you into a job," advised Annette Wachtel, head of design programs for UCLA Extension.

Graduates of design programs usually start at larger clothing manufacturers like California Casuals, Catalina Inc., or Domino of California. But there are many smaller houses in the greater Los Angeles area as well. In fact, sometimes starting at a smaller house can afford greater opportunity to work as a designer with little or no experience than a large house.

FIDM offers both certificate and two-year A.A. degree programs in fashion design, merchandise marketing, apparel manufacturing, and theater costume design, among other areas. Within the fashion design program, students have the option of pursuing either a creative design or production track, said Sharon Diel, FIDM's executive director of industry relations. Tuition at the widely known institute is somewhat pricy: about $10,000 a year. Students who already have four-year degrees may finish the program in only a year, Diel said.

On the creative side, students take classes in textiles, fashion sketching and design, pattern drafting, production techniques, and color theory. After their first year, they're qualified to work as sample makers and sample cutters, gaining the experience necessary to work as a pattern maker.

Pattern making can be a career in itself, but it also can serve as a step toward becoming a designer. Pattern makers, who work under designers, typically make $23,000 to $26,000 a year. At a more senior level, that rate can increase to $1,000 a week or more. "A good pattern maker can earn $50,000 a year," said Wachtel of UCLA Extension.

What's more, with so much attention focused on designers and the fashions they create, fewer and fewer people are sticking with pattern making, Diel said. "It's very difficult to find a good pattern maker these days. A lot of times you'll see good pattern makers earning more than designers. It's a case of supply and demand."

According to Daniel Caudill, an apparel designer with L.A. Gear, the glamorous aspects of fashion—the shows, the introduction of new lines, the write-ups in newspapers and magazines—are only about 2 percent of the job. Still, you have to love the other 98 percent, he said.

"Even though it sounds wonderful to other people, like any job, it's routine," commented Sandra Ow-Wing, a designer with NR-1 clothing in Los Angeles. "Unless you open your own shop, you have to follow the rules. Everything is more structured than it looks. If you're doing a group of clothes, you might be able to offer different options, but that's about it."

Designers draw inspiration from a variety of sources—past designs, cultural trends, pop icons, retail crazes, beach themes, etc.—and develop their ideas for new garments by drawing sketches, cutting patterns, or draping fabric. Next, they select the fabric and any special trimmings, if appropriate, to be used and convert their designs into wash-and-wear reality.

"You need a certain amount of discipline and style," Ow-Wing said. "As far as style goes, I don't think you can develop style. All you can really do is fine-tune it."

A manufacturing business just like any other, fashion involves developing a product conceptually, producing it physically, and then marketing it for people to buy. So there are plenty of opportunities in production and marketing as well. "Now, since it's such a global market, it's crucial to understand the business side of it. The design area is actually a small part of apparel manufacturing," Diel said.

Product management is more customer-driven than design. While designers dream up new outfits by projecting trends and applying their own sense of style, production managers respond to what the customer is asking for. They take the creations of designers and package them as different lines, assessing how a piece of clothing will fit, what the demand for it is, how many pieces can be produced and at what cost.

At some companies, designers are called product managers. They not only develop a clothing line from the conceptual stage but supervise all phases of production and take responsibility for the finished work. Assistant production managers, who monitor shop operations and help set prices, start at $22,000 to $24,000 right out of school. In a few years' time, they can become production managers, ensuring that the production process from pattern making to shipping meets budget and runs according to schedule.

For information about job openings, refer to the classified section of *California Apparel News*, which lists dozens of opportunities each week.

KEY EMPLOYERS OF FASHION DESIGNERS

Body Glove Sportswear
110 E. Ninth Street
Los Angeles, CA 90079
213/489-5636

California Casuals
1401 S. Main Street
Los Angeles, CA 90015
213/746-0555

Camp Beverly Hills
127 E. Ninth Street
Los Angeles, CA 90015
213/629-3364

Campus Casuals of California
1200 S. Hope Street
Los Angeles, CA 90015
213/746-1121

Catalina Inc.
6040 Bandini Boulevard
Los Angeles, CA 90040
213/726-1262

Clothestime Inc.
5325 E. Hunter Avenue
Anaheim, CA 92807
714/779-5881

Cole of California
2615 Fruitland Avenue
Los Angeles, CA 90058
213/587-3111

Contempo Casuals
5433 W. Jefferson Boulevard
Los Angeles, CA 90016
213/936-2131

Domino of California
343 E. Jefferson Boulevard
Los Angeles, CA 90011
213/232-3151

Guess Inc.
123 E. 35th Street
Los Angeles, CA 90011
213/235-7700

International Male
2802 Midway Drive
San Diego, CA 92110
619/226-8751

Jimmy'z
2410 E. 38th Street
Los Angeles, CA 90058
213/583-4944

L.A. Gear
4221 Redwood Avenue
Los Angeles, CA 90066
213/822-1995

Laguna Sportswear Inc.
19032 S. Vermont Avenue
Gardena, CA 90502
213/515-5555

Michelle Lamy
805 Traction Avenue
Los Angeles, CA 90013
213/617-7501

Lane Bryant Inc.
510 W. Seventh Street
Los Angeles, CA 90014
213/627-4824

NR-1
122 E. Seventh Street
Los Angeles, CA 90014
213/627-6367

Ocean Pacific
1200 Valencia Avenue
Tustin, CA 92680
714/731-3100

PROFESSIONAL ORGANIZATIONS

**American Apparel Manufacturers
  Association**
California Mart
110 E. Ninth Street
Los Angeles, CA 90015
213/624-8929

**Coalition of Apparel Industries in
  California**
California Mart
110 E. Ninth Street
Los Angeles, CA 90015
213/623-6064

The Fashion Group
3960 Laurel Canyon Boulevard
Suite 263
Studio City, CA 91614
818/762-9500

Men's Fashion Association
240 Madison Avenue
New York, NY 10016
212/683-5665

**Textile Association of Los Angeles
  (TALA)**
818 W. Seventh Street
Los Angeles, CA 90017
213/627-6173

PROFESSIONAL PUBLICATIONS

California Apparel News (Los Angeles, CA)
Daily News Record (New York, NY)
Fashion Accessories (Bergenfield, NJ)
L.A. Style (Los Angeles, CA)
M (New York, NY)
Men's Guide to Fashion (New York, NY)
Women's Wear Daily (New York, NY)

DIRECTORIES

Apparel Manufacturers: Guide for the L.A. Area (JASA Sewing Contractors Group, Los Angeles, CA)

Fairchild's Textile & Apparel Financial Directory (Fairchild Publications, New York, NY)

Membership Directory (American Apparel Manufacturers Association, Arlington, VA)

TALA Directory (Textile Association of Los Angeles, Los Angeles, CA)

CHAPTER 7

Real Estate

Realtors strike pay dirt
in booming Southland.

As with so many other fields, the real estate industry in Southern California defies the law of averages. The growth of the regional economy, the influx of foreign investment, and the desirability of the area have created an urgent need for space, providing real estate agents with wide-ranging opportunities to sell and lease residential, commercial, and investment properties.

"Overall in the nation, people are very nervous about the real estate industry," said Jack Kyser, chief economist for the Los Angeles Area Chamber of Commerce. "But in Southern California, it's just a completely different world."

Over the last decade, the number of real estate agents and brokers in the L.A. area increased 48.8 percent, from 5,660 in 1980 to an estimated 8,420 in 1990, according to the Employment Development Department. In Los Angeles and Orange counties, their ranks are expected to number over 9,500 by 1992.

A recent study conducted by the Real Estate Research Corp. confirmed that, despite traffic congestion, smog, high housing prices, and formidable regulatory barriers, the Los Angeles area rates as the best market for real estate in the country. The Southland's advantages—economic diversity, job growth, climate, quality of life, and Pacific Rim ties, just to name a few—outweigh its drawbacks, the report said.

That Southern California is the place to get in on the action is indicated by the continuing increase in housing prices. In 1989, the average price of an existing single-family home in L.A. County rose 20.1 percent over 1988, from $179,423 to $215,487, said Lotus Lou of the California Association of Realtors. Coupled with other factors like higher interest rates, this increase in home costs, which had little effect on home buying from 1985 to 1988, resulted in about 13 percent fewer sales in 1989, Lou said.

In the foreseeable future, local real estate experts anticipate a slowdown in the heady buying and selling pace of the last few years. But they point out that this period of relative calm is an opportune time for newcomers to enter the field.

"It might not look as easy as it did the past few years, but the pace will be better," said Ellen Poll, assistant manager of the Jon Douglas Co.'s Santa Monica office. "In the last couple of years, the pressure was intense. As a rule, something would come on the market and if it was good and reasonably priced, it would be sold within a week."

If you are contemplating a career in real estate, there are two main areas to consider: residential and commercial.

Residential real estate offers more opportunity in general for agents and brokers than commercial. Two of the biggest residential firms in Los Angeles County, Merrill Lynch and Jon Douglas, employ around 3,250 and 1,125 agents and brokers respectively. Brokers, who are qualified to open their own office and receive a percentage of total sales, are required to have more education than agents. Agents work out of an office owned by a broker, but essentially sell for themselves.

The competition in residential real estate is keen, but the opportunities are tremendous if you're both driven and good at sales. Successful agents can make six-figure salaries after establishing themselves, especially in high-priced areas such as West Los Angeles and parts of the South Bay, San Fernando Valley, and coastal Orange County.

The average commission in residential real estate is 5 percent, down a notch from 6 percent just a few years ago, mainly due to the escalation in prices.

Not everyone who tries to sell real estate makes a killing. "Real estate is not easy money," said Art Aston, executive vice president of the Los Angeles Board of Realtors. "It takes a lot of time and a lot of effort to be successful. You're seeing the more successful people work 12 to 16 hours a day, seven days a week, for three years to build up their clientele, reputation, and experience. It's not get your license and get rich quick."

What does it take to get into residential real estate? A real estate license, for one, which can be obtained in as little time as two weekends in a crash course if you're familiar with the material, or as long as three months at a normal pace. Real estate schools offer preparation for the state licensing exam. The Anthony Schools, one of the largest, charge $426 for the instruction and allow students to work their own pace.

Real estate professionals warn that the term real estate "school" is a misnomer. Very little about the actual job of matching the right buyer with the right property and filling out the necessary paperwork to complete a transaction is learned at a licensing school. Real training occurs on the job. "It's a job that you learn by doing," said Poll of Jon Douglas. "It's very common for people to flounder. You have to be a self-starter, you have to be able to set your own goals and act on them."

Most large real estate companies provide in-house training, but some are less structured than others. Before hanging your license at an office, inquire about its training program and decide whether it offers enough structure and guidance.

Keeping your license active requires ongoing education as well—a minimum of 45 hours of certified classwork every four years, said Linda Yanders, an agent with RE/MAX Realty in Palos Verdes. "Real estate has become a lot more legalistic than it was 10 years ago. You have to know a lot more about financing, about appraising, about real estate law, even about construction. But still, to be a good realtor, you have to be a good salesperson."

Selling doesn't always necessitate a hard pitch, however. "If you have the right price, you can sell any property. Even a crummy property in a crummy location will sell at the right price," Yanders said. "There is a buyer for everything." But Aston observed: "In real estate, you're not selling homes, you're selling yourself. You're in the people business. You have to be able to handle rejection."

When you're first starting, be sure to have money in the bank. Commission checks can takes months to arrive. "Even if you go to work for a realtor tomorrow, get your first listing tomorrow night, and make your first sale the next morning, you're not going to get paid until escrow closes, and that can take anywhere from 30 to 120 days," Aston said.

Commercial real estate involves the selling and leasing of commercial space—office buildings, shopping centers, industrial buildings, and investment properties—to businesses, developers, and investors. Commercial agents and brokers, like their residential counterparts, work on a commission basis, which is lower than it is for a residential sale. And the commission is usually split 50-50 between the company and the individual agent.

A solid grounding in residential real estate can be a good training base for the commercial side of the business, Aston said. "Commercial real estate is more specialized and takes some additional expertise. The difference is, the home buyer is buying shelter, while the people dealing in commercial real estate are buying investments."

Because working in commercial real estate is generally more complicated than the residential side, it usually requires a college degree with a professional sales background, said Tom Townley, personnel manager for Coldwell Banker Commercial Group. "The great bulk of people who come to our company already have been out in the business world in sales," Townley said.

Although Coldwell Banker accepts a limited number of recent college graduates into its 2½-year training program, the hiring emphasis at commercial firms is on applicants with more experience. "This is a business where the longer the salespeople stay in it, the better they get and the more credibility and prestige they build," Townley said. "Talking to someone who is 35 to 40 years old is not unusual to us at all."

Like the residential side, commercial real estate requires long-term job commitment before a consistently high salary can be attained. New hires at Coldwell Banker, who are required to have a real estate license, enter a one-year training program where they work on a set salary as an assistant to a broker.

"We're asking very experienced professionals to take four or five steps backwards salarywise to eventually look at the big figures. It's hard to get started without the individual being capable and willing to hit the long ball in that regard," Townley said. As a matter of course, he added, Coldwell Banker expects its "people in a three- to five-year period to be in the six-figure range."

Depending on who you talk to, the Southern California real estate market is either rock solid or soft as a marshmallow. Yet despite gloomy predictions about an impending recession that will cause the bottom to drop out of the housing market, properties continue to sell, new construction activity is occurring, and people continue to move here at a robust pace. The 1990s will be as good a time as any to get into the business.

"At this point, the market is good and solid," Aston said. "It's steady. We are seeing a slight slowdown, but nothing marked."

L.A. County's Largest Real Estate Firms
Commercial

Company	Agents	Employees	Property Handled*
Coldwell Banker Commercial Real Estate Services	385	950	$2.75 billion
Cushman & Wakefield of Calif.	119	174	$1.03 billion
Grubb & Ellis Co.	151	252	$1.0 billion
Beitler Commercial Realty Services	74	87	$795.4 million
Julien J. Studley	51	66	$774.0 million

*Ranked by value of property handled in 1989.

Residential

Company	Agents	Offices	Sales Volume*
Jon Douglas Co.	1,675	35	$5.2 billion
Prudential California Realty	1,792	31	$5.0 billion
Fred Sands Realtors	1,300	45	$4.6 billion
Coldwell Banker Residential Real Estate Group	835	36	$4.04 billion
Century 21 Emery Real Estate	642	12	$775.2 million

*Ranked by residential sales volume in 1989.

SOURCE: Los Angeles Area Chamber of Commerce.

KEY EMPLOYERS IN THE REAL ESTATE INDUSTRY

Commercial

CitiPacific
11999 San Vicente Boulevard
Los Angeles, CA 90049
213/471-1212

Cushman & Wakefield
515 S. Flower Street
Los Angeles, CA 90071
213/485-1424

Coldwell Banker
(Commercial & Residential)
533 Fremont Avenue
Los Angeles, CA 90071
213/613-3146

George Elkins Co.
(Commercial & Residential)
499 N. Canon Drive
Beverly Hills, CA 90210
213/272-3456

Grubb & Ellis Co.
18400 Von Karman Avenue
Suite 500
Irvine, CA 92715
213/622-9545

Merrill Lynch Realty
(Commercial & Residential)
1925 Century Park East
Century City, CA 90067
213/201-0023

Fred Sands Realtors
(Commercial & Residential)
11611 San Vicente Boulevard
Los Angeles, CA 90049
213/820-6811

The Seeley Co.
911 Wilshire Boulevard
Los Angeles, CA 90017
213/627-1214

Julien J. Studley
10850 Wilshire Boulevard
Suite 570
Los Angeles, CA 90024
213/475-5761

Residential

Carriage Realty
430 Silver Spur Road
Palos Verdes, CA 90274
213/377-7225

Century 21 Sparrow Realtors
5518 Britton Drive
Long Beach, CA 90815
213/493-6555

Jon Douglas Co.
427 Camden Drive
Beverly Hills, CA 90210
213/859-7007

Herbert Hawkins Co.
230 N. Lake Avenue
Pasadena, CA 91101
818/795-9811

The Prudential California Realty
1925 Century Park East
Los Angeles, CA 90067
213/201-0023

RE/MAX Beach Cities Realty
225 S. Sepulveda Boulevard
Manhattan Beach, CA 90266
213/376-2225

PROFESSIONAL ORGANIZATIONS

American Industrial Real Estate Association
350 S. Figueroa Street
Los Angeles, CA 90071
213/687-8777

California Association of Realtors
525 S. Virgil Avenue
Los Angeles, CA 90020
213/739-8200

Los Angeles County Boards of Real Estate
601 N. Vermont Avenue
Los Angeles, CA 90004
213/668-1973

National Association of Realtors
430 N. Michigan Avenue
Chicago, IL 60611
312/329-8200

Society of Industrial Realtors
601 S. Ardmore Street
Los Angeles, CA 90005
213/387-3768

PROFESSIONAL PUBLICATIONS

California Real Estate Magazine (Los Angeles, CA)
Pasadena Realtor (Pasadena, CA)
Prime Real Estate (Santa Barbara, CA)
Real Estate Review (Palm Desert, CA)
Realty and Building (Chicago, IL)
Western Real Estate News (San Francisco, CA)

DIRECTORIES

Career Planner—Real Estate (VGM Career Horizons, Lincolnwood, IL)
National Directory of 420 Current Real Estate Periodicals and Professional Real Estate Associations, Institutes, Councils and Societies (Real Estate Publishing Co., Sacramento, CA)
National Real Estate Directory (Real Estate Publications, Tampa, FL)
Who's Who in Creative Real Estate (Who's Who in Creative Real Estate Inc., Ventura, CA)

CHAPTER 8

Automotive Marketing and Sales

No. 1 car market offers sales, service opportunities.

More cars are purchased in Southern California than anyplace else in the nation: over 600,000 a year, according to Chris Cedergren, senior analyst for J. D. Power and Associates, a leading automotive research firm in Agoura Hills. "California is by far the No. 1 state in the union when it comes to selling cars," Cedergren said. "Even if you just look at the 13-county Southern California area, we still outperform Texas."

The influx of foreign carmakers that have established corporate beachheads here has created thousands of jobs relating to the sales, marketing, and distribution of cars and, in most cases, the design of new models. "Los Angeles is the prime auto market in the U.S. It's also the trend-setting auto market," said Jack Kyser, chief economist for the Los Angeles Area Chamber of Commerce. "With all the Japanese auto firms here, Los Angeles has a major impact in the auto industry."

The biggest foreign car companies with national sales headquarters in the greater Los Angeles area are Honda, Toyota, Nissan, and Hyundai. Smaller firms including Isuzu, Mitsubishi, Suzuki, and Daihatsu, are carving out a niche for themselves here as well. The General Motors plant in Van Nuys is the only auto manufacturing site left in Southern California. And the fate of that facility, which has been laying off workers in recent years due to slow sales, is uncertain, Cedergren said.

The concentration of so many automotive distributors in one area has resulted in intense competition and a strong emphasis on service and customer satisfaction, Cedergren said. Close to 7,000 people are employed in the corporate or regional offices of these foreign subsidiary companies, which act as intermediaries between the manufacturer and dealer. A dealership, by contrast, is an independent business, a type of franchise operation whose primary function is to sell and service cars. All told, there are about 18,000 jobs in the local automotive industry, Kyser said.

The skills required for working at a subsidiary company are mostly marketing- and service-related, according to Steve Antonoff, employment manager for the Korean giant Hyundai Motor America in Fountain Valley. The bulk of the jobs involve working with bustling car dealerships on a regular basis.

"What they are really doing is helping the dealer increase his sales volume. It's a quasi-sales, quasi-marketing, quasi-promotions kind of job," Antonoff said.

Subsidiaries are divided into several departments, including sales, marketing, parts, service, information systems, quality assurance, human resources, administration, and finance. At the corporate headquarters of most subsidiaries, such as American Isuzu in Whittier, roughly 90 percent of the jobs are either professional or clerical, said Isuzu spokesman Jeff Ringsrud. Most necessitate a college degree. At American Honda in Gardena, the types of positions that come up most often are in the computer division, jobs such as programmer and systems analyst, said Keith Kobular, Honda's employment manager.

The three largest subsidiaries—American Honda Motor Co., Nissan Motor Corp. in USA, and Toyota Motor Sales USA—offer training programs for college-educated, entry-level employees who aspire to management. In Toyota's Field Management Trainee Program, trainees learn firsthand how the various departments in the company's regional offices operate. After gaining experience in sales, marketing, distribution, and customer relations, trainees may then become a district parts or service manager at one of Toyota's nine regional offices nationwide, said Jim Finkel, national personnel operations manager for Toyota Motor Sales in Torrance. Entry-level management jobs in the auto industry generally pay from $25,000 to $35,000 a year, according to Antonoff of Hyundai.

Largest Automotive Employers in Southern California

Company	Employees	Location
Honda	2,600	Gardena
Toyota	1,700	Torrance
Nissan	1,100	Carson
Hyundai	500	Fountain Valley
Isuzu	475	Whittier
Mitsubishi	300	Cypress
Mazda	225	Irvine
Volvo (Concept Center)	120	Westlake Village
Suzuki	100	Brea
Daihatsu	95	Los Alamitos

SOURCE: Los Angeles Area Chamber of Commerce; car companies.

Although specific openings vary with individual companies, the overall job outlook is fairly bright, according to industry experts.

"If you look at the history of the West Coast, there's been a pretty dramatic increase in the auto industry in the last 10 years," Kyser said. "I see really good management opportunities," added Finkel.

Regional or branch offices, which have day-to-day contact with the dealerships, are responsible for training the factory-authorized technicians to work for the dealers as mechanics, Antonoff said. Consequently, a limited number of opportunities are available for service training managers, who are not required to have four-year degrees. Familiarity with auto maintenance and strong organizational abilities are all that's needed for some managerial jobs in the parts or service departments, Ringsrud said. Past experience in car repair always is a plus.

District managers typically oversee 12 to 16 dealerships in their area of specialization, Antonoff said. With one to three years' experience, district or service managers may be promoted to sales manager. Top sales managers with five to seven years of solid performance under their belt can then move on to regional staff manager if the opportunity presents itself, Finkel said.

Education counts and is encouraged for those who want to move up the corporate ladder in the auto industry. "Toyota wants all of its managerial and professional employees to have at least a bachelor's degree. An MBA is desirable, but it's nothing that is mandatory at this time," Finkel said. "People who finish college tend to perform at a higher level and are better employees because of it."

For workers who would like to pursue an advanced degree, many companies offer tuition reimbursement programs that cover up to 80 percent of the costs for tuition and books.

If your idea of work is sitting at a desk and drawing the cars of the future, then L.A.'s the place. Virtually every automobile company, including the Big Three domestic automakers (Chrysler, Ford, and General Motors) and Big Three foreign automakers (Honda, Nissan, and Toyota) have opened design studios in Southern California, Kyser said. The bulk of product design may still be in Detroit, but the number of design jobs in the Los Angeles area is growing, Antonoff said.

Southern California is an important center for automotive design partly because of the Art Center College of Design in Pasadena, the main supplier of creative design talent to the local auto industry, and partly because of the region's diverse mix of cultures and ethnicities. The L.A. area is considered to be fertile ground for finding styles that consumers all across the country can identify with, Cedergren said.

Work at a design center tends to be very secret and theoretical, said Sylvia Voegele, business monitoring manager for Volvo's Concept Center in Westlake Village, which employs about 120 people. Design teams often work seven or eight years in advance on prototypes and three-dimensional car models that reflect projected technical requirements and consumer demands. They are encouraged to draw inspiration from a variety of sources and dream far into the future, producing vehicles that will make today's cars obsolete.

"It's very intense and creative in that we allow designers to run and do their own thing," Voegele said. "We consider the lifestyles and social trends of people living in major metropolitan areas and what is likely to be a good fit for those lifestyles. We cross many disciplines. It involves a lot of strategic planning. Designers are futurists, too, but it's really becoming a more technical field."

The ideal entry-level designer has a good education in design, maybe even in mechanical or electrical engineering, and is a car nut, said Antonoff of Hyundai, the fourth-largest importer of cars into the United States. Depending on their background and level of expertise, beginning designers, who start off as trainees, can make anywhere from $20,000 to $40,000 a year.

Since almost all of the parent companies of local subsidiaries are located in Japan or Korea, specialists in certain departments, especially in product development and engineering, frequently have the opportunity to travel overseas. At Hyundai, Antonoff said, "we have employees who travel to Korea on a regular basis." The willingness to relocate is key, as there is no guarantee that if you start in one zone office you'll end up working there permanently, he added.

With a growing number of people moving to the L.A. area and with dealers continually breaking their own sales records, the city of cars remains a hot prospect for job seekers who want to go corporate. "Southern California appears to be holding its own and gaining," said Ringsrud of Isuzu. "There's definitely movement."

KEY EMPLOYERS IN AUTOMOTIVE MARKETING AND SALES

Corporate Offices

American Honda Motor Co.
100 W. Alondra Boulevard
Gardena, CA 90248
213/327-8280

American Isuzu Motors
2300 Pellissier Place
Whittier, CA 90601
213/949-0611

Daihatsu America
4422 Corporate Drive
Los Alamitos, CA 90720
714/761-7000

Hyundai Motor America
10550 Talbert Avenue
Fountain Valley, CA 92708
714/965-3000

Mazda North America
1444 McGaw Avenue
Irvine, CA 92714
714/261-9429

Mitsubishi Motor Sales of America
Corporate Headquarters
6400 W. Katella Avenue
Cypress, CA 90630
714/372-6200

Nissan Motor Corp. in USA
18600 S. Figueroa Street
Carson, CA 90745
213/532-3111

Toyota Motor Sales USA
19001 S. Western Avenue
Torrance, CA 90501
213/618-4000

Selected Auto Dealerships

Browning Oldsmobile/Subaru
18803 Studebaker Road
Cerritos, CA 90701
213/924-1414

Cormier Chevrolet
2201 E. 223rd Street
Long Beach, CA 90810
213/830-5100

Executive Car Leasing
7807 Santa Monica Boulevard
Los Angeles, CA 90046
213/654-5000

Don Kott Auto Center
21212 S. Avalon Boulevard
Carson, CA 90745
213/518-5770

Longo Toyota
10501 Valley Boulevard
El Monte, CA 91731
213/686-1000

Nugent Chevrolet/Oldsmobile
400 S. La Brea Avenue
Los Angeles, CA 90036
213/939-2131

Penske Cadillac
10700 Studebaker Road
Downey, CA 90241
213/868-9931

Whittlesey Motors
2955 Pacific Coast Highway
Torrance, CA 90505
213/325-7500

PROFESSIONAL ORGANIZATIONS

Automotive Information Council
29200 Southfield Road
Suite 111
Southfield, MI 48076
313/559-5922

**California Automotive Whole-
salers' Association**
4204 Power Inn Road
Sacramento, CA 95826
916/929-9621

**Motor Car Dealers Association of
Southern California**
5757 W. Century Boulevard
Los Angeles, CA 90045
213/776-6144

**Motor Vehicle Manufacturers
Association of the U.S.**
7430 Second Avenue
Suite 300
Detroit, MI 48202
313/872-4311

**National Automobile Dealers'
Association**
8400 Westpark Drive
McLean, VA 22102
703/821-7000

PROFESSIONAL PUBLICATIONS

Automotive Engineering (Warrendale, PA)
Automotive Executive (McLean, VA)

Automotive Fleet (Redondo Beach, CA)
Automotive News (Detroit, MI)
Pacific Automotive News (Laguna Niguel, CA)
Power Report on Automotive Marketing (Westlake Village, CA)
Ward's Auto Dealer (Detroit, MI)
Ward's Auto World (Detroit, MI)

DIRECTORIES

Automotive Age—Buyer's Guide Issue (M. H. West, Van Nuys, CA)
Automobile Dealers Directory (American Business Information Inc., Omaha, NE)
Automotive Marketing—Buyer's Guide Issue (Chilton Co., Radnor, PA)
Directory of Foreign Automotive Companies in the United States (Mead Ventures, Phoenix, AZ)
Ward's Automotive Yearbook (Ward's Communications, Detroit, MI)

Ways to Alleviate Job Stress

Stressed by the job? Health programs can help work it out.

There isn't any job in contemporary society that doesn't cause at least some amount of stress, especially if it's office-related. How you deal with job stress, whether it's physical or psychological, can determine how healthy—and productive—a worker you are, according to medical experts and corporate personnel managers.

"Taking away that stress may make you feel better, sleep better, work better, and function more effectively," said David Shapiro, a professor in UCLA's Department of Psychiatry who studies biofeedback techniques. "Healthy lifestyle habits are going to prolong your life and reduce medical costs," added Dr. Albert Puskas, director of preventive medicine and wellness for Rockwell International in El Segundo.

Some stress, of course, is inevitable. And a certain amount of manageable stress inducers, such as deadlines, may provide some people with the incentive they need to see a task through to completion. But job stress that becomes unmanageable can have many negative side effects, including unnecessary conflict and friction with co-workers, irritability, job dissastisfaction, reduced productivity, even work-related accidents.

"Stress for a while may improve performance, but if it's chronic and ongoing, it can become a law of diminishing returns," said Anthony Reading, a psychologist at Cedars-Sinai Medical Center and director of UCLA's Stress Management Clinic. "Stress may affect the immune system and result in many viral infections. Another important sign of job stress is spin-over that carries into a person's nonwork time. It's common. People may not be aware of the deterioration of the quality of their work, or of their relationships outside of work."

Physically, stress can take a variety of forms, including headaches and stomach aches, abnormal eating habits, a rapid pulse rate, insomnia, fatigue, nervous twitches, dizziness and ulcers. Psychologically, stress can cause nervousness, feelings of worthlessness or hopelessness, depression, anger, mental lapses or lack of concentration, and nightmares, Reading said.

Two obvious ways job stress manifests itself is in muscle tension and frequent illness, said Stephen Sideroff, director of Stress Strategies, a stress reduction program that is part of the Santa Monica Hospital Medical Center's Fit Dimension health clinic. "There is some evidence that stress reduces the effectiveness of the immune system, so people under more stress might get sick more frequently. And when they get sick, they might take longer to recover," Sideroff said.

Many forward-looking companies have recognized that maintaining a vital workforce is good for their bottom line and have established health enhancement programs with workout rooms, exercise classes, and nutrition plans. Not only do these programs keep employees fit and trim and help reduce stress levels, they also help keep the company's health care costs down.

"If we head off the risk employees, we're all better off," said George Wiley, director of employee relations for Rockwell. "We're constantly working to provide our employees with opportunities to be healthy. We want to help them change their lifestyles to practice wellness as a day-to-day activity. We make them our 'health partners.' It's a more productive, sensible approach toward the workforce. It's just a good investment."

Exercise programs are perhaps the best example of how some employers are encouraging their workers to minimize job stress. Sometimes just getting out of the office and working up a good sweat during lunch or after work can make all the difference in one's attitude and stress level.

"Studies have shown that exercise is one of the most effective tools of reducing stress levels. It also helps reduce high blood pressure," said Laurie Bayless, director of employee communications for Transamerica Life Companies in downtown Los Angeles.

At Foodmaker Inc. headquarters in San Diego, corporate employees have free access to a fitness center called Jack's Gym (Foodmaker is the parent company of Jack-in-the-Box restaurants) that includes an exercise room with weights, rowing machines, and stationary bikes. Employees are encouraged to undergo an assessment by the company's fitness director, who will tailor a workout program to meet individual needs, said Durwin Long, Foodmaker's manager of public relations.

Foodmaker also sponsors life improvement classes ranging from aerobics, weight control, and nutrition to how to stop smoking and reduce stress. "We even have classes in meditation and massage," Long said.

Rockwell, which employs roughly 35,000 people in Southern California, maintains workout facilities at its El Segundo, Anaheim, Canoga Park, Downey, and Palmdale locations, Wiley said. The resortlike Anaheim site is replete with a 20-acre park, nine-hole golf course, and Olympic-size swimming pool.

Transamerica, which takes a holistic approach toward its workers' health and welfare, has a wellness policy written into its business philosophy, Bayless said. In addition to a full-service gym with basketball, volleyball, and racquetball courts on the 10th floor of its Broadway building in downtown Los Angeles, Transamerica offers brown-bag luncheon classes on such topics as how to quit smoking, "sit and be fit" (how to exercise while at your desk), and reduce stress.

Jeff deBoer, franchise sales manager for Jack-in-the-Box, says he jogs five miles a day during lunch with a running partner and uses the Jack's Gym fitness center four or five times a week to help alleviate the stress inherent in his high-pressure position (most of his time is spent making sales calls). Jogging every day has helped him relieve his high blood pressure to some degree, deBoer said. "After four hours straight talking on the phone, it's the best release I know for being able to come back in with a new attitude."

Despite elaborate recreational opportunities, which are even extended to retirees and dependents of employees at companies like Rockwell, most employees do not take advantage of them. Of the more than 3,100 people who work at the Transamerica Center, for example, only 500 are gym members. DeBoer said that only 2 out of 10 people in his department work out regularly at the company's facility.

"We probably do not reach more than 20 percent of our employees," concurred Wiley of Rockwell. "I think you will find that true of most companies." Added Puskas: "We have a lot of people who should get involved in athletic programs, but I'd be happy if 50 percent of our people did nothing but watch their dietary intake and lose some weight. Just encouraging people to walk is a tremendous breakthrough."

Besides workout programs, exercise facilities, and recreation classes, companies are helping to alleviate job stress in other ways:

Flexible hours programs, also known as flextime, that give employees the option of coming in to work early and leaving early, thereby beating traffic and allowing time to take care of personal errands, are now common at companies like Transamerica and Hewlett Packard. This affords workers greater control over their working lives, which experts agree is a key factor in reducing stress. Transamerica also has a "short Friday" policy during the summer months, whereby employees are required to work only 5½ hours on Fridays.

Calorie labels are affixed to all the packaged foods at the Rockwell cafeteria so that employees can keep a close watch on their caloric intake and better control their weight, Wiley said. "Most of the reasons we go to doctors are for things that are really brought on by our lifestyles. For people who don't practice good dietary habits, the results are obvious. We want our employees to be the healthiest employees anywhere."

Employee assistance counselors, who offer referral and counseling services in everything from child care and marital problems to financial services and car pool arrangements, are another way companies are trying to make employees' lives less complicated. "Any personal thing can get in the way of work," said Lisa Moriyama, director of employee relations for Transamerica. "When you're worried about transportation and child care, those are stress inducers."

Health fairs are becoming increasingly common at companies like Transamerica, which also stages periodic "stress fairs" that feature experts who give talks on the various factors related to stress. Such programs benefit the company as well as the employee, Bayless said. "By offering services that help employees' personal lives, it helps them concentrate on their work while they're at work." Transamerica also publishes a health enhancement supplement entitled "Well Aware" in the employee newsletter.

While Rockwell, Transamerica, and Foodmaker have integrated programs that incorporate their employees' health and welfare into their daily work routine, most employees are lucky just to receive medical benefits to cover hospital costs. "There is an awareness in the public health area and in industry that good programs that anticipate problems can save money in the long run," said Shapiro of UCLA. "But companies haven't done as much as they should."

Are there ways to prevent stress? Yes—if you're aware of the factors that can contribute to it. Mental stress tends to be most prevalent where the worker has the least control over the work environment, Reading said. Too many interruptions, a high level of pressure, lack of organization, not enough social support, and insufficient autonomy can all contribute to stress. "In terms of job stress, if you have more control, you have less stress," Reading said. "You need people to laugh with, get along with, and share with to have a sense of a caring, trusting environment."

A poor relationship with a superior or co-worker, or the feeling that you aren't being paid what you're worth or being recognized for the good work that you're doing, should not go unattended. Being in constant fear of losing your job—a counterproductive tactic used by all too many bosses—is another major source of stress.

"Stress is a disease of denial," Moriyama said. "The person who is experiencing stress may not admit it." But, Reading added, "it's never too late to reduce stress, even if it's caused the breakdown of a relationship or marriage."

The inability to express anger or concern when exposed to such conflict and uncertainty can only aggravate the stress that already exists, said Shapiro. "There is such a thing as the need to assert yourself. If you're in a situation where you're being confronted by a demanding person making unreasonable demands, that can cause difficulty."

Even if you are powerless over outside factors, such as your job responsibilities, work setting, or management style of your supervisor, you still have control over the way you can inwardly react to these pressures. Namely, you can learn to accept the unchangeable and either not let it bother you or move on to a new job. Prolonged stress can be highly destructive, experts agree.

"If you have a deadline, it's very important that you don't have your stress reaction going for a whole week leading up to that deadline," said Sideroff of Stress Strategies. "You need to stay relaxed at various points leading up to the deadline."

ARE YOU STRESSED AT WORK?

Here are some common signs of stress.

Physical Signs
- Tension or migraine headaches
- Difficulty in falling or staying asleep
- Fatigue
- Overeating or loss of appetite
- Indigestion, ulcers
- Twitches

Psychological Signs
- Nervousness, anxiety
- Irritability, anger
- Depression, nightmares
- Feeling emotionally drained
- Diminished memory and recall
- Loss of sense of humor

Behavioral Signs
- Reduced productivity at work
- Reduced quality of work performance
- Inappropriate mistrust or hostility toward associates
- Missing appointments or deadlines
- Absenteeism or shirking responsibilities
- Indecisiveness

SOURCE: Cedars-Sinai Medical Center.

Advised Reading: "Look at ways of relaxing so that you're not forever pestered by this stress with no respite."

Leaving a situation you are incompatible with and that causes too much stress should not result in feelings of inadequacy. As Reading notes: "It's a fit between the individual, his or her personality, and the nature of the company. One person's ideal job is not another's."

A simple yet effective way of keeping stress under control is to set aside time for yourself whenever possible *while* working, especially if you have a demanding job, said Shapiro. "Just getting up from your desk for 5 or 10 minutes and stretching can help. The most important thing about a coffee break is not the coffee, but the break. The coffee's probably not so good for you."

At the managerial level, Sideroff said, it is important to take an organizational approach to reducing stress, to work within the rules and procedures of the company as a team and not create so much competition among fellow employees that they're suspicious of each other or constantly tense. Unremitting stress can engender a vague fear among employees that something bad or unpleasant is going to happen. Many times, such notions can turn into self-fulfilling prophecies.

"There's a lot of stress at the management level because managers are caught between executives and employees. But if you foster a more sensitive and cooperative atmosphere, you're going to wind up with a better performance out of people," Sideroff said. "If you reward them for good work rather than just criticize them when they don't do a good job, you'll have a much healthier situation for everyone."

And less costly, in both human and economic terms. Mental stress claims against California employers skyrocketed more than 500 percent in the 1980s, costing companies an estimated 4.5 percent of their total payroll, or $1 billion yearly, according to the California Workers' Compensation Institute (CWCI), an independent research organization based in San Francisco.

Surveys, such as those conducted by the American Institute of Stress in New York, routinely identify work situations as the biggest source of personal stress, contributing more to mental tension and emotional strain than any other cause. Stress is now cited as the most common nonphysical work injury in California, said Alan Tebb, CWCI's general manager.

Yet, as recently as the late 1970s, the number of such claims didn't even warrant a separate listing in the state's annual report on occupational injuries and illnesses. "Twenty years ago it was unheard of," said Dr. Allen Enelow, a clinical professor of psychiatry at USC who has a private practice in Santa Monica. "Since then, there has been an increase in awareness of psychological issues in the general public."

In addition to heightened awareness, the mounting number of stress claims is due in part to increased workloads brought on by cutbacks, restructurings, and international competition. The sharp rise in the incidence of job stress over the past decade can also be attributed to the shift from a manufacturing- to service-oriented economy, Enelow said. Service jobs emphasize the employee's ability to interact with customers, clients, and superiors, which is considerably more stressful than operating a machine.

In light of the financial implications of job stress, CWCI counsels employers to identify, and try to eliminate, the causes of stress in the workplace, including insensitive managers, unrealistic deadlines, insufficient training, and failing to provide workers with the opportunity to share their views, Tebb said.

RECOMMENDED READING

Bensen, Herbert and Klipper, Miriam Z. *The Relaxation Response.* New York: Avon, 1976.

Brod, Craig, and St. John, Wes. *Technostress: The Human Cost of the Computer Revolution.* Reading, MA: Addison-Wesley, 1984.

Campbell, Jeremy. *Winston Churchill's Afternoon Nap: A Wide-Awake Inquiry into the Human Nature of Time.* New York: Simon & Schuster, 1987.

Feur, Louis C. *White-Collar Stress: A Comprehensive, Practical Approach to Relieving Stress and Ensuring Professional and Financial Success.* Hollywood, FL: F. Fell Publishers, 1987.

Hanson, Peter G., MD. *The Joy of Stress.* Kansas City: Andrews, McMeel & Parker, 1986.

Hanson, Peter G., MD. *Stress for Success.* New York: Doubleday, 1989.

Ivancevich, John M. *Job Stress: From Theory to Suggestions.* New York: Haworth Press, 1987.

Murphy, Lawrence R. *Stress Management in Work Settings.* New York: Praeger, 1989.

Pelletier, Kenneth R. *Healthy People in Unhealthy Places: Stress and Fitness at Work.* New York: Delacorte, 1984.

Roskies, Ethel. *Stress Management for the Healthy Type A: Theory and Practice.* New York: Guilford Press, 1987.

Shaevitz, Marjorie Helen. *The Superwoman Syndrome.* New York: Warner, 1985.

Taylor, Harold L. *Making Time Work for You: A Guidebook to Effective and Productive Time Management.* New York: Beaufort, 1982.

Veninga, Robert L., and Spradley, James P. *The Work-Stress Connection: How to Cope With Job Burnout.* New York: Ballantine, 1982.

Witkin-Lanoil, Georgia. *The Male Stress Syndrome: How to Recognize and Live With It.* New York: Newmarket Press, 1986.

SECTION 3

Careers in Architecture and Design

CHAPTER 9

Architecture and Landscape Architecture

Los Angeles is in the midst of an architectural renaissance.

Every major city has its time of cultural awakening and architectural renaissance. Florence, Italy, during the 1400s. London in Christopher Wren's time. Paris under the reigns of Louis XIV through Louis XVI. New York in the early 20th century. Now, many prominent architects believe, it's Los Angeles's time.

Architects like Michael Rotondi, director of the Southern California Institute of Architecture and a partner in the avant-garde architectural firm Morphosis, argue that the world is watching, and waiting, for what L.A. will do next. "The advancement of civilization will depend on what we do here. I am absolutely convinced of that," Rotondi recently said in the *Los Angeles Times.*

Los Angeles, one of the world's youngest big cities, is considered by many to be the ultimate architectural laboratory. Architects working here have that rare opportunity to make a bold new statement and leave a lasting impression. As the ephemeral city continues to search for a more permanent identity, architects will play an increasingly important role in shaping its destiny.

Around town, there are now several examples of innovative architecture built to last. They include the distinctive red brick Museum of Contemporary Art designed by Arata Isozaki, the ultramodern Loyola Law School designed by Frank Gehry, and the 73-story white granite library tower designed by I. M. Pei. These are not replaceable buildings, as so many of L.A.'s edifices have been in the past.

"There's a renewed emphasis on design and the quality of buildings," said Jack Kyser, chief economist for the Los Angeles Area Chamber of Commerce. "You have more attention being paid to architecture and more interest in rehabilitation. If you're talented, Southern California is going to be a place to get ahead."

Kyser's assertions are supported by rising employment figures. From 1987 to 1992, the number of architects and landscape architects in Los Angeles and Orange counties is expected to grow from 3,810 to 4,340, a 14 percent gain in just five years. Statewide, the field of architecture is projected to grow 16 percent by 1995, from 11,200 professionals in 1990 to an estimated 13,010 by mid-decade, according to Employment Development Department statistics.

From new construction in the bustling downtown central business district to new housing developments, remodeling jobs, and commercial projects in the sprawling suburbs, architects are directly influencing the city's course. In L.A., they also have more freedom to experiment, dabble in the avant-garde, and try things that aren't allowed in other, stodgier cities.

"There's a much more open environment in Los Angeles (than in the east)," Peter Eisenman, a prominent New York architect, recently told the *Times.* "Clients are willing to take risks with younger architects and more avant-garde projects. It has the spirit of the frontier. Los Angeles is the city of the avant-garde in this country right now, no question. There's nothing happening here in New York in terms of movement forward."

Architects, in essence, create enduring pieces of usable art. They design all manner of structures—dwellings, skyscrapers, hospitals, shopping centers, airports, industrial parks, office complexes, and school campuses. Architects take their cue from clients, meeting with them to determine the purpose and cost limitations of a project. To visualize their concept, they then prepare scale drawings.

Next, blueprints are drawn up, showing exact dimensions and the placement of utilities. Architects also specify building materials and in some cases interior furnishings, although these are usually prescribed by an interior designer. Many large architectural firms employ their own interior designers on staff (see Chapter 10).

In architecture, raw talent is not enough. Architects must

graduate from an accredited degree program, which typically takes five years to complete as an undergraduate or, with a four-year degree already in hand, a year or two at the graduate level. Los Angeles–area schools noted for their architecture programs include USC, UCLA, and Cal Poly Pomona.

Upon graduating, beginning architects can go to work for a small office or large firm and start designing projects at the associate level. Internship experience while still in school helps to get that first important job offer. To become registered, architects must work for at least 2½ years before qualifying to take the state licensing exam. Registered architects can solicit business and act as signatories on project plans.

While architects have to understand design and engineering, they also need management and community relations skills. Projects must be built on schedule and within the budget. Architects not only design a project, they oversee its construction to ensure that contractors are adhering to the plans and using the specified materials.

Further, since most projects require approvals from various government agencies, architects must know how to work with city building departments and planning officials. Increasingly, homeowner associations and private interest groups are having a say in what new projects get approved, especially in areas that are environmentally sensitive. This is where community relations comes in.

"Added scrutiny is changing the field," said Jeffrey Tohl, owner of the Architecture Studio in Los Angeles. "It's becoming more difficult to practice architecture. There's downzoning in many areas and a lot more red tape. So it's important to get hands-on experience in dealing with the agencies and seeing all the pieces come together. You have to be a master of all languages."

The best overall hands-on experience, according to many architects interviewed, can be had at a smaller office rather than a large firm. Small offices afford more opportunity for substantive design work and direct interaction with clients and the different regulatory agencies involved in a project.

At big firms, the duties are more specialized and narrowly defined. Beginning architects usually work under the wing of a senior designer; senior designers under the direction of a project architect; project architects under the guidance of a project designer, ad infinitum.

"In a large firm, unless you're a hotshot designer or senior architect, you're going to be negotiating your ideas and the integrity of your ideas," Tohl said.

The advantages of working for a big firm are the prestige (the experience you gain there looks great on a résumé), the opportunity to work on a wide variety of projects, including high-rise buildings, and, in the long run, job security. Surprisingly, beginning architects at large firms are paid about the same as at a small office, around $22,000 or $23,000 with a bachelor's degree, and $25,000 with a master's. Principals of large architectural firms typically make $100,000 or more.

When interviewing for a job, your portfolio and how well you present your ideas are paramount. This is another reason communication skills are important. The presentation of designs and the thought processes that went into them—the aesthetic and structural justifications—often make the difference between winning or losing a client.

Veteran architects around long enough to have helped plan parts of the Southland agree that L.A. is a city with great potential.

"Of all the cities in the U.S., I think Los Angeles is the most active architecturally," said Raymond Kappe, an architect for 40 years and founder of the Southern California Institute of Architecture (SCI-ARC) as well as Cal Poly Pomona's architecture program. "The Pacific Rim influence and foreign investment that comes into this center have made it much more international than it used to be."

Another aspect of architecture that has been growing in prominence in recent years is landscape architecture, planning the exterior look of a building.

"It's a profession that is really timely," said Donald Tompkins, a senior principal landscape architect for the SWA Group in Laguna Beach. "A lot of people understand how to build buildings, but they don't understand how to build livable environments. I really think the 1990s is going to be *the* decade for landscape architecture."

Like architects, landscape architects need a combination of education and experience for licensing, said Kenneth Nakaba, a professor in the Landscape Architecture Department at Cal Poly Pomona, which offers the only accredited landscape architecture program in Southern California. The extension programs at UCLA and UC Irvine offer unaccredited programs. Landscape architects make an average salary of about $35,000 but can earn much higher, Nakaba said.

SELECTED ARCHITECTURAL FIRMS

Bobrow/Thomas and Associates
1001 Westwood Boulevard
Los Angeles, CA 90024
213/208-7017

Leo A. Daly
3333 Wilshire Boulevard
Suite 200
Los Angeles, CA 90010
213/388-1361

Daniel, Mann, Johnson & Mendenhall
3250 Wilshire Boulevard
Los Angeles, CA 90010
213/381-3663

Ellerbe Becket Inc.
2501 Colorado Avenue
Santa Monica, CA 90404
213/207-8000

Gensler and Associates/Architects
2049 Century Park East
Suite 570
Century City, CA 90067
213/277-7405

Gruen Associates
6330 San Vicente Boulevard
Los Angeles, CA 90048
213/937-4270

The Jerde Partnership Inc.
2798 Sunset Boulevard
Los Angeles, CA 90026
213/413-1030

Kober Cedergreen Rippon
649 S. Olive Street
Suite 1200
Los Angeles, CA 90014
213/623-6661

The Luckman Partnership
9220 Sunset Boulevard
Los Angeles, CA 90069
213/274-7755

Albert C. Martin and Associates
811 W. Seventh Street
Los Angeles, CA 90017
213/683-1900

McClellan Cruz Gaylord & Associates
199 S. Los Robles Avenue
Suite 400
Pasadena, CA 91101
818/793-9119

The Nadel Partnership Inc.
1990 S. Bundy Drive
Los Angeles, CA 90025
213/826-2100

Neptune & Thomas Associates
1550 W. Colorado Boulevard
Los Angeles, CA 91105
213/255-1401

Pereira Associates
6100 Wilshire Boulevard
Los Angeles, CA 90048
213/933-8341

Rochlin Baran & Balbona Inc.
10980 Wilshire Boulevard
Los Angeles, CA 90024
213/879-1474

Starkman + Vidal + Christensen
5657 Wilshire Boulevard
Suite 500
Los Angeles, CA 90036
213/934-1010

PROFESSIONAL ORGANIZATIONS

American Institute of Architects
Los Angeles Chapter
8687 Melrose Avenue
Room M-72
Los Angeles, CA 90069
213/380-4595

**Asian American Architects &
  Engineers**
808 N. Spring Street
Los Angeles, CA 90012
213/625-2520

**Association for Women in
  Architecture**
810 E. Third Street
Los Angeles, CA 90013
213/625-1734

Frank Lloyd Wright Foundation
Taleisin West
Scottsdale, AZ 85261
602/860-2700

**National Institute for Architectural
  Education**
30 W. 22nd Street
New York, NY 10010
212/924-7000

**Society of American Registered
  Architects**
1245 S. Highland Avenue
Lombard, IL 60148
312/932-4622

PROFESSIONAL PUBLICATIONS

Architecture (Washington, DC)
Architecture California (Sacramento, CA)
Architectural Designs Magazine (New York, NY)
Architectural Digest (Los Angeles, CA)
Architectural Record (New York, NY)
Building Design and Construction (Des Plaines, IL)
Progressive Architecture (Stamford, CT)

DIRECTORIES

Accredited Programs in Architecture (National Architectural Accrediting
  Board, Washington, DC)
*Directory of Minority and Women-Owned Engineering and Architectural
  Firms* (American Consulting Engineers Council, Washington, DC)
Macmillan Encyclopedia of Architects (Macmillan, New York, NY)
Pro File: The Official Directory of the American Institute of Architects (Ar-
  chimedia, New York, NY)

KEY EMPLOYERS OF LANDSCAPE ARCHITECTS

Ambrose Associates
430 N. Rodeo Drive
Beverly Hills, CA 90210
213/274-5331

Bionomic Design Associates
1041 E. Green Street
Pasadena, CA 91106
213/681-7082

**Bridgers & Bridgers Landscape
  Architects**
23564 Calabasas Road
Calabasas, CA 91302
818/704-7212

EDAW Inc.
18002 Cowan
Suite 100
Irvine, CA 92714
714/660-8044

Eriksson Peters Thoms (EPT)
1214 E. Green Street
Pasadena, CA 91106
818/795-2008

Fong & Associates
930 W. 16th Street
Costa Mesa, CA 92627
714/645-9444

Galper Baldon Associates
723 Ocean Front Walk
Venice, CA 90291
213/392-3992

Hume Edward & Associates Inc.
17302 Lassen Street
Northridge, CA 91325
818/993-0200

Iwanaga Associates
412 W. Fourth Street
Santa Ana, CA 92701
714/547-3900

Land Images
14025 Panay Way
Marina del Rey, CA 90292
213/822-0043

Lee Newman & Associates
31320 Via Colinas
Westlake Village, CA 91361
818/991-5056

William L. Peacock, Inc.
742 N. Glendale Avenue
Glendale, CA 91206
818/240-0874

Peridian Group
17848 Sky Park Circle
Irvine, CA 92714
714/261-5120

POD/Sasaki
106 W. Fourth Street
Santa Ana, CA 92701
714/953-9443

**Bryan H. Spangle Landscape
  Architects**
11836 Laurelwood Drive
Studio City, CA 91604
818/762-6723

Studio Green
458 S. Wetherly Drive
Beverly Hills, CA 90211
213/278-7437

SWA Group
811 W. Seventh Street
Los Angeles, CA 90017
213/622-7242

Takata Associates Inc.
1017 El Centro
South Pasadena, CA 91030
818/799-7187

Urban Landscape Concepts
458 S. Wetherly Drive
Beverly Hills, CA 90211
213/278-1790

Walt Young Associates Inc.
8949 Reseda Boulevard
Northridge, CA 91324
818/886-8180

PROFESSIONAL ORGANIZATIONS

American Society of Landscape Architects
3151 Airway Avenue
Costa Mesa, CA 92626
714/557-0238

Council of Landscape Architectural Registration Boards
309 S. Franklin Street
Syracuse, NY 13202
315/472-1717

California Council of Landscape Architects
1121 L Street
Sacramento, CA 95814
916/447-4113

Landscape Architecture Foundation
1733 Connecticut Avenue, NW
Washington, DC 20009
202/223-6229

PROFESSIONAL PUBLICATIONS

Interiorscape (Clearwater, FL)
Landscape Architecture (Washington, DC)
The Landscape Contractor (Glen Ellyn, IL)
Landscape Design (Van Nuys, CA)

DIRECTORIES

Guide to Educational Programs in Landscape Architecture (American Society of Landscape Architects, Washington, DC)
Landscape Architects (American Business Information, Omaha, NE)
Members' Handbook (American Society of Landscape Architects, Washington, DC)

CHAPTER 10

Interior Design

Building a career takes hard work, training, and creativity.

Interior design is like most jobs with a glamorous image. Behind the glitter is a lot of hard work. Technical skills and a large dose of business savvy are no less important than creativity and an eye for the next trend. Experienced designers say the field offers the best of both the corporate and artistic worlds—the opportunity to make important business decisions and the chance to be independently creative.

Designers adjust, dress, and shape space in all manner of structures in which people work and play. They take into account factors ranging from weather conditions, available materials, and visual appeal to budgets and deadlines. They might be employed by an interior design or architectural firm, a theme park or large corporation, such as a hotel chain, all of which have continuing interior design needs.

Starting salaries in the interior design field range from $5 an hour for design assistants to upward of $26,000 a year for junior designers, project managers, or draftspeople. Designers make $30,000 to $40,000, while senior designers bill from $50 to $250 an hour and earn $50,000 a year or more.

Los Angeles is the design center of the West Coast, with most design offices concentrated in a five-mile radius extending from the landmark big blue Pacific Design Center in West Hollywood.

"In Los Angeles, you have a tremendous amount of resources for the industry to draw on for materials and training," said Jack Kyser, chief economist for the Los Angeles Area Chamber of Commerce. "It's a good and growing profession. There's a lot of new space out there. That means happy times for interior designers."

While the interior design industry has been steadily growing over the past several years, it's a competitive field that demands a high level of skill and expertise. In the whole of Southern California—from San Luis Obispo to San Diego—there are about 4,500 interior designers.

On the job, designers are part artists, part technicians, part coordinators, part salespeople, and part expediters.

"Maybe 10 percent of our time is spent on design. We have to sell the job, do the ordering, oversee the installation, and follow up," said Jeanne James, senior vice president for Design 1 Interiors in Century City. Added Bret Parsons, executive director of the Los Angeles chapter of the American Society of Interior Designers: "It's highly exacting and tedious work. It's detail-oriented and labor-intensive. And you need a real good business person back at the office if it's not yourself. You need to get that 50 percent down."

Designers who work for sole proprietors usually design home interiors, while those employed by large firms typically plan commercial interiors, including offices, lobbies, and corridors. Home interior designers often work odd hours, accommodating the schedules of their clients. They frequently make presentations at night and on weekends. Commercial, or contract, interior designers usually work during normal business hours.

Beyond matching colors, furniture, and fabrics, designers need to be well-versed in building codes, fire retardant materials, and barrier-free designs for handicapped access. For today's designer, the emphasis now is on practical skills, James said. "Get away from the frills of it and get into the technical part. The job is not going out to lunch with your client and looking at pretty things."

A college degree or certificate in interior design, which takes two to four years to complete, is virtually essential to break into the field. "Very few designers make it big without an education," Parsons said. This is mainly due to the growing importance of drafting—drawing a plan of work to be completed—which takes at least two years to master, he added.

"The most important thing, and I see it lacking in some of my peers, is to get a good foothold on the basic technical skills of design and the history of architectural design," said John Turturro, a designer with the Hilton Hotel Corp.

Since designers often work in tandem with architects on office building interiors, those who are skilled in drafting are highly prized. "When designers go to work for an architectural firm, quite often their ability to draw is a marketable skill that even the architects don't have," said Gaylord Eckles, coordinator of the Environmental Design Department for the prestigious Art Center College of Design in Pasadena.

The L.A. area has several respected design schools. Besides the Art Center, these include Woodbury University in Burbank, UCLA Extension, the Otis Art Institute of Parsons School of Design in Los Angeles, the American College for the Applied Arts in Westwood, the Fashion Institute of Design and Merchandising in Los Angeles, Cal State Long Beach, and Cal State Northridge.

Design curricula are becoming more technical, incorporating classes in drafting and architecture. This sophisticated training reflects the evolution of the field beyond interior decorating. "Designers can become members of the architecture team," Eckles said. "They often play an important part in building decisions. If you're designing it, you're thinking of the entire package, how the space responds to the required need."

The Art Center's program in environmental design entails coursework in interior design, space planning, exhibit and theme park design, architecture, graphic design, product design, drawing, and rendering, Eckles said. "It's practice. What the school looks for is your ability to draw. Learning the day-to-day realistic things, like budgets, will come in time."

Design programs are looked on favorably by the industry because of the technical training they provide. Students also have the opportunity to assemble a portfolio, or collection of drawings and work samples representing their ability, which acts as a calling card to prospective employers.

"In design, the portfolio carries a great deal of weight," said Turturro, a graduate of the UCLA Extension Interior and Environmental Design program. "I was hired as an assistant designer with Hilton in 10 minutes based largely on my portfolio. We're a visual field, so if [employers] see photos and renderings and drawings that show you have a technical skill and maybe some art with it, they know the potential is there."

Just because drawing ability is a prerequisite for some programs doesn't mean the field is closed to people who can't draw naturally. "If someone can follow detail, he or she can learn how to design," said James of Design 1. "Some of our best people started out with absolutely no talent. I'd rather hire a really dependable person who wants to learn than have a talented artist who's not dependable."

Out of school, design graduates have several career options. One jumping-off point is drafting. At Design 1, which does about 60 percent of its business designing the interiors of model homes, "we usually start everybody out in drafting," James said. "They have to understand scale and architecture."

On the commercial side, draftspeople work on technical elements of interior design under the direction of an architect. Residential drafting involves more simplistic tracing and conceptual placement of furniture, James said. A junior draftsperson will typically start out on the residential side.

Another entry-level position in interior design is junior designer. Junior designers work under the guidance of a designer, assembling all the materials for a project and helping make the presentation to the client. After a year or two at the junior level, it's possible to become a full designer and dictate the colors, design, and direction of a project.

Interior designers can also work their way up through the ranks by starting as design assistants, helping to put the designer's look together by gathering the fabrics, wallpaper, accessories, and artwork. They might then become a project manager in charge of tying all the loose ends of a project together, keeping a job within budget, following up on the ordering, and making sure a project's on schedule. "This is a team effort," James said. "We have a lot of deadlines."

Interior designers acting as space planners also work with commercial real estate brokers on large leasing projects, determining the precise amount of space required by office tenants. Due to a flurry of recent building activity, much of this space is new. But a large amount of work involves redesigning existing spaces. Frequently, the same firm that designed the original space is called in to redesign it.

"As their needs change, we can make recommendations," said Dannine Sheridan, regional sales director for PHH Environments, a nationwide interior design firm with an office in Los Angeles. "We'll even come in, take an inventory, and resell their furniture for them. It's much more involved than it used to be."

SELECTED INTERIOR DESIGN FIRMS

Chaix & Johnson International Inc.
7060 Hollywood Boulevard
Suite 1100
Los Angeles, CA 90028
213/461-3761

Cole Martinez Curtis & Associates
308 Washington Street
Marina del Rey, CA 90292
213/827-7200

Design 1 Interiors
2049 Century Park East
Suite 3000
Century City, CA 90067
213/553-5032

Ellerbe Becket Inc.
2501 Colorado Avenue
Santa Monica, CA 90404
213/207-8000

Gensler & Associates/Architects
2049 Century Park East
Suite 570
Century City, CA 90067
213/277-7405

Hellmuth, Obata & Kassabaum Inc.
1999 Bundy Drive
Los Angeles, CA 90025
213/207-8400

Interior Design Inc.
1440 S. Sepulveda Boulevard
Suite 216
Los Angeles, CA 90025
213/473-5358

Interni Design Inc.
523 W. Sixth Street
Suite 347
Los Angeles, CA 90014
213/629-1248

ISD Interiors
818 W. Seventh Street
Los Angeles, CA 90017
213/622-5252

Leason Pomeroy Associates
3780 Wilshire Boulevard
Suite 300
Los Angeles, CA 90010
213/738-7655

PHH Environments
716 S. Olive Street
Los Angeles, CA 90014
213/629-0011

Reback Design Associates Inc.
10960 Wilshire Boulevard
Suite 300
Los Angeles, CA 90024
213/478-0142

Reel/Grobman & Associates
261 S. Figueroa Street
Los Angeles, CA 90012
213/628-9090

Reeves Associates Architects
417 S. Hill Street
Suite 1100
Los Angeles, CA 90013
213/680-3230

Rothenberg Sawasy Architects Inc.
241 S. Figueroa Street
Suite 300
Los Angeles, CA 90012
213/680-1421

Steinmann, Grayson, Smylie
6310 San Vicente Boulevard
Suite 550
Los Angeles, CA 90048
213/933-5050

Widom Wein Cohen Interiors
11801 W. Olympic Boulevard
Los Angeles, CA 90064
213/312-6800

John Wolcott Associates Inc.
3859 Cardiff Avenue
Culver City, CA 90232
213/204-2290

PROFESSIONAL ORGANIZATIONS

American Society of Interior Designers
c/o Pacific Design Center
8687 Melrose Avenue
Los Angeles, CA 90069
213/659-8998

Foundation for Interior Design Education Research
60 Monroe Center, NW
Grand Rapids, MI 49503
616/458-0400

Institute of Business Designers
National Headquarters
341 Merchandise Mart
Chicago, IL 60654
312/467-1950

Interior Design Educators Council
14252 Culver Drive
Suite A-311
Irvine, CA 92714
714/551-1622

PROFESSIONAL PUBLICATIONS

Architectural Digest (Los Angeles, CA)
Interior Design (New York, NY)
Interior Landscape Industry (Chicago, IL)
Interiors (New York, NY)
Interiorscape (Clearwater, FL)

DIRECTORIES

Design Firm Directory (Wefler & Associates, Evanston, IL)
Interior Decorators (American Business Information Inc., Omaha, NE)
Interior Design Programs Accredited by FIDER (Foundation for Interior Design Education Research, Grand Rapids, MI)

CHAPTER 11

Urban Planning

Planners are needed to oversee, manage L.A.'s rapid growth.

Los Angeles is the only big city in the industrial world that is still growing rapidly. New businesses and residents are moving in at a prodigious rate. By the year 2010, the population of the L.A. basin is forecast to swell from today's 14.4 million to an estimated 19 million. From 1984 to 2010, 3 million new jobs should be created in the five-county greater Los Angeles area.

This tremendous expansion translates into opportunity for planners, who are needed to oversee the revitalization of existing communities and manage future growth. The City of Anaheim's Planning Department, for example, has increased from 60 people in 1986 to 86 people in 1990. Overall, there are some 1,100 urban and regional planners in Los Angeles and Orange counties, according to the Employment Development Department.

The role of urban planners is twofold: to help a city chart a course for long-range development, and take those actions necessary to regulate current development. They also try to solve current social, economic, and environmental problems.

Planning is divided into two primary areas: long-range, or advance planning, and current planning, or zoning. Long-range planning encompasses redevelopment, environmental planning, ordinance development, and transportation management. Current planning includes community development, code enforcement, and environmental planning.

"Long-range planners look at how everything fits together,

the balances between residential and commercial. They make sure everything is working. It's a coordination role," said Greg Hastings, zoning division manager for the City of Anaheim. "Current planning, on the other hand, is more reactionary. It's implementing laws that have already been created."

Here's a close-up look at the six specific planning areas:

Redevelopment involves the building or rebuilding of commercial and industrial projects where something else now stands. Typically, areas are targeted that are deemed to be "blighted" or run-down. New construction is then proposed and developers are given low-cost loans and tax benefits to encourage them to build. Many times, "eminent domain" is declared and a city buys back private property for public use.

Environmental planning is an indispensable part of the process. Under the National Environmental Protection Act and the California Environmental Quality Act, planners are required to draw up an environmental impact report, or EIR, for any new project undertaken. The EIR evaluates the effects of a project independently of the project itself. If they are deemed too great, the project can't go through.

"The environmental aspect of planning is growing, primarily due to the evolution of the laws and the fact that most of the easiest parcels of land to develop already have been developed," said Frank Wein, vice president of planning services for Michael Brandman Associates in Santa Ana. "Moreover, the public has latched on to the environmental process as a way to curb and carefully monitor growth."

Within environmental planning, two major areas of concern to local planners are waste management and air quality. Most, if not all, Southland cities are initiating some sort of recycling program in an effort to conserve reusable materials and minimize dumping in landfills. Every city in the L.A. basin also has to comply with the South Coast Air Quality Management District's Air Quality Management Plan, which requires preparation of an air quality element in each jurisdiction's general plan.

Ordinance development entails the technical process of zoning, or partitioning of cities into sections reserved for different uses, such as commercial, residential, or industrial. Zoning can become a hot topic when a developer requests an exemption for an over-sized project in an environmentally sensitive or particularly dense area. Ordinance development also involves the creation of a general plan, which serves as a city's blueprint for long-term development.

Transportation management is another crucial issue facing Southern California, as the population continues to explode and the number of cars on the road (currently around 9 million) proliferates. Planners in this area devise ways to streamline traffic patterns, such as synchronizing traffic signals during rush hour and designating certain streets one-way. Mass transit is an integral component to transportation management, and one that Southland planners are addressing wholeheartedly, with new freeways, rail systems, and bus lines all in the works.

Community development is the part of current planning that deals with subdividing tracts of land into specific building lots. While its role is minimal in metropolitan Los Angeles, it's vitally needed in such rapidly developing outlying areas as Palmdale, Lancaster, and the Antelope Valley. In Orange County, growth areas include east Anaheim, east Orange, and unincorporated parts between Irvine and Laguna Beach.

Code enforcement is the regulatory work of current planners. Enforcement comes at various stages of the building process, and planners who act in this role make sure that zoning ordinances are adhered to, height limits aren't exceeded, and a project turns out the way it was approved. In this sense, they act as building inspectors, but in a broader capacity.

Managing the Southland's vast urban and suburban sprawl is no easy task. Urban and regional planners must have a strong combination of technical skills and analytical ability. The ideal educational background for planning is a master's degree in urban and regional planning, although a bachelor's in urban studies or a closely related area can get you into a planning department. Los Angeles–area schools known for their planning programs include USC, UCLA, Cal State Northridge, and Cal Poly Pomona.

Beginning planners work for various local and regional agencies, typically city or county government, and usually start as junior planners or planning aides. The title may sound bantam-weight, but they still make $25,000 to $28,000. With a master's degree, many earn over $30,000 to start. The next few promotions, to assistant and then associate planner, are fairly routine and come within a few years of each other. So do raises.

The jump to senior planner is competitive and takes longer to attain. In the City of Anaheim, senior planners make from $45,103 to $62,017. Senior planners who distinguish themselves are often in line for the division manager slots that open up, and they in turn are prime candidates for the planning director position. Anaheim's planning director can make anywhere from $69,970 to $96,208.

Studies conducted by planners incorporate the location of streets and highways, water and sewer lines, existing buildings, open spaces, public facilities, and recreational sites. Working from this information, they map out ways to redesign certain areas or use undeveloped land. Finally, they prepare materials showing how their programs can be carried out and at what cost. Frequently, this means making presentations at city council hearings and planning commission meetings.

Planners work closely with the power structure of a city or area, taking direction from elected officials, conferring with developers, and meeting with community leaders. The job, as one might well imagine, is oftentimes political, as planners must balance the leanings of the city council and planning commission, the desires of private developers, and the sentiments of the community.

"Planners work for the city, so they're not advocates, but certainly they're advocating good planning," said Bob Paternoster, director of planning and building for the City of Long Beach. "They provide a good technical analysis of the issues."

Ultimately, planners who work in the public sector are generalists. In fact, they are encouraged to gain experience in as many different areas as possible. "As you move up in the organization, we want people to have a broad range of experience," said Jeff Taylor, regional planning administrator for the County of Los Angeles. "When you start, you're a specialist. But as you move up, you become more of a generalist. If you work at a small city, you do everything anyway."

Small cities with high growth rates like the City of Palmdale are great places to learn. But after you reach a certain level, the opportunities for advancement narrow because the department is so small. Consequently, about the only way to move up is by moving out, to another city.

Another option is to work for a private planning consulting firm. In consulting, planners work for numerous agencies—whoever their clients are—and have the opportunity to specialize.

"If you work in the public sector, with very few exceptions, you're a generalist," said Wein of Michael Brandman Associates. "But with all these changing laws, there's a need for specialists in areas like grading, hazardous materials, noise control, and traffic management. A private firm can afford those types of experts on staff. Once they're done with one job, they go on to the next client and the next. At a public agency, it's not like that."

Wein went on to say that private planning consultants earn salaries on par with public sector planners.

KEY EMPLOYERS OF URBAN PLANNERS

Public Sector

City of Anaheim
Planning Department
200 S. Anaheim Boulevard
Anaheim, CA 92805
714/999-5100

City of Burbank
Planning Department
275 E. Olive Avenue
Burbank, CA 91502
818/953-9721

Culver City
Planning Department
9770 Culver Boulevard
Culver City, CA 90232
213/202-5777

City of Fullerton
Planning Department
303 W. Commonwealth Avenue
Fullerton, CA 92632
714/738-6300

City of Garden Grove
Planning Department
11391 Acacia Parkway
Garden Grove, CA 92640
714/638-6639

City of Lancaster
Planning Department
44933 N. Fern Avenue
Lancaster, CA 93534
805/945-7811

City of Long Beach
Planning Department
333 W. Ocean Boulevard
Long Beach, CA 90802
213/590-6812

City of Los Angeles
Personnel Office
111 E. First Street
Los Angeles, CA 90012
213/485-2442

City of Riverside
Planning Department
3900 Main Street
Riverside, CA 92501
714/782-5492

City of Santa Ana
Planning Department
20 Civic Center Plaza
Santa Ana, CA 92701
714/647-5200

City of Torrance
Planning Department
3031 Torrance Boulevard
Torrance, CA 90503
213/618-5990

Private Sector

Community Systems Associates Inc.
1717 S. State College Boulevard
Anaheim, CA 92806
714/978-8887

EIP Associates
80 S. Lake Avenue
Pasadena, CA 91106
818/568-1363

J. A. King & Associates
550 Newport Center Drive
Newport Beach, CA 92660
714/759-0669

Krueper Engineering & Associates
568 N. Mountain View Avenue
San Bernardino, CA 92401
714/884-2159

Michael Brandman Associates (MBA)
2530 Red Hill Avenue
Santa Ana, CA 92705
714/250-5555

Phillips Brandt Reddick
18012 Sky Park Circle
Irvine, CA 92714
714/261-8820

Turrini & Brink Planning Consultants
1920 E. 17th Street
Santa Ana, CA 92701
714/835-1691

PROFESSIONAL ORGANIZATIONS

American Planning Association
California Chapter
1121 L Street
Sacramento, CA 95841
916/736-2434

American Society of Consulting Planners
1667 K Street, NW
Suite 750
Washington, DC 20006
202/659-2727

Center for Design Planning
1208 N. McKinley Street
Albany, GA 31701
912/888-1606

Southern California Urban and Regional Information Systems Association
c/o Glenn Johnson
Planning Department
City of Los Angeles
200 N. Spring Street
Room 550
Los Angeles, CA 90012
213/485-3472

PROFESSIONAL PUBLICATIONS

Journal of the American Planning Association (Washington, DC)
Journal of Planning Literature (Columbus, OH)
Long Range Planning (Elmsford, NY)
Planning (Chicago, IL)
Planning Review (Oxford, OH)
The Western Planner (Soldotna, AK)

Career Counseling

*Professional guidance can help identify your talents,
determine your interests, and explore your options.*

Nothing is forever. But when it comes to careers, many people remain in a bad situation rather than actively trying to find more satisfying work. The majority of American workers are better at performing their job than they are at finding a career that suits them. Even some of the most outwardly successful professionals—doctors and lawyers included—are inwardly miserable about their work.

Up to 75 percent of workers nationwide are reportedly unhappy with their current position, said John Stevenson, head of John Stevenson & Associates, a vocational consulting firm in Los Angeles. But relatively few people do anything to find out why they're bored or dissatisfied with a particular occupation.

"Most people make career choices strictly by chance. The majority of people just get a job or start working in the field and are unhappy," Stevenson said. "The misery comes from just not figuring it out."

Where does one look to take those first daring steps toward that long-contemplated and probably inevitable job change? Perhaps the best place to look for new direction is a career counseling service, whose business is to provide job seekers with the resources and knowledge they need to find a new career. A multitude of career counselors have offices in the Los Angeles area.

"My advice would be for people to analyze what they're doing," Stevenson said. "If they're unhappy, see a specialist. What the professional will do is open up a lot of other areas and show them what they have the aptitude for. The majority of people don't understand that what they're doing has a lot to do with whether they're happy or not. Career guidance can make the difference."

94

Career counseling typically consists of a highly structured program of career assessment, personal evaluation, and job counseling sessions combined with advice and information about specific career fields. Counseling is available in group or individual sessions through colleges, continuing education programs, adult schools, counseling centers, and private consultants. Most programs are open-ended, lasting anywhere from a few weeks to several months depending on how long it takes a person to find a suitable new job.

Susan Miller, a certified career consultant with a private practice in Los Angeles, said she divides the career transition process into three phases. "The first is self-assessment: determining a client's talents and options through interviews, assessment exercises, and vocational testing, if needed. Next, I help clients explore possible careers by structuring their library research and setting up information interviews for them. The last phase is the job search. At this point, clients are ready to undertake a self-marketing campaign with a résumé, cover letter, and all the rest."

Career counselors may also offer advice on how to best approach a job interview and suggest how present yourself in the best possible light to a prospective employer. At Forty Plus of Southern California, a nonprofit career guidance service for displaced workers aged 40 and over who earned a salary of at least $30,000, job seekers have the option of videotaping mock interviews to review the way they come across in person.

"The interviewing process is the most important part of finding a new job," said Philip W. Hauhuth, president of Forty Plus of Southern California. "Within 45 seconds your impression is made—good, bad, or indifferent."

At the UCLA Extension Career Counseling Center, participants are given three personality interviews by a psychologist to determine what career options might enable them to achieve their career objectives as well as personal goals. In addition, they are given a series of tests that measure interests, needs, aptitudes and, abilities, said Aida Hillway, the Career Counseling Center's associate director.

"Often people will have the ability to do what they're doing, but they won't have the personality for that kind of work, or their interests are in another area," Hillway said. "Our objective is to help people evaluate their strengths and weaknesses and relate them to a career field."

Private vocational counseling services may be supportive and instructive, but they're not free. Costs for group counseling range from $10 for an introductory seminar to $30 for a two- or three-hour workshop to over $100 for an all-day affair. Private career counselors charge anywhere from $50 to $75 an hour. Even nonprofit programs like Forty Plus require a $350 initiation fee and a $50 monthly user fee. Most initial screening interviews at career counselors are free, however.

Be wary of counseling programs that require several thousand dollars up front. You'll have to do most of the actual work involved in a career transition anyway (sending out letters, meeting with people, finding the right company, etc.), so there's no sense in doling out a good chunk of your savings to pay someone else for nonexistent services, Miller advised.

When shopping for a career counselor, check to see whether they're licensed or certified by a national or state professional association. A Nationally Certified Career Counselor (NCCC), for instance, has to meet certain prescribed conditions. Among these, the counselor has earned a graduate degree in counseling or a related field, acquired at least three years of career development work experience, and successfully completed a knowledge-based certification exam.

The National Career Development Association in Alexandria, Virginia, (703) 823-9800, keeps a list of some 17,000 counselors, 1,000 of whom are career specialists, and offers consumer guidelines for selecting a career counselor.

With people living and working longer than ever before, many career programs are now offering specially tailored programs for older age groups. The UCLA Career Counseling Center, for example, periodically offers a seminar for workers 55 and over who are either facing retirement, seeking a career change, or wishing to come out of retirement.

Judith Sommerstein, a certified career counselor who conducts frequent seminars for UCLA Extension called "Job Options for the 55+," said her program is aimed toward providing those who are entering the next phase of their working lives with an opportunity to plan new work areas that lend themselves to flexible lifestyles and continued growth.

"A recurring theme in the field of preretirement planning is that many baby boomers now reaching their 40s will not be able to retire on schedule," Sommerstein said. "More people are staying in the labor market longer than ever before. This trend will only intensify in the years to come."

Aside from specialty seminars, UCLA Extension offers two main career exploration and counseling programs that vary in price and intensity for those contemplating job changes. The fee for the first, which entails three months of testing and counseling and offers a written summary of conclusions, is $660. A shorter workshop consisting of two group meetings, 15 hours of individual testing, and a counseling interview is offered for $325, Hillway said.

Less intensive, cost-free career evaulation services are available to the public at most community colleges and at selected state Employment Development Department (EDD) offices with Experience Unlimited Job Club centers, including the Fullerton and West Covina locations.

The EDD centers, which provide office space, equipment, and part-time staff to match members' skills with job openings, is available to displaced professional, managerial, and technical workers who have suddenly found themselves out of work due to a merger, acquisition, or leveraged buyout. EDD counseling also is available for workers who have had disabling, industrial injuries and need to find new jobs.

If you are considering a career move in the Los Angeles area, the job prospects will remain excellent in the decade ahead. Regionally, the total number of jobs is expected to grow from 6 million in 1984 to 9 million by 2010, according to the Los Angeles Area Chamber of Commerce. This breaks out to over 115,000 new jobs being created each year. Two industries that are expected to grow substantially are fashion—women's clothing in particular—and the computer field, said Jerry Hawbaker, the EDD's Los Angeles County labor market analyst.

On the downside, the aerospace industry will continue to scale down and the financial services sector will experience ongoing cutbacks and restructuring, according to Gerry Corrigan, a partner in the Los Angeles outplacement firm McCarthy Resource Associates. But, when you're going after a new job, numbers aren't everything, Corrigan said. In fact, they sometimes lie. "Statistics, even on a local level, are in a sense meaningless. If you're good at what you do, there's a role for you," he said.

SELECTED CAREER COUNSELORS IN THE L. A. AREA

Eileen Brabender, MA
Brabender Career Management
 Associates
6363 W. 80th Street
Los Angeles, CA 90045
213/417-8189

Business Solutions Group
548 S. Spring Street
Los Angeles, CA 90013
213/688-8727

Career Counseling and Assessment
 Associates
9229 W. Sunset Boulevard
Los Angeles, CA 90069
213/274-3423

Career Planning Center
1623 S. La Cienega Boulevard
Los Angeles, CA 90035
213/273-6633

Career Transition Group
12100 Wilshire Boulevard
Los Angeles, CA 90025
213/820-4992

Experience Unlimited Job Club
Employment Development
 Department
233 E. Commonwealth Avenue
Fullerton, CA 92632
714/680-7800

Forty Plus of Southern California
3450 Wilshire Boulevard
Los Angeles, CA 90010
213/388-2301

Marjorie Golter, MS
20121 Ventura Boulevard
Suite 325
Woodland Hills, CA 91367
818/884-5581

The Guidance Center
2116 Wilshire Boulevard
Santa Monica, CA 90403
213/829-4429

Huffine & Associates
229 N. Central Avenue
Suite 400
Glendale, CA 91203
818/956-1855

Elaine Kaback Career Consultants
24222 Hawthorne Boulevard
Torrance, CA 90505
213/373-4484

Pricilla Smith, MS
Career Solutions
1145 Artesia Boulevard
Manhattan Beach, CA 90266
213/376-7799

Judith Sommerstein & Associates
Career Consultants
24520 Hawthorne Boulevard
Suite 110
Torrance, CA 90505
213/373-4249

John Stevenson & Associates
12304 Santa Monica Boulevard
Los Angeles, CA 90025
213/477-6731

UCLA Extension Career
 Counseling Center
10995 Le Conte Avenue
Room 413
Los Angeles, CA 90024
213/825-2934

Vocational Training Consulting
 Services
6363 Wilshire Boulevard
Suite 210
Los Angeles, CA 90048
213/651-5102

Also try the career counseling office of the community college in your area. For a
listing of community colleges, see "How to Choose a Vocational School" at the end
of Section 13. In addition, most universities have career planning and placement
centers for use by students and alumni. This list is not an endorsement of the people
or agencies listed.

Careers in Health Care

CHAPTER 12

Health Care

Clerks, technicians, and other skilled
professionals are in great demand.

Mention careers in health care, and most people think of doctor and registered nurse. The greatest opportunities in the field, though, will lie elsewhere over the next few years. By the mid-1990s, a surplus of doctors is likely, forcing many to become administrators. And while there's always a need for nurses, the demand for non-nursing personnel will be growing as well, according to health care educators and administrators.

The streamlining of hospital operations, the growing number of physicians in private practice, the aging of the population, and the rise of home health care have created incredible demand for the gamut of health care workers: insurance billers, pharmacy clerks, records technicians, medical assistants and transcriptionists, therapists, radiologists, lab technicians, and home health care workers, just to name a few.

"All of these areas are really booming," said Dr. Joy Albert, dean of life and health sciences at El Camino College in Torrance. "The whole health care industry is booming." Added Judi Hansen, director of regional recruitment services for Kaiser Permanente: "Health care is a burgeoning field. It's phenomenal. It's called job security."

Indeed, the state Employment Development Department (EDD) ranks health care as one of the fastest-growing occupational fields in Southern California. The number of medical workers employed in Los Angeles and Orange counties is expected to rise from a combined total of 302,075 in 1987 to an estimated 342,775 in 1992, according to state projections.

One reason the demand for medical support staff will remain

high is that for every new doctor entering the field, more than a dozen health care workers are required. The number of doctors in Los Angeles and Orange counties is projected to grow from 19,780 in 1987 to an estimated 21,220 in 1992, according to EDD figures.

"There is a great demand for medical workers," affirmed Pamela Honish, associate director of nursing at USC's Kenneth Norris Cancer Hospital. "Trained workers are even in more demand because of their readiness for the job. There are a wide range of opportunities, from clerical to the very technical."

Perhaps the best place for entry-level workers to break into the health care field is at a community hospital, which can't always demand the same degree of experience as a well-endowed medical center. Indeed, community hospitals often provide their own on-the-job training, Honish said.

Demonstrating a positive, caring attitude and a willingness to take on added responsibility can open the door to advancement. "A lot of it has to do with your personality and desire to learn. If they see some glimmer of potential in you, they'll train you," Honish said. So a motivated orderly who expresses interest might become a unit secretary or ward clerk, maintaining patients' files and keeping the front desk organized.

Moving up the basic skills ladder, opportunities are available for instrument and pharmacy technicians, as well as for staffing clerks and medical transcriptionists. Staffing clerks ensure that staffing on hospital wards is adequate, while medical transcriptionists, who must be intimately familiar with medical terminology, transcribe dictated chart information and physicians' orders.

As a starting point, applicants without experience should scour the classified section of the newspaper to see what positions are available. Ronni Cooper, a job counselor at Doctor's Corner staffing agency in Los Angeles, recommends taking whatever job you can find and staying there for at least six months. At that point, a medical employment service like hers has good success in placing applicants. "As long as they have experience and can think, I can send them out," Cooper said.

At a more skilled level, there are openings for billing clerks, admitting counselors, lab technicians, and radiologists. Most of these specialized hospital positions require a year or two of training at an accredited school or college. East Los Angeles College in Monterey Park and El Camino College in Torrance, for example, offer medical records classes that teach record keeping and insurance coding procedures.

With hospitals under pressure to control costs, there's been a big jump in opportunities on the financial side, particularly for people who are familiar with hospital billing methods, said Betty Hartwig, assistant dean for nursing at Los Angeles Trade-Technical College. "Insurance billing and medical records have been a very undersupplied category for some time."

Medical records clerks assemble information about patients, locating previous medical records and organizing patient files. Some transcribe reports of operations, examinations, and treatments given to patients. Medical records technicians perform slightly more advanced duties, coding and recording illnesses, operations, and therapies to compile patient histories for later review by doctors. They also periodically prepare reports on medical operations, including the types of illnesses treated, surgeries performed, and level of bed capacities.

The nine campuses of the Los Angeles Community College District all offer classes in life and health sciences that can lead to a certificate or two-year associate degree in health care. These programs vary in scope and length, with the position of radiologist or X-ray techinician requiring the most training, according to Dr. Donald Visintainer, director of radiology at El Camino College.

The cost of health care training can vary greatly. Private schools that offer health care instruction, such as the Bryman Center, may charge upward of $9,000 a year for a particular course of study. Community colleges, on the other hand, charge a maximum of $50 per semester, plus books and uniforms. Health care education can enhance an applicant's job prospects and promotional opportunities, but the school you attend doesn't make a whole lot of difference—as long as it is reputable, Cooper said. (For more information, see the article on vocational schools at the end of Section 13.)

"If anyone is trying to get into the health care field, I would suggest that they contact a community college first to see what programs are available," said Hartwig of L.A. Trade-Tech.

Health care is generally touted as a low-paying but saintlike field in which personal satisfaction is derived from helping people recover from sickness or injury. But in reality the money isn't all that bad either. A fully licensed X-ray tech can earn up to $2,400 a month, while the salary for billers ranges anywhere from $1,700 to $2,100. In private practices, front office workers make between $1,600 and $1,900, and office managers running a busy doctor's office can command upward of $3,000 a month.

"You'll probably make more money in a hospital, but there is a lot more pressure and irregular hours" than at a clinic or private office, Cooper said.

With the average cost of inpatient care running about $800 a day and rising, more and more hospitals are treating and releasing patients on an outpatient basis when they can rather than admitting them. Statewide, annual hospital outpatient visits rose from 19.1 million in 1982 to 25 million in 1987.

"People don't want to be in hospitals anymore because of the expense and inconvenience. They'd rather be with their families," said Honish of USC's Norris Hospital. "What they're in the hospital for is high-tech nursing, diagnostic testing, and surgery. The rest can be done at home or at a day care center."

This focus on outpatient, or ambulatory, care has opened the door for a host of home health care providers, including physical therapists, respiratory therapists, speech therapists, and home health aides. These specialists typically work through a nurses'

In Demand: The Hardest-to-Fill Health Care Jobs at Kaiser Permanente

Position	Hourly Pay
Pharmacist	$21.23–$23.31
Psychiatric social worker	$15.05–$17.57
Medical/lab technologist	$14.84–$17.93
Physical/occupational therapist*	$14.05–$18.84
Occupational therapist	$14.05–$18.84
Telecommunications technician & planning engineer	$12.17–$24.43
Data processor	$11.16–$27.41
Respiratory care practitioner	$10.94–$12.06
Radiologic technician	$10.59–$13.29
Staffing clerk	$ 9.48–$10.06
Medical transcriptionist	$ 9.02–$10.59
Ward clerk	$ 7.49–$ 9.43

* Employees have the option of being hired in through the Alternate Compensation Plan, without benefits, for $18.27–$24.49 per hour.

SOURCE: Kaiser Permanente.

registry or one of the numerous community care organizations cropping up in the Los Angeles area.

With a projected 57 percent annual national growth rate through the year 2000, physical therapy is one of the most sought after occupations in health care. Licensed physical therapists evaluate patients and carry out a course of treatment in cooperation with a doctor. Their job is to restore bodily functions, relieve pain, or help prevent permanent disability following a disabling injury or illness.

To become licensed, physical therapists must complete a four-year college degree program and pass a state licensing exam. Southland schools that offer degrees in physical therapy include Cal State Long Beach, Cal State Northridge, Loma Linda University, and USC. A physical therapist may work for a hospital, HMO, or private clinic, or for an athletic team as a trainer. At Kaiser Permanente, physical therapists make $14 to $25 an hour.

Physical therapist assistants, who typically receive their training through a community college, work under the supervision of a licensed physical therapist, carrying out the prescribed patient treatment plan. The opportunity for physical therapists and physical therapist assistants is "wonderful," according to Lois Magette, physical therapy department adviser at Cal State Long Beach. "We can't possibly turn out the number of students to match the job opportunities."

KEY EMPLOYERS IN HEALTH CARE

CaliforniaCare (Blue Cross)
21555 Oxnard Street
Woodland Hills, CA 91367
818/703-2345

Care America Health Plans
20520 Nordhoff Street
Chatsworth, CA 91311
818/407-2222

CIGNA Health Plans of California
505 N. Brand Boulevard
Glendale, CA 91209
818/500-6262

**Daniel Freeman Home Health
  Agency**
301 N. Oak Street
Inglewood, CA 90301
213/673-0288

**Greater Los Angeles Home Health
  Services**
1104 W. Redondo Beach Boulevard
Gardena, CA 90247
213/217-9903

Health Net
21600 Oxnard Street
Woodland Hills, CA 91367
818/719-6800

**Hospital Home Health Care
Agency of California**
2601 Airport Drive
Torrance, CA 90505
213/530-3800

**Kaiser Permanente Medical Care
Program**
393 E. Walnut Street
Pasadena, CA 91188
818/405-3279

Maxicare of Southern California
5200 W. Century Boulevard
Los Angeles, CA 90045
213/568-9000

National Medical Enterprises
11620 Wilshire Boulevard
Los Angeles, CA 90025
213/479-5526

Olsten Health Care Services
5757 Wilshire Boulevard
Los Angeles, CA 90036
213/933-2273

PPO Alliance
5252 Orange Avenue
Cypress, CA 90630
714/761-9771

PacifiCare of California
5995 Plaza Drive
Cypress, CA 90630
714/952-1121

**Physical Therapy Provider Net-
work Inc.**
21243 Ventura Boulevard
Suite 241
Woodland Hills, CA 91364
818/883-7876

Summit Health Ltd.
1800 Avenue of the Stars
Los Angeles, CA 90067
213/201-4000

Upjohn Healthcare Services
4751 Wilshire Boulevard
Los Angeles, CA 90010
213/659-8322

For a listing of hospitals, see Chapter 13 on nursing.

PROFESSIONAL ORGANIZATIONS

**American Association of Medical
Assistants**
20 N. Wacker Drive
Suite 1575
Chicago, IL 60606
312/899-1500

American Health Care Association
1201 L Street, N.W.
Washington, DC 20005
202/842-4444

American Medical Association
535 N. Dearborn Street
Chicago, IL 60610
312/645-5000

**American Medical Records
Association**
875 N. Michigan Avenue
Suite 1850
Chicago, IL 60611
312/787-2672

**American Physical Therapy
Association**
1111 N. Fairfax Street
Alexandria, VA 22314
703/684-2782

American Society of Allied Health Professionals
1101 Connecticut Avenue, NW
Suite 700
Washington, DC 20036
202/857-1150

Health Careers Information Center
Hospital Council of Southern California
201 N. Figueroa Street
Los Angeles, CA 90012
800/234-0080

PROFESSIONAL PUBLICATIONS

Health Care Systems (New York, NY)
Health Week (Emeryville, CA)
Home Healthcare Nurse (East Norwalk, CT)
Hospitals & Health Services Administration (Ann Arbor, MI)
Modern Healthcare (Chicago, IL)
U.S. Healthcare (Lakewood, CO)

DIRECTORIES

Allied Health Education Directory (American Medical Association, Chicago, IL)
Careers That Count (American Hospital Association, Chicago, IL)
Directory of the Health and Human Care Agencies in Los Angeles County (Los Angeles County Department of Health Services, Los Angeles, CA)
Guide to the Health Care Field (American Hospital Association, Chicago, IL)
200 Ways to Put Your Talent to Work in the Health Field (National Health Council, New York, NY)

CHAPTER 13

Nursing

Unprecedented demand for nurses
affords job security and flexibility.

Florence Nightingale, or at least her modern counterpart, is a hot property nowadays. If you are a caring person who likes to help others get well, who values job security and flexibility, good wages, and working in a challenging profession that can make the difference between life and death, then consider a career in nursing. When you're a nurse, you work.

According to the California Nurses Association (CNA), there is an unprecedented local, state, and nationwide demand for nurses that is expected to continue well into the next century. By the year 2000, the country will face an anticipated shortage of 1.4 million nurses. On average, hospitals in Los Angeles have openings in 15 percent of their budgeted nursing positions, according to a recent study by the Commonwealth Fund.

Behind the demand for nurses are changing demographic trends and technological advances. As the population grows older and lives longer, a greater percentage of people will need medical care. At the same time, strides in medicine leading to more complex procedures and operations will require a higher level of care and nursing expertise both during and after surgery.

"There's a great need in the critical care area," said Ana Root, regional nurse recruiter for Kaiser Permanente, which employs over 6,000 registered nurses (RNs) at 10 Southern California hospitals. "The opportunities are almost unlimited. We need more nurses at the bedside taking care of patients."

But on the supply side, enrollments in nursing schools have been on the decline. Part of the reason for this decline is demographic: due to the "baby bust," there are fewer students today than in the past. Moreover, career opportunities have opened up for women in other areas in recent years. Although nursing traditionally has been a women's field, that is starting to change, the Commonwealth Fund reported.

About two-thirds of all nurses work in hospitals. At local hospitals, the majority of the more than 6,200 openings for registered nurses are concentrated in surgical units and emergency departments, said CNA spokeswoman Maureen Anderson. But openings also exist at home health providers, private clinics, hospices, schools, even large companies with their own medical staff—virtually any type of work environment one could desire.

Three basic types of nurses are involved in direct patient care: RNs, licensed vocational nurses (LVNs), and practical nurses.

Registered nurses, the most skilled of the three nursing groups, have the most job opportunity, are the highest paid, and are in the most demand. RNs must go through two to three years of specialized training involving both clinical and classroom instruction. In addition, RNs are required to hold clinical internships at medical centers to gain firsthand experience in their field before becoming licensed.

After a year of generalized training, RNs may specialize in such areas as pediatrics (the care of infants and children), obstetrics (childbirth), or psychiatric (mental health) nursing.

Los Angeles County–USC Medical Center, the world's largest medical teaching facility with approximately 1,700 nurses and 2,100 beds, offers a demanding diploma program in nursing. Students are required to intern 16 hours a week their freshman year and progress to 24 hours a week by their senior year.

"County-USC graduates are in very high demand because of what they learn here," said Javier Trejo, nurse recruiter for County-USC. "Our students put in more clinical hours than anywhere. They have to put in an eight-hour day during school. They're holding a full-time job, really."

To be eligible to apply for County-USC's competitive RN program, which costs $600 tuition per semester, applicants must be high school graduates and have coursework in anatomy, microbiology, and chemistry. (If these science courses weren't taken in high school, they can easily be picked up at a community college, Trejo said.) County-USC accepts anywhere from 70 to 120 students a semester for the two- to three-year program.

Upon finishing their training, RNs are required to take a state licensing exam. After passing the two-day state boards, RNs are qualified to provide general patient care, administer intravenous (IV) medications, and dispense oral medications ordered by a doctor. RNs, who oversee a patient's bedside treatment, have more responsibility than other types of nurses and are likely to hold supervisory positions.

With a year or more experience, RNs can apply and train for specialty units within hospitals, such as intensive care, surgery, or the emergency room, earning more money and receiving what essentially is a promotion.

Job latitude and competitive salary levels are greatest at large medical centers like Cedars-Sinai and County-USC. "The thing that's so great about nursing is that people continually have the opportunity to change directions," said Jane Ramseyer, director of nursing operations for Cedars-Sinai Medical Center. "Once you have your basic training, you can be certified in another area."

For instance, an RN on the surgical ward at a Kaiser hospital could go through the labor and delivery training program and later take a course to become a maternal nurse practitioner. Nurse practitioners work directly under a doctor and can perform complete physical examinations and use diagnostic and health-assessment skills beyond those of regular nurses.

RNs have the most promotional opportunities of any nursing group, Ramseyer said. Besides nurse practitioner, a registered nurse may be promoted to nursing supervisor, assistant director, and, eventually, director of nursing services. But first things first. "You can't enter directly into management," said Root of Kaiser Permanente. "You have to have some clinical experience. You have to enter at the bedside."

Hospital staff nurses who are RNs start at an annual salary ranging from $25,000 to $30,000 in Los Angeles, while experienced hospital nurses can make up to $50,000 a year, according to Anderson of CNA.

Licensed vocational nurses, also called licensed practical nurses, are also in high demand. "Right now we have a shortage of RNs and we're almost to the same point with LVNs," said Lorraine Puleikis, executive director of PRN Nurse's Registry in Santa Monica. "But we have an overabundance of practical nurses."

LVNs receive training that is more clinical, or hands-on, than theoretical. (RNs are taught the clinical *and* theoretical aspects of nursing.) The duties of LVNs, who are required to have a year of school, usually at a community college, are more limited than those of RNs. For instance, they are licensed to dispense oral medications, but not IVs. They perform a variety of patient-related tasks, such as bathing and recording temperatures.

LVNs typically do not hold supervisory positions at the hospital level, but they can help manage smaller medical clinics, where they might prepare patients for examination and treatment, administer medications, apply dressings, and teach patients health care regimens. LVNs always have the option of returning to school for RN training.

"I would encourage them to go all the way," said Ramseyer of Cedars-Sinai. "In addition to the (RN) shortage in the routine areas, we're now performing more advanced procedures, such as heart, lung, and liver transplants, that require even more experience and care expertise after the surgery."

Because of constantly changing technology in the medical field and the introduction of new approaches to health care, nursing requires continuous education. RNs and LVNs must complete 30 units of continuing education every two years to renew their licenses. The state board exam for LVNs takes only a day.

Practical nurses, also referred to as certified nurse assistants, are not required to be licensed, but many have training either from an adult school or community college. Practical nurses may feed patients, provide physical therapy, or keep bandaged areas clean. Home health aides may perform similar duties in a home care setting. While their responsibilities are similar to other nurses', practical nurses aren't allowed to dispense any medications or administer injections.

Because hospitals need staffing around the clock, nursing can offer very flexible hours. Locally, some 39 percent of hospitals offer nurses the opportunity to work partial shifts, the Commonwealth Fund study found. Hospital nurses usually work 4-, 8-, or 12-hour shifts.

One of the drawbacks to the nursing profession is that nurses tend to suffer from a relatively high rate of burnout. Among the reasons nurses cite for leaving the field are boredom, lack of upward mobility, low pay, and stress from always working on the front line of a hectic hospital environment.

Yet for all the complaints you hear about nursing, there is a very low percentage of dropouts. "About 80 percent of those who are licensed [RNs and LVNs] are still working as nurses," said Mary Canobbio, assistant clinical professor at the UCLA School of Nursing. "It's hard work and there's low pay, but they're still satisfied with their profession."

Because nurses often deal with crisis situations, nursing can be a physically, intellectually, and emotionally demanding job. At different times, nurses may act as patient advocates, surrogate parents, and counselors. But there are definite rewards when patients make recovery.

"We have to be sad and cry with the husband whose wife just died, but at the same time we have to go into the next room and be happy and joyous with the lady who just found out that she doesn't have cancer," said Trejo of County-USC. "You have to be all of these things to the patient and the family at different times. It's not an easy profession, [but] you feel good about yourself. The impact a doctor or nurse has on people can affect them for the rest of their lives."

There are opportunities for nurses in education and research as well. A master's degree in nursing, for example, provides nurses with the option of either teaching at the college level or conducting research at a medical school or a large research-oriented hospital, Canobbio said. "There are a lot of alternatives for nurses today."

Nurses with advanced degrees may also enter into a collaborative private practice with a physician and assist with the follow-up treatment and counseling of patients, she added. Schools that offer master's degree programs in nursing include Azusa Pacific College, Cal State Los Angeles, Cal State Long Beach, Loma Linda University, and UCLA.

Salaries for Registered Nurses (RNs)

Experience Level	Hourly Pay*
No experience	$13.91–$14.21
1–2 years	$14.33–$14.63
2–3 years	$15.05–$15.34
3 or more years	$15.82–$16.07
Specialty Units: critical care, operating room, emergency room, etc.	
1–2 years	$14.97–$15.14
2–3 years	$15.34–$15.71
3 or more years	$15.82–$16.64

* Includes differential for evening shifts. Full medical and dental benefits extended to full-time and part-time nurses who work a minimum of 16 hours per week. Nurses also have the option of accepting 30 percent higher salary in lieu of benefits.

SOURCE: Kaiser Permanente.

SELECTED HOSPITALS AND MEDICAL CENTERS IN THE L.A. AREA

Anaheim General Hospital
3350 W. Ball Road
Anaheim, CA 92804
714/827-6700

Cedars-Sinai Medical Center
8700 Beverly Boulevard
Los Angeles, CA 90048
213/855-5000

Children's Hospital of Los Angeles
4650 W. Sunset Boulevard
Los Angeles, CA 90027
213/660-2450

City of Hope Medical Center
1500 E. Duarte Road
Duarte, CA 91010
818/359-8111

Daniel Freeman Memorial Hospital
333 N. Prairie Avenue
Inglewood, CA 90301
213/674-7050

Harbor-UCLA Medical Center
1000 W. Carson Street
Torrance, CA 90509
213/533-3234

Huntington Memorial Hospital
100 Congress Street
Pasadena, CA 91105
818/440-5000

Kaiser Foundation Hospital
4867 Sunset Boulevard
Los Angeles, CA 90027
213/667-4011

Robert F. Kennedy Medical Center
4500 W. 116th Street
Hawthorne, CA 90250
213/973-1711

Martin Luther King Jr./Drew Medical Center
12021 S. Wilmington Avenue
Los Angeles, CA 90059
213/603-3689

Little Company of Mary Hospital
4101 Torrance Boulevard
Torrance, CA 90503
213/540-7676

Long Beach Memorial Medical Center
2801 Atlantic Avenue
Long Beach, CA 90801
213/595-2311

Los Angeles County-USC Medical Center
Nurse Recruitment Office
1200 N. State Street
Los Angeles, CA 90033
213/226-4664

Rancho Los Amigos Medical Center
7601 E. Imperial Highway
Downey, CA 90242
213/940-7511

St. John's Hospital
1328 22nd Street
Santa Monica, CA 90404
213/829-5511

St. Joseph Medical Center
Buena Vista at Alameda
Burbank, CA 91505
818/843-5111

Santa Ana Medical Center
1901 N. Fairview Street
Santa Ana, CA 92706
714/531-1653

Torrance Memorial Hospital Medical Center
3330 W. Lomita Boulevard
Torrance, CA 90505
213/775-6334

UC Irvine Medical Center
101 The City Drive South
Orange, CA 92668
714/634-5496

UCLA Medical Center
10833 LeConte Avenue
Los Angeles, CA 90024
213/825-1911

Valley Presbyterian
15107 Vanowen Street
Van Nuys, CA 91405
818/782-6600

Veterans Administration Medical Center
11000 Wilshire Boulevard
Los Angeles, CA 90073
213/478-3711

For other health care providers, see Chapter 12 on health care. Also see the Yellow Pages for a listing of Nurses Registries.

PROFESSIONAL ORGANIZATIONS

Accrediting Bureau of Health Education Schools
Oak Manor Offices
28089 U.S. 20 West
Elkhart, IN 46514
219/293-0124

American Hospital Association
840 N. Lake Shore Drive
Chicago, IL 60611
312/280-6000

California Association of Hospitals and Health Systems
1023 12th Street
Sacramento, CA 95805
916/443-7401

California Nurses Association
5410 Wilshire Boulevard
Los Angeles, CA 90036
213/826-4407

Health Careers Information Center
Hospital Council of Southern California
201 N. Figueroa Street
Los Angeles, CA 90012
800/234-0080

Los Angeles County Medical Association
1925 Wilshire Boulevard
Los Angeles, CA 90057
213/483-1581

National Association for Practical Nurse Education and Service
1400 Spring Street
Suite 310
Silver Spring, MD 20910
301/588-2491

National Federation of Licensed Practical Nurses Inc.
Post Office Box 18088
Durham, NC 27703
919/781-4791

PROFESSIONAL PUBLICATIONS

California Nurse (San Francisco, CA)
California Nursing Review (Santa Clara, CA)
Hospitals & Health Services Administration (Ann Arbor, MI)
Hospitals (Chicago, IL)
Journal of Nursing Staff Development (Philadelphia, PA)
Modern Healthcare (Chicago, IL)
Nursingworld Journal (Weston, MA)
Public Health Nursing (Cambridge, MA)

DIRECTORIES

Critical Care Choices (Springhouse Corp., Springhouse, PA)
Nursing Career Directory (Springhouse Corp., Springhouse, PA)
Nursingworld Journal Nursing Job Guide (Prime National Publishing Corp., Weston, MA)
Saunders Health Care Directory (W. B. Saunders, Philadelphia, PA)

Health Care Field Facing an Acute Shortage

From hospitals to HMOs, the health care profession is welcoming medical workers with open arms.

Faced with a chronic shortage of nurses and other professionals, the field of health care has become its own seemingly incurable patient. Unable to attract and retain an adequate number of qualified medical support staff, hospitals, health maintenance organizations (HMOs), private clinics, and other health care providers are threatened with a decline in the quality of patient care and a reduction in the current level of services, according to several studies documenting the shortage.

Despite efforts to offset the shortage, many hospitals and health care providers have been forced to cut services, reduce bed capacities, close units, and send patients to other medical centers for treatment.

"Hospitals and patients already feel the effects of personnel shortages," said Carol McCarthy, president of the American Hospital Association (AHA) in Chicago. "If left unchecked, these shortages can threaten our ability to respond" to the nation's health care needs.

Many forces are converging to create the health care labor shortage, McCarthy said. Among the most prominent: the demand for health services is growing; demographics are shifting; new career opportunities are opening up for women; the health care field is battling to overcome an image problem; wages are compressed and relatively stagnant; and competition is growing within the health care industry for qualified professionals.

By the year 2000, the country may face a shortage of 1.4 million nurses. And while there are more nurses than ever before—some 213,000 in California alone—patients' needs are becoming more acute than ever. Patients now occupying hospital beds require more highly skilled professionals to take care of them. In 1972, hospitals got by with a ratio of 5 nurses to every 10 patients. In 1986, that number rose to 9.1 nurses for every 10 patients, McCarthy said.

Moreover, increasingly sensitive and sophisticated medical equipment, such as fetal monitors and life-support systems, are demanding a higher level of training from health care workers. In addition, today's hospital patient is likely to be older—a trend that is expected to continue. By 2025, people aged 65 and older will outnumber teenagers two to one. And as life expectancy increases, so does the risk of illness.

In Southern California, the delivery of health care is further complicated by a scarcity of state and local funding for public hospitals and nonprofit clinics. Budgetary shortfalls have already placed severe strains on medical facilities throughout the Southland, causing several trauma centers to close down and 17 private, nonprofit family planning centers to suspend operations during the 1980s in Los Angeles County alone.

The health care shortage involves not just nurses but workers in the allied health professions, including such disciplines as audiology, radiology, X-ray technology, medical technology, occupational and physical therapy, respiratory care, dietetics, and EKG/EEG technology, among others.

Here are the 10 health care occupations with the highest vacancy rates at California hospitals as identified in a 1988 survey by the American Hospital Association:

Occupation	Vacancy Rate
Registered nurse anesthetist	15.9%
Physical therapist	15.7%
Physical therapist assistant	13.6%
Ultrasound technologist	11.3%
Occupational therapist	10.4%
Medical transcriptionist	8.9%
Radiologic technologist	8.2%
Respiratory therapist	7.7%
Nuclear medicine technician	7.4%
Licensed vocational nurse	7.3%

Nationwide, of the 20 occupational categories expected to have the most job growth from 1988 to 2000, 11 are health-related professions. Here are the hottest health care jobs for the 1990s as identified by the U.S. Bureau of Labor Statistics:

Occupation	National Growth Rate, 1988–2000
Medical assistant	70.0%
Home health aide	67.9%
Radiologic technologist & technician	66.0%
Medical records technician	59.9%
Medical secretary	58.0%
Physical therapist	57.0%
Surgical technologist	56.4%
Physical & corrective therapy assistant	52.5%
Occupational therapist	48.8%
Human services worker	44.9%
Respiratory therapist	41.3%

To illustrate just how dire the need is for certain health care professionals, the American Academy of Physician Assistants in a recent survey found that there were seven jobs available for every graduate from the 51 accredited physician assistant programs around the country.

Among the health care workers in shortest supply are those needed to care for the growing disabled and dependent elderly population. But these chronic care workers, mainly nursing and home health aides, have a high rate of turnover due to low pay, poor benefits, stressful working conditions, limited advancement opportunities, and low status in the health care hierarchy, according to a 1988 study by the Older Women's League. Nevertheless, the nation's health care providers will need some 500,000 new chronic care workers by the year 2000.

While a growing number of men are entering the profession, the majority of health care workers are still female. According to the Bureau of Labor Statistics, women represent 88 percent of all occupational therapists, 77 percent of clinical laboratory techs, 72 percent of physical therapists, 67 percent of radiologic techs, and 61 percent of respiratory therapists. Most nurses are women, too.

Yet women are now looking to a wide variety of professions to pursue satisfying careers. Traditionally male-dominated professions, such as law enforcement, construction, law, and finance, for instance, are seeing increasing numbers of women joining their ranks at the expense of the health care field, McCarthy said.

In the 1980s, student enrollment in health care programs experienced a sharp decline. Between 1983 and 1987, nursing school enrollments in California decreased an average of 5 percent per year. Fewer college freshmen want to become nurses. In 1974, 10.2 percent of the state's students expressed an interest in nursing, compared to 8.4 percent in 1983 and only 4 percent in 1987, the California Nurses Association reported.

Health care professionals stress that the issue of salary cannot be ignored. A recent study by the Institute of Medicine found that in many health occupations, salaries over the life of a career are so compressed, there is little incentive to stay in the field. Compensation is reported as the No. 1 problem in retaining nurses, according to the California Association of Hospitals and Health Systems.

The difference between entry-level and senior-level pay in the nursing profession, for example, is negligible. At Kaiser Permanente, registered nurses are paid $13.91 an hour to start, while the salaries of the most experienced senior RNs with at least three years on the job and training in a specialized area start at only $16.64—less than $3 more an hour.

To some analysts, the most pressing human resources problem in health care is the retention of qualified employees. In a nationwide survey of 857 hospitals, the Hay Group, a management consulting firm, found that more than 30 percent of all nurses were likely to leave their jobs in the first year and close to 40 percent planned to leave by their second year.

To help combat the dire health care shortage, the Hospital Council of Southern California, which represents 225 hospitals and medical centers from Santa Barbara to San Bernardino, recently established a Health Careers Information Center to promote health care and inform the public about career options.

"People don't know what opportunities are available at hospitals. They think hospitals employ nurses and doctors and that's it," said Kathy Barry, the Information Center's director. During the center's first year (1989), some 5,600 people made inquiries to the information center. Of these, about 4 percent enrolled in a health care educational program, Barry said.

The Hospital Council is searching for long-term solutions to the health care crisis, including reaching out to the nontraditional health care labor force of senior citizens, second-career seekers, and men. "We encourage people to contact us," Barry said.

For more information about specific occupations, write the Health Careers Information Center in care of the Hospital Council of Southern California, 201 N. Figueroa Street, Los Angeles, CA 90012. The center's toll-free phone number is (800) 234-0080.

A growing number of opportunities, with varying educational requirements, are available to those interested in pursuing a career in health care, Barry said. "For the individual who wants to work in health care, Southern California has it all—from small rural community type hospitals to large medical centers to huge, multi-hospital corporations."

Careers in Law and Translation

CHAPTER 14

Lawyer

Real-life opportunities abound in L.A. law.

Thanks to the popular television show "L.A. Law," Los Angeles is perhaps the most overpublicized place to practice law. Its image notwithstanding, Southern California *is* one of the most legally active areas in the country and among the highest-paying for attorneys anywhere.

L.A. lawyers commonly charge $200 to $300 an hour for legal services. Large corporate law firms bill as much as $400 hourly for the services of their senior partners. Salaries for first-year associates at the largest firms are pushing $65,000 to $72,000 a year, while partners garner considerably more than that.

The spiraling cost of wooing top law school graduates is partially due to the arrival of many high-paying New York law firms in the L.A. area, people in the industry note.

But behind the glamour and high salaries for the select few are the sobering facts of professional life for the great many. Most attorneys wind up working 60 hours a week, or more, under tremendous pressure. Legal cases require extensive research and analysis, frequent meetings with clients, regular correspondence with the court and opposing counsel, appearances on motions, and pretrial deposition meetings.

There are two main divisions within law: civil and criminal. Civil law has several subdivisions, including corporate law, communications law, entertainment law, labor law, real estate law, and tax law. Criminal cases involve either misdemeanor or felony offenses.

"You have to be a lot better on your feet in criminal law," said Mary O'Keefe, an attorney at Overland, Berke, Wesley, Gits, Randolph & Levanas in Santa Monica. "You have to be a bit tougher. It's not as civilized as civil law. You're dealing with people's lives, not their money or businesses."

Few civil lawsuits ever make it to court (most are settled out of court before the trial date), only a few litigation attorneys ever participate in the drama of the courtroom, and only a few top-notch lawyers make over $100,000 a year.

Yet despite the harried, pressure-laden nature of the work, more people than ever are going into law, increasing competition to record levels. For the 190 spaces in its 1989 entering class, the USC Law Center received some 3,500 applications. (The average GPA was 3.5; the median LSAT score 42.) At UCLA's School of Law, 9,000 applications were received for little over 300 spaces.

Why go into law? A lot of attorneys ask themselves that very question after they've been in practice for a few years. The money potential is an obvious answer, but hardly justification in itself. Moreover, it doesn't always pan out. Some attorneys cite the intellectual attraction of their work, or, in the public sector, the satisfaction derived from performing a public service. Still others say that being a lawyer is a way of turning idealism into concrete action.

"I know people who want to change the world, clean up the environment, eliminate discrimination from society," said George Ruiz, a first-year law student at UCLA's School of Law. "A lot of other students are interested in the discussion and debate generated by a thoughtful analysis of the law. I don't think anyone's doing it just to be rich."

Statewide, there were 122,642 attorneys eligible to practice law in January 1990, including 48,430 in Los Angeles and Orange counties. That's a 24 percent increase since 1985, according to the State Bar of California. Eligible attorneys are those who have not been disciplined or disbarred.

The main reason for this growth in the legal profession is the escalating need for legal services, which at the Los Angeles County Public Defender's Office increases about 20 percent yearly. The 565-attorney Public Defender's Office handles some 550,000 criminal matters each year, said David Meyer, an assistant public defender in Van Nuys.

The demand for legal services is rising steadily in the civil arena as well. The Los Angeles County Superior Court now has about a five-year backlog of nonpriority civil suits. "We live in a very litigious society, one that encourages people to get the most from the least," said Blane Prescott, vice president of Hildebrandt Inc., a San Francisco–based consulting firm.

A burgeoning area for lawyers in the 1990s is environmental law, Prescott said. "Environmental law will be a phenomenal practice over the next 20 years. By the year 2000, as many as 7 percent of all lawyers nationwide could be dealing with environmental issues. The magnitude of toxic waste problems that have built up is enormous."

Industry analysts note that corporate law should see some retrenchment in the 1990s, especially in securities trading, mergers, and acquisitions. But there will be increased opportunities for bankruptcy lawyers to deal with the creditors of the nation's failing savings and loan industry. "There will continue to be a huge amount of bankruptcy work," Prescott said.

The qualifications for attorneys are pretty standard: a four-year bachelor's degree, a three-year law degree on top of that, and a passing score on the state bar examination. But where you go to law school can make a big difference in what form your career takes.

Leading corporate law firms, such as Gibson, Dunn & Crutcher, the largest law firm in Los Angeles (and California), look for the highest-quality candidates in the top 10 percent of their class, preferably with law clerk *and* law review experience. Public employers like the Los Angeles County District Attorney and Public Defender's offices aren't quite so selective, although the DA's Office restricts its opportunities for graduates of law schools with lesser academic reputations to the top 20 or 25 percent of their class.

Within the law school hierarchy, there are three basic levels of quality, Prescott said. So-called first-tier schools, the finest in the country, include the eight Ivy League universities back east and, on the West Coast, Stanford and UC Berkeley. Second-tier schools in the Los Angeles area include USC, UCLA, Loyola, Pepperdine, Southwestern, and Whittier universities. In the third-tier are night law schools, correspondence schools, and the like, Prescott said.

One thing to keep in mind about elite private law schools is their almost uniformly high cost. At private universities like USC and Loyola, tuition runs $15,500 to $17,500 a year (multiply that times three for your total time there), while public institutions such as UCLA charge little over $2,000 a year.

In law school, there are two basic ways students can distinguish themselves: by their grades or involvement in extracurricular activities, namely, law review and moot court. The law review is a given law school's publication, which serves as a forum for analysis of important decisions. Moot court is a simulated courtroom setting in which students prepare briefs and present oral arguments, sometimes in state or national competitions.

After their first and second years of school, law students typically work as a summer associate or clerk for a judge, performing legal research and other attorney-related tasks. The combination of experience and a strong academic record enhances their prospects upon graduation. As Ruiz notes: "Most employers want to see some example of excellence in academics."

"The $65,000 salary you hear about for first-year associates is true for graduates of first- and second-tier law schools who graduate in the top half of their class," Prescott added. "The people who don't, end up in the much smaller firms making less. I know of lawyers who, starting out of school, are making $30,000. The reality is, of the total number of law school graduates in any one year, about a third end up in low-paying jobs or go into another field altogether.

"Law school credentials follow you around for the rest of your life, so it really pays to go to the best school possible. Unfortunately, so many people learn that either after they graduate or in mid-life."

Qualified attorneys who have passed the bar can always start their own practice or go into business with another independent attorney, but both of these propositions are a little precarious right out of school. Attorneys need time to learn how to operate effectively within the legal system and build a reputation for themselves. For information on opening a law office, write the California Young Lawyers Association, c/o The State Bar of California, 555 Franklin Street, San Francisco, CA 94102.

Attorneys who go to work for large corporate law firms rarely handle cases directly, but assist other, more senior attorneys during their first few years. It generally takes seven or eight years to make partner. Partners are responsible for running the office, bringing business to the firm, and for overseeing cases. As such, they receive a percentage of the total profits in addition to their normal salary. But with increased competition and pressure to keep costs down, fewer partnerships are opening up.

"As a young lawyer in a big place, you're at the bottom of a huge team of people. There's a lot of grunt work," said O'Keefe of Overland, Berke. O'Keefe previously worked for O'Melveny & Myers, the second-largest law firm in L.A. "What's good about going to a big firm is that you get great experience. Once you get that name on your résumé, it opens a lot of doors."

At smaller firms, O'Keefe said, attorneys are generally afforded more independence. They also have the opportunity to work on both civil and criminal proceedings. At big firms like Gibson, Dunn & Crutcher, which is divided into four practice areas—litigation, corporate law, labor law, and tax law—there is little crossover between departments, although associates are exposed to each through a two-year rotation program, said Willard Z. Carr, a partner in the firm.

If you're eager for action, then you might want to consider the county Public Defender's Office, recently described by *California Lawyer* as the "Marine Corps" of the law profession. Deputy public defenders, who start at $39,400 and top out at $89,500, represent indigent defendants in criminal trials, striving to obtain the least onerous consequence for their clients as possible.

Working for the Public Defender, or the District Attorney (who is on the prosecuting side of the law) is one of the quickest and most direct ways of seeing the inside of a courtroom. There is some training and orientation, but usually within six months of being hired, deputy public defenders and district attorneys start handling jury trials. Over the years, they work their way up from preliminary hearings and misdemeanor trials to full-blown felony proceedings and, ultimately, death penalty cases.

"We look for people with some grit and hide," said Meyer of the Public Defender's Van Nuys office. "It's not easy to be a public defender. I need somebody who can stand up under fire and apply the law right then and there, who can speak loudly and clearly and make cogent decisions under a lot of pressure. This is the most exciting thing there is in law. But I wouldn't try to talk anybody into doing it. You either want to go to court and do battle or you don't."

KEY EMPLOYERS OF LAWYERS, PARALEGALS, AND LEGAL SECRETARIES

Private Sector Law Firms

Buchalter, Nember, Fields & Younger
700 S. Flower Street
Los Angeles, CA 90017
213/626-6700

Fleming, Anderson, McClung & Finch
24012 Calle de la Plate
Laguna Hills, CA 92653
714/768-3601

Gibson, Dunn & Crutcher
333 S. Grand Avenue
Los Angeles, CA 90071
213/229-7000

Haight, Brown & Bonesteel
201 Santa Monica Boulevard
Santa Monica, CA 90401
213/458-1000

Jones, Day, Reavis & Pogue
355 S. Grand Avenue
Los Angeles, CA 90071
213/625-3939

Latham & Watkins
555 S. Flower Street
Los Angeles, CA 90071
213/485-1234

Lewis, D'Amato, Brisbois & Bisgaard
261 S. Figueroa Street
Los Angeles, CA 90012
213/628-7777

Lillick & McHose
725 S. Figueroa Street
Los Angeles, CA 90071
213/488-7452

Loeb & Loeb
1000 Wilshire Boulevard
Los Angeles, CA 90017
213/688-3400

Manatt, Phelps, Rothenberg & Phillips
11355 W. Olympic Boulevard
Los Angeles, CA 90064
213/879-1610

McCutchen, Black, Verleger & Shea
600 Wilshire Boulevard
Los Angeles, CA 90017
213/624-2400

McKenna, Conner & Cuneo
444 S. Flower Street
Los Angeles, CA 90071
213/687-8000

Mitchell, Silberberg, Knupp
1377 W. Olympic Boulevard
Los Angeles, CA 90064
213/312-2000

Morgan, Lewis & Bockius
801 S. Grand Avenue
Los Angeles, CA 90017
213/612-2500

Musick, Peeler & Garrett
One Wilshire Boulevard
Los Angeles, CA 90017
213/629-7600

O'Melveny & Myers
400 S. Hope Street
Los Angeles, CA 90071
213/669-6000

Paul, Hastings, Janofsky & Walker
555 S. Flower Street
Los Angeles, CA 90071
213/489-4000

Sheppard, Mullin, Richter & Hampton
333 S. Hope Street
Los Angeles, CA 90071
213/620-1780

Skadden, Arps, Slate, Meagher & Flom
300 S. Grand Avenue
Los Angeles, CA 90071
213/687-5000

Wyman, Bautzer, Christensen, Kuchel, Silbert
2049 Century Park East
Los Angeles, CA 90067
213/556-8000

Public Sector

California State Attorney General's Office
3580 Wilshire Boulevard
Los Angeles, CA 90010
213/736-2304

Los Angeles City Attorney's Office
200 N. Main Street
Los Angeles, CA 90012
213/485-5441.

Los Angeles County District Attorney's Office
320 W. Temple Street
Los Angeles, CA 90012
213/974-3535

Los Angeles County Public Defender's Office
210 W. Temple Street
Los Angeles, CA 90012
213/974-2811

United States Attorney's Office
Department of Justice
312 N. Spring Street
Los Angeles, CA 90012
213/894-2434

PROFESSIONAL ORGANIZATIONS

American Bar Association (ABA)
750 N. Lake Shore Drive
Chicago, IL 60611
312/988-5000

Association of American Law Schools
One Dupont Circle, NW
Suite 370
Washington, DC 2003
202/296-8851

California Attorneys for Criminal Justice
311 S. Spring Street
Suite 502
Los Angeles, CA 90013
213/620-1081

Los Angeles County Bar Association
617 S. Olive Street
Los Angeles, CA 90014
213/627-2727

National Association of Women Lawyers
750 N. Lake Shore Drive
Chicago, IL 60611
312/988-6186

State Bar of California
333 S. Beaudry Avenue
10th Floor
Los Angeles, CA 90017
213/975-1200

PROFESSIONAL PUBLICATIONS

ABA Journal (Chicago, IL)
California Law Review (Berkeley, CA)
California Lawyer (San Francisco, CA)
Los Angeles Daily Journal (Los Angeles, CA)
Los Angeles Lawyer (Los Angeles, CA)
The National Law Journal (New York, NY)
Orange County Reporter (Santa Ana, CA)
Southern California Law Review (Los Angeles, CA)
Women Lawyers Journal (Chicago, IL)

DIRECTORIES

ABA Directory (American Bar Association, Chicago, IL)
Barron's Guide to Law Schools (Barron's Educational Series, Hauppauge, NY)
Martindale-Hubbell Law Directory (Martindale-Hubbell, Summit, NJ)
Parker Directory of California Attorneys (Parker & Son Publications, Los Angeles, CA)

CHAPTER 15

Paralegal

*Growth in the legal services field
has made this the fastest-growing
profession in the country.*

Just two decades ago, the job of paralegal barely existed. Now, with 75 percent projected national growth through the year 2000, it's rated by the U.S. Bureau of Labor Statistics (BLS) as the fastest-growing profession in the country. It's also one of the most lucrative. Industrious paralegals at the largest law firms can make upward of $80,000 a year.

Paralegals, also called legal assistants, are trained nonlawyers who work under the supervision of a lawyer. Nationwide, there are over 83,000 paralegals. Their numbers are expected to almost double in the 1990s, to an estimated 145,000 by the turn of the century, BLS projections show. In California, paralegals' ranks are expected to exceed 15,000 by mid-decade, a whopping 122 percent increase since 1985. Spurring this growth are factors that create a need for legal services, such as increased international trade and contentious air quality issues.

"It's a burgeoning field. It's really taken off in the last few years," said Doris Childs, director of the 1,200-member Los Angeles Paralegal Association (LAPA). Indeed, BLS didn't even recognize the occupation of paralegal as a job category until 1982. "And the salary range is fantastic."

According to Employment Development Department calculations, the number of paralegals in Los Angeles and Orange counties is projected to grow from 4,050 in 1987 to an estimated 5,650 by 1992, a growth rate of almost 40 percent. When taking part-timers into account, the figures are even greater, Childs said.

So how do you become a paralegal? "The best way is to get

a good, solid education," said Childs, noting the LAPA distributes a list of reputable paralegal programs in the greater Los Angeles area.

As of this writing, only four schools that offer paralegal certificate programs in Southern California were accredited by the American Bar Association: the extension programs of UCLA and UC Irvine, Cal State Los Angeles, and the University of West Los Angeles. Still, many other programs are well worth their salt.

"The point is to investigate the teaching facilities, the curriculum, the books, the library," Childs said. "Check into the school's reputation, ask what percentage of paralegals have graduated and are working."

UCLA Extension offers a demanding, broad-based program that covers legal terminology, the drafting of documents, and basic research. Students are introduced to important precedent cases and taught how to understand legal forms, statutes, and regulations. They can specialize in either corporate law or litigation. To be admitted to UCLA Extension's Attorney Assistant Training Program, applicants must have a bachelor's degree or two years of college plus work experience, said Sydney Goines, the program's administrator.

A scaled-down version of law school, the typical paralegal program isn't cheap. The UCLA program, which takes 5 to 12 months to complete, costs $3,000. The amount spent on education is quickly earned back once the job commences, however. Entry-level paralegals in Los Angeles make an average base salary of $2,400 per month, Goines said. Working overtime can boost earnings 10 to 25 percent.

After completing a certificate program, beginning paralegals are qualified to index and digest depositions, keep corporate minutes, draft interrogatories, supervise routine real estate transactions, organize trial materials, and prepare exhibits for trial. With experience, paralegals may take on more difficult assignments, such as drafting motions, researching case law, writing briefs, interviewing witnesses, and analyzing transcripts of testimony and other legal documents.

"The function of the paralegal is to free up the attorney to allow him to do his job," Childs said. "There is nothing a paralegal cannot do that an attorney can do except give legal advice and appear in court."

Another way college degree holders can become paralegals is by finding a law firm that offers on-the-job training.

Before he started as a paralegal at the downtown L.A. office of Skadden, Arps, Slate, Meagher & Flom, Shaun O'Sullivan said he knew comparatively little about business and law. A psychology major in college, he planned to go into broadcast news. But, disillusioned by the odd hours and low pay of his first job as an assistant night producer at Cable News Network, he contacted a friend at Skadden—one of the largest private law firms in the country—who helped arrange an interview.

Within his first year, O'Sullivan said, he had mastered most aspects of the job and, with overtime, was earning a salary of over $35,000. Learning about the overlapping business and legal worlds has been an integral part of his training. Employed by a firm whose client list reads like the Fortune 500, O'Sullivan said he feels like he has been an eyewitness to the changing structure of corporate America.

"Every time I open the business section of the paper, it seems like 9 out of 10 times I see an item about a deal I'm working on," said O'Sullivan, now a senior legal assistant. "If I were a legal assistant at a smaller law firm, I don't think I'd be exposed to what I've been exposed to."

For all the advantages of working for a big firm (including the opportunity to travel), the demanding pace of L.A. law and the endless flood of paperwork can be overwhelming at times. When a case is scheduled to go to court, or when a closing needs to be completed, there's just no stopping. "Sometimes the long hours start getting to you, especially at a firm this size,' O'Sullivan said. "When you're working on your 30th hour, you start to get a little fuzzy. The upside is that you're compensated fairly well."

Working for a smaller firm may pay less, but it can result in more latitude and recognition. Paralegals aren't easily lost in the corporate shuffle or necessarily limited to one area of the law. They may perform work related to civil proceedings as well as criminal cases. Rather than spending months, or even years, reviewing and indexing documents without ever leaving the office, paralegals at small firms tend to see more action. They may draft briefs or assist attorneys at hearings and even trials.

"You pick up more rounded experience at a small firm," said Edgar Regalado, a paralegal at Overland, Berke, Wesley, Gits, Randolph & Levanas, a Santa Monica law firm with a staff of about 10 attorneys. "It's also more personal. You work daily with attorneys on a very personal basis. You're involved with cases where you have a good understanding of what's going on."

In hiring paralegals, law firms generally look for applicants who are enthusiastic about the profession, have a college degree or paralegal training, and can continue to be effective while working the long hours common to the business.

"We're looking for intelligence and physical stamina, and the ability to be very organized and efficient and to get along with a wide variety of people and different personalities at all different levels," said Louise Gittelson, Skadden's director of legal assistant services. "Basically, we're looking for someone who won't cause a lot of problems. We're there for the lawyers to do the most effective job they can."

Indeed, part of a paralegal's job is to make sure things flow smoothly around the office and to head off potential complications before they become full-blown problems. "It's definitely stress management," O'Sullivan said. "A lot of times, you're a facilitator trying to tie all the loose ends together. The one thing you don't want to do is make enemies. When you're in a bind, you might need someone's help."

Like other legal careers, working as a paralegal requires a fair amount of professional ethics. Paralegals can't practice law, appear in court, solicit business, or set fees. But like attorneys, they must maintain a high degree of confidentiality. This is especially important in the world of corporate law, where paralegals must keep their insider's knowledge about multimillion- and multibillion-dollar transactions to themselves.

Working as a paralegal doesn't have to be dead-end. Some paralegals use their experience as a stepping-stone to a career as a lawyer and, after a year or two, enroll in law school. Others advance into law firm administration, becoming senior paralegals, paralegal coordinators, director of paralegal services, or even office managers.

Another way paralegals can advance is by working in the legal department of a large corporation, such as a bank, insurance company, or energy supplier. ARCO, for example, has introduced a career ladder for paralegals, establishing five job grades, each with its own title, responsibilities, and salary scale. At some corporations, senior paralegals may advance to the position of manager of litigation support, overseeing such functions as document analysis, data processing, document retrieval, quality assurance, micrographics, and computer support.

KEY EMPLOYERS OF PARALEGALS

See Chapter 14 for a listing of major L.A. law firms.

PROFESSIONAL ORGANIZATIONS

American Bar Association
Standing Committee on Legal
  Assistants
750 N. Lake Shore Drive
Chicago, IL 60611
312/988-5000

**Legal Assistant Management
  Association**
Post Office Box 40129
Overland Park, KS 66204
913/381-4458

Los Angeles Paralegal Association
Post Office Box 24350
Los Angeles, CA 90026
213/387-7175

**National Association of Legal
  Assistants**
1601 S. Main Street
Suite 300
Tulsa, OK 74119
918/587-6828

**National Federation of Paralegal
  Associations**
10 S. Pine Street
Post Office Box 629
Doylestown, PA 18901
215/348-5575

PROFESSIONAL PUBLICATIONS

California Lawyer (San Francisco, CA)
Legal Professional (Dallas, TX)
Los Angeles Daily Journal (Los Angeles, CA)
Southern California Law Review (Los Angeles, CA)

DIRECTORIES

Career Guide for Paralegals (Monarch Press, New York, NY)

CHAPTER 16

Legal Secretary and Court Reporter

Nimble fingers, sharp minds are needed for these demanding jobs.

A boom in the legal profession has created an unprecedented number of attorneys. But there are plenty of other opportunities in the high-paid legal field that don't require seven years of schooling. Two promising careers in the growing legal services industry are legal secretary and court reporter.

The demand for both is expected to remain high as society in general and Southern California in particular become increasingly litigious. A crowded court system means more jobs for court reporters. And for every two attorneys at a busy law firm, there is at least one legal secretary.

From 1985 to 1988, the legal services industry grew over 20 percent in Los Angeles County, from 38,900 to 49,800 jobs, said Jack Kyser, chief economist for the Los Angeles Area Chamber of Commerce. The number of legal secretaries in Los Angeles and Orange counties is expected to number nearly 20,000 by 1992, according to Employment Development Department projections.

Legal secretaries are among the most proficient and well paid of any type of secretary. They must be able to type from 65 to 85 words per minute. At modernized law offices, they must be familiar with the WordPerfect word processing program and, at New York–based law firms, be able to take dictation using shorthand.

That's just the foundation. Since legal secretaries are frequently asked to draft a letter or complaint, prepare a summons or subpoena, or proofread a contract, they also need excellent grammar and communication skills. In addition, some handle administrative duties, such as bookkeeping, billing, and keeping time sheets.

Being a legal secretary has always meant more than just answering the phones. In today's hectic legal environment, the job requires superb organizational skills and the ability to stay on top of complicated scheduling matters. A thorough grounding in legal terminology and knowledge of court procedures are essential as well.

"We look for assertive individuals, people who can think on their feet and who don't have to be supervised," said Karen Chiba, personnel recruiter for the 216-attorney law firm of Latham & Watkins.

Experienced legal secretaries can make $3,000 or more monthly. For temps, the hourly rate varies between $12 and $20, said Nelle Benfell, a counselor for Legal Temps, an employment service in North Hollywood.

For both temporary and permanent legal secretaries, past experience as a secretary, preferably in the legal field, is key. Most law firms and employment agencies require at least three years' experience. "Applicants must have a proven record that they are meticulous and capable of dealing with the myriad details that arise," Benfell said.

There are several ways to gain direct experience as a legal secretary. They include applying to a trainee program at a large law firm, starting at a small law office, or enrolling in a school for legal secretaries.

Trainee programs are offered by some of the large downtown law firms, including O'Melveny & Myers, Latham & Watkins, and Paul, Hasting, Janofsky & Walker. Secretaries hired as trainees usually spend a few months in classroom-type training before they start working for an attorney on their own.

At many of the big law firms, secretaries who don't have much experience, or who have other secretarial experience, usually start in corporate or real estate law, said Anice Hurley, human resources supervisor for Dewey, Ballantine, Bushby, Palmer & Wood.

Starting at a small law office is another possibility, but small offices usually pay less than large firms. One tradeoff is that, depending on their caseloads, lawyers at smaller offices may be willing to spend more time training a secretary than attorneys at large firms. Another advantage is that the work pace tends to be less hectic and more personalized at a smaller law office with only a handful of attorneys than at a big firm.

Vocational schools are a third option. The 10-month legal secretary program at Watterson College in Pasadena teaches students shorthand, typing, court documentation, and office procedures as well as transcription, legal terminology, and word processing, said Gail Ballew, Watterson's director of admissions. Watterson's program costs around $5,000.

"When prospective secretaries go into an attorney's office untrained, that attorney has the upper hand to pay them a lower wage," Ballew said. "When they have education and training under their belt, they then have more leverage and opportunity when it comes to finding a job."

The demand for legal secretaries is particularly high in the area of litigation—the actual trying of lawsuits, said Chiba of Latham & Watkins. Of all the areas within the legal field, litigation demands the greatest amount of knowledge and expertise from secretaries. However, not very many have that necessary breadth of experience, Hurley said.

"Litigation secretaries are specialized. They need to know the court system. They need to know how to do filings. And they need to know all the legal terms," Hurley said. They also are responsible for calendaring—marking court dates and keeping track of deposition appointments.

The job requires that legal secretaries display grace under pressure. Since attorneys spend much of their time on the front line going to bat for their clients, they work under a lot of stress. This tension, in turn, gets passed on to their staff. "Because of the high volume, it's usually stressful. Things have always got to be done now," Benfell said. "Understanding priorities and deadlines is terribly important."

Legal secretaries need to develop a positive, can-do attitude toward the numerous demands placed on them by their bosses. This is especially true in large corporate law firms with hierarchical corporate cultures. As Kyser puts it: "They're dealing with lawyers, who can be real prima donnas."

As top-notch legal secretaries become increasingly hard to find, loyalty tends to be amply rewarded in the form of salary and job security. "When I'm looking for secretaries to hire, I want those who stay at a firm for a long time to show that they are dedicated," Hurley said. "Stay and grow with the firm.

Legal secretaries can become more administrative as time goes on. A lot of times they become office managers."

Court reporters, like paralegals, can earn sizable salaries. "If you're a principal in a court reporting agency, you can make up to $80,000 a year," said Richard Colby, president of the Los Angeles County Court Reporters Association. "The money is largely dependent on how hard you want to work."

Statewide, there are about 7,000 licensed court reporters, said Neil Ferstand, executive director of the California Court Reporters Association in Sacramento. Southern California has about 1,100 court reporters and room for a lot more.

"It's definitely a growing field," said Ben Hyatt, managing partner of Noon & Pratt, a nationwide court reporting agency with some 100 employees in the Los Angeles area. "Now is an excellent time to be in it. There's more than enough work."

Court reporters are charged with taking down every word of official court proceedings (except those stricken from the record) on stenotype machines, and reproducing transcripts of them upon request. Court reporters also are present at depositions—in which attorneys question potential witnesses and obtain testimony before a trial—and sit in on arbitration meetings.

"It's for those who like to have a front row seat. Every day, you're subject to a different witness and field, and every day, it's like a course in college," said Colby, a 30-year court-reporting veteran. Like interpreters, court reporters must get it right the first time. "We get stuff thrown at us on first blush, one time only and that's it, so the stress level is pretty high. You have to be quick and nimble mentally," he added.

Because of their important yet neutral role, court reporters are required to have a high degree of impartiality and professional ethics, Colby said. They must be licensed by the state and, if they work in Los Angeles County, also must pass a county-administered test.

The two-day state test, given every May and November, consists of two parts: academic ability and technical skills. Would-be court reporters must be able to type at least 200 wpm with 97 percent accuracy on a stenotype machine and take four-voice dictation in the form of reporting a mock trial. Experienced court reporters can type 225 to 400 wpm, Colby said.

The state exam also tests English comprehension, vocabulary, and knowledge of court procedures and civil code sections that pertain to the court reporting field. The pass rate for the state test, which is similar in content to the county exam, is fairly low—only about 30 to 50 percent, Ferstand said.

Usually at most state tests, private court reporting agencies set up informational tables to describe current openings and network with potential reporters, Ferstand said. Job opportunities also appear in a trade magazine for court reporters called *CaliGrams*, published in Sacramento.

To be licensed by the state, at least 18 months of formal training is required. It takes most people two to three years to go from zero to 200 wpm on a stenotype machine, said Nancy Patterson, director of the Bryan College of Court Reporting in Los Angeles.

The Bryan College's program, which claims a perfect, 100 percent placement rate, costs $780 per quarter and lasts two to three years depending on how long it takes students to get up to speed, Patterson said.

In addition to stenotyping—learning to spell phonetically— students take classes in English, punctuation, court procedures, and word processing. Court reporting has now entered the age of high technology, and advanced stenotype machines are capable of interfacing with personal computers, which then translate phonograms (a character or symbol used to represent a word, syllable, or letter) into real words.

In addition to private vocational schools, many community colleges offer associate degrees in court reporting.

What qualities should court reporters possess? "Excellent spelling and English skills, an innate curiosity, a high level of concentration, and certainly above-average intelligence," summed up Hyatt of Noon & Pratt. An understanding of legal and medical terms is also important.

Court reporters generally work in three capacities: as employees of a municipal or superior court system; as independent contractors for a single court reporting agency; or as freelancers. The most money—and opportunity—is in the latter two areas. Independent contractors are typically assigned to do deposition work by their home agency, which receives job orders from law firms. They are generally paid 50 percent of whatever the agency bills its client.

"They're essentially their own boss. There are no benefits, but there is a chance to make more money and they also have the option to stay off calendar," Hyatt said. The main drawback, he added, is that "there are odd hours because you're at the behest of whatever law firm you're working for."

Salaries for Legal Secretaries in Los Angeles

Level	Years' Experience	Monthly Salary
Secretary to newer associate	1–2	$1,151–$2,301
	3+	$1,976–$2,301
Secretary to junior partner	1–2	$2,301
	3+	$2,301–$2,701
Secretary to partner	1–2	$1,976–$2,501
	3+	$2,501–$3,101
Secretary with quasi-paralegal responsibility	1–2	$2,501–$2,901
	3+	$2,901–$3,301

SOURCE: 1988 National Law Office Compensation Survey, Institute of Continuing Legal Education, Ann Arbor, MI.

Court reporters who freelance for government agencies, law firms, or court reporting agencies typically buy their own office equipment, which may include one or more computers and stenotype machines, a printer, and a photocopy machine.

The Los Angeles County Superior Court system offers among the highest salaries and most opportunities for court reporters of any court system statewide, Ferstand said. Currently, court reporters for Superior Court are paid between $3,797 and $4,465 a month plus fees for their transcription services, Colby said.

*KEY EMPLOYERS OF COURT REPORTERS

Selected Court Reporting Agencies

Abkin Newman & Palter
Suite 205
8060 Melrose Avenue
Los Angeles, CA 90046
213/653-3800

Stan Brink & Associates
1655 Beverly Boulevard
Los Angeles, CA 90026
213/250-8972

Coleman, Haas, Martin & Schwab
3600 Wilshire Boulevard
Los Angeles, CA 90010
213/480-1234

A. Edelist Deposition Service
15300 Ventura Boulevard
Sherman Oaks, CA 91403
818/788-3376

Gillespie Reporting Services
6840 Indiana Avenue
Riverside, CA 92506
714/683-0977

Kerns & Gradillas Inc.
400 S. Beverly Drive
Beverly Hills, CA 90212
213/556-1136

Lacey Shorthand Reporting Corp.
695 S. Harvard Boulevard
Los Angeles, CA 90005
213/386-1108

Los Angeles Court Reporters
714 W. Olympic Boulevard
Los Angeles, CA 90015
213/749-4565

McKay Court Reporters
1223 Wilshire Boulevard
Santa Monica, CA 90403
213/250-8129

Noon & Pratt
3810 Wilshire Boulevard
Los Angeles, CA 90010
213/381-5110

Pelletier & Jones Court Reporting
3138 S. Rita Way
Santa Ana, CA 92704
714/641-8451

**Racklin, Bernstein, Minjares &
   Associates**
3400 W. Sixth Street
Suite 200-A
Los Angeles, CA 90023
213/382-0829

South Bay Court Reporters
3655 Torrance Boulevard
Torrance, CA 90503
213/543-0343

Gerry B. Wilcox & Associates
2740 W. Magnolia Boulevard
Burbank, CA 91505
213/849-6886

Public Sector Employers

**Los Angeles County Superior
   Court**
Court Reporter Services
111 N. Hill Street
Los Angeles, CA 90012
213/974-5451

Orange County Superior Court
700 Civic Center Drive W.
Santa Ana, CA 92701
714/834-3226

Santa Monica Municipal Court
1725 Main Street
Santa Monica, CA 90401
213/458-5434

South Bay Municipal Court
825 Maple Avenue
Torrance, CA 90503
213/533-6500

United States District Court
312 N. Spring Street
Los Angeles, CA 90012
213/894-3118

*For employers of legal secretaries, see the Chapter 14 listing of major law firms in the Los Angeles area.

PROFESSIONAL ORGANIZATIONS

**California Court Reporters
Association**
1809 19th Street
First Floor
Sacramento, CA 95814
916/443-5090

**National Association of Legal
Secretaries**
2250 E. 73rd Street
Suite 550
Tulsa, OK 74136
918/493-3540

**Los Angeles County Court
Reporters Association**
111 N. Hill Street
Los Angeles, CA 90012
213/485-1519

**National Shorthand Reporters
Association**
118 Park Street, SE
Vienna, VA 22180
703/281-4677

PROFESSIONAL PUBLICATIONS

CaliGrams (Sacramento, CA)
Docket (Tulsa, OK)
The National Shorthand Reporter (Vienna, VA)

DIRECTORIES

California Legal Directory (Legal Directories Publishing Co., Dallas, TX)
Parker Directory of California Attorneys (Parker & Son Publications, Los
Angeles, CA)

CHAPTER 17

Translator and Interpreter

*The work is difficult but
the rewards are ample.*

Southern California's growing multilingual and multicultural population is rapidly expanding the job market for interpreters and translators. They're in high demand in almost every field, from business to the courts, government, social services, and the private sector.

"We have a countywide shortage," said Ed Johnson, director of interpreter and translator services for the Los Angeles County Superior Court system, the largest employer of interpreters and translators in the Los Angeles area. The court, one of the heaviest users of court interpretation services in the country, is short an average of 10 interpreters a day, and many times more, Johnson said. "The demand is basically for Spanish-language interpreters. They can pretty much work every day."

Interpreters convert one language to another verbally, usually while someone is talking. They translate speeches, conversations, and conference proceedings to an audience unfamiliar with a given tongue in the presence of the speaker. **Translators** work with the written word, rendering letters, manuals, reports, court cases, and books or manuscripts into one or more different languages.

Both interpreters and translators must be highly trained and deadly accurate, since the stakes in courtroom settings, business transactions, and diplomatic situations can be very high. For their expertise, interpreters and translators can make $40,000 to

$50,000 a year or more depending on their workload. Starting salaries for interpreters are about $18 to $20 an hour.

Most interpreters and translators are independent contractors. As such, they have the advantage of choosing their own hours. The main drawback is that they generally do not receive benefits.

Over 300 interpreters and translators are used each day at the county's 60 different superior and municipal court, jail, and psychiatric hospital locations. The court currently employs about 480 interpreters and translators on a freelance basis—a dramatic jump from the 5 it had back in 1962. Large international law firms also employ their own interpreters.

Superior Court interpreters, who currently make $174 a day, work in a variety of settings, including courtrooms, visiting rooms at jails, and law offices, to help facilitate interviews and discussions between lawyers and clients. Translators may transcribe documents written in a foreign language or cassette recordings made by undercover agents to be used as evidence in criminal proceedings, Johnson said.

Apparently, no private agency has tallied the total number of translators and interpreters and the U.S. Department of Labor Statistics claims their numbers are too few to be counted. But the statewide California Court Interpreters Association has about 600 members. The nationwide American Translators Association has some 2,200 members. Considering the number of people who don't join professional organizations, there probably are a lot more.

Contributing to growth in the interpreting and translating field are developments such as a more crowded court system and a recent court ruling stipulating that each participant in a trial is entitled to his or her own interpreter, to increased trade with Pacific Rim countries and an influx of foreign residents to the greater Los Angeles area, said Jack Kyser, chief economist for the Los Angeles Area Chamber of Commerce.

But a difficult state certification test, which has only a 4 percent passing rate, has limited the number of people qualified to become interpreters, said Alexandre Rainof, head of UCLA Extension's translation and interpretation program. Added Johnson: "There is a misconception that simply because someone is bilingual they can be an interpreter. Being an interpreter requires a higher level of linguistic skills. We have people on staff who are college professors."

In Los Angeles County, interpreters are also required to pass a two-part county-administered exam that tests for grammar and knowledge of legal terms, as well as actual interpreting ability in a simulated courtroom setting, Johnson said. The county court system requires state certification in particular languages, including Spanish, Arabic, Japanese, Chinese, Korean, Vietnamese, and Tagalog.

Federal court interpreters and translators earn even more than interpreters for the county—$225 a day—but they are required to pass a stringent federal test, which even experienced state- and county-certified interpreters are said to have difficulty passing.

Besides Spanish, Los Angeles–area court systems have a great need for interpreters and translators in several Asian languages, including Korean, Vietnamese, Chinese, and, to a lesser extent, Japanese, Johnson said. Laotian and Armenian are other languages in which demand is growing.

Another large employer of interpreters and translators is the Berlitz Language and Translation Centers, the nation's largest commercial translation service. Some 150 employees (not all of them interpreters and translators) work out of Berlitz's production facility in Woodland Hills, said Mary Lou Kirkpatrick, the company's director of operations. "Our interpretation business is growing very, very rapidly. We're always recruiting."

The languages with the biggest demand at Berlitz are Spanish and Japanese, she said. "If you're a Spanish interpreter, you'll always be busy in the Southern California area," said Kathy Boyer of Euramerica International Business Translators, which was recently acquired by Berlitz. Interpreters can increase their earnings by working on call at a variety of agencies, Boyer said.

Occasionally an interpreter with special qualifications, for instance someone with a background in technical sciences who can translate Korean to English, may be flown across the country on interpreting assignments, making upward of $1,000 a day during the assignment, Kirkpatrick said. High-level interpreters known in diplomatic circles also have occasion to travel. They go wherever world events take them, such as the United Nations in New York or to Geneva, Malta, or even Moscow for summit meetings.

"It's challenging. Interpreters find themselves in all types of different situations. We provided someone when Gorbachev came (to New York City) to visit in 1988," Kirkpatrick said. "We have some people who are flown all over the country because they're really in demand. They can make $1,000 a day plus airfare."

The work performed by interpreters and translators may seem closely related, but the skills required are vastly different. Top-notch translators seldom make first-rate interpreters and good interpreters aren't always able to translate well, said Rainof of UCLA Extension.

Both interpreters and translators need to know their "target" language, the one they're translating into, virtually as well as they know their native language. Since words and expressions often cannot be translated directly in different languages, in-depth knowledge of the subtleties of both languages is required.

In general, the level of fluency needed for interpreting and translating requires at least four or five years of intensive study of the target language, plus a year or more of living in the country, language experts say. Life experience also helps. "The level of knowledge and experience that a person needs to bring to translation is not there for a person who is in his or her early 20s," Kirkpatrick said.

The same principle of familiarity also applies to technical translation. "Unless you've grown up in Japan, it's almost impossible to translate a technical document from Japanese to English," said Keiko Isshiki, a court-certified interpreter and translator who teaches Japanese through UCLA Extension and is able to both translate and interpret. "You have to know about the culture and nuances and idioms, and all of that cannot come from textbooks."

Students taking the UCLA Extension program, which is limited to English and Spanish, learn some 3,000 words in both languages across a range of legal, technical, and medical subjects.

The program teaches students how to interpret consecutively and simultaneously, said Rainof. Consecutive interpreting takes less time to learn because it moves at a slower, stop-and-go pace; the speaker speaks and then stops, while the interpreter interprets. In simultaneous interpretation, the interpreter may be only a word or two behind the speaker.

More than being able to speak two languages, interpreters must do five things at once: listen and make sense out of what they're hearing, translate that into a different language, repeat what they heard out loud and then remember what has just been said, Rainof said. "They're linguistic athletes," remarked Johnson of the county court system.

A college degree is not necessary to work as an interpreter or translator. However, education is available. But applying to a respected school is competitive. The UCLA Extension program, one of the few in California to offer state-accredited intepreter training, receives six applications for every one accepted, Rainof said. For more information, call (213) 825-1898.

The well-respected Monterey Institute of International Languages in Monterey, California, offers a master's degree in interpreting and translating, as does Georgetown University in Washington, D.C. Internationally, Berlitz has training centers in Mexico City and Caracas, Venezuela. The University of Geneva in Switzerland also offers a world-renowned interpreting and translating degree program, Rainof said.

Translating between English and Spanish or one of the other Romance or Germanic languages is difficult enough. But Asian languages require even more study because of the different alphabets and pronunciations that are used. Some sounds common to English-speaking peoples simply don't exist in Japan, and vice versa, Isshiki said.

Japanese interpreters at this time are mostly needed for business meetings and technical conferences, especially in the computer, medical, and telecommunications fields. "There aren't too many qualified interpreters around," Isshiki added.

Pay Scale for Translators and Interpreters

Position	Wage
Private interpreters	$18–$30/hour
Interpreters for government agencies	$90/day
L.A. County court interpreters	$174/day
	$117/half day
State court interpreters	$108/day
Federal court interpreters	$225/day
International conference interpreters	$380/day
Translators	7–12 cents/word

SOURCE: Los Angeles County Superior Court; Berlitz Translation Centers; UCLA Extension.

KEY EMPLOYERS OF TRANSLATORS AND INTERPRETERS

Private Sector

American Translators International
3600 Wilshire Boulevard
Los Angeles, CA 90010
800/443-2444

Berlitz Translation Services
6415 Independence Avenue
Woodland Hills, CA 91367
818/347-8282

Bilingual Services
1888 Century Park East
Suite 10
Los Angeles, CA 90067
213/556-0446

Continental Communications Agency
7120 Hayvenhurst Avenue
Van Nuys, CA 91406
818/782-4711

Inlingua
3255 Wilshire Boulevard
Los Angeles, CA 90010
213/386-9949

International Documentation
1801 Avenue of the Stars
Suite 419
Los Angeles, CA 90067
800/336-9898

International Translation Bureau Inc.
125 W. Fourth Street
Los Angeles, CA 90013
213/629-1990

Intex Translation Agency
Suite 205
9021 Melrose Avenue
Los Angeles, CA 90069
213/275-9571

Japanese Interpreters & Translators Service
2126 Barry Avenue
Los Angeles, CA 90025
213/879-8881

Japanese Translators
800 W. First Street
Los Angeles, CA 90012
213/687-7500

Omni Lingual Services Inc.
973 Westlake Boulevard
Westlake Village, CA 91361
800/543-4244

Poly Languages Institute
350 S. Lake Avenue
Pasadena, CA 91101
213/380-4270

Transcontinental Language System
1901 Avenue of the Stars
Los Angeles, CA 90067
213/478-5337

Trans-World Interpreters
3434 Amesbury Road
Los Angeles, CA 90027
213/662-3522

Public Sector

Los Angeles County Superior Court
Court Interpreter Services
111 N. Hill Street
Los Angeles, CA 90012
213/974-5363

Los Angeles Municipal Court
Personnel Office
110 N. Grand Avenue
Los Angeles, CA 90012
213/974-6105

Orange County Superior Court
700 Civic Center Drive W.
Santa Ana, CA 92701
714/834-3226

State of California Court of Appeal
3580 Wilshire Boulevard
Los Angeles, CA 90010
213/736-2391

United States District Court
312 N. Spring Street
Los Angeles, CA 90012
213/894-3118

Also see Chapter 14 for a listing of major law firms in the
Los Angeles area.

PROFESSIONAL ORGANIZATIONS

**American Literary Translators
 Association**
Post Office Box 830688
University of Texas, Dallas
Richardson, TX 75083
214//690-2093

American Society of Interpreters
Post Office Box 9603
Washington, DC 20016
301/657-3337

American Translators Association
109 Croton Avenue
Ossining, NY 10562
914/941-1500

**National Association of Judicial
 Interpreters and Translators**
Post Office Box 506
Albuquerque, NM 87103
505/242-8085

National Translators Association
Post Office Box 628
Riverton, WY 82501
307/856-3322

Western Interpreters Association
8665 Florin Road
Sacramento, CA 95828
916/381-4620

DIRECTORIES

Directory of Translators (Association of Professional Translators, Pittsburgh, PA)

Membership Directory (American Translators Association, Ossining, NY)

Membership List (American Society of Interpreters, Washington, DC)

Translations Index (Materials Information, Metals Park, OH)

Job Sharing

*Splitting responsibilities and working half-time
is gaining as a viable work option.*

With housing prices soaring, the cost of living rising, and the burden of making ends meet becoming heavier each year, many working couples cannot afford to give up half their income when they decide to raise a family. Rather than sacrificing a rewarding career for a satisfying home life, many people in the workforce have found an alternative that allows them to continue working *and* be attentive parents at the same time: job sharing.

Job sharing, where two people share one position, dividing the salary, job responsibilities, and work hours, is slowly gaining ground among forward-looking employers who would rather let two valuable employees each work part-time than not have them work at all. It's also becoming more popular among working mothers.

Nationwide, between 3 and 10 percent of companies have some job sharers, according to *Personnel Administrator* magazine. That number is expected to rise sharply in the 1990s. The Work in America Institute estimates that as many as half of all working Americans are currently involved in some kind of part-time or alternative work schedule, such as flextime (coming in early and leaving early) or four-day work weeks.

A variety of factors, including an increased number of women in the workforce and a shrinking labor pool, are combining to push companies toward adopting more accommodating schedules.

Changing demographics are also providing employees with the clout to suggest job sharing as a viable work option. "More and more women who are having children want to continue working in some way," said Maria Laqueur, executive director of the Association of Part-Time Professionals (APTP) in McLean, Virginia. "At the same time, many people are easing into retirement. Managers are having to look at job sharing because they're being asked about it."

Job sharing isn't just for women; an increasing number of men are beginning to job share for parental, avocational, or health reasons. At New Ways to Work, a work-time options research and training center in San Francisco, about a third of all people who inquire about reducing their work time are men, said Suzanne Smith, who shares the directorship of her organization.

Until recently, most people who shared jobs were clerical or technical workers. Now, interest in job sharing is growing in professional and managerial groups, especially among those trying to juggle the demands of their careers with the needs of their children. "Jobs where you're required to supervise a large number of people are more difficult to share," Laqueur said. "But we're seeing more and more of it at the professional level."

There are professors, personnel administrators, bank vice presidents, and members of the clergy who job share—everybody from attorneys to zookeepers. "It's simply a matter of two individuals being able to put a package together and sell their employer on it," Laqueur said. "In most cases it involves full-time employees who are now choosing to work part-time."

A few Los Angeles–area employers with job sharers on staff include the City of Santa Monica Recreation Services Department, the state Attorney General's Office, and the Los Angeles County District Attorney's Office—all from the public sector. "The public sector has been head and shoulders above the private sector in adapting to alternative work schedules, particularly when it comes to giving part-timers benefits," noted Susan Miller, a career counselor with Vocational Training Consulting Services in Los Angeles.

That's mainly because government agencies aren't as profit-conscious. Yet while job sharing is typically viewed as benefiting the employee, there are advantages to the employer as well. Experts argue that job sharing can help reduce job burnout and increase efficiency by enabling workers to be more focused during their shifts. It's also a way to retain the skills of veteran employees rather than losing them altogether.

"Job sharing makes people feel good about their company, that they're not a slave to it, that they have options," said Miller. "It makes the workplace much more humane."

The District Attorney's Office employs five pairs of deputy district attorneys (all of whom happen to be women with young children) on a permanent, part-time basis, said Ann Burnett, a personnel officer in the DA's Office. Each job sharer works 20 hours a week, performing tasks that usually take only a day to complete, Burnett said.

"Most of them are in it with the thought that it's only temporary," Burnett said. "It's a more realistic approach to the workplace. It has been very successful."

The DA's Office doesn't extend benefits to job sharers. But other employers, like the City of Santa Monica, allow job sharers to split their vacation time, sick leave, and holiday pay. Each employee also receives a full set of medical and dental benefits.

Miller suggests the following seven steps as a guideline for people who want to job share:

1. Endear yourself to your employer as a full-time employee *first* so you are a valuable commodity. Proven ability is perhaps the most important bargaining chip you can bring to the table when negotiating for a job sharing arrangement. Seniority helps, but it's not mandatory.

   "Essentially, you have to be very good at what you do. You have to be very knowledgeable. In fact, you almost have to be better than anyone else if you want to go on part-time status because the employer has to feel that they don't want to lose you," Miller said.

2. Find a partner with whom you are comfortable and can communicate well, and who has skills that complement your own. Job sharing has been likened to marriage in that it requires an intense level of commitment and communication between partners. Communication is paramount because one partner usually has to pick up right where the other has left off without missing a beat.

3. Draw up a proposal or course of action that outlines how you intend to implement your job-sharing plan and what you expect out of it. Do you want to work half days, or eight-hour shifts every other day? Do you expect to receive full benefits, or are you willing to share one set and pay a prorated amount to obtain full health coverage?

   Think out your proposed arrangement fully so you can make a convincing presentation to your boss. Don't expect management to have a ready-made plan of action. That's your responsibility. Be armed with as much informational ammunition as you can muster.

Reference material on job sharing is available from APTP in McLean, Verginia, and from the National Council for Alternative Work Patterns in Washington, D.C. In addition, New Ways to Work publishes a job-sharing handbook, and Catalyst, a women's employment resource center in New York, publishes a comprehensive bibliography of alternative work patterns. (See the reference list at the end of this chapter.)

4. Keep careful track of your responsibilities in your current job so you'll know precisely which duties you'll want to perform as a part-timer and which responsibilities you'll want your partner to handle. Many times, your boss or supervisor might not even know the totality of what you do. Pulling your job description apart and putting it in outline form shows your employer that you're organized and have thought out how a job-sharing arrangement could be reasonably implemented.

5. Ask yourself whether you have the temperament and willingness to share a job. Job sharing requires a great deal of trust and confidence between partners. When your shift is done, you must be able to let go and give the work over to your partner. "If what you are is very attached to your work and you don't really think anybody else can do it, you won't be able to job share," said New Ways to Work's Smith.

Job sharers also should be prepared to pick up the slack when their partner is sick or away (and by the same token be responsible enough not to take advantage of the other person's charity), and be flexible enough to attend company or departmental meetings that aren't scheduled during normal work hours to show that they are still dedicated to the company or organization.

6. Get to know the different departments and managers within your company or organization. If your immediate supervisor is not open to a job-sharing arrangement, try a manager in another department. A transfer could be the impetus you need. Establish contacts and make yourself visible. The more people you talk to, the better feel you will have for the opportunities available.

7. Finally, be diplomatic. Sometimes office co-workers don't take to a job-sharing arrangement very well. They might

SELF-ASSESSMENT FOR JOB SHARING

Susan Miller, M.A., a Los Angeles career consultant, advises potential job sharers to ask themselves the following questions to determine whether they are likely candidates for a job-sharing arrangement:

- Can you define what you offer at your job?
- Are you basically satisfied with the job?
- Are your reasons for wanting to job share acceptable to your place of employment?
- Are you a valuable employee to the organization?
- Do you have the patience and determination to go through the lengthy process of restructuring the job?
- Do you possess the confidence and assertiveness necessary to sell management on your idea?
- Are you prepared to give up half the job and half the salary?
- Are you flexible and adaptable to change?
- Are you willing to spend extra time and effort to develop solid, trusting relationships and good communications with co-workers?

harbor resentment toward other employees who appear to be leading the easy life by operating under a separate set of rules. (Never mind that job sharers earn only a part-time salary.) To help minimize morale problems, announce what you're doing. But be careful not to flaunt your new-found independence.

"If you're a part-time, re-entry career woman with three kids at home, you have to make it clear that you're not playing in your other time. When you leave work, you're going to your other job, essentially," Miller said.

PROFESSIONAL ORGANIZATIONS

Association of Part-Time Professionals
7700 Leesburg Pike
Suite 216
Falls Church, VA 22043
703/734-7975

Catalyst
250 Park Avenue South
New York, NY 10003
212/777-8900

**The National Council for
  Alternative Work Patterns**
1925 K Street, NW
Suite 308-A
Washington, DC 20006
202/476-4467

New Ways to Work
149 Ninth Street
San Francisco, CA 94103
415/552-1000

The Society for Work Options
c/o FOCUS
509 10th Avenue E.
Seattle, WA 98102
206/329-7918

RECOMMENDED READING

Alter, JoAnne. *A Part-Time Career for a Full-Time You.* Boston: Houghton Mifflin, 1982.

California State Senate. *Flextime, Reduced Worktime and Jobsharing: Interim Hearing.* Sacramento: Joint Publications, 1986.

Lee, Patricia. *The Complete Guide to Job Sharing.* New York: Walker, 1983.

Meltz, Noah M. *Sharing the Work: An Analysis of the Issues in Worksharing and Jobsharing.* Toronto: University of Toronto Press, 1981.

Olmsted, Barney, and Smith, Suzanne. *The Job Sharing Handbook.* New York: Penguin Books, 1983.

DIRECTORIES

Employer Directory (Association of Part-Time Professionals, McLean, VA)
Job Sharing: A Bibliography (Vance Bibliographies, Monticello, IL)
Part-Time Employment: A Bibliography (Vance Bibliographies, Monticello, IL)

SECTION
6

High-Tech
Careers

CHAPTER 18

Careers
in Space

*With the space station, lunar, and Mars
initiatives on the boards, all systems are
go to launch a career in astronautics.*

Space—the final frontier—is opening up as a new job frontier.
From the National Aeronautics and Space Administration (NASA)
to private contractors like TRW and Rockwell International, space-
related careers are taking off. The once-distant dream of working
in space is now becoming more and more a reality.

President Bush's recently announced Space Station Freedom
and space exploration plans, added to the success of the Voyager
deep space probe and the reintegration of the space shuttle
program, have generated an excitement and interest in space not
felt since the crew of Apollo 11 first set foot on the moon July
20, 1969. And with the recent launch of the Hubble space telescope,
at no time in recorded history have eyes been so heavenly fixed.

Space veterans from the days of the Mercury, Gemini, and
Apollo moon missions of the 1960s and early 1970s note that
the 1990s are likely to provide more opportunities for space
careers, and more day-to-day discussion about space, than all
the previous decades combined.

"A large number of people who entered at that time are now
in senior positions and will be retiring," said Alan Silcock, human
resources director for Rockwell International's Space Transportation Systems Division in Downey. "We are aggressively recruiting talent to fill that need. We look at our future very brightly.
I think the future in this kind of work is absolutely phenomenal."

Besides projected mass retirements of a whole generation of professionals in the space community, there is a renewed national emphasis on space exploration spearheaded by President Bush that promises to bolster opportunities. Bush in a recent address set three goals: the placing of a space station in permanent orbit around the Earth; the establishment of a manned laboratory on the moon; and a manned trip to Mars by the year 2019—the 50th anniversary of the first moon landing. (History buffs will note that it was President John F. Kennedy who initially proclaimed America's commitment to space in a famous 1962 speech following the Soviet Union's successful launch of the first Sputnik orbiter in 1957.)

"It's another age of exploration. It's another big jump," declared Robert Vredenburgh, recruitment supervisor for the California Institute of Technology's Jet Propulsion Laboratory (JPL) in Pasadena. JPL, under contract to NASA to carry out unmanned exploration of the solar system and interplanetary space, has two major programs on the boards: CRAF (Comet Rendezvous/ Asteroid Fly-by) and the Cassini space probe, which is designed to explore Saturn's planetary system, Vredenburgh said.

"The CRAF and Cassini projects are going to cause a big upturn in our business," Vredenburgh said. "From late this year [1990] on, it looks very rosy. Unless Congress does a complete turnaround and won't fund the president's programs, I see nothing but good times ahead. If it goes as planned, the next 10 to 20 years will be absolutely phenomenal for people in the space industry."

NASA Administrator Richard Truly recently announced plans to boost the space agency's budget from $12.3 billion in 1990 to $19.3 billion by 1993—nearly 60 percent, and more than twice what the agency received in 1988. NASA's 1990 spending created an estimated 237,000 private-industry jobs nationwide, spurred some $23 billion in sales by contractors, and resulted in $2.4 billion in corporate profits, according to a report released by the NASA Alumni League.

Southern California, the largest aerospace center in the country, was the biggest benefactor. Statewide, $6.7 billion in sales were generated by NASA spending in 1990 alone. These expenditures created directly or indirectly an estimated 70,332 private sector jobs in California—nearly 30 percent of all space-related opportunites nationwide. The Los Angeles area, no doubt, receives the lion's share of that spending.

At JPL, Vredenburgh said, the majority of the 7,000-member workforce (including contractors) are engineering types— electrical, mechanical, aeronautical, and optical. As a minimum, most are required to have at least a bachelor's degree and, preferably, an advanced degree (either a master's or PhD). "Advanced degrees are really another form of experience," said Silcock of Rockwell.

JPL also employs a number of astronomers, physicists, mathematicians, and computer scientists, Vredenburgh said. "The computer-related fields—people who can work with concurrent or simultaneous processing, the supercomputing-type functions— that's wide open. So are image and infrared processing, which are offshoots of electrical engineering and physics. They're both very much in demand right now."

Southland universities noted for their engineering and/or science departments include Cal Tech, USC, UCLA, Cal Poly Pomona, Cal State Los Angeles, and Cal State Northridge, Vredenburgh said.

JPL staff have a perk unique to the space industry: they are the first to see any photographs transmitted from outer space and they are privy to a good portion of space shuttle missions, not just snippets and sound bites.

At TRW's Electronic Systems Group in Redondo Beach, maker of space satellites, "systems analysts and engineers are in the most demand," said Gary Jong, group placement manager. Systems analysts plan efficient ways of processing data by computer and interpreting the results, while systems engineers design the whole system (see Chapter 21). "The ideal systems engineer for us understands both hardware and software," Jong said.

"Materials and composites people and manufacturing engineers are also needed," he continued. "They can have a variety of backgrounds, from physics and chemistry to mechanical engineering. Those who understand computer-integrated manufacturing are critical. While the environment is moving more toward specialists, we also need people with cross-training."

Most of TRW's project leaders and even program managers have master's degrees in their respective fields, Jong said. More and more have PhDs. "We try to hire as many people with advanced degrees as we can. Systems analysis won't even hire you unless you plan to participate in their fellowship program or already have a master's degree." TRW employs about 20,000 people in the Los Angeles area.

Beginning engineers with a bachelor's degree, at least a B+ average, and some experience start at $630 to $670 a week, Jong said, adding that with a master's degree or PhD, the salary rises to $680 to $770 a week. Starting salaries for members of JPL's technical staff range from $650 to $1,000 a week. Mid-career managers typically earn a $50,000 to $70,000 salary. Previous experience increases an applicant's marketability as well as salary potential and can be gained through an internship while still in college. This holds true for most aerospace companies.

Rockwell International, a major player in the space industry and one of the prime contractors for the space shuttle, space station, and national aerospace plane projects (McDonnell Douglas is another), has set out on a nationwide search for students with skills in such emerging technologies as robotics and artificial intelligence, skills needed to turn our space dreams into reality, Silcock said.

Engineers working on the national aerospace plane, which will take off like an airplane and fly into space at roughly 25 times the speed of sound (approximately 18,500 mph), face profound technical challenges, particularly in the areas of materials, propulsion, and guidance. The aerospace plane and space station are scheduled to be operational by the late 1990s.

"As our national objectives are defined, oftentimes the specifics of how we're going to get there are totally unknown because we've never done it before," Silcock said. "On the space station, for example, one of the key criteria is that the people tending it should be minimized and the self-repair capability maximized. This is relatively new stuff. It gets down to Stanley Kubrick's famous movie *2001*."

Rockwell, which provides extensive in-house training for its 35,000 employees in Southern California, hires mostly electrical engineers for its Space Transportation Systems Division (STSD) and looks for a "handful" of mechanical engineers, increasingly in the orbital mechanics area, said Sandy Adkisson, STSD's manager of professional employment. On the nontechnical side, a limited number of opportunities are available for business and financial analysts, Adkisson added.

Not everyone who works in the space field is a rocket scientist. When it comes to manufacturing a new spacecraft, much of the credit for completing the job must be given to the technicians, who apply the drawing-board plans of scientists and engineers to actual situations. At many aerospace companies, an A.S. degree from a technical college can open the doors for an electronic or prototype technician. But the vast majority of space-related careers require at least a bachelor's degree.

In space, one career reigns supreme: astronaut. Currently, there are only about 90 astronauts in the entire space program. Nevertheless, NASA has an ongoing need for pilot and mission specialist astronaut candidates to support the space shuttle program, according to a NASA career announcement. A space shuttle crew normally consists of five people—the commander, pilot, and three mission specialists, all of whom are NASA astronauts.

Pilot astronauts, who usually have military flight backgrounds, serve as both space shuttle commanders and pilots. Commanders are the mission leaders, responsibile for the vehicle, crew, mission success, and safety of the flight. Pilots assist with controlling and operating the spacecraft. Mission specialists are the on-board scientists, typically astrophysicists, medical scientists, engineers, and the like, who carry out experiments during a flight mission.

Since space missions are primarily military or scientific in nature at this point, there is little room for astronauts without test pilot or scientific backgrounds, said Billie Deason, spokeswoman for the Johnson Space Center in Houston.

"Once we get the space station in orbit with people there all the time, you'll see a larger number of U.S. astronauts going into space. But we're not going to send construction workers into space. That's just not feasible. Space is a very hostile environment. It takes a good deal of very specific, intense training to learn to live and work in that environment. The space station crews will be working scientists."

Civilian applications for the Astronaut Candidate Program are accepted on a continuous basis and can be obtained by writing to NASA, Johnson Space Center, Astronaut Selection Office, Attn: AHX, Houston, TX 77058.

KEY LAUNCHING PADS OF SPACE CAREERS

California Institute of Technology (Cal Tech)
Jet Propulsion Laboratory
1201 E. California Boulevard
Pasadena, CA 91105
818/354-4321

Hughes Aircraft Co.
Space & Communications Group
909 N. Sepulveda Boulevard
El Segundo, CA 90245
213/648-2345

McDonnell Douglas
Astronautics Company
5301 Bolsa Avenue
Huntington Beach, CA 92647
714/896-3311

National Aeronautics and Space
Administration (NASA)
Pasadena Office
4800 Oak Grove Drive
Pasadena, CA 91109
818/354-5359

Rockwell International
Rocketdyne Division
Professional Staffing
6633 Canoga Avenue
Canoga Park, CA 91303
818/710-6300

Rockwell International
Shuttle Integration & Satellite
  Systems Division
2201 Seal Beach Boulevard
Seal Beach, CA 90740
213/594-3311

TRW
Space & Technology Group
One Space Park Drive
Redondo Beach, CA 90278
213/536-2000

United States Air Force
Space Division
Civilian Employment Office
200 N. Douglas Street
El Segundo, CA 90245
213/643-0616

Also see Chapter 19 for a list of major defense contractors.

PROFESSIONAL ORGANIZATIONS

Aerospace Education Foundation
1501 Lee Highway
Arlington, VA 22209
703/247-5839

Aerospace Industries Association
  of America
1250 I Street, NW
Washington, DC 20005
202/371-8400

American Institute of Aeronautics
  and Astronautics
370 L'Enfant Promenade, SW
Washington, DC 20024
202/646-7400

National Space Society
922 Pennsylvania Avenue, SE
Washington, DC 20003
202/543-1900

Planetary Society
65 N. Catalina Avenue
Pasadena, CA 91106
818/793-5100

United States Space Education
  Association
746 Turnpike Road
Elizabethtown, PA 17022
717/367-3265

PROFESSIONAL PUBLICATIONS

Aerospace America (Washington, DC)
AIAA Journal (Washington, DC)
Aviation Week & Space Technology (New York, NY)

Business & Commercial Aviation (White Plains, NY)
Final Frontier (Minneapolis, MN)
NASA Tech Briefs (New York, NY)
Space News (Springfield, VA)

DIRECTORIES

Aviation Week & Space Technology, Buyers Guide Issue (McGraw-Hill Publishing, New York, NY)
Directory (American Astronautical Society, Springfield, VA)
Roster (American Institute of Aeronautics and Astronautics, Washington, DC)
Space Information Sourcebook (Space Trends Publishing, Penacook, NH)
Space Station Directory and Program Guide (Pasha Publications, Arlington, VA)

CHAPTER 19

The Defense Industry

Despite recent cutbacks, some firms are still hiring.

The defense industry in Southern California is massive and, even in this era of the Cold War thaw and Department of Defense cutbacks, so are the opportunities if you apply to the right companies.

L.A. is one of the largest, if not *the* largest, aerospace centers in the country. Seven of the biggest space and defense firms in the nation—Hughes Aircraft, Rockwell International, McDonnell Douglas, Northrop Corporation, TRW, General Dynamics, and Lockheed—have corporate headquarters in Los Angeles County, which receives about 43 percent of all the major Defense Department contracts awarded in California and about 8 percent nationwide.

In the five-county greater Los Angeles area, including L.A., Orange, Riverside, San Bernardino, and Ventura counties, aerospace and high technology is an $18-billion-a-year industry, ranking only behind business services and tourism in its importance to the Southern California economy, said Jack Kyser, chief economist for the Los Angeles Area Chamber of Commerce. Regionally, some 411,800 people are employed in defense-related industries.

The key to finding employment with long-term security, industry experts say, is to be selective, as opportunities are spread unevenly among the Southland's numerous aerospace firms. Companies that assign priority to their commercial endeavors and emphasize civilian applications for their technologies are generally more secure than those that rely mostly on military contracts.

"It's more a question of which company you go to" than which job you apply for, said Gordon Palmer, principal economist with the Southern California Association of Governments. "When a particular project goes, they usually cut back on staffing."

The "aerospace" industry is really an aggregation of eight different fields: missiles, space vehicles, instruments, communications systems, aircraft and parts, computers, electronics, and semiconductors, said Brad Williams, director of economic and revenue forecasting for the Commission on State Finance in Sacramento.

Aerospace insiders quip that there are three types of jobs available in the defense industry: engineer, engineer and, if you look hard enough, engineer. And indeed, most opportunities at high-technology and space-oriented contractors are for degreed applicants in engineering-related fields, including aerospace engineering, electrical engineering, and computer science, said Professor Robert Liebeck of USC's Department of Aerospace Engineering.

Entry-level engineers typically start at around $27,000 at large aerospace companies. With five to seven years' experience, they can earn $40,000 to $50,000. In addition to professional openings, there are opportunities for technical, clerical, and administrative staff as well, especially with companies that are heavily involved in mass production aircraft projects, such as Hughes Aircraft, Lockheed, and McDonnell Douglas.

Despite cutbacks in other areas, the demand on the manufacturing side of the defense industry has gotten to the point where many aerospace companies actually have a shortage of skilled crafts workers in such areas as tool design, production, quality assurance, machine operation, machine electronics, and assembly planning, said Northrop spokesman James Hart. Skilled workers generally make between $10 and $15 an hour.

Technological advances in microelectronics, robotics, and computer operations require today's production worker to be highly specialized, familiar with math, and able to read engineering blueprints and technical manuals, Hart added.

"This is not just working on an assembly line," said TRW spokesman John Booth. "It's working with very specialized tools making very specialized equipment. It requires very specialized training." Typically, this training can be had by pursuing a two-year degree at community colleges that offer manufacturing technology programs, including El Camino College in Torrance, Long Beach City College, and Cerritos College.

Production work is only a small part of the total job picture. At aerospace firms with a high-technology orientation like TRW, nondegreed employees account for less than a third of the company's workforce, Booth said.

At TRW, a diversified aerospace company with operating groups in space and technology, electronic systems, avionics, and surveillance and systems integration (computer hardware and software), the corporate survival strategy is to improve existing microelectronic components and build new satellites and surveillance systems to help the military become more efficient.

During the defense buildup of the Reagan administration, the Southern California aerospace industry experienced tremendous growth that experts say won't be matched in the forseeable future. As defense spending gradually declines over the next few years, job openings are expected to dry up. (Defense Secretary Richard Cheney has called for $180 billion in spending cuts from 1992 to 1994. Defense budgets have been running at about $300 billion annually.)

In the principal defense sectors of aircraft manufacturing, missiles systems, and space technology, Department of Defense cutbacks are expected to eliminate an estimated 25,000 positions out of a total of 200,000 in the Los Angeles area by 1995, according to Stephen Levy, director of the Center for the Continuing Study of the California Economy in Palo Alto. Indeed, many defense jobs have already vanished.

Individual companies that may be hard hit by the shrinking defense budget include Northrop, which has been banking on the massive B-2 Stealth bomber project and next-generation Stealth fighter plane, and Lockheed, builder of the C-5 transport plane and F-117 Stealth fighter. Northrop receives a whopping 90 percent of its revenues from military contracts—half of those from the politically sensitive Stealth bomber—while Lockheed is 78 percent dependent on the Defense Department. Another project that has been isolated as a potential budget target is the C-17 transport plane made by McDonnell Douglas.

In the 1980s, the largest cutbacks occurred at Hughes and Rockwell. In 1986, Rockwell began laying off some 12,600 workers in Southern California who had been assigned to the B-1 bomber project. Three years later, Hughes announced that it had trimmed

9,300 jobs in an effort to reduce costs. The Hughes layoffs came in the midst of a declining market at a time when Northrop, Lockheed, and General Dynamics were also laying off workers. In 1988, TRW reduced its workforce by about 1,000 people.

Ironically, the same companies that initiate wholesale layoffs often find themselves short of workers in some areas and must turn around and advertise for new employees or bring in temporary workers through employment services. In many instances, employees laid off from one project are rehired for another. For instance, about 2,100 of the 9,300 jobs pared at Hughes may have been lost only temporarily, said Hughes spokesman Ray Silvius.

While the number of jobs directly tied to defense contracts will continue to shrink, an estimated 130,000 positions in communications-related fields will not be affected, Levy said. Nor will the regional economy feel an appreciable impact from the trimming of the defense budget. As big as the high-tech and defense industries are, they still account for just 6 percent of total nonagricultural employment in the five-county Southern California area, Kyser added.

"We expect the L.A. economy to continue to outperform the national average despite leveling in the defense industry," Levy said.

Job openings in the defense industry may fluctuate, but opportunities in the related fields of commercial aircraft design and production as well as satellite and communications systems are in steady supply.

The greatest job stability can be found at companies that have a healthy military-commercial business mix such as Rockwell, the prime contractor for the space shuttle, and McDonnell Douglas, whose Long Beach–based aircraft division has enough commercial airline orders to carry it through the year 2002.

"Right now we can't make airplanes fast enough," said USC's Liebeck, who has worked for McDonnell Douglas since 1961. "The commercial area is booming. I've never seen business doing as well as it's doing now. Douglas is pretty darn stable."

Security is an important consideration in the defense industry. Employees assigned to work on classified or "black" projects undergo extensive background checks. To obtain a security clearance, job applicants cannot have a criminal record, be a member of the Communist Party, or have relatives, friends, or contacts who live in unfriendly foreign nations.

The Largest Aerospace Contractors*

Firm	Employees	Military-Commercial Business Mix
McDonnell Douglas	50,000	30–70
Northrop Corp.	41,000	90–10
Hughes Aircraft Co.	35,000	75–25
Rockwell International Corp.	35,000	40–60
TRW (Space & Defense Groups)	20,000	90–10
Lockheed Corp.	14,000	78–22
Allied-Signal Aerospace Co.	9,000	50–50
Litton Industries Inc.	7,000	60–40
Teledyne Inc.	6,000	20–80
The Aerospace Corp.	4,200	100–0
Logicon Inc.	1,851	80–20

* Ranked by size of Los Angeles area workforce.
SOURCE: Companies.

Even the apparently minor blemish of having an open-container violation on one's driving record can hinder an employee from getting a security clearance and being promoted to a better job later. "It is all looked at. Their background is thoroughly checked. People don't just walk in off the street in aerospace. They usually have experience. They know what they're looking for," Booth said.

KEY EMPLOYERS IN THE DEFENSE INDUSTRY

Aerojet ElectroSystems
1100 W. Hollyvale Street
Azusa, CA 91702
818/812-1000

Aeronautical Systems Co.
2555 N. Hollywood Way
Burbank, CA 91520
818/847-6121

The Aerospace Corp.
2350 E. El Segundo Boulevard
El Segundo, CA 90245
213/336-5000

Allied-Signal Aerospace Co.
Headquarters Location
2525 W. 190th Street
Torrance, CA 90504
213/323-9500

Ford Aerospace Corp.
5757 W. Century Boulevard
Los Angeles, CA 90045
213/645-8443

Garrett General Aviation
1515 Hughes Way
Long Beach, CA 90810
213/568-3700

General Dynamics Corp.
2250 E. Imperial Highway
El Segundo, CA 90245
213/640-6163

Honeywell Inc.
1200 E. San Bernardino Road
West Covina, CA 91790
213/331-0011

Hughes Aircraft Co.
Corporate Headquarters
7200 Hughes Terrace
Los Angeles, CA 90045
213/568-7200

Litton Industries
360 N. Crescent Drive
Beverly Hills, CA 90210
213/859-5000

Lockheed Corp.
Administrative Offices
2627 N. Hollywood Way
Burbank, CA 91520
818/847-6121

Logicon Inc.
3701 Skypark Drive
Torrance, CA 90505
213/373-0220

McDonnell Douglas Corp.
Douglas Aircraft Co.
3855 N. Lakewood Boulevard
Long Beach, CA 90808
213/593-5511

Northrop Corp.
Corporate Headquarters
1840 Century Park East
Los Angeles, CA 90067
213/553-6262

Rockwell International Corp.
Corporate Offices
2230 E. Imperial Highway
El Segundo, CA 90245
213/647-5000

Teledyne Inc.
1901 Avenue of the Stars
Los Angeles, CA 90067
213/277-3311

TRW Inc.
Defense Systems Group
One Space Park Drive
Redondo Beach, CA 90278
213/536-2000

Wyle Laboratories
128 Maryland Street
El Segundo, CA 90245
213/322-1763

PROFESSIONAL ORGANIZATIONS

Aerospace Education Foundation
1501 Lee Highway
Arlington, VA 22209
703/247-5839

Aerospace Industries Association
of America
1250 I Street, NW
Washington, DC 20005
202/371-8400

American Institute of Aeronautics
and Astronautics
370 L'Enfant Promenade, SW
Washington, DC 20024
202/646-7400

International Association of
Machinists & Aerospace Workers
214 S. Loma Drive
Los Angeles, CA 90026
213/483-6630

Women in Aerospace
6212-B Old Keene Mill Court
Springfield, VA 22152
703/866-0200

PROFESSIONAL PUBLICATIONS

Aerospace America (Washington, DC)
Aerospace and Defense International Product News (New York, NY)
Aviation Week & Space Technology (New York, NY)
Defense & Foreign Affairs (Alexandria, VA)
Defense Daily (Potomac, MD)
Defense News (Springfield, VA)

DIRECTORIES

The Aerospace Careers Handbook (Career Press, Hawthorne, NJ)
Aviation Week & Space Technology, Buyers Guide Issue (McGraw-Hill Publishing, New York, NY)
Defense Aerospace Information Sources Directory (Phillips Publishing, Potomac, MD)
Major Defense Systems Producers—USA (Noyes Data Corp., Park Ridge, NJ)

CHAPTER 20

Engineering

*Flexibility can pay off in
lucrative field, experts say.*

Most budding engineers have it made. Finding a secure, high-paying position isn't hard. Recent studies indicate a nationwide shortage of engineers due to declining interest levels and an aging workforce.

In the booming and highly diversified Southern California economy, opportunities for engineers abound in almost every industrial field—from the aerospace and automotive industries to telecommunications, industrial parts making, and petroleum refining. "Any manufacturing company needs this expertise now," said Northrop spokesman James Hart. Indeed, roughly half of all engineers work in manufacturing fields.

Regionally, the overall number of engineers is expected to grow substantially in the next few years. In Los Angeles and Orange counties, the Employment Development Department (EDD) projects 22.8 percent job growth between 1987 and 1992, during which time the number of engineers is expected to swell from 113,910 to 139,830. Within the engineering disciplines (the EDD identifies 14), the largest categories include aeronautical and astronautical engineers, electrical and electronic engineers, civil engineers, and mechanical engineers.

Because so many major aerospace companies are concentrated in Los Angeles County—seven of the largest space, aircraft, and defense firms in the nation are headquartered here—the local engineering community tends to be dominated by this industry. However, engineers are employed by a diverse range of employers in the public and private sectors and the specific type of work they perform varies greatly.

An aerospace engineer, for instance, might work on the navigational system of a new fighter plane or on the design of a space shuttle component. The electronics engineer, meanwhile, may try to develop a faster, smaller computer or better stereo receiver. Petroleum engineers spend their time attempting to find more efficient methods of extracting and refining oil. Civil engineers may work on the design of buildings or public infrastructure systems, such as sewers and freeways.

Median salaries for entry-level engineers with a bachelor's degree and less than a year's experience exceeded $30,000 in 1988, according to the American Association of Engineering Societies. The average salaries for mid-level engineers ranged from $37,000 to $44,000. But high-level engineering managers can command much more money.

Being consistently promoted and gaining entrance into the upper echelons of the corporate hierarchy isn't automatic, however. As companies adopt increasingly sophisticated design, manufacturing, and production technologies to improve quality and competitiveness while reducing costs, many engineers who have worked in a specific area for several years are now finding themselves overspecialized and unpromotable.

"You're seeing people whose expertise is so narrowly defined that it can be detrimental in the long run to their career," said Spike Booth, executive director of Russell Reynolds Associates, an executive search firm in downtown Los Angeles. "It's important to have your love and specialization, but you've got to remain flexible."

According to a recent special report in *Aviation Week & Space Technology* magazine, entry-level engineers who are trained to solve specific problems in college often ignore the "systems thinking" approach that looks at how an apparently isolated problem fits into the larger engineering picture. When this tunnel-vision mentality is combined with a lack of knowledge about the manufacturing side of engineering, opportunity for advancement becomes limited.

"What happens is you get a guy who's 50 years old who has been in a very narrow niche for his entire career being pushed from behind by a 37-year-old whiz kid who's diversified," Booth said. "Sometimes the old guy just gets canned."

To avoid being pigeonholed in certain types of jobs and stuck on a salary plateau, industry experts say, working engineers must be active in their quest for knowledge, taking the time to regularly read professional publications to stay abreast of new developments in their area of specialization and related fields as well. To further strengthen their position, engineers should take advantage of continuing education and in-house training programs whenever possible, Booth said.

Los Angeles–area schools noted for their engineering departments include Cal Tech, USC, UCLA, and Cal State Long Beach. But in today's high-tech climate, where design engineering teams work closely with manufacturing engineers and production departments, cross-knowledge of these divisions, as well as an advanced degree in your particular area of interest, is increasingly vital.

Engineers who want to get ahead also have to be vocal at times.

"You have to take it upon yourself to stay current and make your interests known," said Alan Nakamura, an electrical engineer in the Hughes Corporate Rotation Program. "You have to read the literature and talk to management. It's easy to be labeled a programmer or something and then get cast in that mold. If you have a broad background, it helps because a lot of fields these days are merging. Engineers in design and manufacturing have to know a little about the other guy's field."

In essence, engineers apply scientific principles and theories to practical technical problems to find suitable solutions. Frequently, their work provides the link between a scientific discovery and its application to real life. In addition to designing and developing a product or system, engineers may also work on its testing, production, operation, and maintenance. According to working engineers, hands-on experience is becoming more and more important.

"Engineers experienced in manufacturing can visualize problems much quicker than those who don't have experience in manufacturing and only know how to design," said Jeff Mirich, manager of computer-aided design and manufacturing (CAD/CAM) at Northrop's B-2 (Stealth bomber) Division in Pico Rivera. "It's this interdisciplinary approach that makes them so valuable to the company."

From looking over countless executive résumés, Booth of Russell Reynolds Associates has come up with a composite of a successful engineer. He described an engineer with three years' experience and a master's degree who goes on to be a manager of a specific component on a project. From there, this hypothetical engineer might become an assistant program manager.

With another five or six years of experience, plus an MBA degree and a grounding in accounting and finance, Booth's archetypal engineer is now qualified for the position of project director or vice president of business development. "The guy's now 40-ish and probably earning $100,000 to $125,000 a year, plus bonuses," Booth said. "On the other end of the spectrum, you get a lot of engineers who like sitting at a bench and just creating."

Moving up the corporate hierarchy and salary scale generally requires a combination of ambition, advanced education (frequently a master's degree), and effective communication skills—something many engineers lack, Booth added. Even so, it is not always necessary to be a "Great Communicator."

"The outgoing personality, long-term drive, and commitment to personal success are important," Booth said. "But I know a lot of executives who are not the most conversant, most personable type of guys. Yet they're still successful. People in engineering tend to be a little more precise, a little more focused. They're scientists by training. That can work to their benefit."

Recognizing the need for versatile engineers who know how to manage, leading universities like USC have developed graduate-level "bridge" programs designed to make engineers more well-rounded. USC's yearlong Engineering Management Program, a joint effort between the School of Engineering and the Graduate School of Business Administration, allows engineering graduates with some experience to enhance their technical skills while learning about team approaches to problem solving and how to coordinate efforts between different departments.

Graduates of the program are qualified to work not only as project managers but also as inter-project liaisons between different departments, said Robert Karasek, associate professor of industrial and systems engineering and director of the Engineering Management Program at USC.

Key up-and-coming areas for people contemplating engineering careers are CAD/CAM systems (computer-aided design and computer-aided manufacturing processes) and computer-aided graphics, which are slowly replacing conventional drafting skills, Northrop's Mirich said. Computer technology now plays an prominent role in both aerospace and architectural engineering, which utilize three-dimensional computer databases to produce lifelike graphics.

Engineering Growth Trends in Los Angeles and Orange Counties

Types of Engineers	Number Employed		Percent Change
	1987	1992	
Aeronautical & astronautical engineers	16,310	19,710	20.8%
Agricultural engineers	100	120	20.0%
Chemical engineers	2,130	2,600	22.1%
Civil engineers	9,930	11,430	15.1%
Electrical & electronics engineers	45,680	57,860	26.7%
Industrial engineers	9,040	10,620	17.5%
Marine engineers	250	300	20.0%
Mechanical engineers	13,210	16,170	22.4%
Metallurgists & metal engineers	690	850	23.2%
Mining engineers	120	160	33.3%
Nuclear engineers	380	470	23.7%
Petroleum engineers	650	760	16.9%
Safety engineers	1,170	1,400	19.7%
Other engineers	14,250	17,380	22.0%
Total engineers	113,910	139,830	22.8%

SOURCE: Employment Development Department.

KEY EMPLOYERS OF ENGINEERS

Engineering Firms

Boyle Engineering Corp.
1501 Quail Street
Newport Beach, CA 92660
714/476-3400

CDI Corp./West
15760 Ventura Boulevard
Suite 1110
Encino, CA 91436
818/981-1811

Leo A. Daly
3333 Wilshire Boulevard
Suite 200
Los Angeles, CA 90010
213/388-1361

Engineering Science Inc.
75 N. Fair Oaks Avenue
Pasadena, CA 91103
818/440-6000

Engineering Service Corp.
6017 Bristol Parkway
Culver City, CA 90230
213/417-7999

Jacobs Engineering Group
251 S. Lake Avenue
Suite 204
Pasadena, CA 91101
818/449-2171

LPL Technical Service
6151 W. Century Boulevard
Suite 1200
Los Angeles, CA 90045
213/645-7820

Albert C. Martin and Associates
811 W. Seventh Street
Los Angeles, CA 90017
213/683-1900

James M. Montgomery Engineers Inc.
250 N. Madison Avenue
Pasadena, CA 91109
818/796-9141

SCS Engineers
3711 Long Beach Boulevard
9th Floor
Long Beach, CA 90807
213/426-9544

Sikand Engineering Associates
19230 Burbank Boulevard
Van Nuys, CA 91411
818/787-8550

Also see Chapter 24 for a list of aerospace firms.

Oil Companies

Atlantic Richfield Co. (ARCO)
515 S. Flower Street
Los Angeles, CA 90071
213/486-3511

Chevron USA Inc.
302 E. El Segundo Boulevard
El Segundo, CA 90245
213/615-5000

Exxon Chemical Co. USA
5199 E. Pacific Coast Highway
Long Beach, CA 90804
213/597-8491

Occidental Petroleum Corp.
10889 Wilshire Boulevard
Los Angeles, CA 90024
213/208-8800

Shell Oil Co.
511 N. Brookhurst Street
Anaheim, CA 92801
213/591-8513

Unocal (76) Corp.
1201 W. Fifth Street
Los Angeles, CA 90017
213/977-7600

Public Sector

City of Los Angeles Public Works Department
Engineering Bureau
200 N. Spring Street
Los Angeles, CA 90012
213/485-5821

County of Los Angeles Public Works Department
Personnel Division
900 S. Freemont Avenue
Alhambra, CA 91803
818/458-3609

United States Army Corps of Engineers
Los Angeles District Office
300 N. Los Angeles Street
Los Angeles, CA 90012
213/894-5340

PROFESSIONAL ORGANIZATIONS

American Institute of Plant Engineers
3975 Erie Avenue
Cincinnati, OH 45208
513/561-6000

American Society of Civil Engineers
2550 Beverly Boulevard
Los Angeles, CA 90057
213/386-6291

American Society of Mechanical Engineers
626 N. Garfield Avenue
Alhambra, CA 91801
213/283-1986

California Society of Professional Engineers
1005 12th Street
Sacramento, CA 95814
916/442-1041

National Association of Architectural Engineers
Post Office Box 395
Lawrence, KS 66044
913/864-3434

National Society of Professional Engineers
1420 King Street
Alexandria, VA 22314
703/684-2800

Society of Women Engineers
9832 Flower Street
Bellflower, CA 90706
213/867-6500

PROFESSIONAL PUBLICATIONS

Aerospace Engineering (Warrendale, PA)
California Engineer (Berkeley, CA)
Civil Engineering (New York, NY)
Computer-Aided Engineering (Cleveland, OH)
Electronic Engineering Times (Manhasset, NY)
The Engineer of California (Alhambra, CA)
Engineering Journal (Chicago, IL)
ENR: Engineering News Record (New York, NY)
Manufacturing Engineering (Dearborn, MI)
Mechanical Engineering (New York, NY)
The Professional Engineer (Raleigh, NC)
USC Engineer (Los Angeles, CA)
U.S. Woman Engineer (New York, NY)

DIRECTORIES

Employment Guide for Engineers and Scientists (Institute of Electrical and Electronic Engineers, New York, NY)

ENR—Directory of Top 500 Design Firms (McGraw-Hill, New York, NY)

Membership Directory (Society for Computer-Aided Engineering, Rockford, IL)

Official Register (American Society of Civil Engineers, New York, NY)

Who's Who in Engineering (American Association of Engineering Societies, New York, NY)

CHAPTER 21

The Computer Field

A job in the computer industry is a logical career choice: sales, programming, and consulting opportunities are growing.

The greater Los Angeles area may not be as entrenched in the production of microchips as the Silicon Valley, but when it comes to the sales, use, and application of computers, the Southland job market is wide open. From account executive positions at computer retail stores to systems engineering, programming, and analyst jobs at computer consulting and high-technology firms, the demand for the computer-literate professional is proliferating at about the same rate as new programs.

"The opportunities are excellent, especially within our company," said Anthony Barthel, marketing manager for the Personal Computer Centre in Lawndale, a leading Southern California computer dealer. "The field is getting tougher, but it's growing if you know what you're doing. We have some very good jobs available."

The number of people employed in the computer field jumped significantly in the last decade and continues to climb steadily. In Los Angeles County, 86,760 people were employed in computer programming, repair, operations, software development, and research in 1987, according to the state Employment Development Department. By 1992, the number of computer-related jobs is expected to grow 29 percent, to an estimated 111,830. In Los Angeles and Orange counties, an estimated 140,260 people will be employed in computer-related careers by 1992.

Statewide, an additional 151,050 people are projected to enter the computer field between 1985 and 1995, increasing the size of the workforce a whopping 63.5 percent. The number of computer jobs in California, 237,780 in 1985, should grow to 388,830 by 1995, EDD statistics show.

"The computer industry in general is experiencing considerable growth, so companies like ours are looking for all kinds of people who are trained in the fields of computer science, engineering, mathematics, and business," said Scott Sharp, vice president of human resources for the Computer Sciences Corp.

The Computer Sciences Corp., a professional computer services company with private sector and government contracts, has some 600 employees in Los Angeles County and 20,000 workers nationwide. But most computer firms are a lot smaller. Of the 802 computer programming and software businesses in L.A. County in 1987, 62 percent had one to four employees, said Jack Kyser, chief economist for the Los Angeles Area Chamber of Commerce.

Companies that manufacture and sell computer systems and then provide support services generally employ four groups of workers: development, sales, support, and repair. Within these departments are the main occupations of systems analyst, programmer, engineer, account executive, and service technician.

Systems analysts and applications programmers, who start in the mid-$30,000 range, are trained to recommend and design programs. Systems analysts work in a variety of high-tech fields ranging from telecommunications to scientific research. These specialists analyze a given problem or task to be performed, devise a new system that will solve it, and then translate the requirements of the system into the capabilities of a computer.

Applications programmers, who usually work from descriptions prepared by systems analysts, write specific programs by breaking each step into a series of coded instructions using one of the languages specifically designed for the computer. After checking to see that the program will work as intended and correcting any errors ("debugging" the system), the applications programmer prepares an instruction sheet for the computer operator, who then runs the program.

Systems programmers work in the specific context of the computer itself, designing and maintaining the inner workings and utilities that control the operation of the machine, such as DOS or UNIX, two popular operating systems. Their goal is to optimize the capabilities of their particular brand of machine. They lay the foundation on which applications programmers then create programs. Lead systems and applications programmers, who can become project managers, make upward of $40,000 and beyond.

"For someone who is looking to become a programmer, you would start out with some basic courses in data processing, then learn some specific computer languages. You would then go on to get your computer science degree at college and get the specific languages down," said Phyllis Boyajian, head of AT&T's technical support group in Los Angeles.

Systems engineers work in both retail and corporate settings. At the retail level, they serve as resident experts and answer whatever support or technical questions customers may have. They provide advice on which products would best serve the needs of the customer and, depending on the company, may also train customers on the use of the computer system after the sale.

Systems engineers, who can make from $40,000 to $70,000 a year, are normally required to have a degree in electrical engineering or computer science, especially for large companies like Hewlett Packard. In addition to cutting-edge technical knowledge, would-be systems engineers need strong people skills.

Account executives in the sales division work either at the retail or commercial level. At the retail or store level, account executives aren't required to have a college degree. But some background in computers and previous sales experience in home electronics or big-ticket items like photocopy machines are desired, Barthel said.

Retail salespeople need good communication or people skills combined with some technical expertise. "We don't want someone who's completely incompetent, but at the same time, we're not looking for a 'techie.' We try to reach a happy medium," Barthel said. "You don't have to be an expert. We have experts in-house. Our job is to sell."

In the rapidly changing computer world, where new systems are continuously introduced and upgraded, rendering old ones obsolete in only a few years, it's important to be adaptable and receptive to ever-changing technology and terminology. In the 1980s, personal computing took several turns. For instance, basic XT technology introduced in 1981 was enhanced by the widespread introduction of hard disk drives, but was soon replaced by the more advanced AT, or 286, system. In turn, the short-lived 286 model quickly gave way to 386 and 486 series computers.

Innovators are now trying to design neural networks and analog microprocessors based on biological models, and computer manufacturers are following IBM's lead into Dynamic Random Access Memory (DRAM) chips and Reduced Instruction Set Computer (RISC) technology, which is faster than current systems and capable of running multiple programs at the same time. DOS, the heretofore standard disk operating system, is capable of running just one program at a time.

If anything, careers in the computer field require the ability to learn quickly and stay open to new ideas. "There are so many companies competing to come up with the latest and the greatest that machines sold five years ago are obsolete," said Tom Gebhart of HW Computers in Northridge. Gebhart said HW Computers stocks 20 to 25 types of computers and over 1,000 peripheral (printers, modems, etc.) product lines.

The most lucrative sales arena in the computer field isn't in the store, though, it's selling to commercial clients. Retail salespeople typically start at around $1,500 a month. However, if you're employed in commercial or outside sales, you can make up to six figures working solely on commission. "We have one person who made $150,000 in commissions-only last year," Gebhart said.

Selling directly for a computer manufacturer can require both education and experience. The ideal candidate for a commercial sales position at Hewlett Packard, for example, has a degree in computer science or electrical engineering, previous sales experience, *and* an MBA degree.

"We look for people with some experience in those markets that we sell into," said Sharon Shaw, Hewlett Packard's regional sales staff manager. "This helps them to understand our customers' needs. They can make recommendations more knowledgeably. We also look for people who are experienced in computer sales, or at least in large-ticket, capital-equipment items."

The widespread acceptance of computers into the workplace and home has created a new breed of sophisticated buyers who are more discriminating than ever before. Consequently, computers sales positions demand a certain level of professionalism. "This has to be what you want to be doing," Barthel said. "It's no longer just come in and sell computers for six months. You have to be good at it. You have to know your stuff."

Service technicians work in the repair departments of computer manufacturers and large retail stores. A four-year degree in electrical engineering is usually required to become a service tech, although most repairs at the retail level aren't all that complicated. Warranty work on IBM, Apple, and Hewlett Packard computers, for instance, usually entails parts swapping rather than repairing systems, Barthel said. Previous repair experience in electronics is desirable, he added.

One of the prime evolving technologies in the computer industry, and one of the biggest areas of job growth besides support services, is networking, said George Bekey, chairman of USC's Computer Science Department.

Networks link computers together so information can be shared simultaneously by large groups of people in different departments or different companies. Using a network, scientists, engineers, and programmers are able to solve problems collectively rather than individually, greatly enhancing their speed and effectiveness, Bekey said. "Today, the design of an airplane may involve 1,000 design engineers working around the country."

Within networking, an aspect of increasing concern is computer security—controlling the levels of access that computer users have to information. Most protocols, or security codes, are designed by computer theorists who have graduate degrees in computer science, Bekey said.

"Network computing is the future," agreed AT&T's Boyajian. "That's one of the areas we are working very strongly in." Boyajian said she looks for applicants who are "multi-tasking" in their abilities—people who understand the fundamental concepts of computing and can apply them to specific situations.

"You have to have a technical mind but a marketing personality so you can talk to customers and work with them, so you can tell what a customer is really trying to say if he isn't expressing it," Boyajian said. "I look for the person who takes ownership of a problem and searches for the answers. It is a very unique individual who is successful in that situation."

In some professions, the higher you advance, the less opportunity there is. But in the computer field there is a dire need for senior-level project or systems managers to run company data centers and corporate management information strategies (MIS) departments, said Sharp of the Computer Sciences Corp. MIS directors at large companies are paid from $61,000 to $81,000 a year, according to a recent study by Robert Half

What Those Abundant Computer Jobs Pay

Position	Salary
Manager/supervisor, systems analysis & programming	$57,000
Lead programmer/analyst, project manager	$47,800
Senior programmer/analyst	$39,500
Programmer/analyst	$33,100
Manager/supervisor, applications programming	$56,400
Lead applications programmer	$47,500
Senior applications programmer	$37,700
Applications programmer	$30,600
Manager/supervisor, systems analysis	$52,100
Lead systems analyst	$44,300
Systems analyst	$36,000

SOURCE: 1988 *Data Processing Salaries Report*, Administrative Management Society, Trevose, PA.

International, a financial, accounting, and data processing search firm.

A major employer of computer programmers and systems engineers not to be forgotten is the aerospace industry, which is becoming increasingly computer-oriented. Engineers, for example, frequently design computer hardware and software packages. "Generally, you think of an aerospace company not being a software firm," said John Wilhite, manager of corporate college relations for Hughes International. "That's an incorrect observation. More and more software packages are being developed in conjunction with specific projects that we're working on."

KEY EMPLOYERS IN THE COMPUTER FIELD

Selected Manufacturers

Apple Computer Corp.
100 Corporate Pointe
Culver City, CA 90230
213/645-3011

Compaq Computer Corp.
535 Anton Boulevard
Costa Mesa, CA 92626
714/546-2044

Epson America
2780 W. Lomita Boulevard
Torrance, CA 90505
213/539-9140

Hewlett Packard Co.
5651 W. Manchester Avenue
Los Angeles, CA 90045
213/337-8000

IBM Corp.
Central Employment Office
355 S. Grand Avenue
Los Angeles, CA 90012
213/621-6700

NEC Information Systems Inc.
150 N. Santa Anita Avenue
Arcadia, CA 91006
818/447-8947

Packard Bell
9425 Canoga Avenue
Chatsworth, CA 91311
818/773-4400

Wang Laboratories Inc.
6701 Center Drive West
Los Angeles, CA 90045
213/337-6200

Zenith Data Systems
11925 E. Pike Street
Santa Fe Springs, CA 90670
213/695-0721

Selected Retailers

First Computer
1740 Westwood Boulevard
Los Angeles, CA 90024
213/470-2501

L.A. Computer Center
17013 Hawthorne Boulevard
Lawndale, CA 90260
213/542-3501

MicroAge Computer Stores
8501 Wilshire Boulevard
Beverly Hills, CA 90211
213/652-7770

Personal Computer Centre
16811 Hawthorne Boulevard
Lawndale, CA 90260
213/516-6969

Sun Computers Inc.
1000 E. Dominguez Street
Carson, CA 90746
213/538-8338

PROFESSIONAL ORGANIZATIONS

**ADAPSO: The Computer Software
and Services Industry Association**
1300 N. 17th Street
Suite 300
Arlington, VA 22209
703/522-5055

**Association of Computer
Professionals**
230 Park Avenue
Suite 460
New York, NY 10169
212/599-3019

**Association of Computer
Programmers and Analysts**
15269 Mimosa Trail
Dumfries, VA 22026
703/690-3843

**Association for Computing
Machinery**
Los Angeles Chapter
Post Office Box 90698
Los Angeles, CA 90009
213/480-3311

**Professional Software
Programmers Association**
1405 Civic Center Drive
Santa Clara, CA 95050
408/985-2181

**Semiconductor Industry
Association**
4320 Stevens Creek Boulevard
San Jose, CA 95129
408/246-1181

PROFESSIONAL PUBLICATIONS

BYTE (Peterborough, NH)
California Computer News (Sacramento, CA)
Macworld (San Francisco, CA)
MicroTimes (Oakland, CA)
PC/Computing (Cambridge, MA)
PC Magazine (New York, NY)
PC World (San Francisco, CA)
Personal Computing (Hasbrouck Heights, NJ)
UNIX Review (San Francisco, CA)
Your Computing Career (Park Ridge, IL)

DIRECTORIES

Directory of Computer Software and Services Companies (ADAPSO, Arlington, VA)

Directory of Systems Houses, Value Added Resellers and Computer Original Equipment Manufacturers (McGraw-Hill, Dallas, TX)

ICP Software Directory (International Computer Programs, Indianapolis, IN)

Yearbook/Directory (Semiconductor Industry Association, San Jose, CA)

CHAPTER 22

Data
Processing

Keyboard skills and computer knowledge
can keep your career options open.

If any skill can keep your career options open, it's data processing. Data and word processors are needed in almost every department of every modernized company, no matter the size—from multinational banks and giant defense contractors to small retail stores and home-based marketing businesses.

"Every office that's automated has data entry needs, even if it's just inputting a mailing list," said Ellen Finver, office manager for United Personnel Services in Los Angeles.

As more and more offices become automated and store their information by computer instead of filing cabinets, the need for data processors will continue to grow. Being automated essentially means utilizing a computer, typically a micro, or personal, computer (PC), to store and retrieve information that otherwise would be kept manually.

"Word processing, database, spreadsheet functions—any type of skill on a computer is in short supply right now," said Theresa Jordan, regional office automation manager for Kelly Temporary Services. "What we're finding is that in any office situation, wherever there *was* a typewriter, there are now PCs. Even in the reception area, a lot of functions like phone messages are now automated."

The state Employment Development Department forecasts that the number of data entry operators, word processors, computer operators, and peripheral equipment (printers, fax machines, etc.)

operators in Los Angeles and Orange counties will grow from 42,320 in 1987 to an estimated 46,160 in 1992. Growth in the data processing and computer services field was far more dramatic in the early 1980s, which witnessed the widespread introduction of the personal computer into the workplace.

Gauging the precise number of people employed in data processing is difficult. The above job categories, for instance, leave out the multitude of data and word processors working in clerical capacities or through temporary employment services. Kelly Temporary Services, which has 16 branch offices in Southern California, employs a pool of temporary data processing workers numbering in the thousands, Jordan said.

A low unemployment rate in the Southern California area combined with a limited pool of experienced computer-literate workers have made data processing jobs relatively easy to find, she added. In the field of data entry, the two main positions with the most opportunities are word processor and data entry operator.

Word processing is the most sophisticated form of data processing and has the highest demand for workers, according to Finver. Most employers require word processors to type 55 to 60 words per minute (wpm). Word processors must know the proper form of a business letter and multipage reports and have good grammatical skills, for in addition to inputting information into a computer, they often edit and proofread text once it is stored.

Technical composition is a more specialized form of word processing. Composers create business forms, such as purchase orders, ledgers, and checks, by translating the size and dimensions of a desired form into computer language and inputting that information into the system much like a programmer would execute a series of commands to create a program. Composers need a certain amount of editing skills to guard against grammatical mistakes and help ensure the proper phrasing of passages of text.

Word processors can make anywhere from $8 to $15 an hour—or slightly more—depending on their speed, efficiency, and familiarity with different software packages. Their place of employment can also make a difference, Jordan said. The word processing departments of large law firms, which employ teams of up to 30 or 40 legal word processors, tend to pay the most.

Knowing how to use more advanced word processing and desktop publishing functions involving document merges, layout and font (typeface) changes and how to format multipage documents is a definite advantage and adds to one's earning potential. "The pay varies drastically depending on their skills and whether they know multiple software packages," Jordan said.

The most common word processing programs for IBM and IBM-compatible computers, which still dominate the business world, include WordPerfect, Display Write, and Microsoft Word, according to Finver and Jordan. Other word processing programs worth knowing include WordStar and MultiMate, Jordan said. The most common word processing program for Macintosh computers and Mac-compatibles is the Mac version of Microsoft Word.

Data entry operators primarily input information, such as figures from a report or addresses for a mailing list, word for word into a computer system using a keyboard and a electronic display screen. "Production (high-volume) data entry people are very good at inputting exactly what they see," Finver said. "There's no creativity necessarily involved." However, Jordan added: "It's no longer mindless work. You have to be more well-rounded than that."

Data entry operators must be able to type accurately, though not as fast as word processors since they usually input bits and pieces of information rather than large blocks of text. Because data entry operators are routinely asked to update company spreadsheets, they should be familiar with Lotus 1-2-3, the most common spreadsheet program for IBM compatible PCs. For Macintosh computers, the most common spreadsheet program is Excel.

Data entry operators start at around $6 an hour and can make up to $10 hourly, Jordan said.

In addition to the above programs, word processors and data entry operators stand to benefit by knowing some database and data management functions. The most common data management program currently in use is dBase III, said Earl Perry, assistant dean of electronics and computer science at Los Angeles Trade-Technical College.

In data processing, the more computer literate you are, the more marketable you become. Knowing one word-processing program makes cross-training for others relatively easy, while familiarity with numerous software packages as well as knowing how to operate both IBM- *and* Macintosh-type computers will maximize your job opportunities.

At the professional or supervisory level, data processing jobs increase in pay, ranging from the low- to high-$30,000 range, according to a nationwide survey by the Administrative Management Society in Trevose, Pennsylvania. The survey found that data processing managers earn $40,000 and up.

Data processing training is available on the job, at temporary employment services, through community colleges, and at private vocational schools.

Computer companies such as IBM, which employs some 4,000 workers in Southern California, provide advanced job training in addition to formal education courses. A four-year degree is not necessary to work at IBM, but applicants for data processing positions should know how to use a keyboard, type at least 45 wpm, and have a technical orientation, said Gloria Mallet, manager of IBM's Central Employment Office in Los Angeles.

"We look for good keyboard skills and an applicant who is articulate, personable, and flexible in dealing with people and situations," Mallet said. "They should have an aptitude for math, computer science, or the physical sciences or a combination of those skills. Training at a data entry or computer operations school is adequate, as virtually every position at IBM benefits from on-the-job training and continuing education courses."

Temporary employment services, including both Kelly and United, train their workers (who are hired out on a temporary basis to other companies) on a wide range of data processing programs in exchange for agreeing to work a certain number of hours at the home office.

"We have training and testing on 23 different software packages. We can take top-notch secretaries who know phones and how to take shorthand and dictation and all those skills that take years to develop and train them on word processing," said Jordan of Kelly Temporary Services.

Outside of free on-the-job training, perhaps the most affordable way to learn data processing skills is through one of the Southland's numerous community colleges, which charge only $5 per unit, and not more than $50 a semester. L.A. Trade-Tech's Electronics and Computer Science Department offers a word processing option as part of its office administration major.

Private schools that specialize in computer repair and word processing, such as the American Technical Institute (ATI) in Van Nuys, tend to offer more intensive instruction in a single subject area. ATI offers a six-month certificate program in word processing that prepares students for the job market.

The main drawback to private schools is their cost—some certificate programs run upward of $5,000 or more. While many technical schools, ATI included, are well respected and deliver what they promise, it never hurts to check around before you spend your money. (For more information on vocational schools, see the article at the end of Section 13.)

The Bottom Line for Data Processing

Position	Salary
Manager/supervisor, computer operations	$41,900
Lead computer operator	$26,500
Senior computer operator	$24,100
Computer operator	$20,200
Data entry supervisor	$31,100
Lead data entry operator	$21,500
Senior data entry operator	$19,100
Data entry operator	$17,100

SOURCE: *1988 Data Processing Salaries Report*, Administrative Management Society, Trevose, PA.

KEY EMPLOYERS OF DATA PROCESSORS

Accu-Data Systems
3500 Wilshire Boulevard
Los Angeles, CA 90010
213/386-2143

Ade/Data Processing
5741 Rostrata Avenue
Buena Park, CA 90621
714/739-1265

Alpha Beta Data Service
1501 Wilshire Boulevard
Los Angeles, CA 90017
213/413-3282

American International Data
3121 W. Temple Street
Los Angeles, CA 90026
213/487-5095

Applied Data Services Inc.
1550 Flower Street
Glendale, CA 91201
213/245-0183

California Data Services
2409 N. Sepulveda Boulevard
Manhattan Beach, CA 90266
213/546-2484

Century Data Systems
1270 N. Kraemer Boulevard
Anaheim, CA 92806
714/632-7500

CompuServe Information Services
1000 Corporate Pointe
Culver City, CA 90230
213/216-5867

**Control Data Business Management
   Services**
18831 Von Karman Avenue
Irvine, CA 92715
714/851-5620

Dataccount Corp.
19320 Van Ness Avenue
Torrance, CA 90501
213/775-3645

Data Products Corp.
6200 Canoga Avenue
Woodland Hills, CA 91365
818/887-8000

EDP Services Co. Inc.
2930 W. Imperial Highway
Inglewood, CA 90303
213/757-4101

Express Data Services
1151 Magnolia Avenue
Anaheim, CA 92801
714/229-9311

GTE Data Services
4750 Lincoln Boulevard
Marina del Rey, CA 90291
213/821-0511

National Data Services
21835 Nordhoff Street
Chatsworth, CA 91311
818/882-7360

Pacific Keypunch Service
15515 San Fernando Mission
   Boulevard
Suite 2
Mission Hills, CA 91345
213/698-0211

Pyramid Information Services
10801 National Boulevard
Los Angeles, CA 90064
213/475-4611

United States District Court
Data Processing Section
312 N. Spring Street
Los Angeles, CA 90012
213/894-7163

Unisys
10920 Wilshire Boulevard
Los Angeles, CA 90024
213/208-1511

Also see Chapter 14 for a listing of major law firms
in the Los Angeles area.

PROFESSIONAL ORGANIZATIONS

**Association of Data Center Owners
   & Managers**
Post Office Box 7623
Van Nuys, CA 91049
213/988-5670

**Association of Data Processing
   Service Organizations**
c/o ADAPSO: The Computer Software and Services Industry
   Association
1300 N. 17th Street
Suite 300
Arlington, VA 22209
703/522-5055

**Data Processing Management
   Association**
362 Arguello Boulevard
San Francisco, CA 94118
415/387-1550

Society of Certified Data Processors
2200 E. Devon Avenue
Suite 268
Des Plaines, IL 60018
312/299-4270

PROFESSIONAL PUBLICATIONS

Data Communications (New York, NY)
Datamation (Newton, MA)
Data Processing Digest (Los Angeles, CA)

DIRECTORIES

Data Communications Buyers Guide (McGraw-Hill, New York, NY)
Data Entry Services Directory (Morgan-Rand Publications, Philadelphia, PA)
Datamation—Top 100 U.S. Companies Issue (Cahners Publishing Co., Des
   Plaines, IL)
Data Processing Services Directory (American Business Directories, Omaha,
   NE)

The Office of the Future

People are still needed to run the high-tech machinery.

Twenty-five years ago, it was widely assumed that time-saving technologies would all but eliminate the need for general clerical workers in the office of the future. The new technology has eliminated a lot of the drudge work, but not the people who keep a company running. In the decade ahead, the demand for office workers as well as support personnel will remain strong, according to industry experts.

"We receive job orders on a daily basis," said Robert Henry, chairman of the Business and Office Administration Department at Los Angeles Trade-Technical College. "We have open positions in all of these areas continuously. These areas are definitely on the increase." Industries with large numbers of general office job opportunities include banking, insurance, and accounting.

The availability of these positions is likely to expand with the continuing shift from a manufacturing to a service-oriented economy, said Jack Kyser, chief economist for the Los Angeles Area Chamber of Commerce. "There has been incredible growth in the service sector, especially in business services."

Within business services, the biggest growth areas include communications, computer support, data processing, and personnel supply, Kyser said. These fields grew by about 25 percent in the last decade, ranking general office occupations among the largest areas of job growth in Los Angeles County.

The L.A. area's more than 80,000 service firms (retail, finance, consulting, etc.) will employ an estimated 2.26 million professional and clerical workers in 1992, compared to 1.96 million in 1987, according to Employment Development Department statistics. In Orange County, the overall number of service workers is expected to increase from 565,225 in 1987 to an estimated 660,300 in 1992, for a 16.8 percent rate of growth, state projections show.

While the introduction of personal computers, interactive computer networks, modems, facsimile machines, and electronic mail hasn't made the people who operate these machines obsolete, the new technology has created a need for workers at both the professional and technical levels who are more skilled and technically oriented than ever before.

"New technology won't eliminate [office workers], but it will change the content of what they do," said Lynne Markus, an assistant professor at UCLA's Graduate School of Management. "We see secretaries doing a lot less typing, but they have more of a role in managing documents. They're putting drafts of reports together. They're information managers, really."

Perhaps more than anything, computers have enabled workers to gain more control over their work, according to Robert Kling, professor of information and computer science at the University of California, Irvine. "They've gotten rid of tasks, but they haven't gotten rid of work," said Kling, who has studied the effects of computers in the workplace.

Tora Bikson, senior behavioral scientist for the Rand Corp. in Santa Monica, agrees with Markus that new technologies have changed skill levels required of general office workers. Bikson recently worked on a study for the U.S. Office of Technology Assessment (OTA) to determine the effects new technologies have on workers.

The roles of general office workers are changing and expanding, Bikson learned. "We found a number of employees whose title was secretary but whose duties were that of systems operator or computer systems maintenance worker. If employees are being taken advantage of, it's because they're doing more and not getting paid a high enough salary for their extra duties, and they're not getting new job titles to add to their prestige."

The OTA study examined whether technology decreased skill levels by only requiring monitoring and maintenance—drone work, essentially—rather than interactive use, thereby limiting the need for workers. It concluded that just the opposite was occurring: increased use of technology required a higher level of competence from employees and had no apparent effect on the number of jobs, Bikson said.

"We've seen a lot of job evolution, but we haven't necessarily seen a net decrease in the number of white collar workers. When a clerk leaves a firm, the employee might be replaced with a higher-skilled worker and the former job eliminated," Bikson said.

"Data processing used to be the exception, not the rule. Now it's the rule," said Julie Bradley of the Administrative Management Society in Trevose, Pennsylvania. "When you come into a company, you have to know how to use a computer. What maybe 10 years ago was done by a computer programmer is now being done by a word processor."

Older workers who still consider computers to be the exclusive domain of programmers and scientists are particularly at risk in this new age of almost mandatory computer literacy, which seems to favor those who are adaptable and bring to the workplace a willingness to learn high-tech skills.

"A lot of people in their mid- to late 50s are afraid to use personal computers," Kyser said. "There's still a lot of people who love to shuffle paper and type and pore over memos. But almost anyone who wants to get ahead as a secretary, moving up to administrative assistant and into management, is going to have to be computer literate."

An estimated 25 percent of the nation's 5 million white collar work groups, consisting of clerical and professional employees, are now computerized, said Kling of UC Irvine. (The nation's current labor force of over 122 million includes more than 70 million office workers total.) In response to this growing need for computer knowledge in the workplace, schools are now integrating word processing and computer operating classes into their curricula.

"People who don't get the education are going to find jobs harder and harder to find," said Scott Sharp, vice president of human resources for the Computer Sciences Corp. in El Segundo. "We are becoming a high-tech society."

For the entry-level general office worker just beginning a career, continued development of "user-friendly" computer technology should make it easier to become computer literate. But the increasing sophistication of new programs will require an even higher level of skill from senior employees who, in addition to their broader management-related duties, must understand and keep pace with new technological developments, Kling said.

The need for computer literacy has long been recognized by many temporary employment services. Manpower Temporary Services, for example, has an office automation training program that makes prospective employees without computer training instantly more marketable by giving them basic instruction in word processing, electronic mail, and computer file management procedures.

"The age of the high-power administrative assistant/secretary is here," said Al Durant, branch manager for Manpower in Century City. "Employers expect employees to walk in with all these different skills because that is what the market is asking for. You have to be able to receive mail without ever opening a letter."

Indeed, with each new technological development, the office moves closer and closer toward a paperless state, futurists contend. There are glimpses of this already, with computer message centers, integrated databases, voice mail, and electronic paychecks, which increase efficiency while saving time and money. "The idea of the paperless office—that's now," Durant said.

"The future is now," emphasized Sharp of the Computer Sciences Corp.

As a minimum, job seekers looking for general office work should be able to type 45 to 50 words per minute, possess some computer skills, and have at least a high school education, although a diploma doesn't carry very far at most large companies, Henry said. Applicants with a bachelor's degree or even a two-year A.A. degree from a community college have a considerable edge over those who haven't attended college, he added.

Especially important for people just entering the job market is the ability to express their ideas clearly and communicate effectively. "At some point, a career person needs to be proficient at representing the company in an oral and written capacity," Henry said. "Being able to punch a keyboard is not enough."

RECOMMENDED READING

Drucker, Peter F. *The Changing World of the Executive.* New York: Times Books, 1982.

Drucker, Peter F. *The Frontiers of Management.* New York: Harper & Row, 1986.

Drucker, Peter F. *The New Realities: In Government & Politics, in Economics & Society, in Business, Technology & World View.* New York: Harper & Row, 1989.

Naisbitt, John, and Aburdene, Patricia. *Re-inventing the Corporation: Transforming Your Job and Your Company for the New Information Society.* New York: Warner, 1985.

Naisbitt, John, and Aburdene, Patricia. *Megatrends 2000: Ten New Directions for the 1990s.* New York: William Morrow, 1990.

SECTION
7

Careers in
Management
and Office
Administration

CHAPTER 23

Civil Service: City and County Jobs

Government jobs aren't just for politicians: Civil Service workers are paid well, advance quickly.

Public service can often result in personal gain. Careers in local government pay better than the name implies. And the jobs are by no means dead-end. What's more, because city and county governments are among the largest employers in Southern California, there are always hundreds, if not thousands, of jobs available for qualified applicants.

The County of Los Angeles—the Southland's single largest provider of jobs—employs around 77,000 workers who are part of a government staff larger than that of 42 states. (Orange County, by contrast, employs about 14,000 people.) Within L.A.'s county government are divisions ranging from administration to public works to social and health services, according to Effeta Williams, chief of the county's personnel contract services division, which provides testing and other human resources services for client cities.

The City of Los Angeles, with a slightly smaller bureaucracy than the county, employs about 54,000 people, but has an equally bewildering array of job categories—1,200 in all—including everything from professional jobs that require specialized training and education to trade and technical jobs that don't require any previous experience.

In Los Angeles and Orange counties, there are 111 incorporated cities, each employing its own staff of municipal workers. Including the two county administrations, there were 185,900 people working in city and county government in 1987. That number is expected to increase to 189,425 by 1992, according to Employment Development Department projections.

"If you enjoy a challenge, the opportunities are there," said Williams of the county. "There is a lot of flexibility as far as being able to transfer from one occupation to another if you have the minimum educational requirement. I think county government is exciting and these are exciting times."

Unlike private industry, which may hire an outsider for a top-ranking position, most jobs with the city and county are protected under the civil service system that limits promotions to current employees through a competitive examination process and ensures job security through seniority.

At the county, promotions upward depend on what division you're in. In a small division that has a dedicated staff, opportunities to advance may be rare. In some cases, it may behoove county employees on their way up to make a lateral move to another department that has more room for climbers.

As an example, Williams said that she started out as a social worker in the county's Department of Public Social Services, but couldn't see herself working there her entire career. So she transferred to a job in human resources and was quickly promoted. The chance for both vertical and horizontal movement is "one of the things that make the county a good employer," she said.

While L.A. County continually has job openings due to attrition, promotions, and transfers, few new jobs have been created recently. Times are tight due to repeated budgetary shortfalls over the last several years. As a consequence, the county does a lot of selective recruiting rather than mass broadcasting of hard-to-fill positions, Williams said.

Even with budgetary constraints, roughly 15,000 people are hired or move into new positions each year because of attrition, transfers, and promotions, Williams added. The county has a relatively high annual job turnover rate of around 20 percent. The city's, by contrast, is about 12 percent, said James Nishimuro, assistant chief of the city's recruitment division.

Visiting the L.A. County personnel office in the Hall of Administration in downtown Los Angeles confirms the availability of scores of jobs in a variety of departments at a range of different skill and salary levels.

Among the openings a spot check revealed were: a Spanish-speaking community worker for $1,447 to $1,802 a month; a Los Angeles Municipal Court secretary for $1,749 to $2,180 a month; and an electronics communications technician for $3,399 a month. Moreover, city and county employees who are bilingual in their jobs are often paid extra.

What does the county look for in an applicant?

Besides versatility, "someone who is enthusiastic, who has integrity, who is industrious, and who is an idealist. We think those attributes still have value," Williams said. "Anyone who works for a governmental agency also has to be service-oriented. We're a service organization."

The county personnel office has a listing of current job opportunities and detailed information sheets about specific positions that are open. Most jobs require an aptitude and skills examination. Once hired, county employees are placed on probation for six months, after which time they are eligible for promotion.

"The jobs change every day," said Ameila Guerrero, a clerk at the personnel office. "If you call one day and can't find anything you're interested in, you should come down the next day because there might be five new openings."

The county also has a 24-hour recorded message of job opportunities. The number is (213) 974-2711. In addition to current openings with the county, the personnel office has a notebook stuffed full of job listings at various government agencies throughout Southern California.

A brief look at this resource uncovers hundreds more jobs, including such positions as journeyman plumber with the City of Compton for $2,778 to $3,240 a month, workers' compensation and safety officer with the South Coast Air Quality Management District for $3,255 to $4,033 a month, and affirmative action specialist/personnel analyst for the City of Glendale for $2,959 to $3,663 a month.

Most, if not all, government agencies now emphasize their equal opportunity, affirmative action hiring policies and in many instances actively recruit minority applicants. The City of Los Angeles, for example, has a separate affirmative action unit.

Many jobs at the City of Los Angeles that don't require any special training or experience pay as well as some jobs that do. For instance, the positions of police service representative, electrical craft helper, and meter reader, which fall into this category, all start at over $1,900 a month, according to the city's Personnel Department. Police service reps, the highest paid of these four occupations, start at $2,175 a month.

As with the county, one of the best—and easiest—entry points for people who are contemplating a career of public service with the city is that of clerk typist, which pays $1,510 a month to start, said Himiko Nishiyama, a recruitment officer with the city.

"We constantly have a need for clerk typists. And you can go anywhere you want with it, too," Nishiyama said. "A person who starts out as a clerk typist without a high school diploma, but who accumulates experience on the job, has as much opportunity (to advance) as a person with a master's degree."

Having a master's degree is by no means a hindrance. It enables an applicant to enter at a higher level and earn a higher salary. The city allows master's degree holders to waive the written test during the application process and proceed straight to the interview, after which time they are automatically placed on a waiting list.

Applicants with a bachelor's degree, who typically enter at the management assistant level, are required to take the written test. A management assistant job with the city pays anywhere from $24,000 to $30,000 a year. But the competition can be keen. The city administered some 62,000 tests in 1988, eventually hiring about 6,500 full-time employees, said Bill Eagleson, senior personnel analyst for the city.

To enable employees without college degrees to compete with degree-holding candidates, the city offers what are known as "bridge classes" to teach them management skills.

But in order to advance, an employee had better score high on the promotions test. For the coveted positions, there are always equally ambitious co-workers one must compete against. "It's how well you do on the exam that dictates when you'll hear from us," said Nishimuro of the city's recruitment division.

In addition to standard public service–type jobs, the city offers some nontraditional positions as well. For instance, the Department of Water and Power (DWP) needs aqueduct and reservoir keepers to measure the amount of snowfall in the mountains. The Harbor Department regularly hires deckhands and boat operators. The Parks and Recreation Department needs tree surgeons. And the Department of Airports needs security officers. "A lot of people don't realize how spread out we are," said Nishimuro.

Job opportunities with the City of Los Angeles can be explored by visiting the personnel office in Room 100 of City Hall South at 111 E. First Street downtown. The city also has a 24-hour job information number: (213) 485-2441.

Working Your Way up the Ladder: A Career Path with the City
Here is a possible career path in the personnel department of
the City of Los Angeles both for an applicant without a
college education and one with a four-year degree*

Position	Salary	Years on the Job Needed to be Promoted (Minimums)
Without a college degree:		
Clerk typist	$18,120–$22,512	1
Senior clerk typist	$21,060–$29,496	2–3
Management aide	$23,856–$29,660	1–5
Principal clerk	$25,308–$31,440	1
With a college degree or equivalent experience:		
Management assistant	$23,856–$29,660	1
Personnel analyst I	$28,501–$35,412	1
Personnel analyst II	$33,554–$41,697	1
Senior personnel analyst I	$39,755–$49,381	1
Senior personnel analyst II	$49,214–$61,136	1
Chief personnel analyst	$59,153–$73,497	Indefinite

* An equal, if not greater, number of clerical and management
opportunities are available at the County of Los Angeles.

SOURCE: City of Los Angeles Personnel Department.

KEY EMPLOYERS OF CIVIL SERVICE WORKERS

City of Anaheim
200 S. Anaheim Boulevard
Anaheim, CA 92805
714/999-5100

City of Beverly Hills
9298 W. Third Street
Beverly Hills, CA 90210
213/550-4856

City of Burbank
275 E. Olive Avenue
Burbank, CA 91502
818/953-9721

Culver City
9770 Culver Boulevard
Culver City, CA 90232
213/202-5750

City of Glendale
613 E. Broadway
Glendale, CA 91206
818/956-2110

City of Huntington Beach
Civic Center
2000 Main Street
Huntington Beach, CA 92648
714/536-5226

City of Inglewood
One Manchester Boulevard
Inglewood, CA 90301
213/412-5460

City of Lancaster
44933 N. Fern Avenue
Lancaster, CA 93534
805/945-7811

City of Long Beach
333 W. Ocean Boulevard
Long Beach, CA 90802
213/590-6812

City of Los Angeles
111 E. First Street
Los Angeles, CA 90012
213/485-3920
Job Hotline: 213/485-2441

City of Monterey Park
320 W. Newmark Avenue
Monterey Park, CA 91754
818/307-1255

City of Orange
300 E. Chapman Avenue
Orange, CA 92666
714/532-0341

City of Palmdale
708 E. Palmdale Boulevard
Palmdale, CA 93550
805/273-3162

City of Santa Ana
20 Civic Center Plaza
Santa Ana, CA 92701
714/647-5200

City of Santa Monica
1685 Main Street
Santa Monica, CA 90401
213/458-8246
Job Hotline: 213/458-8697

City of Torrance
3231 Torrance Boulevard
Torrance, CA 90503
213/618-2960

County of Los Angeles
Hall of Administration
Room 493
500 W. Temple Street
Los Angeles, CA 90012
213/974-1311
Job Hotline: 213/974-2711

PROFESSIONAL ORGANIZATIONS

**American Federation of State,
County and Municipal
Employees**
1625 L Street, NW
Washington, DC 20036
202/429-1144

**International City Management
Association**
1120 G Street, NW
Suite 300
Washington, DC 20005
202/626-4600

Los Angeles County Employees Association
950 W. Washington Boulevard
Los Angeles, CA 90015
213/589-7300

Southern California Association of Governments
600 S. Commonwealth Avenue
Los Angeles, CA 90005
213/385-1000

National League of Cities
1301 Pennsylvania Avenue, NW
Washington, DC 20004
202/626-3000

PROFESSIONAL PUBLICATIONS

American Review of Public Administration (Kansas City, MO)
Public Administration Review (Washington, DC)
Public Administration Times (Washington, DC)
Public Budgeting and Finance (New Brunswick, NJ)
The Public Employee (Washington, DC)
Public Management (Washington, DC)
Public Personnel Management (Alexandria, VA)

DIRECTORIES

Braddock's Federal-State-Local Government Directory (Braddock Communications, Washington, DC)
Compleat Guide to Finding Jobs in Government (Planning/Communications, River Forest, IL)
Complete Guide to Public Employment (Impact Publications, Manassas, VA)
Moody's Municipal and Government Manual (Moody's Investors Service, New York, NY)

CHAPTER 24

Social Service Careers

Gain meaningful payoffs in social services by helping those in need.

Some of the most rewarding job opportunities can be found in areas that pay the least. Just ask one of the nearly 105,000 people who work for social service and nonprofit organizations in Los Angeles and Orange counties. "If anything can get you into heaven, this can," said Creola Howard, personnel director and 23-year employee of United Cerebral Palsy/Spastic Children's Foundation.

The opportunities range from volunteer work to part-time jobs to full-time career positions at charities, relief organizations, and public social service agencies. Working in the nonprofit world of social services requires a big heart, sympathy for the abused or downtrodden, professional training where appropriate, and the desire to make the world a better place to live. Perhaps the essence of social service is doing unto others as you would have them do unto you.

"I haven't gone home early one day this week," said Barbara Wilks, acting director of the Los Angeles chapter of the American Red Cross, which stays busy by helping coordinate the local relief and rescue efforts for calamities around the world. "When you're working these extreme hours, you may be worn out and tired and stressed, but what balances it out is that you're helping people who lost everything."

Many former private industry types who have decided to switch gears welcome the respite that social services offer from the dog-eat-dog world of corporate competition. They say their new jobs allow them to focus on bettering, rather than getting a competitive edge on, their fellow man.

"There's a lot of satisfaction in actually doing something for somebody," said Dick DeMattos, a former advertising copywriter who now serves as director of media relations for the Salvation Army in Los Angeles. "The world is so full of inequities. We're doing the best we can to help improve it."

But even the nonprofit sector can become competitive, especially in the area of fundraising. There are about 3,000 nonprofit and charitable organizations in Los Angeles and Orange counties that must compete for the same limited pool of donor funds. The biggest percentage of donations comes from individuals, not corporations, according to Jack Kyser, chief economist for the Los Angeles Area Chamber of Commerce.

"Nonprofits are really hurting," Kyser said. "In the past, they were able to tap a lot of volunteers. But with the emergence of the two-earner household, those types of volunteers have disappeared. Nonprofits are really facing a lot of challenges, especially in the health services area. There's all kinds of social programs cropping up for child care, AIDS, and the homeless at a time of declining volunteerism. There's just limited resources."

While low fundraising levels may spell lean times ahead for charities, the increased financial pressures nonprofit social service organizations are facing suggest a demand for competent managers who know how to raise funds and carefully manage programs. The need for effective managers of nonprofit organizations is recognized by a growing number of university business schools. The MBA program at the University of Southern California, for instance, offers a nonprofit emphasis.

That fundraising has become an integral part of operating a social service organization is indicated by the expanding membership of the National Society of Fundraising Executives, which has grown from a few hundred members during the late 1970s to over 10,000 members today, said Joe Bryant, director of development for the Braille Institute in Los Angeles. At the YMCA, adult volunteers now split their time between fundraising activities and leading boys' groups, said John Medler, senior vice president of the YMCA of Metropolitan Los Angeles.

As with other fields, opportunities in social services vary with each organization. In general, however, there is an ample supply of paid positions in the areas of nursing and health care. United Cerebral Palsy, for example, which has 17 facilities throughout Los Angeles County, continually needs physical and occupational therapists, social workers, counselors and nurses.

One of the, if not *the,* largest employers of social workers in Southern California is the County of Los Angeles, which provides financial aid and services to those in need of public assistance. Some 8,000 people, including close to 1,000 social workers, work for the county's Department of Public Social Services (DPSS) and Department of Children's Services.

Social workers investigate, evaluate, and attempt to rectify reported cases of abuse, neglect, endangerment, illness, or domestic disputes. They intervene when necessary and provide counseling and referral services to individuals and families. In extreme instances, they may arrange for conservatorships.

As part of their job, social workers sometimes act as career counselors and financial advisers, assisting clients with solving their housing, health care, employment, or money management problems. Social workers at DPSS work independently, referring only their most complex, sensitive, or controversial cases to their social services supervisor, said David Miyashita, a DPSS administrative services manager.

Social work is a professional career and, at the county, requires a minimum of a four-year degree plus a year's experience at a recognized social service agency. Social workers with a master's degree in social work, family or psychological counseling, psychology, or gerontology earn a starting salary of $2,115 to $2,630 a month.

Within DPSS, an even larger occupational field is eligibility work. The county's 3,400 eligibility workers and 550 supervisors are responsible for evaluating whether individuals or families qualify for public assistance and for authorizing the amount of financial aid.

Eligibility worker applicants are hireable with either a two-year associate in arts degree from an accredited community college (at least nine units must be in social sciences) or three years of specialized job experience. Entry-level eligibility workers make between $1,532 and $1,710 a month.

Working for a charitable organization like United Cerebral Palsy, which provides support services for the developmentally disabled, is similar to working for a hospital or any other health care organization: it requires some professional training and a compassionate personality. The bulk of United Cerebral Palsy's direct care staff are nurse assistants, said Howard.

"Normally, we look for people who want to help other human beings. You try to make their lives as comfortable and normal from their standpoint as you can. I see that happen on most occasions," she said.

To help them become more understanding care providers, the staff of United Cerebral Palsy are required to undergo sensitivity training, which includes spending time in a wheelchair to see the world from the patient's point of view, Howard said. Some people, while giving in nature, just aren't cut out to work with the severely disabled, she added. "It has to be something you can cope with. If you get to the crying stage, the feeling-sorry-for-you stage, we can't use you here."

The biggest reward from the job, Howard said, is the personal satisfaction derived from helping others, knowing "that you brought just a little more joy to someone who didn't have a choice in life."

. . . .

From Harvard Law School to the Salvation Army: How One Man Found a Higher Calling by Helping Others

He graduated from Harvard Law School and came to Los Angeles to pursue a career in corporate real estate law. Now he doesn't even have a guaranteed salary. But Lt. Kenneth Hodder of the Salvation Army is doing exactly what he wants to do.

With superlative credentials, Hodder was almost certainly destined for a partnership in the downtown law firm of Brobeck, Phleger & Harrison. But the self-effacing ex-attorney said his career switch to the Salvation Army wasn't unusual or unprecedented. He's a sixth-generation "Salvationist," with ancestors who were among the first followers of Salvation Army founder William Booth in the 1860s.

Hodder, 32, who heads the Salvation Army's modest

Glendale post, said he decided to abandon his career in corporate law in favor of a lifetime commitment to the corps mainly on spiritual grounds. A look at the future changed his course.

"I can distinctly recall the day when I looked around my office and tried to imagine where I would be in about 35 to 40 years," Hodder said. "After some thinking, I was able to figure out: it would probably be down the hall in a somewhat larger office with a pile of paper representing the sum total of my professional life. I didn't think that was enough. I really felt that God had something else in mind for me."

Hodder entered the Salvation Army's School for Officers Training in the fall of 1986 and, with his wife, Jolene—a former department manager for the Broadway—studied to become an Army officer. (Married couples must serve together.) They were both commissioned as lieutenants in June 1988, but not before Hodder was elected president of his class and given the school's highest honor, the Commissioner's Award.

"It was truly life-changing," he said.

Some who know Hodder, like Dick DeMattos, director of media relations for the Salvation Army in Los Angeles, say he is destined to become the legal secretary, if not commanding general, of the Salvation Army. His undergraduate thesis on the organizational development of the Salvation Army may be published as a history book. But Hodder is modest about his future.

"It's important for a Salvation Army officer to abandon all sense of ambition when you become an officer," Hodder said. "The officers are going to be sent when and where needed. The Army's success as a social organization and as a church has been its ability to respond quickly. It's a commitment to 24-hour service. It's a commitment to people."

Although Hodder has turned his back on the profit-driven corporate world, he still has some of the trappings of his former career, including an executive suite complete with his own secretary. His office, furnished with bookshelves containing volumes on history and religion, still seems somewhat lawyerly.

But whether behind his desk or in front of a group of bell ringers about to be sent out on a Yuletide mission, the youthful-looking lieutenant with eyes full of optimism projects a sense of heartfelt enthusiasm about his multifaceted job, which he says is a calling.

"A Salvation Army officer is a lot of things," Hodder said. "First and foremost, he is a pastor. In addition, an officer is a business manager, public relations person, and social services worker. In large part, that's where the excitement of being an officer lies—in the different hats you get to wear."

From coordinating volunteer efforts to organizing a Christmas party for the homeless, Hodder's commitment to helping people serves as his guiding light. One of his main frustrations, he said, is not being able to do enough.

"There's always one more person out there who needs help, always one more need to be met. That's the frustrating thing. You work and work and work and the need gets even greater," Hodder said.

SELECTED SOCIAL SERVICE ORGANIZATIONS

American Cancer Society
601 S. Ardmore Street
Los Angeles, CA 90005
213/386-6102

American Heart Association
2405 W. Eighth Street
Los Angeles, CA 90057
213/385-4231

American Red Cross
Los Angeles Chapter Headquarters
2700 Wilshire Boulevard
Los Angeles, CA 90057
213/739-5200

Braille Institute
741 N. Vermont Avenue
Los Angeles, CA 90029
213/663-1111

California State Department of Social Services
Personnel Board
107 S. Broadway
Los Angeles, CA 90012
213/620-4192

City of Los Angeles
Social Services Department
200 N. Spring Street
Los Angeles, CA 90012
213/485-5003

County of Los Angeles
Public Social Services Department
3000 W. Sixth Street
Los Angeles, CA 90020
213/738-3517

Easter Seal Society
209 E. Alameda Street
Suite 102
Burbank, CA 91502
818/848-5999

**Goodwill Industries of Southern
California**
342 San Fernando Road
Los Angeles, CA 90031
213/223-1211

March of Dimes
Los Angeles Chapter
1111 S. Central Avenue
Glendale, CA 91204
818/956-8565

NAACP Watts Branch
8823 S. Central Avenue
Los Angeles, CA 90002
213/587-2114

Oriental Service Center
213 S. Hobart Boulevard
Los Angeles, CA 90004
213/386-3605

Para Los Ninos
845 E. Sixth Street
Los Angeles, CA 90021
213/623-8446

Salvation Army
Divisional Headquarters
900 W. Ninth Street
Los Angeles, CA 90015
213/627-5571

**United Cerebral Palsy/Spastic
Children's Foundation**
2628 Brighton Avenue
Los Angeles, CA 90018
213/737-0303

United Way Inc.
Corporate Office
621 S. Virgil Avenue
Los Angeles, CA 90005
213/736-1300

Volunteer Center of Los Angeles
621 S. Virgil Avenue
Los Angeles, CA 90005
213/385-4244

Volunteers of America
3600 Wilshire Boulevard
Los Angeles, CA 90010
213/389-1500

**YMCA of Metropolitan Los
Angeles**
625 S. New Hampshire Avenue
Los Angeles, CA 90005
213/380-6448

PROFESSIONAL ORGANIZATIONS

Center for Human Services
7200 Wisconsin Avenue
Bethesda, MD 20814
301/654-2550

**National Association of Social
Workers**
7981 Eastern Avenue
Silver Spring, MD 20910
301/565-0333

**National Organization for Human
Service Education**
2840 Sheridan Road
Evanston, IL 60201
312/256-5150

**United States Conference of City
Human Services Officials**
1620 I Street, NW
Washington, DC 20006
202/293-7330

PROFESSIONAL PUBLICATIONS

Charities USA (Washington, DC)
Health and Social Work (Silver Spring, MD)
The Journal of Contemporary Human Services (Milwaukee, WI)
Social Service Review (Chicago, IL)
Social Work (Silver Spring, MD)

DIRECTORIES

Directory of the Health and Human Care Agencies in Los Angeles County
(Los Angeles County Department of Health Services, Los Angeles, CA)
Human Services Organizations (American Business Information, Omaha,
NE)
National Directory of Children's and Youth Services (Marion Peterson,
Longmont, CO)
National Directory of Private Social Agencies (Croner Publications, Queens
Village, NY)

CHAPTER 25

Customer Service

If you're good with people, try the customer service field.

From coast to coast, the bottom line for forward-looking companies in the service industry is pleasing customers. At businesses as diverse as financial institutions, parcel delivery services, department stores, and restaurant chains, keeping customers happy has become job No. 1, whether that means having an unconditional return policy, footing the delivery bill, or installing a 24-hour customer service line.

"It used to be a rarity [for a customer] to be treated with anything but total disregard and utter disdain," said Jon Hughes, president of Local-Carr Business Machines in New York. "But now we're finding that in order to maintain any kind of competitive edge, a business has to go beyond that."

The growth of service-related jobs in the local and state economy combined with increased competition in the service industries and a growing similarity of products have given customer service a prominent new role, one that some experts say should permeate an organization.

"In the past, so many businesses perceived customer satisfaction as the role of either management or sales," Hughes said. "But customer satisfaction is everybody's business. It's an attitude that applies even to something as simple and basic as answering the telephone."

The service industries, including everything from business and financial services to architecture and retailing, are made up of some 80,000 firms in the Southern California area, which employ about 25 percent of the entire greater Los Angeles workforce (including Orange County) of more than 5.5 million. They are among the fastest-growing major occupational groups in the Southland, according to Employment Development Department statistics.

Hughes, who conducts seminars on customer satisfaction for the National Office Machine Dealers' Association, said attentively responding to customer needs is one way for a company to improve its competitive posture. Weak customer service policies and philosophies can cost a company business.

"Products are becoming less different from one another, so often the only thing that really differentiates one company from another is the level of service they provide," affirmed Sue Joseph, vice president of customer service for L.A. Cellular in Los Angeles. "The customer service representative is the primary contact for any company."

This contact had better be good—indeed, better than the competition—if a company wants to increase its clientele and continue to please loyal customers. In the competitive global marketplace of the 1990s, companies that fail to deliver customer satisfaction may find themselves dead in the water.

Pushed by rising expectations of time-constricted customers and challenged by the successful example of such service-intensive retailers as Nordstrom department stores, many businesses are adopting aggressive customer service policies to increase their appeal. "It's the level of service that gets you new customers or loses old customers," said Janice Wainright, manager of First Interstate Bank's downtown Los Angeles branch.

These measures haven't been taken just to be nice. According to a widely heeded study of customer service and complaint handling conducted by the Technical Assistance Research Programs Institute, a Washington-based consulting group, some 95 percent of customers who were disgruntled with the service they received took their business elsewhere, never bothering to lodge complaints. The study also found that it costs companies five times more to bring in new customers than to keep old ones. Some cost estimates run even higher.

"Customers today are more sophisticated than ever before. They realize they deserve good service. They're expecting a lot more and demanding a lot more from a company—not just a quality product, but somebody and something to stand behind that product to make sure they get it on time and that it's serviced properly and with a smile," said Madalyn Duerr, director of the International Customer Service Association in Chicago.

Customer service is no longer an entry-level job in a company's operations department, used as a springboard to other departments. Many companies are establishing career tracks in service positions, affording ample supervisory and management opportunities. "Customer service manager is probably the second [highest] position at most of our branches," Wainright said.

What's more, customer service experience in one field frequently translates into potential job opportunities in another. "Every industry now has customer service occupations, so if a service representative trains for one industry, he or she could easily move into another," said Regina Mahmoodi, administrator for the Travel & Trade Career Institute in Long Beach, which offers a customer service program. "We've had graduates who have gone to work for various companies as customer service reps and now they're managing a department. It's a good way to get into sales, too."

The changing perception and new respectability of customer service have created new hurdles for job seekers at larger companies. Namely, big firms are increasingly requiring previous on-the-job experience. "A lot of times customer service *is* the promotion," Joseph said. "It isn't always the best first job" for entry-level employees.

When they're ready, beginning customer service employees usually work as an account or customer service representative whose primary job is to handle inquiries by phone. At AT&T, an account representative can earn a starting salary from $300 to $425 a week and receive pay increases every 6 months, said Sandi Johnson, AT&T's employment manager. After 18 months, customer service employees at AT&T are eligible for a raise and promotion into a sales or management position.

Occasionally, AT&T's 18-month waiting period can be shortened if an employee demonstrates sales or managerial abilities. "Any time management identifies a person who has the potential to become a manager, they can put him or her in a training program," Johnson said. "If we find people who have sales skills, they may be promoted early."

Besides fielding calls from irate customers and answering questions after the initial sale, customer service reps are now being required to have sales skills and in-depth knowledge of their company's products, procedures, and policies. "The customer service person has to learn the entire company, to understand every department," said Joseph of L.A. Cellular. "In order to satisfy the customer, you need to handle the situation on the spot."

What do employers look for in a prospective customer service employee? A combination of patience, helpfulness, experience in dealing with the public, clarity of speech, the ability to type and to be a good listener, and, perhaps most important, an unflappable demeanor.

"Usually, we look for someone who has some selling skills, experience in dealing with the public, and an outwardly positive attitude," said Shirley Perkins, senior vice president of human resources for First Interstate Bank. "A financial services rep, for example, is familiar with all the products at the branch. As you are talking about your various products, it's in an organization's best interest to make them attractive for a client to buy, whether it's a compact disc player or an IRA account."

Added Wainright: "You have to have a real enthusiasm to work with others and the ability to not get rattled. You can't please everybody all the time. You do have customers who get upset, but you can't take that personally. It requires a lot of professionalism. Mostly, it's the love of working with people."

A college degree generally is not essential to work in the customer service field, but management positions are usually filled by college graduates. Some larger companies, such as AT&T, offer tuition aid programs for promising employees who want to further their education.

"We don't rule anyone out (for a job)," said Johnson of AT&T. "They would not even need a high school diploma. As long as they're over the age of 18, they can get a job here. We're not requiring them to come in with loads and loads of skills and experience. But we are looking for individuals who are bright and articulate."

KEY EMPLOYERS OF CUSTOMER SERVICE REPRESENTATIVES

For a list of customer service employers, see Chapter 1 on the banking industry, Chapter 5 on the retail industry, Chapter 37 on the airline industry, or any other service-oriented field.

PROFESSIONAL ORGANIZATIONS

*International Customer Service
  Association (ICSA)
401 N. Michigan Avenue
Chicago, IL 60611
312/321-6800

National Association of Service
  Managers
650 W. Algonquin Road
Second Floor
Des Plaines, IL 60016
312/640-8133

* For a list of local ICSA chapters, call ICSA headquarters.

PROFESSIONAL PUBLICATIONS

ICSA News (Chicago, IL)

RECOMMENDED READING

Davidow, William H., and Uttal, Bro. *Total Customer Service—The Ultimate Weapon: A Six-Point Plan For Giving Your Company the Competitive Edge in the 1990s.* New York: Harper & Row, 1989.

CHAPTER 26

Personnel Management

*Placement supervisors needed
for a growing workforce.*

Helping others find employment can be a career in itself. Given a scarcity of talent and an abundance of jobs in the opportunity-laden Southland, the job placement field has blossomed from a smattering of loosely organized companies into a highly structured industry employing more than 75,000 people.

The employment business has three basic types of specialists: service or evaluation supervisors, executive recruiters, and outplacement consultants.

Evaluation supervisors at employment agencies screen and select applicants for temporary and permanent work assignments, sometimes arranging for job training, and supply workers to client companies. They also solicit new business by pitching large companies targeted as potential clients.

Recruiters at executive search firms conduct managerial and executive-level searches at a broad range of companies, making dozens of phone calls, conducting numerous interviews, and frequently traveling, in an effort to find the best-qualified candidates for senior positions at client companies.

Consultants at outplacement firms counsel laid-off employees who are out of work due to cutbacks and plant closings. They administer interest and aptitude tests, sometimes offering individual counseling, and set up job search programs to help displaced members of the workforce find new employment.

Despite their differences, most jobs in personnel services

involve interviewing and screening people who are in the market for new employment. Because of the regular one-on-one contact personnel specialists have with potential job candidates and clients, good communications and people skills are a must.

So is the ability to analyze data and prepare reports, make sales presentations, design specialized job-search programs tailored for individual employees, and provide constructive advice to laid-off workers. According to industry experts, a degree in business administration or one of the social sciences, such as psychology or sociology, is a good foundation for employment in the field.

Temporary Services

The rapidly growing temporary employment services industry is highly competitive. As employers with heavy workloads begin to rely more on temps (who are cheaper to hire than permanent employees in the long run, primarily because they aren't entitled to health insurance, retirement, and other benefits), the demand for temporary personnel specialists and managers will go up.

The number of people employed in personnel supply services in the Los Angeles area—about two-thirds of whom are in the temporary help category—grew an amazing 73.2 percent in the last decade, from 44,856 people in 1980 to an estimated 77,696 in 1990, according to the state Employment Development Department.

Getting your foot in the door of a temporary services company may mean starting as a receptionist for $7 to $8 an hour. Within a year, this starting position can lead to an interviewing or coordinating position, called service or evaluation supervisor.

Evaluation supervisors interview applicants and match people they've interviewed with the job orders they've received. They also help solicit new business by calling on potential client companies.

"We're looking for people who are dependable and very aggressive," said Katherine Arbolida, office manager for Apple One's temporary division for the Los Angeles International Airport and South Bay area. "You have to be good on the phone and self-disciplined. You need drive. It's extremely fast-paced."

Supervisors, who receive a base salary plus commission, make in the low- to mid-$20,000 range depending on their territory. In the Los Angeles area, companies located downtown, along the Wilshire corridor, and in Westwood/West L.A. pay the best rates.

There is a lot of movement in temporary services—upward, lateral, and out the door. About 40 percent of those who try working in temporary services don't make it past their three-month probationary period, Arbolida said. The competitive market demands hard work and dedication. Apple One's offices are open from 7:30 a.m. to 5:30 p.m. But supervisors frequently work longer. "You don't take a lunch if you're busy, and you sometimes take work home," she said.

Promotions occur every few years for top performers, and within 5 years it's possible to move from supervisor to office manager, making around $30,000 a year. In another 7 to 10 years, the manager of a top-performing office may be promoted to a regional managing position.

Top-producing supervisors may also become sales reps, who spend most of their time in the field making sales calls and pitching their employment service to potential client companies. Most reps at Apple One are hired with past sales experience, frequently from other employment services, Arbolida said. They can make from $35,000 to $65,000 a year, depending on their sales and territory.

Large employment services have several divisions, including temporary and permanent job placement, clerical support, executive recruiting, banking and finance, and affirmative action. Although the industry is large, individual offices are small, which can limit job movement. There usually is little movement between different divisions as well, Arbolida said.

Executive Search

Like temporary employment services, the executive search field has grown by leaps and bounds in recent years. "There's a growing acceptance and necessity of using executive recruiters," said Lee Van Leeuwen, managing partner of Korn/Ferry International in Los Angeles. "It's an excellent field, particularly in Southern California. The demand for recruiting is probably higher here than for any place else in the nation."

Executive recruiters, or headhunters, as they are more crassly known, find and place senior managers, from vice presidents to chief executive officers, on a retainer basis. The job requires a certain amount of intuition and the ability to visualize how skills from one industry can apply to another. A marketing executive from a soft drink company, for example, may be just the person to fill an opening at a financial institution because both positions involve product marketing.

"A good recruiter is able to assess that fit. If you become overly analytical, you'll miss the person who has the right chemistry for the target company," Van Leeuwen said. Recruiters also should have a high energy level, enjoy extensive contact with people, and be an excellent judge of character, he added.

Entry-level recruiting associates typically have a college degree plus around five years' business experience. Salaries start at $30,000 and can eventually reach six figures. "Entry-level recruiters do a lot of phone work, then a lot of interviewing, then take on client-contact responsibilities," Van Leeuwen said. "Then, as a partner or vice president, they have the responsibility of bringing business to the firm."

Increasingly, executive recruiters are specializing in particular industries, usually a field that they themselves have worked in. Line experience in such high-demand fields as information technology, higher education, and health care can provide recruiters with inside expertise that can translate into a competitive advantage. Although, Van Leeuwen said, "There's probably a niche for anyone who has a basic business background."

Recruiters typically work on 6 to 8 assignments, each of which takes about four months to complete. On average, they conduct 15 to 20 searches a year, Van Leeuwen said.

Another way of joining a recruiting firm is as a researcher. Researchers, who make $25,000 to $35,000 a year, assist recruiters by developing strategies for job searches, scouring files for background information about potential candidates, and performing other legwork tasks important to the search.

Outplacement Consulting

Nonexistent 25 years ago, the outplacement industry has surged in recent years, mainly due to downsizing, plant closings, mergers, acquisitions, restructuring, and other changes that result in layoffs. As the wave of mergers and acquisitions continues to roll over corporate America and as overgrown companies further downsize to increase their efficiency, more and more employees will be displaced, creating work for outplacement specialists.

"In the last five years, outplacement has grown from about

12 companies in Southern California to about 35," said Budd Carr, executive vice president and partner of the Career Transition Group in Los Angeles. "Companies are relying on it more. They feel if they treat people decently, there won't be a backlash of employees filing wrongful-termination suits."

Outplacement consultants are hired by companies to selectively counsel displaced employees at all levels, from the blue-collar to senior-management ranks. Frequently, they are on site at the time of mass terminations and plant closings to counsel designated workers, set up job-search programs, and distribute resource materials. They also conduct job seminars and small group workshops and offer individual counseling.

As part of individual counseling, outplacement specialists may administer a series of career evaulation tests and psychological inventories to assess a person's abilities, usually emphasizing positive qualities over negative ones. Essentially, consultants act as career counselors, instructing out-of-work employees how to market themselves and interview.

They are highly experienced professionals who typically have 15 to 20 years of business experience before they start working in outplacement. Many have prior personnel experience or were in training and development. Almost all have college degrees, frequently in psychology. Some outplacement firms also prefer their consultants to have experienced a job loss and undergone outplacement counseling themselves.

"It's a job for someone who is middle-aged or older, because those are the people you're dealing with in most cases," Carr said. "You want to have that rapport, respect, and confidence. The youngest person on my staff is 38 years old."

For their experience, consultants at outplacement firms are well compensated. Salaries start at around $50,000 a year plus a bonus and, depending on the company, sometimes commissions.

One of the main objectives of an outplacement consultant is to get laid-off employees thinking positively about tomorrow rather than negatively about yesterday. This aspect of the job necessitates a certain amount of preparedness and understanding on the part of the consultant. "You have to be able to respond to every possible reaction they're going to have to a job loss," Carr said, "from anger to suicide."

SELECTED EXECUTIVE SEARCH FIRMS
AND EMPLOYMENT SERVICES

Executive Search Firms

**Business and Professional
Consultants**
3255 Wilshire Boulevard
17th Floor
Los Angeles, CA 90010
213/380-8200

Robert Half of Southern California
3600 Wilshire Boulevard
Los Angeles, CA 90010
213/386-6805

Korn/Ferry International
1800 Century Park East
Suite 900
Los Angeles, CA 90067
213/879-1834

Mitchell, Larsen & Zilliacus
523 W. Sixth Street
Suite 1228
Los Angeles, CA 90014
213/489-7120

National Recruiters Corp.
22222 Sherman Way
Suite 200
Canoga Park, CA 91303
818/702-8000

Purcell Group
11845 W. Olympic Boulevard
Suite 880
Los Angeles, CA 90064
213/477-4433

Russell Reynolds Associates
333 S. Grand Avenue
Suite 4200
Los Angeles, CA 90071
213/620-1643

Sales Consultants Inc.
300 Corporate Pointe
Suite 100
Culver City, CA 90230
213/670-3040

Search West
1875 Century Park East
Los Angeles, CA 90067
213/203-9797

Spencer Stuart
400 S. Hope Street
Los Angeles, CA 90071
213/620-0814

Employment Services

Accountemps
11845 W. Olympic Boulevard
Los Angeles, CA 90064
213/312-8649

Apple One Temporary Services
725 S. Figueroa Street
Los Angeles, CA 90017
213/623-8558

Kelly Services
3600 Wilshire Boulevard
Los Angeles, CA 90010
213/381-7951

Manpower Temporary Services
2951 28th Street
Santa Monica, CA 90405
213/452-5801

Norrell Temporary Services
725 S. Figueroa Street
Los Angeles, CA 90017
213/623-5455

Thor Temporary Services
4055 Wilshire Boulevard
Suite 250
Los Angeles, CA 90010
213/487-0130

PROFESSIONAL ORGANIZATIONS

American Society for Personnel Administration (ASPA)
606 N. Washington Street
Alexandria, VA 22314
703/548-3440

Association of Professional Personnel Agencies
3255 Wilshire Boulevard
Los Angeles, CA 90010
213/387-9690

Employment Management Association
5 W. Hargett Street
Suite 1100
Raleigh, NC 27601
919/828-6614

International Association for Personnel Women (IAPW)
5820 Wilshire Boulevard
Suite 500
Los Angeles, CA 90036
213/937-9000

PROFESSIONAL PUBLICATIONS

California Management Review (Berkeley, CA)
Human Resource Executive (Fort Washington, PA)
Human Resource Management (New York, NY)
Personnel (New York, NY)
Personnel Administrator (Alexandria, VA)
Personnel Journal (Costa Mesa, CA)
Personnel Management (Washington, DC)
Recruitment Today (Costa Mesa, CA)

DIRECTORIES

Employment Marketplace Resource Directory (The Kimberly Organization, St. Louis, MO)
Membership Directory (International Personnel Management Association, Alexandria, VA)
Membership Roster (International Association for Personnel Women, Los Angeles, CA)

Trends in Middle Management

Versatility is key in a field where demand is on the decline.

In *The Great Job Shake-Out*, economic forecaster Marvin Cetron warns of a worldwide depression in the 1990s that will eclipse the Great Depression of the 1930s and cause cataclysmic upheaval in the working lives of most Americans. Middle managers, already reeling from cost-cutting measures designed to eliminate unnecessary layers of management, will be the hardest hit, Cetron asserts. Managerial opportunities in the shrinking job market will all but dry up for them.

Cetron's predictions are the extreme, but managers *have* been hard hit in recent years, according to management consultants and industry experts. "The demand for middle management has been down over the last two or three years," confirmed Bill Mangum, president of Thomas Mangum Co., a leading executive search and management consulting firm in Los Angeles. "Companies are going through very substantial tightenings of the belt."

The recent flurry of multimillion- and multibillion-dollar corporate mergers and acquisitions is expected to cause companies to streamline, if not sell off part of their operations and reduce overhead costs in order to make their huge debt payments. Reducing overhead frequently means closing satellite operations and laying off that part of the workforce considered only marginally necessary.

Moreover, increased foreign competition in such fields as automotive manufacturing and high-technology development is pushing many American companies to be more efficient. They're paring any job—and division—that might be disposable. If a division isn't vital to a company's overall mission, why keep it? Similarly, if one person can get the job done, why hire two?

"Inefficiency and complacency were fine when you didn't have international competition," said Jack Kyser, chief economist for the Los Angeles Area Chamber of Commerce. "But now you need to be competitive. Marginal performers are the first to go."

Despite this bleak jobs forecast, prominent members of the Southern California business community contend that, even with the potential chaos and bad times ahead, there will be new job opportunities for those in management with enough foresight to make themselves fire-proof.

"I don't see the future of middle management being that dim," said Bill Davidson, associate professor of management and organization at USC's School of Business Administration. "But I do see the jobs changing. Either people in those jobs will have to change, or upper management will have to change those people."

In addition to the ability to manage people effectively and control costs, one of the key qualities a middle manager must possess is versatility. Job functions are being delegated more broadly than before so that instead of performing a very small range of activities in a single department, managers must increasingly be able to handle many assignments in a variety of situations, Davidson said.

"There will always be work for people who have the flexibility to reorient themselves and work in multifunctional teams on short-term projects," Davidson said. "Middle managers have traditionally viewed themselves in very vertical terms. Now managers are thinking more horizontally. Teams are being created and disbanded on an as-needed basis."

In a traditional, eight-layer corporate hierarchy, middle management is defined as layers three, four, and five. In the future, there is likely to be less differentiation, Davidson said. "What I see taking shape is not a flattened organization, but one that looks more like a diamond. In this new setting, there won't be so much distinction between different layers of management. The issue of status kind of disappears."

Redefining the role of managers is also changing the way managers are rewarded. The age of entitlement—the period of the past four decades when middle managers received increased benefits and guaranteed annual pay increases—is coming to an end. The 1990s, said Gary Teesdale, vice president and western regional director of compensation consulting for Hay Management Consultants, will be the age of performance.

According to Mangum, middle managers can do several things to improve their net worth:

- Assess how your company fits into the overall market. Learn the broad scope of your firm's operations. Refuse to be content in a dead-end position, even if the work pace is leisurely. The more productive you are, the more valuable you are to the company—in good times or bad. "Don't sit back and assume that whatever you're doing is all you're capable of doing," Mangum said.

- Think of ways to improve your company's competitive posture, both in terms of its operational capability and market position, then pitch your ideas to your boss. Don't be afraid to make suggestions and show some initiative. Even if you are the junior member of a staff, present your ideas. They may win out.

- Try to avoid working in a department that is almost sure to be trimmed in a restructuring plan, such as corporate planning and forecasting. Managers who desire real staying power should look to more basic, indispensable business functions, such as manufacturing and operations management. The divisions that produce a company's product or service and get it out the door and delivered to customers will always be needed.

  Fields that are the least likely to be eliminated during a downsizing—indeed, those that capitalize on corporate restructuring—remain good prospects for middle managers. For instance, there is a stable demand for management jobs in the areas of accounting and finance, according to Bob Kyle, vice president of Financial Search Associates.

  "The market right now for Southern California is actually very good, particularly in the accounting area," Kyle said. "Accounting is always needed, whether a company's making a profit or not. Those figures have to be reported."

- Continually update yourself with new information about your field. Take advantage of in-house training programs and attend continuing education classes. In today's fast-forward society, there is hardly a professional job left that doesn't require at least some ongoing education. Enhance your marketability by staying on the cutting edge.

- Be quality conscious, whether you work in the manufacturing or service sector.

- Finally, don't rule out the possibility of switching to a field with better opportunity. Good long-term prospects include health care, international marketing, especially to Japanese firms, and high-tech industries, such as electronics, computer software, and biotechnology. Be persistent. There's plenty of work to be had, if you just pair your abilities with the right company.

Just as today's middle managers must be versatile in what they do, they also must be flexible in their search for employment, Kyle said, particularly when it comes to where they are willing to work. Some geographical areas simply afford more opportunities than others. Growing suburban areas, such as Orange County, the San Fernando Valley, and the South Bay area of Los Angeles, are rife with opportunities, especially at smaller, entrepreneurial-type organizations, Kyle said.

Projections by the state Employment Development Department confirm the demand for managers who are numbers-oriented. In a recent survey of the Los Angeles and Orange County labor markets, accounting and financial management were listed among the top 30 occupational fields with the largest absolute job growth. From 1987 to 1992, the total number of management and administrative positions in Los Angeles and Orange counties is expected to grow from 333,060 to 383,540, according to state projections.

While an MBA degree is virtually essential for seasoned professionals who aspire to the senior executive ranks at older-thinking, hierarchical organizations, a standard four-year college education is all the formal training required of most middle managers relatively new to the job market. "MBA programs produce very fine technicians, but they really don't teach people how to lead or manage," Kyle said.

A less rigorous academic background, often consisting of an associate in arts degree or certificate of proficiency from a technical school or community college, is expected of would-be managers in the trades, who must first become experienced journeymen or master craftsmen in their specialty area.

Even in professional fields, education by itself is not enough to land a job, let alone follow a management track. Experience, outside activities, organizational abilities, communication, and leadership skills are all looked at and factored into the hiring or promotion equation, Mangum said. As long as the economy remains healthy, the middle manager's fate will remain very much in his or her own hands.

"There's a lot of opportunities out there for talent," Mangum said. "Times have been better for middle managers, but they're still not bad."

RECOMMENDED READING

Bennis, Warren. *On Becoming a Leader.* Menlo Park, CA: Addison-Wesley, 1989.

Drucker, Peter F. *The Changing World of the Executive.* New York: Times Books, 1982.

Drucker, Peter F. *The Effective Executive.* New York: Harper & Row, 1967.

Jenks, James M. *Managers Caught in the Crunch: Turning a Job Crisis Into a Career Opportunity.* New York: Franklin Watts, 1988.

Korn, Lester. *The Success Profile.* New York: Simon & Schuster, 1989.

Lundy, Jim. *Lead, Follow or Get Out of the Way.* San Diego: Avant Books, 1986.

MacKay, Harvey B. *Swim with the Sharks Without Being Eaten Alive.* New York: William Morrow, 1988.

Neuharth, Al. *Confessions of an S.O.B.* New York: Doubleday, 1989.

Peters, Tom, and Waterman, Robert H. *In Search of Excellence.* New York: Warner Books, 1982.

Procaccini, Joseph. *Mid-Level Management: Leadership as a Performing Art.* Lanham, MD: University Press of America, 1986.

Safire, William, and Safir, Leonard. *Leadership.* New York: Simon & Schuster, 1990.

Tomasko, Robert M. *Downsizing: Reshaping the Corporation for the Future.* New York: AMACOM, 1987.

SECTION
8

Careers in Education

CHAPTER 27

Elementary and Secondary School Teaching

The field's image and pay scales are improving, and the demand is growing.

Not too long ago, teaching was one of the most undervalued professions in America. In the materialistic climate of the 1980s, it suffered considerable setbacks. But despite the perception of education as a low-paying, thankless career, teachers are starting to earn salaries more on a par with other professionals. What's more, they're in extremely high demand.

"Our graduates have had no problems getting jobs," said Lamar Mayer, associate dean of Cal State Los Angeles's School of Education. "We're having growth of the population in California, and we have an aging teaching population. For the most part, school districts are growing rapidly. And half the teachers in California will be retiring in the next few years. I think it's a good time to get into the field."

Expanding student enrollments and year-round education schedules adopted by many school districts have created an urgent demand for educators. In addition, resignations and retirements open up thousands of new jobs each year.

In Los Angeles and Orange counties, the number of elementary and secondary schoolteachers is expected to increase from 91,510 in 1987 to an estimated 100,970 by 1992, according to Employment Development Department projections.

With an average daily attendance of 627,000 students and a combined teaching and certificated staff (administrators and teaching assistants) of nearly 73,000, Los Angeles Unified is the second-largest school district in the nation, smaller only than New York. And Southland schools are growing at an astonishing rate. During the 1990s, the number of schoolchildren throughout Los Angeles County's 82 school districts, including Los Angeles Unified, will increase an estimated 22.6 percent, bringing the number of students in the state's single largest K–12 population from 1.3 million in 1988 to 1.6 million in 1998, according to the state Department of Finance.

This population explosion of school-age children—the biggest since the post–World War II baby boom—has created a shortage of schools and teachers (for more information, see the article at the end of Section 8). In the face of urgent staffing needs, many new teachers have been hired under an emergency credentialing system whereby prospective educators with college degrees in high-demand fields, such as math, science, and English, are hired first and given the opportunity to earn their preliminary teaching credentials on the job.

Emergency teaching credentials are issued on a one-year, renewable basis to qualified college graduates. To receive emergency credentials, would-be teachers must pass the state-administered California Basic Education Skills Test, or CBEST. To have their credentials renewed, teachers with emergency credentials are also required to complete nine quarter units of college study in education during their first year on the job.

Another way potential teachers can gain employment with L.A. Unified is through a two-year district internship, or alternative certification program, in which the district provides the training and education needed for the preliminary teaching credentials, said Michael Acosta, the district's head of teacher recruitment. Under this arrangement, the expenses for the additional education are picked up by the school district rather than the teacher. So far, L.A. Unified has trained over 1,000 teachers through this program, Acosta said.

To be accepted into L.A. Unified's alternative certification program, prospective elementary schoolteachers need only to have completed a general liberal arts degree. High school teacher candidates are required to have graduated with a specific college major and a minor area of study as well, Acosta said. Since teachers with emergency credentials carry the same teaching load as veteran teachers, they must be prepared to work hard.

In order to receive preliminary teaching credentials, which represents the next step toward the full credentials, teachers must accumulate at least two quarters of student teaching or regular teaching experience, Mayer said. "It used to be that a person could get a credential and it would be good for life. Now the state wants teachers to accomplish a certain amount of professional growth."

To receive full credentials, teachers must complete 45 quarter units of college coursework beyond their preliminary credentials. One way to accomplish this is by pursuing a master's degree in education. Some accelerated programs, like the one offered by USC's School of Education, allow bachelor's degree holders to work toward a teaching certificate and a master's degree while working full-time in a salaried teaching position.

To stay sharp and keep pace with current trends in education, all teachers must regularly attend workshops and educational seminars.

While the emergency credentials program offers prospective teachers who are already college graduates quick entry into the field, the traditional method of becoming a teacher is to gear your education toward that outcome while still in college.

At Cal State Los Angeles, the educational home to one of the largest pools of future teachers in Southern California, about 2,000 students are enrolled in the five-year credential program, Mayer said. To be admitted to Cal State L.A.'s program, students who want to become teachers must score at or above the median grade level in their major field.

After five years of experience and after earning their full credentials, working teachers may achieve master status and serve as mentors to those just starting out. Mentor teachers at L.A. Unified earn a regular teacher's salary—$23,440 to $40,871 a year depending on experience—plus a $4,000 differential for their expertise and added responsibilities.

Augmenting these earnings is the fact that teachers are entitled to more vacation time than almost any other class of professionals—an average of about three months out of the year at both standard-schedule *and* year-round districts. And if teachers do decide to teach during their time off, they get paid extra for it, Acosta said. Additionally, periodic negotiations between teachers' unions and school district administrations result in regular pay increases.

Both special education and bilingual teachers are in such demand that they are virtually assured of a job. Throughout the Southland, the languages that are most needed are Spanish, Cantonese, Korean, Armenian, and Vietnamese, Acosta said.

"If you're in one of these fields, you can go to just about any major city in the country and get a job," he said. "A good teacher can teach anywhere, whether it's in the suburbs or the inner city. Here, we look for teachers who are sensitive to a multicultural situation because this is Los Angeles, and Los Angeles is very diverse."

Bilingual teachers receive a $2,000 bonus if they are certified by the state, and another $1,000 bonus if certified by the district. Teaching specialists in reading or special education, who are required to have an extra credential and therefore more education, earn from $44,179 to $55,002 a year.

Besides the extra monetary compensation, special education carries with it other rewards. Because they are specialists working with children who have learning problems, special education teachers typically have small classrooms of 8 to 10 students and are assisted by a teacher's aide to reinforce what they teach. On top of instruction, the job entails a certain amount of record-keeping, testing, and report writing.

The emphasis in special education is on individual success, no matter how small, for kids who aren't used to succeeding, said Beth Bacon, a special education teacher at Westport Heights Elementary School in Westchester.

"I see myself as helping people. My students are made to feel special. When they come in here, they have already hit their low point, so I try to give a lot of positive reinforcement," Bacon said. "Parents are really thankful when their child is getting some special help, especially the ones who see progress. When you see a child succeeding, everybody's eyes light up."

With increased attention to the importance of educating the nation's youth, the image of teaching is gradually improving. A recent study conducted by the Higher Education Research Institute at UCLA confirmed that interest in teaching is starting to gain impetus among college freshmen.

"People still view teaching as a job that's not compensated enough for the amount of work and responsibility it carries," Acosta said. "That has been the perception, but once people

Teaching Salaries at L.A. Unified School District

Position	Salary
Teacher's assistant	$8.09/hr.
Teacher	$23,440–$40,871
Counselor	$23,440–$40,871
Mentor teacher	Teacher salary plus $4,000
Bilingual teacher	Teacher salary plus $2,000 (for state certification)
School psychologist	$36,294–$45,186 (reg. school year) $44,435–$55,321 (year round)
Teaching specialist	$44,179–$55,002

SOURCE: Los Angeles Unified School District.

get into teaching, they find out it's a good-paying job and that there's a lot of personal reward."

Even with the limitations inherent in teaching, educators assert that theirs is an interesting and satisfying career that gives them an important role in nurturing young people's lives and minds. "In working with the kids you get fresh approaches. Each class looks at things differently. New issues come up," said Carol Perry, who has taught for 22 years at Huntington Park High School. "It's hard for me to think of doing anything else."

SELECTED ELEMENTARY AND SECONDARY SCHOOL DISTRICTS

Anaheim Elementary
890 S. Olive Street
Anaheim, CA 92805
714/535-6001
Enrollment: 12,300

Anaheim Union High School District
501 Crescent Way
Anaheim, CA 92803
714/999-3511
Enrollment: 21,500

Beverly Hills Unified
255 S. Laskey Drive
Beverly Hills, CA 90212
213/277-5900
Enrollment: 4,800

Garden Grove Unified
10331 Stanford Avenue
Garden Grove, CA 92640
714/663-6000
Enrollment: 36,000

Glendale Unified
223 N. Jackson Street
Glendale, CA 91206
818/241-3111
Enrollment: 21,000

Hacienda/La Puente Unified
15959 E. Gale Avenue
Post Office Box 1217
La Puente, CA 91749
818/333-2201
Enrollment: 21,300

Inglewood Unified
401 S. Inglewood Avenue
Inglewood, CA 90301
213/419-2500
Enrollment: 26,000

Long Beach Unified
701 Locust Avenue
Long Beach, CA 90813
213/436-9931
Enrollment: 66,300

Los Angeles Unified
450 N. Grand Avenue
Post Office Box 3307
Terminal Annex
Los Angeles, CA 90012
213/625-6000
Enrollment: 705,000

Montebello Unified
123 S. Montebello Boulevard
Montebello, CA 90640
213/726-1225
Enrollment: 51,500

Orange Unified
370 N. Glassell Street
Orange, CA 92666
714/997-6100
Enrollment: 24,000

Pasadena Unified
351 S. Hudson Avenue
Pasadena, CA 91109
818/795-6981
Enrollment: 22,600

Santa Ana Unified
1405 French Street
Santa Ana, CA 92701
714/558-5501
Enrollment: 37,000

Santa Monica/Malibu Unified
1651 16th Street
Santa Monica, CA 90404
213/450-8338
Enrollment: 9,300

Torrance Unified
2335 Plaza Del Amo
Torrance, CA 90509
213/533-4200
Enrollment: 19,200

PROFESSIONAL ORGANIZATIONS

American Federation of Teachers
Elementary and Secondary Division
2511 W. Third Street
Los Angeles, CA 90057
213/487-5560

**California School Employees
  Association**
548 S. Spring Street
Los Angeles, CA 90013
213/727-7243

California Teachers Association (CTA)
5757 W. Century Boulevard
Suite 400
Los Angeles, CA 90045
213/642-6622

National Education Association (NEA)
1201 16th Street, NW
Washington, DC 20036
202/833-4000

PROFESSIONAL PUBLICATIONS

American Teacher (Washington, DC)
The California School Employee (San Jose, CA)
Education Week (Washington, DC)
Excellence in Teaching (Flagstaff, AZ)
Instructor and Teacher (Duluth, MN)
Teacher (Washington, DC)
Teaching/K-8 (Norwalk, CT)

DIRECTORIES

Career Information Center (Glencoe Publishing Co., Mission Hills, CA)
Directory of Organizations Related to Teacher Education (American Association of Colleges for Teacher Education, Washington, DC)
Educational Placement Sources (Educational Information Sources, Newton, MA)

CHAPTER 28

College and University Faculty Positions

Mass retirements and a student boom mean opportunities for college professors are on the rise.

Educating the nation's youth has never been more important. Global competition, the whirlwind pace of world events, leaps in technology, and the need to place it all in historical perspective have thrust education into prominence as the linchpin to advancement.

Education is no longer a luxury; it's a necessity. In today's fast-forward society, leading academics and business leaders agree, education is the difference between progress and stagnation. Strides being made by other developed nations primarily due to education are chipping away at America's dominance on virtually all fronts.

"There is a need for people to look at teaching as a career," said John K. Roth, professor of philosophy at Claremont McKenna College, who was voted Professor of the Year by the Carnegie Foundation for the Advancement of Teaching in 1989. "If someone's looking for meaningful work, I can certainly recommend teaching. A professor's life has a lot of attractions for a person who is interested in ideas and wants to work with people. You have a tremendous amount of freedom. And, perhaps equally important, you have time."

In the job market of the 1990s, opportunities for college and university professors throughout California will be remarkably abundant, as higher education undergoes a massive personnel changeover. Projected mass retirements of a whole generation of instructors, combined with an influx of new college-age students, will create a need for some 34,000 full- and part-time faculty in California's public colleges and universities by the year 2000.

The state's public postsecondary system, including the University of California, State University system, and community colleges, will need to replace some 64 percent of its current faculty in the decade ahead. Independent colleges and universities are in a similar bind, one that will not occur again for roughly 30 years, according to a report by the California Postsecondary Education Commission (CPEC).

"All of higher education, especially in California but throughout the U.S., is going to be hurting because there aren't enough people to fill the need," said Paul West, spokesman for the University of California (UC) in Berkeley. "There will be a lot of job opportunity for qualified people." The UC system projects hiring 7,000 new faculty for its nine campuses over the next 10 years, an average of about 700 professors a year.

As California moves toward becoming the first state without a single racial majority, colleges and universities increasingly will be engaged in a hiring effort aimed at diversifying faculties, namely, adding more women and minorities. What's more, salaries are going up because quality faculty are in short supply, West said. The 1990s bode well for would-be professors: Not only will there be a plethora of openings in the near future, but new college and university professors will make more money than ever before.

"Just because it doesn't pay as well (as the private sector) doesn't mean it doesn't pay," said Dr. Ennis Layne, provost and senior vice president for academic affairs at the University of Southern California. "You can make a living. It's not so terrible."

Indeed, if you are outstanding in your field, higher education pays quite well. As of March 1990, there were 166 UC faculty statewide earning salaries over $100,000, 146 of them working only nine months out of the year, the CPEC report said. Keep in mind that these prized professors are often Nobel laureates, Field Medal scholars, Pulitzer Prize winners, National Academy of Science scholars, or other premier researchers and teachers with national reputations.

On a more accessible level, salaries for full UC professors are expected to average $75,916 for the 1990–91 academic year. Including associate and assistant professors, the average income is projected to be $65,540. Tenured professors at Cal State schools should make $62,680 in 1990–91, while the average professorial income will be an estimated $52,544.

Salaries for deans and administrators are considerably higher in many instances. Vice chancellors at the Coast Community College District in Orange County, for example, can make over $81,000 with a PhD, while divisional or associate deans with master's degrees can garner $65,000, said John Renley, vice chancellor of human resources for the district.

In general, teaching at a two-year community college requires at least a master's degree in a given area of specialization, while at four-year colleges and universities that award bachelor's, master's, and doctorate degrees, a PhD is requisite for employment. As Roth says, the PhD degree has become the teaching credential of the higher-education field. There are some exceptions to this rule in such "performance" fields as art, drama, dance, creative writing, cinema, and journalism, however.

Community colleges, open to any resident over age 18, offer two-year associate degrees with credits that are transferable to four-year universities. At the community college level, the emphasis for faculty is on teaching. Instructors typically carry a heavy teaching load—an average of 15 lecture hours a week, plus four office hours daily. For every hour in the classroom, one hour of outside preparation is required, Renley said.

Four-year colleges and universities are more selective about whom they admit. They tend to cater to a younger student, usually fresh out of high school, and make enrollment decisions based on a combination of factors, including grade point average, test scores, personal essays, and extracurricular activities.

Cal State University professors are required to teach at least 12 hours a week, and hold 3 weekly office hours, while UC faculty carry a lighter teaching load—a minimum of 3 lecture hours a week, said Jack Munsee, professor of physics at Cal State Long Beach and associate vice president of the California Faculty Association.

The tradeoff is that UC professors are expected to conduct original research and periodically publish their findings in scholarly journals or in the form of books: "Publish or perish," the saying goes.

Increasingly, California State University schools are expecting their faculty to also find time to conduct research, Munsee said. "By and large, people now are expected to do research during the summer." During the school year, a professor's week consists of teaching, holding office hours, preparing for lectures, grading homework, serving on committees, and conducting research. "It's a 50- to 60-hour work week," Munsee said.

Other academics may put in even more time. "I'm working basically seven days a week, 12 hours a day with what I have to do," said Roth of Claremont McKenna College. Roth, a professor since 1966, looks at research in a positive light, as a way to learn and remain active.

"It's important to keep up in your field so what you have to say isn't old and dead," he said. "The best professors use their research time to enhance their teaching. And the best teachers are the ones who have this kind of infectious enthusiasm about what they're doing. You almost have to have a passion or sense of calling about what you're doing, whether you're a mathematician, physicist, history professor, or philosopher."

Another plus to the research aspect of academic life is that much of it can be done at home. Being an academic allows you to define your own work schedule and spend time being a parent. Professors from community colleges to major universities also cite the enjoyment derived from teaching and working with students, helping them develop their own potential and find their way intellectually, as a reason for going into the field.

"It's the idea of turning people on, to open their eyes," said Thomas Silliman, professor of art history at East Los Angeles College. "I enjoy bringing something so esoteric as art down to the ordinary person's level. I like educating the housewife, the kid off the street. I enjoy lighting fires in people. It's a kind of evangelism for me."

Quality of instruction and quantity of research are two key ways professors are evaluated. Service is another. In fact, serving on committees is a definite path toward gaining notoriety and, ultimately, respect around a department. Dean Edward A. Alpers of UCLA's Division of Honors said he was in line for the deanship when it opened up, in part, because he had served as vice-chair in his department (history) and had agreed to chair the Academic Senate Committee's graduate council.

"These are the parts of academic life people don't tell you about beforehand," Alpers said. "There's a lot of paper pushing that goes on. You make yourself known by virtue of getting the job done."

Beginning professors at most colleges start at the assistant level, making $30,000 to $40,000 a year. At USC, tenure-track faculty members are subject to a seven-year probationary period, at the end of which they are either granted tenure or asked to leave, said Layne, USC's provost. The criteria for nomination? "A good teaching record, some examples of service, and national importance as a scholar," Layne said.

Typically, professors are eligible for promotions every 5 years. The second step is to associate professor, at which point college educators earn $40,000 to $50,000, and it usually takes at least 10 years to make full professor. Opportunities for professors can be found in the *Chronicle of Higher Education* as well as academic journals specific to a given field of inquiry.

SELECTED PUBLIC AND PRIVATE COLLEGES AND UNIVERSITIES

California Institute of Technology (Cal Tech)
1201 E. California Boulevard
Pasadena, CA 91106
818/356-6811
Enrollment: 2,000

Cal Poly Pomona
3801 W. Temple Avenue
Pomona, CA 91768
714/869-7659
Enrollment: 20,000

Cal State Dominguez Hills
1000 E. Victoria Street
Carson, CA 90747
213/516-3300
Enrollment: 8,000

Cal State Fullerton
800 N. State College Boulevard
Fullerton, CA 92631
714/773-2011
Enrollment: 23,000

Cal State Long Beach
1250 N. Bellflower Boulevard
Long Beach, CA 90840
213/498-4111
Enrollment: 35,000

Cal State Los Angeles
5151 State University Drive
Los Angeles, CA 90032
213/224-0111
Enrollment: 21,000

Cal State Northridge
18111 Nordhoff Street
Northridge, CA 91330
818/885-1200
Enrollment: 31,000

Cal State San Bernardino
5500 University Parkway
San Bernardino, CA 92407
714/880-5000
Enrollment: 10,900

The Claremont Colleges:
 Claremont McKenna College,
 Harvey Mudd College, Pitzer
 College, Pomona College,
 Scripps College, Claremont
 Graduate School
747 N. Dartmouth Avenue
Claremont, CA 91711
714/621-8000
Total enrollment: 5,000

Loyola Marymount University
7101 W. 80th Street
Los Angeles, CA 90045
213/642-2700
Enrollment: 6,500

Occidental College
1600 Campus Road
Eagle Rock, CA 90041
213/259-2500
Enrollment: 1,700

Pepperdine University
24255 W. Pacific Coast Highway
Malibu, CA 90265
213/456-4000
Enrollment: 7,100

University of California, Irvine
University Drive
Irvine, CA 92715
714/856-5011
Enrollment: 14,000

University of California, Los
 Angeles (UCLA)
405 Hilgard Avenue
Los Angeles, CA 90024
213/825-4321
Enrollment: 35,000

UC Riverside
900 University Avenue
Riverside, CA 92512
714/787-1012
Enrollment: 5,200

University of Southern California
 (USC)
University Park
Los Angeles, CA 90089
213/743-2111
Enrollment: 30,000

Whittier College
13406 Philadelphia Street
Whittier, CA 90601
213/693-0771
Enrollment: 1,500

Also see the article at the end of Section 13 for
a listing of community colleges.

PROFESSIONAL ORGANIZATIONS

American Association for Higher
 Education
One Dupont Circle
Suite 600
Washington, DC 20036
202/293-6440

American Association of University
 Professors
1012 14th Street, NW
Suite 500
Washington, DC 20005
202/737-5900

American Federation of Teachers
College Guild Local 1521
617 W. Seventh Street
Los Angeles, CA 90017
213/629-1631

Association of California State
  University Professors
9010 Reseda Boulevard
Northridge, CA 91324
818/886-1196

National Education Association
  (NEA)
1201 16th Street, NW
Washington, DC 20036
202/833-4000

PROFESSIONAL PUBLICATIONS

Chronicle of Higher Education (Washington, DC)
Community, Technical and Junior College Journal (Washington, DC)
Journal of College Science Teaching (Washington, DC)
Journal of Higher Education (Columbus, OH)
NEA Today (Washington, DC)

DIRECTORIES

Annual Guide to the Best Schools (U.S. News and World Report Inc., Washington, DC)
The College Handbook (College Board Publications, New York, NY)
Peterson's Guide to Four-Year Colleges (Peterson's Guides, Princeton, NJ)
Public Ivys: A Guide to America's Best Public Undergraduate Colleges and Universities (Viking-Penguin, New York, NY)

The Teacher Shortage

Southland schools are facing a tidal wave of students.

Blame it on the baby boomers. Public school populations statewide, particularly in Southern California, will explode in the 1990s, creating an urgent need for new schools and additional teachers at the elementary and college levels to educate the biggest influx of school-age children since the post–World War II baby boom. "Schools are needed everywhere. Absolutely. No question about it," said Janice Noreen, a classroom and housing consultant for the San Bernardino County School District.

California's K–12 enrollment is expected to swell 35 percent in the coming decade, from 4.5 million students in 1988 to an estimated 6.1 million in 1998, according to the state Department of Finance. At the college level, an additional 180,000 students will push enrollment in the Cal State University system up almost 50 percent, from the 361,000 students currently enrolled to 541,000 by the year 2005, education officials say.

According to the "Report for Growth in the Years 1990 to 2005," at least 5 new campuses will have to be added to the 20-campus system—3 or more in the southern half of the state—and 14,000 to 15,000 new tenure-track faculty members hired, to accommodate this surge of college students. If current projections are accurate, the growth for Cal State schools in the 1990s will be reminiscent of the boom years from 1960 to 1975, when nine campuses were added and statewide enrollment mushroomed from 95,000 to 311,000 students, said Frank Jewett, Cal State University growth planning project director.

This new wave of incoming students, coupled with a statewide population increase and the approach of retirement age for a generation of faculty members, raises the question of how to accommodate the state's growing student body and attract enough new qualified instructors at a time when interest in teaching is at a record low.

The demand for teachers and new school facilities is especially pressing at elementary school districts in the state's high-growth counties, including virtually the whole of Southern California: Los Angeles, Ventura, Orange, Riverside, San Bernardino, and San Diego counties. According to estimates by Cal State Los Angeles's School of Education, up to half the teachers in the state will be retiring over the next few years.

"The elementary field is where our biggest growth is occurring. Math, science, English, and ESL (English as a second language) teachers are needed at all levels," said Michael Acosta, head of teacher recruitment for the massive, 627,000-student Los Angeles Unified School District, which employs about 27,000 teachers. "Our growth is all over Los Angeles. In addition, because we're so big, we face resignations and retirements amounting to a turnover rate of about 5 to 6 percent per year. We hired about 2,000 teachers in 1989 alone."

During the 1990s, the number of schoolchildren throughout Los Angeles County's 82 school districts, including L.A. Unified, is projected to increase 22.6 percent, augmenting the state's single largest K–12 population by 300,000 students—from 1.3 million in 1988 to an estimated 1.6 million in 1998, according to Department of Finance statistics.

But while L.A. County schools may experience the largest growth in terms of sheer student population figures, other regional school systems will have a faster growth rate. The elementary student population in Riverside County is expected to have the highest growth rate of any county statewide in the 1990s: 88.8 percent. Right behind Riverside is San Bernardino County, projected to grow 78.4 percent by 1998. The number of students in neighboring San Diego County should swell 46.2 percent, while in Orange County, kids' ranks are expected to rise 27 percent.

"When I started teaching in 1947, we had 1,500 teachers. Now we have 15,000. That's a phenomenal increase in just a few decades," said Robert Peterson, Orange County's superintendent of schools. "We have districts, largely at the high school level, that have stabilized or are declining in growth. In the elementary grades, an increase is occurring. If it continues, we will need to build a considerable number of new schools. Already, districts are going out of state to recruit teachers."

School planners say the population explosion was anticipated, but perhaps not in time. Compounding the problem is a slow-moving state legislature, which, education officials charge, has been sluggish in its effort to find adequate long-term funding solutions for the construction of new schools.

"Growth has exceeded expectations. California continues to be a magnet, attracting new residents from across the country and around the globe," Bill Honig, state superintendent of public instruction, said at a widely publicized 1989 press conference.

If California is a magnet, Southern California is its strongest point of attraction. Indeed, no other metropolitan region in the nation saw a larger population explosion during the 1980s than Los Angeles, Orange, and Riverside counties, according to the U.S. Census Bureau. From 1980 to 1988, the number of people living in the three-county area grew by 2.3 million, pushing the total number of residents over 13.8 million.

"In addition, more and more California women, from all socioeconomic groups, are having babies," Honig said. "The nature of public education is quite simply put: a baby born today needs a school desk in just a few years. From 1990 through the 1995–96 school year, between 170,000 and 200,000 new students will be added to our schools each year. That's the equivalent of a brand-new city of Stockton or Riverside each year."

A sizable number of the state's incoming students are the children of, or are themselves, first-generation immigrants, Honig said. Two prime examples of this new wave of students are the Garden Grove and Santa Ana school districts in Orange County. In the Garden Grove district, more than 60 different languages are spoken by students: in Santa Ana, students speak over 30 languages, Peterson said.

"I know of one third grade teacher who arrived in her class and not a single student spoke English," Peterson said. This increase in students who speak foreign tongues has created unique opportunities for teachers who are bilingual. (For more information, see Chapter 27 on teaching.)

As the number of students continues to skyrocket, school districts are having to patiently wait their turn for state funding to build new schools. More than $5 billion worth in applications for local school construction are awaiting state assistance, and the backlog is expected to grow by about $100 million per month over the next few years, Honig said.

"We're looking at almost 10,800 classrooms that need to be built by 1996," said Matthew Spies, a building analyst with the L.A. County Office of Education. "The cost to provide these new facilities is roughly $1.2 billion, and that's on the low side. It's tough to come up with that amount of money." State lottery revenues have provided some additional funding for schools, but not nearly enough, education experts say.

In the years ahead, experts say, growth will prove more difficult than it was in past decades when the state was less populated and there was much more room to build.

"The crisis confronting California [schools] is equal to any of the state's needs and will directly affect our economy," Honig asserted. "Business leaders know how vital it is to have a well-educated workforce. And the state's educators are committed to making our state second to none. But you can't do that without first putting a roof over [students'] heads."

"We're between a rock and a hard place," added Rich Roberts, facilities fiscal officer for the Riverside County Office of Education, where the growth rate is the highest. "Individual school districts are caught in a big bind of having a large increase in enrollment and not having enough classrooms to put them in. New schools are going up daily. But a lot of parents are still wondering where they're going to send their kids."

To help alleviate crowding problems, the state's elementary schools are increasingly moving toward solutions like year-round schedules, in which four students can be educated in the space normally occupied by three. L.A. Unified has adopted a year-round schedule that will take effect in 1991. Temporary, relocatable classroom facilities are another remedy.

Despite the challenges facing them in the years ahead, educators remain fundamentally optimistic about the field of education and the prospects of those who aspire to enter the teaching profession. "I think it's a wonderful time to get into the field," said Lamar Mayer, associate dean of Cal State L.A.'s School of Education. "Job opportunities continue to be very good if you live in the greater Los Angeles area."

SECTION
9

Sports-
Related
Careers

CHAPTER 29

Sports Information Director

The PR specialists of athletics help provide the play-by-play.

Ever wonder how Los Angeles Dodgers announcer Vin Scully knows the number of RBIs every baseball player coming to bat has hit in the last season, or how the Monday football announcers astutely recall the minutiae of a running back's college career? Or, in the print media, how a newspaper reporter's account of a sporting event can be so exhaustively detailed?

Many times, their memory serves them well. But more often than not, there's a sports information director (SID) in the picture who provides detailed information before and during the game, and then facilitates player interviews after it's over.

For instance, for a football game, a team or athletic department's sports information office supplies the press with a media guide. During the game, a detailed play-by-play account of the event is periodically issued to all reporters covering the event while it is happening, so they can be freed up to watch the game's broader developments. Afterward, reporters follow the players into the locker room for interviews.

Sports information directors are the public relations specialists of sports. During their sport's season, they interact with the media on a day-to-day basis, write weekly press releases, promote their team, pitch stories, and put together game day programs. It's a hectic job that entails a lot of travel—to all of the away games— and working when other people are playing, literally.

"In sports, you're working when most people are working, and you're working when they're in their leisure time," said Mike Williams, director of publicity for the Los Angeles Dodgers. "It's important to understand that the industry has tremendous benefits, but also a tremendous amount of work. It's not just getting to know all the players on a first-name basis."

During the season, sports information directors work upward of 60 to 80 hours a week, from 9 o'clock in the morning until the end of a game at night, said Terri Nealy, public relations assistant for the L.A. Rams. "You're always on the go," she said. But their job is really year-round. During the off-season, they write the team's annual media guide, yearbook, and preseason prospectus, including highlights of past seasons, biographies on the players, and an analysis of the coming season.

There are two main facets of sports information: college and professional sports. Sports information directors at the college or university level are responsible for handling a number of different athletic programs. In professional sports, public relations directors, as they are called, oversee the publicity for their team only. The pressure is generally more intense in professional sports, although some college teams like USC and UCLA garner as much attention as many pro teams.

The crush of media requests that follows a successful team or athletic program can place sports information directors in the hot seat. They must try to satisfy the media's seemingly insatiable appetite for interviews and information while maintaining good relations with the coaching staff and players. Sometimes, sports information involves counseling athletes on how to deal with the press. Other times, the SID acts as spokesperson for the team.

"It's like being a press secretary for the president," said Steve Vanderpool, director of athletic publications for USC's Sports Information Office. "You're the information source, the go-between, and the image maintainer."

The field of sports information has evolved over the years from a sportswriter type of job to the full-service public relations position it is today, said Fred Nuesch, sports information director for Texas A&I University in Kingsville and president of the 1,650-member College Sports Information Directors of America. Writing is still one of a sports information director's strongest suits, however.

"Writing skills are important, but not mandatory," Vanderpool said. "There are some sports information directors who could write for *Sports Illustrated*, then there are others who would have a hard time putting together a press release. What it comes down to is having a background in public relations with an emphasis in writing."

Most people entering the sports information field today have a bachelor's degree in either public relations or journalism, plus experience in sports information or as a sportswriter. Many schools, such as USC, now offer special concentrations in sports information or sports studies through the journalism school or department of physical education.

Because the market for sports information directors is so small—Nuesch estimates there are only 3,000 college SIDs nationwide—it is imperative to gain internship experience while still in school if sports information is the career path you want to take, Williams said.

"I always tell people that an internship is the best way to get started," Williams said. "Through internships, you can learn how different organizations operate and decide what you like best. Once you get into the job market, it's pretty hard to switch around. There are so many people who want to get into the business that there are very few openings. There isn't a lot of turnover."

An average sports information office has a staff of about three people. Many teams and university athletic departments, such as Texas A&I, may have only one career publicist. Major universities known for their athletic excellence like UCLA have five SIDs, a director for men's and women's athletics, plus three assistants. Beginning assistant SIDs are initially assigned to the "lower sports"—golf, tennis, water polo, etc.—and move up to the more prominent arenas of basketball and football as they progress, eventually becoming the head of the entire sports information office.

Experienced college SIDs are occasionally recruited to ranks of professional sports, Vanderpool said. Take the example of Nick Salata, current director of media relations for the Los Angeles Kings hockey team. Salata interned as a graduate assistant at USC's sports information office while pursuing his master's degree. Upon graduating, he was hired as assistant SID for track and basketball. After proving himself at USC, he was picked by the Kings to head their media relations office, Vanderpool said.

Professional sports organizations like the Dodgers staff a

publicity director plus five full-time assistants and four interns just to handle all the media calls. But that is the exception, not the rule. An NBA basketball team might have only one or two publicists, Nuesch said. Nevertheless, a position will eventually open up if you make enough contacts, gain enough experience, and show ample enthusiasm and expertise in the sport.

"The No. 1 thing I look for is brainpower, a high energy level, and a positive outlook on things," Williams said. "It's not absolutely essential to have a journalism or PR degree. Many of the skills are generated through common sense."

Although the opportunities are limited, the greater Los Angeles area is home to as wide an array of professional sporting teams and college athletic departments as you will find any place in the country. There are eight professional teams based here, plus at least 29 community colleges and 30 four-year colleges and universities, most of which have athletic departments. Women's athletics is one area on the rise, Nuesch said.

"In the last 10 years, there has been growth in prestige and opportunities," Nuesch said. "The growth of women's athletics has doubled the need for sports information directors in that area. It's continuing to grow even now. The membership of our organization has grown each year."

Since sports is generally considered to be a glamour field with great visibility, there are certain tradeoffs to working in sports information. The chief drawbacks are long hours, limited opportunities, and a modest pay scale. At the entry level, sports information assistants are paid $17,000 to $20,000 a year. Directors of a department make around $20,000 to $25,000 a year, while sports information directors overseeing the entire show earn anywhere from $25,000 to $50,000 annually.

These salaries, people working in sports information admit, are paltry compared to what public relations specialists can make in the business sector (see Chapter 42). Another negative aspect to sports information is that a major part of it, compiling statistical records, can become very tedious. "If you don't like sports, it can be a very drudging job. We deal in lots of statistics and details," Vanderpool said.

On the upside, SIDs are in the unique position to experience the thrill of victory, along with the agony of defeat, as part of the team. At the college level, SIDs are increasingly becoming integral members of the school's athletic administration, serving as assistant athletic directors as well as SIDs, Nuesch said.

The greatest joy of being in sports information comes when the team is winning and heading toward a championship season. Then the job is not only easier, but also pays more in the form of playoff bonuses. It also results in added recognition.

"It's great to be with a successful organization, especially when you're in publicity, because it's easy to sell what we have to offer," said Williams of the Dodgers, the winner of six World Series titles, the most recent in 1988. "When we experience the success of postseason play, that makes all the efforts you go through worthwhile. That doesn't happen every year, so you appreciate that a great deal. There's great pride to winning something like the World Series."

KEY EMPLOYERS OF SPORTS
INFORMATION OFFICERS

Golden West Baseball Co./Angels
2000 State College Boulevard
Anaheim, CA 92806
714/937-6700

Los Angeles Clippers
3939 S. Figueroa Street
Los Angeles, CA 90037
213/748-8000

Los Angeles Dodgers
1000 Elysian Park Avenue
Los Angeles, CA 90012
213/224-1500

Los Angeles Kings
3900 W. Manchester Boulevard
Inglewood, CA 90305
213/419-3160

Los Angeles Lakers
3900 W. Manchester Boulevard
Inglewood, CA 90305
213/419-3121

Los Angeles Lazers
401 S. Prairie Avenue
Inglewood, CA 90301
213/412-5000

Los Angeles Raiders
332 Center Street
El Segundo, CA 90245
213/322-3451

Los Angeles Rams
2327 W. Lincoln Avenue
Anaheim, CA 92801
714/535-7267

UCLA Sports Information Office
405 Hilgard Avenue
J.D. Morgan Center
Los Angeles, CA 90024
213/206-6831

USC Sports Information Office
103 Heritage Hall
University Park
Los Angeles, CA 90089
213/743-2224

Also see Chapter 28 for a listing of four-year colleges, and the article at the end of Section 13 for a listing of two-year colleges.

PROFESSIONAL ORGANIZATIONS

American League of Professional Baseball Clubs
350 Park Avenue
New York, NY 10022
212/371-7600

College Sports Information Directors of America
c/o Fred Neusch
Campus Box 114
Texas A&I University
Kingsville, TX 78363
512/595-3908

National Basketball Association (NBA)
645 Fifth Avenue
New York, NY 10022
212/826-7000

National Collegiate Athletic Association (NCAA)
Nall Avenue at 63rd Street
Mission, KS 66201
913/384-3220

National Football League (AFC & NFC)
410 Park Avenue
New York, NY 10022
212/758-1500

National Hockey League (NHL)
960 Sun Life Building
1155 Metcalfe Street
Montreal, Canada H3B 2W2
514/871-9220

National League of Professional Baseball Clubs
350 Park Avenue
New York, NY 10022
212/371-7300

Public Relations Society of America
7080 Hollywood Boulevard
Los Angeles, CA 90046
213/461-4595

PROFESSIONAL PUBLICATIONS

American Sports (Rosemead, CA)
California Football Magazine (Redondo Beach, CA)
Goal (Montreal, Can.)
Hoop (New York, NY)
Inside Sports (Evanston, IL)
The National (New York, NY)
Sport Magazine (New York, NY)
The Sporting News (St. Louis, MO)
Sports Afield (New York, NY)
Sports Illustrated (New York, NY)

DIRECTORIES

Blue Book of Senior and Junior and Community College Athletics (Rohrich Corp., Akron, OH)

Directory (College Sports Information Directors of America, Kingsville, TX)

Directory (National Collegiate Athletic Association, Mission, KS)

New American Guide to Athletics, Sports and Recreation (New American Library, New York, NY)

The Sports Address Book (Simon & Schuster, New York, NY)

CHAPTER 30

Coaching

Experience the thrill of victory and the agony of defeat while shaping young lives.

Legendary football coach Vince Lombardi of the Green Bay Packers said it best: Winning isn't everything, it's the only thing. Top professional and college coaches live and die by this axiom, changing teams and losing jobs as often as new television shows debut and get canceled. However, not all coaches are in the spotlight. At the lower levels, the pressure to win isn't so intense.

For the vast majority of coaches, who work as assistants or the heads of high school and lesser-known college programs, coaching affords at least some stability and allows them to be near the sport they love while helping to shape young lives.

"Winning is important, but it's not the most important thing," said Dan McGee, head basketball coach for West High School in Torrance since 1962. "We're not like the NBA. We're not out there to see how much money we can make. We're trying to educate kids. That's the joy of coaching, seeing your players progress and develop."

In coaching, the opportunities are determined by the number of teams a given sport can sustain. Take football. Nationwide, there are about 10,000 high school teams, 650 college squads, and 28 professional football organizations. For the entire NFL, there are just under 400 coaches, counting head coaches, assistants, and trainers. A professional team may staff 10 or more assistant coaches, including 4 for defense, 6 for offense, and 1 for special teams. A college team may staff 8.

"To start coaching in high school with the assumption that you're [eventually] going to make it as an NFL coach is very poor arithmetic," commented Al LoCasale, executive assistant for the Los Angeles Raiders.

In Los Angeles and Orange counties, there were 1,640 total coaches and umpires in 1987, according to the Employment Development Department. By 1992, only 380 more slots are expected to open up.

As the numbers suggest, the opportunities are greatest at the high school level. In basketball, for instance, there are about 450 high school teams from Santa Maria to Orange County, McGee said. Full-time high school coaches are hired as teachers and must possess a valid California state teaching certificate before they can be considered for employment. (For more information about teaching, see Chapter 27.)

Walk-on coaches, on the other hand, are employed on a part-time, seasonal basis and are paid a small stipend, usually $1,200 to $1,500 for the season. They may serve as assistant coaches, or as is increasingly the case, head coaches of freshman or junior varsity teams. Some walk-ons even act as head coach of such high school sports as golf, tennis, or volleyball.

Full-time coaches are required to teach four classes a day and a two-hour fifth period for their respective sport's practice, McGee said. They typically are paid a percentage of their base salary (around 8 percent or so) for their coaching duties, so a full-time coach making $40,000 a year as a teacher may earn an additional $3,200 for his or her coaching duties.

Most head high school coaches have previous coaching experience, although occasionally a standout college performer may start directly as the head coach of a high school varsity or junior varsity team.

Prospective coaches without a playing background can learn the basics through a local recreation department or by attending sports clinics, camps, and workshops run by experienced coaches during the off-season. These coaching seminars are advertised in such magazines as *Scholastic Coach*. Observing other coaches and volunteering at practices offer further exposure.

A. J. Matel, a former junior varsity head coach at West High, said he coached for three years through the Torrance Parks and Recreation Department and assisted in a high school summer basketball league before starting as an assistant freshman high school coach. Matel said he then became the head freshman coach and, the next year, the junior varsity head coach—all while attending Pepperdine University in Malibu.

"At the freshman level, you can get on with basic knowledge," Matel said. "You don't have to be an X and O strategist. I learned by going to varsity practices. I worked in a summer league and attended clinics. I went as far as I could while I was going to school." After graduating, Matel said, he was offered a graduate assistant position with the Pepperdine basketball team, but opted instead for a job in sales. "It's hard to make a living coaching," he explained. However, Matel said his current job as senior account executive for Telecom*USA allows him the flexibility to continue coaching on a part-time basis.

Full-time coaching positions begin at the middle school or junior high school level, which can be a good jumping-off point into a high school coaching career, said McGee, who coached eighth-graders before getting on at West High. "With coaching, there has to be a teaching job available first," he said.

In theory, coaches stay only an hour or two longer after school than regular teachers. But in reality, coaching is considerably more time-consuming, especially when there are away games that involve travel. The time commitment is even more intense in college athletics, where coaches double as recruiters and represent their school's program at fundraising activities.

"Coaching collegiately is very much like being an executive officer at a corporation. We're all our own bosses and we're in a setting that is competitive," said Lisa Love, head coach for USC's women's volleyball team. Love said she spends about two hours each day recruiting. "It's a phenomenal time commitment. During the season, every weekend is obligated, and when you have matches during the week, you might work until 11 p.m."

Occasionally, a head high school coach with a superb win-loss record may become an assistant coach with a Division 1 college team, or assume the head coaching responsibilities at a community college or lesser-known four-year school. Love said she became the head of the USC women's volleyball team after putting together a winning program at the University of Texas, Arlington.

Graduating to the college ranks can be a mixed blessing, coaches say. On the upside, head coaches and even assistants at big-name schools aren't required to teach. The prestige and notoriety are certainly greater, but so are the pressure to win and the obligations off the field, namely, with recruiting. At a big-name school—virtually any Division 1-level program—the onus is on the coach to put together a winning program. And no matter how good a coach you are, you can't win if you don't have the talent. Another drawback is that advancement frequently requires moving to another city or state.

"We have coaches here who have been at 10 different schools," noted Bob Donlan, associate athletic director at Cal State Long Beach, who said the average lifespan of a Division 1 head coach in a high-profile sport isn't very long. "After 15 years here, I've become accustomed to the fact that coaches come and go. If you stay too long, the end result is you're going to get fired. You don't see people like [former University of Alabama football coach Paul] 'Bear' Bryant who stay at the same school for 35 years anymore, because of the pressure. You're only as good as your last game or last season. It's tenuous at best."

At Cal State schools, assistant coaches are generally hired in at professor salaries, from $30,000 to $60,000 a year, but they don't receive tenure. "As an assistant, what you're coming up against is the head coach either being let go or moving up to another head job," Donlan said. "We have a lot of turnover at our school because people move up."

The majority of professional and Division 1 college coaches have played the sport either in college or the pros. The level a player tops out at is usually his or her most logical starting point as a coach, said Tony Fuller, an assistant basketball coach at UCLA. Without playing experience, it's possible to move up either from the high school ranks or by becoming a graduate assistant.

Fuller, who played basketball at Pepperdine University in Malibu, said he returned to the team as a graduate assistant upon graduating and finishing his eligibility as a player.

After working for two years as a part-time assistant while pursuing his graduate degree, Fuller became a full-time assistant under coach Jim Harrick. Then, when Harrick was chosen to head UCLA's basketball program in 1988, Fuller came over to UCLA with him, landing his current position. (The other assistant coach at Pepperdine, Tom Asbury, became the new head coach there.)

Fuller, whose job entails some scouting and preparing game plans for upcoming games, said he relearned basketball from a coach's perspective by working at clinics and camps, watching other coaches, studying game films, and observing other teams. His initial break came, in part, because he was a known commodity.

"It's like any job. When someone becomes the head coach,

he wants to go with people he knows personally or by reputation," said LoCasale, a former high school and college coach who worked his way into the professional ranks by becoming a scout and then director of player personnel for the San Diego Chargers and Cincinnati Bengals. "In the NFL, there are some coaches who haven't played pro ball, but they have to come recommended from a college or professional coaching staff."

The select few coaches who do make it to the pros are well compensated but, like Division 1 college coaches, have short professional lifespans—under 10 years on average. In football, some head coaches make as much as star players—$250,000 to $1 million a year, while assistant coaches can be paid anywhere from $50,000 to $200,000 or $300,000, depending on their experience and win-loss record, LoCasale said.

Assistant coaches in professional sports have at least some semblance of security. In the NFL, for instance, assistants who transfer from team to team also transport their experience under the league's retirement plan. "Pension is based on 15 years of coaching," LoCasale said. "Most assistants make it to their pension."

The coaching profession historically has been dominated by men. But with the rise of women's athletics has come increased opportunities for female coaches. "The atmosphere in hiring now is very pro-women," said USC's Love. "There is a huge push to get women involved in sports. The positions are there. There just aren't the numbers. I would advise young women to pursue coaching as a profession. We need them and they have a tremendous lot to offer."

KEY EMPLOYERS OF COACHES

See Chapters 27 and 28 plus the Career Trends article at the end of Section 13 for a listing of high schools, colleges, and universities, and Chapter 29 for a listing of professional sports teams.

PROFESSIONAL ORGANIZATIONS

American Baseball Coaches Association
Post Office Box 3545
Omaha, NE 68103
402/733-0374

American Football Coaches Association
7758 Wallace Road
Suite I
Orlando, FL 32819
407/351-6113

American Hockey Coaches Association
c/o Bruce Delventhal
Achilles Rink
Union College
Schenectady, NY 12308
518/370-6134

Association of Professional Ball Players of America
(Baseball)
12062 Valley View Street
Suite 211
Garden Grove, CA 92645
714/892-9900

National Association of Basketball Coaches in the U.S.
Post Office Box 307
Branford, CT 06405
203/488-1232

National Coaches Council
c/o National Association for Girls and Women in Sport
1900 Association Drive
Reston, VA 22091
703/476-3450

National High School Athletic Coaches Association
Post Office Box 1808
Ocala, FL 32678
904/622-3660

National Youth Sports Coaches Association
2611 Old Okeechobee Road
West Palm Beach, FL 33409
407/684-1141

PROFESSIONAL PUBLICATIONS

Basketball Weekly (Branford, CT)
Coaching Digest (Omaha, NE)
The Extra Point (Orlando, FL)
National Coach (Ocala, FL)
Scholastic Coach (New York, NY)
Youth Sports Coach (West Palm Beach, FL)

DIRECTORIES

Blue Book of Senior and Junior and Community College Athletics (Rohrich Corp., Akron, OH)
Clell Wade Coaches Directory (Clell Wade Coaches Directory Inc., Cassville, MO)
Directory (National Collegiate Athletic Association, Mission, KS)
National Directory of High School Coaches (Athletic Publishing Co., Montgomery, AL)

Easing the Transition from the Playing Field to the Job Market

Athletes need to prepare for the inevitable end of their sporting careers.

For professional and student athletes alike, one of the biggest life adjustments they will ever face comes when their playing days end. Some make the transition gracefully, moving into a new career with relative ease. But many flounder, suffering what sociologist Harry Edwards calls "disengagement trauma"—the bewildering sense of loss, confusion, and lack of self-worth that accompanies the end of all too many sporting careers.

What accounts for the difference? In a word, preparation, according to sports psychologists, former athletes, and athletic and career counselors.

"Athletes need to diversify," said UCLA sports psychologist William Parham. "They need to have positive relationships outside of sports. They need to develop several sources to draw self-esteem energies from. They shouldn't let sports be the fundamental part of who they are. Believe in the statistics rather than the dream. There are a lot of factors in our control, but making it professionally isn't one of them."

The statistics are indeed bleak. Only about 1 or 2 percent of all Division 1 college football and basketball players ever make it to the pros. Even when they do, their playing lives are incredibly short. The average NFL career lasts just over three years. In the NBA, it's slightly less than four years. In major league baseball, a player is lucky to see more than four seasons of play.

Professional football has one of the highest casualty rates of any sport. The average NFL football player lives to be only 55 years old. And even though salaries are astronomical by most people's standards (in 1988, professional football players earned an average of $239,000), careers are so short, lifestyles are often so extravagant, and planning so neglected that many ex-players wind up with little or no savings after it's over. Some 60 percent of all former NFL players go into bankruptcy.

"All of this adds up to the need to look for more realistic career opportunities," said Keith Zimmer, athletic/career counselor at the University of Nebraska.

Despite the grim figures, student athletes by the droves continue to believe in the dream, Zimmer said. "Regardless of the sport, you still see that idealism. We have football players who have never played a down here, but they still think they're going to get an agent and make it to the show. Athletes give so much to their sport that they neglect career planning."

Several programs are now emerging to help student and professional athletes lead fulfilling lives after sports. PACE Sports in San Diego offers career guidance to all NBA players and certain amateur athletes. The PACE (Professional Athletes Career Enterprises) program has two phases: an assessment phase to identify a player's career interests and learning abilities, and an action phase to develop skills and home in on specific post-playing opportunities.

Frequently, job preparation requires vocational training, said Ron Stratten, executive vice president of PACE Sports. "Some players may have $500,000 in income but only $20,000 worth of marketable skills," Stratten said. But many athletes are either reluctant to admit they lack knowledge in certain areas or too prideful to get the training they need, he added.

"A lot of players are very stubborn. These are gifted people. They have high comprehension levels, but they don't have much patience," Stratten said. "If you want to be a businessman, you'd better acquaint yourself with business skills. The people who focus are successful. Unfortunately, the people who need us most are the last ones to seek us out."

Steve Garvey, former star first baseman for the Los Angeles Dodgers and San Diego Padres, said he started laying the groundwork for his life after sports early in his baseball career. Only three years into the big leagues, Garvey said, he became a spokesman for Pepsi-Cola. But instead of using the soft drink company solely as a vehicle for self-promotion, he took the opportunity to develop a good understanding of the business side of sales and marketing.

"The PR was a minor part of it," said Garvey, a 10-time National League All-Star who now heads the Garvey Marketing Group in Los Angeles. "I told them I wanted to learn about the business. I did everything. I went on a truck and delivered it, watched how it was made and packaged, and served as an advance salesman. I did a lot of speaking, too."

By working full-time in the off-season, Garvey, who now also helps place former professional athletes in corporate positions through PACE Sports, said he was able to gain enough experience and know-how to eventually branch out on his own—long before his 19-year professional career was over.

"Athletes have to understand that they have to prove themselves in a business environment," Garvey said. "It requires a different state of mind. It takes time, patience, perseverance, and hard work. There also has to be a certain amount of reality. The athlete who has been playing sports his whole life can't realistically expect to step into a management job that has taken someone else going to college four to six years to prepare for."

According to Parham, there are two ways an athlete's career can end: either expectedly or unexpectedly. The latter instance, typically resulting from a sudden injury, is the more traumatic. Indeed, athletes abruptly prevented from playing the sport they have dedicated their lives to undergo a grieving process similar to the steps associated with death and dying: denial, anger, bargaining, depression, and, ultimately, acceptance.

Sometimes, the adjustment period takes a downward spiral into gloom and despair, or leads to a chemical dependency problem—or worse. At least three former NFL players have committed suicide, according to the NFL Players Association. No organization currently offers professional football players counseling to help make the transition, although some teams, like the San Francisco 49ers, provide off-season instruction in finance and investment.

"There's a loss of self-esteem that goes along with this change," Stratten said. "Your social life changes. No one wants to talk to you. You may deny the fact that it's happening, but when it does happen, it's tragic. Athletes who recognize that they're getting down to the line are much better able to deal with this tragedy."

Even an anticipated withdrawal from the playing field can have severe side effects, especially when sports has become an inseparable part of an athlete's identity.

"When you can no longer draw self-esteem from that source, you're going to feel trapped and alone, like nobody cares," Parham said. "There's going to be an overwhelming sense of loss. Change happens every day, but it turns out to be the one thing we can't deal with very well. Bringing an athletic career to a close and starting all over is really, really difficult."

UCLA's Placement and Career Planning Center offers a special four-year counseling program called Career Pathing for Student Athletes that each year teaches the university's nearly 200 new athletes how to match their course requirements to their skills and interests. The program, offered for the duration of their college career, starts with assessment exercises to identify possible majors and career choices.

In their sophomore and junior years, student athletes are taught interviewing techniques, résumé writing, and how to research potential employers. The summer after their junior year, they are encouraged to hold a full-time internship in a career field that interests them. With graduation comes placement assistance and introduction to the school's alumni referral network, said June Millet, educational liaison for UCLA's Placement and Career Planning Center.

Proper guidance can make all the difference in a student athlete's success off the playing field, said Zimmer of the University of Nebraska, whose athletic counseling unit closely resembles UCLA's.

"If they know what their academic and career goals are from the very beginning, we've found they are much more motivated as students," Zimmer said. "This is something high school counselors should be addressing. Unfortunately, it's not occurring there. Intervention needs to occur at an early age, even as early as junior high school."

Parents of child prodigies also need to share the responsibility of stressing the importance of education to their kids, no matter how athletically talented they are, Parham added. "Some parents get drawn into living through their children. They really need to participate more and help to develop some options for them, even at a young age."

One of the most important areas past and present athletes should focus on is the value of transferable skills—qualities and abilities learned on the field that are directly applicable to the business world, Millet said. Such skills include leadership, discipline, perseverance, time management, and communication skills. They also include the ability to motivate others, make level-headed decisions under pressure, and remain dauntless in the face of adversity, just to name a few.

"It always amazes me how a 21-year-old kid can make decisions with 90,000 people watching and then perceive himself as incompetent," Millet said. "It doesn't make sense. Many athletes are very bright, disciplined people who have just bought into the dumb-jock stereotype. They just haven't been socialized to express themselves."

Millet said she would help direct any former professional or college athlete who seeks career guidance. Her number at UCLA's Placement and Career Planning Center is (213) 825-2981.

Garvey noted that he has had success placing former athletes in corporate positions precisely because of their athletic experience. "Athletes have certain skills that are attractive to human resource directors," Garvey said. "Oftentimes, they will have the upper hand in an interview. They have a certain presence about them."

In life—the most important game of all—it's how former athletes develop and apply the skills they have while playing that will determine their success when the fans stop cheering.

"Even for the most successful, the end of a sports career is inevitable and comes at an early age," Parham said. "Thirty-five is pushing it. People like Kareem Abdul Jabbar are rare. The average athlete is finished at age 27 or 28. The average person lives to be about 80 or 85. You've got to do something with the rest of your life. The buzzword for me is 'options.' Go as far as sports will take you, but have a Plan B and Plan C ready."

See the Career Trends article on job loss at the end of Section 14 for a recommended reading list.

Careers in Entertainment

CHAPTER 31

Talent Agent

Make the deals that make stars,
and make a good living.

Entertainment is an unpredictable industry. Some performers struggle along for years, even lifetimes, without much luck, while other actors, musicians, and even screenwriters appear out of the blue and achieve stardom almost overnight. How is a star born? Very often, genuine talent is the common denominator of success. But frequently, there is a talent agent in the picture who has spotted the ability and found the right venue for it to shine.

Talent agents are part of the hidden machinery of the motion picture, television, music, and publishing industries. Before and after most stars are "discovered," they are in the hands of an agent who attempts to find work on their behalf, whether that involves booking an engagement, suggesting possible acting roles, arranging a record deal, or selling a manuscript to a production company or publishing house. (Talent agents also represent athletes and models, but these areas are really beyond the scope of the entertainment industry and, hence, this chapter.)

In Hollywood, the large talent agencies have five main departments: motion pictures, TV/video, music, commercials, and variety shows, said Toby Berlin, director of business administration for Triad Artists Inc. In New York, talent agencies also encompass the theater, publications, lectures, and appearances, Berlin said.

What does it take to make it as an agent? Business savvy, an eye or ear for talent, and a persuasive personality, to start with. For literary agents, some literary judgment is in order. Sales and bargaining skills are vital for all types of agents, since they must first find work for their clients and then negotiate the terms of their contracts. They stipulate services to be performed, the hours their clients will work, how much they will be paid, and the amount of promotion to be done on their behalf.

Of all the areas within an agent's purview, compensation is perhaps the hardest to negotiate. Discussions over money not only concern actual wages, but also share of gate (total admission receipts), residuals (payment for reruns), bonuses, fringe benefits, and expenses. When it comes to settling on an agreeable sum, agents must be realistic about the demand for their client's "product," or talent, a determination that is subjective, though partly influenced by the market.

"Being an agent is being a creative deal-maker," said Steven Glick, vice president of television for the famed William Morris Agency. "You're putting together people and ideas and forming relationships."

Talent agents typically earn a commission of 10 percent on each contract they arrange. Literary agents are usually paid 10 percent of an author's or screenwriter's advances and royalties. Earnings vary wildly, depending on an agent's client list. With top screenplays selling to the major studios for $300,000 or more, it's easily possible to make $30,000 on just one deal.

Finding such talent is rare. But it's not unusual for a talent agent to make a decent salary. In 1987, artist and entertainer managers (i.e., agents) earned an average salary of $52,900, up from only $31,150 in 1982, said Jack Kyser, chief economist for the Los Angeles Area Chamber of Commerce. In 1987, there were 292 firms employing 2,215 artist and entertainment managers in the Los Angeles area, Kyser said.

"No one expects you to sit down with a phone and bring in the next Meryl Streep. It's more just placing your existing talent in the positions that are open," said Rima Bauer Greer, a literary agent with Writers & Artists Agency in Brentwood. Added Glick: "All we can do is get them the opportunity for the job. We're not the buyers."

Typically, the buyers of talent are motion picture producers and television network executives—the moguls of the entertainment industry. Selling these big shots on a client is one of the talent agent's toughest jobs.

"It's a business of diplomacy. You're constantly on the phone talking to producers and matching scripts with actors and actresses," said Chris Andrews, an assistant talent agent at International Creative Management, or ICM, a leading talent agency.

"If you want to find a new client, you have to work that much harder than the next guy."

Due to the difficult, often aggravating task of pairing clients with projects and negotiating contracts, 10- to 12-hour work-days are common. For many agents, the all-consuming nature of their job becomes inseparable from the rest of their lives. "You're committing to a lifestyle," Glick said. "If that means reading a script every night, then that's what it takes. You can get a call at 7 o'clock in the morning ... or midnight."

How do agents discover new talent? Usually, it comes to them—in the form of manuscripts, portfolios, references, or demo tapes. In the music industry, they might be asked to watch a certain band or musician perform. Literary agents occasionally initiate contact with new fiction writers who appear in prestigious magazines like the *New Yorker* or with reporters who cover news stories of great intrigue. Mostly, though, it's by word of mouth and personal introductions.

"It's a business that revolves around contacts," affirmed Ana Adler, ICM's office manager. "If I'm referred to someone by a name, as a rule, I always see them."

For newcomers, much of this information can be gleaned from "the trades"—publications like *Variety, Drama Logue* and the *Hollywood Reporter.* The two main trade magazines for the music industry are *Billboard* and *Music Connection.* Insiders typically pass important news along by word of mouth, however, oftentimes over breakfast with a client at the Beverly Hills Hotel's famous Polo Lounge, or while doing lunch at such industry eateries as Musso and Frank Grill, Spago, or Chasen's.

Agents' backgrounds vary. Most tend to be college educated, especially at the large, established agencies, including Triad Artists, William Morris, and ICM. Each of these influential agencies offers trainee programs for would-be agents. Typically, the larger agencies look for a college degree from a big-name school and a combination of confidence, assertiveness, tact, and enthusiasm. People skills go without saying.

"I look for someone who's aggressive but not oppressive," said Lee Rosenberg, a founding partner of Triad Artists in Los Angeles. "I like to see that their area of supposed expertise is true, and that they can speak intelligently about whatever area they claim to be an expert in. Trustworthiness is another important factor. The ultimate test of all this is the first sale."

Trainee positions pay very little—from $100 to about $300

a week tops—and initially involve a lot of "grunt work." Trainees who make the grade can, after 18 months' to three years' experience, move up to an assistant position. In their first few years on the job, trainees are encouraged to read any and all memos, screenplays, and scripts that pass their way to absorb as much about the business and the key players as possible. They also attend regular conferences and dinners with senior agents and company executives.

Eventually, capable assistants are promoted to junior agent status and begin handling their own clients. After a five- to seven-year apprenticeship, they finally become full-fledged agents and in turn are assigned an assistant of their own.

Talent agents frequently come from other professions, such as business management, consulting, human resources, accounting, or law. When making a mid-career move into agenting, many agents advise, start at a small- to medium-size agency. Otherwise, they say, you may end up working for someone who is 10 years younger, and making 10 times more, than you are.

Since there are more people interested in working in the entertainment industry than there are jobs, becoming an agent is not an easy proposition. Besides daunting odds to gaining employment, talent agents also face intense pressure. "You're responsible for someone else's life and career," Rosenberg said.

Another drawback to the talent agency business is that, in the closed-door society of Hollywood's power brokers, opportunities for women are still somewhat limited, women in the industry say. "It's a boys' club," said Debbie Kotick, who works in William Morris's development department. "You have to jump up and down and yell and let yourself be known." Sometimes, it can be easier to make a name for yourself at a smaller agency.

Veteran agents say the personal fulfillment derived from discovering talented young performers and nurturing their careers is well worth the sacrifices necessary to eventually succeed. "I found Robin Williams and Tom Hanks before anyone knew who they were," said Alan Iezman, vice president of motion pictures at William Morris. "That can be very gratifying."

One of the best places to gain initial exposure to the talent agency business, and the entertainment industry in general, is UCLA Extension's many seminars, extension classes, and panel discussions on specific entertainment industry topics. For more information about upcoming programs, call UCLA Extension at (213) 825-8895.

KEY EMPLOYERS OF TALENT AGENTS

Abrams Artists & Associates
9200 Sunset Boulevard
Suite 625
Los Angeles, CA 90069
213/859-0625

Irvin Arthur Associates
9363 Wilshire Boulevard
Beverly Hills, CA 90210
213/278-5934

Bauer Benedek Agency
9255 W. Sunset Boulevard
Suite 716
Los Angeles, CA 90069
213/275-2421

Contemporary Artists
132 Lasky Drive
Beverly Hills, CA 90212
213/278-8250

Creative Artists Agency
1888 Century Park East
Suite 1400
Los Angeles, CA 90067
213/277-4545

Evergreen Agency
723 N. Cahuenga Boulevard
Los Angeles, CA 90038
213/650-3136

Harris & Goldberg
2121 Avenue of the Stars
Suite 950
Los Angeles, CA 90067
213/553-5290

**International Creative
Management (ICM)**
8899 Beverly Boulevard
Los Angeles, CA 90048
213/550-4000

Leading Artists Inc.
445 N. Bedford Drive
Beverly Hills, CA 90210
213/858-1999

Major Clients Agency Inc.
2121 Avenue of the Stars
Los Angeles, CA 90067
213/277-4998

William Morris Agency
151 El Camino Drive
Beverly Hills, CA 90212
213/274-7451

Triad Artists Inc.
10100 Santa Monica Boulevard
16th Floor
Los Angeles, CA 90067
213/556-2727

Variety Artists
2980 Beverly Glen Circle
Suite 302
Los Angeles, CA 90077
213/475-9900

Writers & Artists Agency
11726 San Vicente Boulevard
Suite 300
Los Angeles, CA 90049
213/820-2240

All of the above-mentioned talent agencies are franchised
by the Screen Actors Guild. For a complete list, call the
Screen Actors Guild at (213) 465-4600.

PROFESSIONAL ORGANIZATIONS

Association of Talent Agents (ATA)
9255 W. Sunset Boulevard
Suite 318
Los Angeles, CA 90069
213/274-0628

Independent Literary Agents Association
c/o Ellen Levine Literary Agency
432 Park Avenue South
Suite 1205
New York, NY 10016

National Association of Performing Arts Managers and Agents
c/o Pentacle
104 Franklin Street
New York, NY 10013
212/226-2000

Society of Authors' Representatives
10 Astor Place
Third Floor
New York, NY 10003
212/353-3709

PROFESSIONAL PUBLICATIONS

American Film Magazine (Los Angeles, CA)
Back Stage (New York, NY)
Billboard (New York, NY)
Cashbox (New York, NY)
Drama Logue (Los Angeles, CA)
Film Comment (New York, NY)
Hollywood Reporter (Los Angeles, CA)
The Literary Agent (New York, NY)
Music Connection (Los Angeles, CA)
Premiere (New York, NY)
Variety (Los Angeles, CA)

DIRECTORIES

Blue Book (Hollywood Reporter, Los Angeles, CA)
Film Producers, Studios and Agents Guide (Packard Publishing, Beverly Hills, CA)
Literary Marketplace (R. R. Bowker, New York, NY)
Pacific Coast Studio Directory (Pacific Coast Studio, Hollywood, CA)
Who's Who in the Motion Picture Industry (Packard Publishing, Beverly Hills, CA)
Who's Who in Television (Packard Publishing, Beverly Hills, CA)
Writer's Market (Writer's Digest Books, Cincinnati, OH)

CHAPTER 32

The Music Industry

The hours are long but the rewards are melodious in the radio and recording business.

The Southern California music industry isn't called an industry for nothing. There are about 650 recording studios, 235 video production facilities, 135 record companies, and 84 radio stations clustered in the Los Angeles area, not to mention a slew of ancillary services vital to the business. The local radio advertising market alone is worth $400 million a year, making L.A. the biggest radio market in the country.

Music is an exciting, fast-paced field that prizes experience and extends few opportunities to outsiders. Breaking in frequently boils down to who you know and what music-related jobs you've held. "It's a Catch-22," said Marjorie Gayle, personnel manager for CBS Records. "To be hired, you already have to be established in the music industry."

Despite the close-knit nature of the business, opportunities are available at record companies, recording studios, and radio stations—if you find a way to create your own value.

Record Companies

Record companies scout and sign new groups, and then produce, print, release, distribute, and promote their albums. At the major record companies, the heart and soul of the music industry, the most stability can be found on the business side. On the creative end, even top executives work under short contracts. When they are let go, so are their staffs.

Some major labels also house smaller mini-labels that focus on specific types of music: classical, jazz, new age, country, easy listening, heavy metal, classic rock, alternative rock, or urban contemporary. Sometimes, it's possible to get hired at a mini-label and then move up to the parent label with experience.

Short of being a rock star, one of the more glamorous entry-level jobs in music is A&R (artist and repertoire) representative. A&R reps listen to demo tapes, sign bands, and match artists with songwriters. Their job takes them into nightclubs, rehearsal sessions, and boardrooms, where they argue the merits of a particular band they feel deserves a record deal.

"Most of the time they strike out," Gayle said. "It's just finding the right talent that 3 percent of the time. A&R is a hard department. There's no guarantees. But everybody and their mother wants to get into it." Experience can be gained at small labels or by interning while in college and enticing radio stations to play a record company's artists on the air.

One area record companies have difficulty staffing is A&R administration, Gayle said. This entails keeping track of contracts, watching how money is spent, and determining how much will be allocated for an album project based on past returns and future projections. "If you're in A&R administration, you can almost write your own ticket anywhere."

The downside is that once you're pegged as a numbers person, the opportunities to cross over into a creative department, such as promotions, are limited. Promotions is one of the more capricious facets of the music business. Promotion executives are often held responsible for the success or failure of an album. Consequently, they are among the first to be replaced when a division isn't performing well.

"They just go from one company to another," Gayle said. "Most people here have worked at MCA, Warner, or Atlantic Records. And a lot of our people have been going to Capitol. In the music industry, especially in promotions, you really don't need a lot of reason to get rid of someone. It just sort of doesn't work out and they're let go. It's just the nature of the business."

The upside to the industry's topsy-turvy employment practices is that someone who starts as an entry-level secretary or administrative assistant at one company may leave, gain experience at another label, and in time return as a manager or vice president of a department.

"One day they're making $20,000. The next day you see an announcement and they're making $70,000," Gayle said. "On the other hand, there are people here for years who never go anywhere. It all depends on whether they think you have that spark or genius. It's a strange business. I wouldn't recommend it to anybody unless they have a love for the industry, a thick skin, and can roll with the punches."

Recording Studios

At recording studios, entry-level openings usually are limited to runner or trainee positions. Trainees learn from staff engineers, called second engineers. During a recording session, a second engineer assists the first engineer, usually a freelancer, to make sure "the session from a technical standpoint proceeds with as little downtime and difficulty as possible," said Craig Hubler, general manager of Sunset Sound in Hollywood.

Recording engineers are responsible for the sound quality of a recording session. Depending on their area of expertise, they mix soundtracks, dub in lyrics or dialogue, or produce voice-overs, adjusting the volume, tone, and speed to desired levels. Besides mixing records, engineers may also work on advertising jingles, television shows, and, increasingly, movie soundtracks.

"With the popularity and demand for better audio in films, a lot of the motion picture companies are turning to the recording studios because we've had decades of experience," Hubler said.

Most second engineers, who make up to $10 or $12 an hour, have some formal training or a technical degree in recording engineering from a trade school, community college, or university extension program. But even with training, beginning engineers must still pay their dues and start as trainees, working under the wing of a second engineer.

"I would rather have someone with 80 percent the right personality and 20 percent the right technical background," Hubler said. "Personality takes you a long way in this business as an assistant engineer. The second engineer often determines whether the guest engineer or producer will return to the studio."

After four or five years as a second assistant, engineers may start working with artists on their own and branch out as freelancers. New freelance engineers charge $40 to $50 an hour, while top engineers command $100 to $125 an hour and, occasionally, a small percentage of a recording's profits, Hubler said. "Some engineers become absolute artists on the console. They bring technical tricks and wizardry to the sound."

The best engineers eventually become producers, developing the concept for an album or soundtrack and orchestrating the recording session. "The producer is the ultimate boss during the session," Hubler said. "He hires the freelance engineer for the gig, and the engineer books a studio he is comfortable with."

Since engineers work in the studio with artists and producers in close confines for hours on end, they need to be accommodating and adopt a teamwork mentality. "The creative aspect of the studio combined with the technical requirements places a lot of pressure on everybody," Hubler said. "It's very much a collaborative effort."

In recording, there currently is a major shortage of qualified maintenance technicians, the people who monitor the tape machines, microphones, and consoles and then repair the equipment when it breaks down. Sunset Sound employs three or four maintenance techs 24 hours a day to handle problems that arise, Hubler said.

"If you want to get into the studio business, become a maintenance tech. The door is wide open if you're good," Hubler said. Because of the shortage, qualified techs are paid top dollar. Chief techs make upward of $50,000 a year. With the increasing sophistication of the equipment, training to become a tech now entails getting an associate or bachelor's degree in engineering technology from an accredited college or university.

Radio Stations

Finally, after a band is signed, the music recorded, and an album released, the songs, if they're catchy, receive airplay at a radio station. Like the music industry as a whole, radio is a volatile, profit-driven enterprise. Consequently, if a station is not receiving high ratings and bringing in adequate revenues, its format is likely to be scrapped in favor of something else.

"This business is run by accountants. They don't care about your ideas unless they make money," said David Crowle, manager of creative services for KABC-AM (790).

Recent years have witnessed the trimming of many radio staffs and complete format changes at numerous stations. Nevertheless, there are a small number of off-air positions that do open up in sales, programming, and promotions. Without experience, about your only way into the oversaturated L.A. radio market is in a clerical capacity or as an unpaid part-time programming or promotions assitant.

Program assistants volunteer their time to work on a specific show, answering calls and responding to listener requests for the deejay or host. Promotions assistants help with remotes—promotional broadcasts from popular locations like record stores, beaches, and concert venues. "In the summertime, we need people every weekend," said Jill Gregory, assistant promotions director for KLSX-FM (97.1). "There are lots of ways to work into this business."

If your sights are set on working in L.A. radio, you are perhaps best advised to first gain experience in an outlying area like Ventura, Riverside, or San Bernardino and then come back to the market as a more valuable commodity. If you aspire to be an on-air producer, disc jockey, or show writer, your chances of getting airtime are greater outside Los Angeles than they are if you stay here.

"Every day it's the same old thing. I see people come in here and think, 'I'm going to write and produce.' I say, 'Yeah, you're going to type and file,'" said KABC's Crowle. "For every job there are 30 to 40 people looking to get hired. Coming out of school with a degree and good grades, you'll be lucky to get a job that pays $17,000 and works you 50 hours a week."

KEY EMPLOYERS IN THE MUSIC INDUSTRY: RADIO STATIONS AND RECORD COMPANIES

Radio Stations

KABC-AM (790)
3321 S. La Cienega Boulevard
Los Angeles, CA 90016
213/840-4958

KFI-AM (640)
610 S. Ardmore Avenue
Los Angeles, CA 90005
213/385-0101

KIIS-FM (102.7)
6255 Sunset Boulevard
Los Angeles, CA 90028
213/466-8361

KLOS-FM (95.5)
3321 S. La Cienega Boulevard
Los Angeles, CA 90016
213/840-4840

KLSX-FM (97.1)
3580 Wilshire Boulevard
Los Angeles, CA 90010
213/383-4222

KMPC-AM (710)
5858 Sunset Boulevard
Los Angeles, CA 90078
213/460-5672

KOST-FM (103.5)
610 S. Ardmore Avenue
Los Angeles, CA 90005
213/385-0101

KPWR-FM (105.9)
6430 Sunset Boulevard
Suite 418
Los Angeles, CA 90028
818/953-4210

KROQ-FM (106.7)
3500 W. Olive Avenue
Suite 900
Burbank, CA 91505
818/953-7667

KRTH-FM (101.1)
5901 Venice Boulevard
Los Angeles, CA 90034
213/937-5230

KTWV-FM (94.7)
5746 Sunset Boulevard
Los Angeles, CA 90028
213/466-9283

Record Companies

A&M Records
1416 N. La Brea Avenue
Los Angeles, CA 90028
213/469-2411

Arista Records Inc.
8370 Wilshire Boulevard
Beverly Hills, CA 90211
213/655-9222

Atlantic Records
9229 Sunset Boulevard
Los Angeles, CA 90069
213/205-7450

Capitol Records
1750 N. Vine Street
Los Angeles, CA 90028
213/462-6252

Columbia (CBS) Records
1801 Century Park West
Los Angeles, CA 90067
213/556-4700

Chrysalis Records
9255 W. Sunset Boulevard
Los Angeles, CA 90069
213/550-0171

Elektra Records
9229 W. Sunset Boulevard
Los Angeles, CA 90069
213/205-7400

EMI-Manhattan Records
1750 N. Vine Street
Los Angeles, CA 90028
213/462-6252

MCA Records Group
70 Universal City Plaza
Universal City, CA 91608
818/777-4000

Polygram Records
3800 W. Alameda Avenue
Suite 1500
Burbank, CA 91505
818/955-5200

RCA Records
6363 W. Sunset Boulevard
Los Angeles, CA 90028
213/468-4039

Warner Brothers Records
4000 Warner Boulevard
Burbank, CA 91522
818/954-6000

PROFESSIONAL ORGANIZATIONS

American Federation of TV and Radio Artists
6922 Hollywood Boulevard
Los Angeles, CA 90028
213/461-8111

American Society of Composers, Authors and Publishers (ASCAP)
6430 W. Sunset Boulevard
Suite 1002
Los Angeles, CA 90028
213/466-7681

Audio Engineering Society
60 E. 42nd Street
Suite 2520
New York, NY 10065
212/661-8528

Broadcast Music Inc. (BMI)
8730 W. Sunset Boulevard
Los Angeles, CA 90069
213/659-9109

Music Industry Conference
c/o Music Educators National
Conference
1902 Association Drive
Reston, VA 22091
703/860-4000

Southern California Broadcasters Association
1800 N. Highland Avenue
Los Angeles, CA 90028
213/466-4481

PROFESSIONAL PUBLICATIONS

ASCAP Today (Los Angeles, CA)
BAM Magazine (Oakland, CA)
The Beat (Highland, IN)
Billboard (New York, NY)
Music Connection (Los Angeles, CA)
Radio and Records (R&R) (Los Angeles, CA)

DIRECTORIES

International Buyer's Guide (Billboard Publications, New York, NY)
Music Business Directory (Music Industry Resources, San Anselmo, CA)
The Recording Industry Sourcebook (Ascona Communications, Los Angeles, CA)
Yellow Pages of Rock (Album Network, Burbank, CA)

Veteran Deejays' Secrets of Success

Their personalities are as varied as their voices, from opinionated to demure. They are compromisers and idealists, all somewhat fearful of losing their jobs in a fickle market. Meet the dinosaurs of the rock and roll airwaves, most of whom are struggling to postpone their inevitable extinction.

But don't call them obsolete; they still have a few good years left in them—as many, perhaps, as such Precambrian music legends as Mick Jagger of the Rolling Stones and Roger Daltry of the Who, whose songs still receive the kind of airplay they did 25 years ago.

Despite basic differences in style, disc jockeys around since the early days of FM radio in the late 1960s have at least one thing in common: they are survivors who have seen it all come and seen it all go.

Boss Radio. Free Format. Disco Fever. New Wave. New Age. Punk Rock. Album Rock. Classic Rock. Rap. Heavy Metal. Urban Contemporary. And, don't forget the latest craze, the "new" sound of Oldies. The technology has evolved, too—from LPs, EPs, 45s, and 8-tracks to cassette tapes, compact discs, and, soon, digital audio recordings.

Just as the music has changed, the stations themselves have changed. In 1989, a benchmark year for local radio, the FM dial underwent radical transformation.

First, KNX-FM (93.1), once upon a time KKHR, became KODJ, while KIQQ-FM (100.3) vanished to make room for KQLZ, "Pirate Radio." Then KMPC-FM (101.9), redubbed KEGD, "The Edge," for eight months, gave way to K-LITE. Perhaps most dramatically, classical stalwart KFAC-FM (92.3)—a tradition since 1934—was replaced by rock station KKBT. Finally, on New Year's Day 1990, jazz station KKGO-FM (105.1) switched to an all-classical format, filling the void created by KFAC's departure.

To the veteran disc jockeys who give L.A. radio its distinctive sound, that year's maelstrom of format changes was just a passing phase, an exciting, if not welcome, period of upheaval in what was considered to be a stagnating market.

"About every five years you go through a period like this," Bob Coburn, a deejay of 21 years, said during his midday shift at KLOS-FM (95.5), L.A.'s oldest FM rock station. "There's so much money at stake that people are willing to stay only so long with a format and then once it begins to go a little sour, they're ready to jump off the bandwagon and go on to something else."

If the dinosaurs aren't fearful about losing their jobs, it's because they're all refugees from other stations who have endured past shakeouts and intrusions of new talent and, despite it all, have carved out a relatively secure niche for themselves in the second-largest but most lucrative radio market in the country. Advertising revenues total around $400 million annually.

In radio, and throughout the entertainment industry, it's not what you know that carries you, but who you know—and who listens to you.

"Everybody has their core group of faithful listeners," said KLSX-FM (97.1) deejay Dusty Street, who started her on-air career in 1968 at KMPX in San Francisco, the country's first FM rock station. "People have grown up with us, and they insist that we stay."

Far from breeding contempt, familiarity often works to a deejay's advantage. Indeed, KLSX program director Tom Yates employed familiarity as a successful marketing strategy when first putting together an on-air staff for the station. When the classic rock station replaced KHTZ, "K-Hits," in 1986, Yates looked for experience, signing veteran L.A. deejays Shana, Damion, Billy Juggs, Frazier Smith, and Dr. Dimento, among others, in search of an older audience.

"We're targeting 25- to 49-year-old males, so I'm basically talking to the same audience (and playing the same songs) as I did when they were young, long-haired, Levi's-wearing hippies," said Damion, KLSX's balding and graying afternoon jock. "As we all grow older here, they're growing older with us."

Except for the morning, when the revelry of on-air

personalities takes precedence over the music, rambling, self-important banter between musical sets can be the kiss of death for a deejay, especially in a crowded field like Southern California.

Geno Michellini, KLOS's popular drivetime jock known for his "5 O'Clock Funnies" show, maintains deejays can lengthen their on-air lifespans by serving their audience rather than their own egos.

"It's not a case of how you want to be perceived by your audience, it's how they perceive you," Michellini said. "When I'm on the air doing my show, I keep in the back of my mind that if I'm talking to people in their car, I'm competing with background noise, the air conditioner, the dog in the backseat. Whatever I say I try to make understandable and short so it doesn't become just a distant hum."

Brevity can ensure longevity. Knowing how to pronounce place names properly and read the city's personality also helps. Even so, listeners can be fickle. "You don't have to be born and raised here, but you do have to know the town and its moods," said Robert W. Morgan, a local radio staple since 1965.

Rodney Bingenheimer, the iconoclastic weekend deejay of KROQ-FM (106.7), said he manages to survive by remaining totally oblivious to radio wars and playing only what he personally thinks is good. "When I'm away from KROQ, I don't even think about radio," said Bingenheimer, a new-music tradition on Saturday and Sunday nights for the past decade. "I'm not even aware there's a competition going on."

Disc jockeys, it seems, generally fall into two categories: idealists or compromisers. Compromisers make up the overwhelming majority of deejays who agree to play a predetermined list of songs approved by a program director. Idealists are the much, much smaller contingent of record spinners who insist on playing their own format, or at least sneak in a few songs of their own choosing each shift.

Room for the idealists has diminished over the years as stations have increased in value and program directors, unwilling to stake their livelihoods on the unpredictable tastes of individual deejays, have streamlined playlists.

"There's usually better tracks on the album than what the program director selects," said Bingenheimer, the only deejay left on the local commercial airwaves who is free to play whatever he wants. (Even then, it's only for three hours a week on Sunday nights.)

Jim Ladd, a familiar FM rock-and-roll voice over the past two decades, most notably at the now-defunct KMET-FM and more recently at KEDG before it was supplanted by K-LITE, is another example of this dying breed of idealists. When KMET (94.7) went off the air in 1987 and became the New Age station KTWV, "The Wave," Ladd went to archrival KLOS. But soon after being promised complete creative control to select songs of his own choosing, Ladd said, he was fired for refusing to adhere to a playlist.

The maverick FM deejay said it was against his principles to play a list of songs arranged by someone else. He laments the constraints—and hype—introduced to the FM bank during the late 1970s and 1980s when station owners realized that FM radio was an enormously profitable business and not just an outlet for renegade rockers.

"The whole essence of rock and roll is freedom," Ladd said. "If you don't know enough to put the music together correctly, why should you be on the air? FM radio originally was almost an art form. It had to do with the way you put the music together, the bands you played, how you related to the audience. None of it had to do with big-money contests, giving away cash prizes, or a playlist, for God's sake."

Ladd's ideals have apparently outlived their usefulness, however, as he is no longer a player in the L.A. market. His obsolescence has sent a message to other radio relics on the musical endangered species list: compromise or else. Most already have.

"I feel quite comfortable with a format—*honestly*," said Damion of KLSX. "My own tastes may fall flat on their face with an audience. My job is to be the human bridge between the music and the radio station, not to set myself up as a kind of music mentor who can turn listeners on to tunes that can change their lives. That was cute back in the '60s, but it ain't workin' in the '90s."

Whether they're fighters or passivists, many dinosaurs are patiently waiting for their turn on the Ferris wheel of radio to reach the zenith of popularity again.

"You're on top for a cycle, then you're down. Then you're coming back up," said Charlie Tuna, a deep-voiced radio veteran of the AM and FM bands who recently switched as morning deejay from KRLA-AM (1110) to KODJ-FM. "I've seen a lot of jocks come and a lot go. I'm content because I'm still here. I'll just wait for my time again."

CHAPTER 33

Motion Pictures

Hooray for Hollywood! The movie business is tough, but tenacity and knowledge of the industry can improve your chances.

Making it in Hollywood has never been easy. For every success story there are countless unfulfilled dreams and deflated egos. But if you desire a career in movies, some routes you can take offer more promise than others. Still, nothing is absolute. There are as many different ways to make it in this business are there are people in the industry.

In Los Angeles County, an estimated 220,000 people are employed directly or indirectly by the film and entertainment industry, said Michael Walbrecht, associate director of the California Film Commission in Los Angeles. Little under half work in ancillary services—everything from catering to costume designing—providing the necessary creative and administrative support to keep Hollywood running, Walbrecht said.

Although there is growing concern about films being shot elsewhere—so-called runaway productions—Los Angeles is still the movie capital of the world. In 1989, Southern California filmmakers dished out a record $5.25 billion on movies, cable programs, television shows, and commercials. More than 90 percent of that remained in the L.A. area. New York filmmakers, the second-largest group of spenders, invested around $2.5 billion on productions, Walbrecht said.

The motion picture industry converges in Hollywood. This is

mainly due to the presence and pull of the six major studios: Columbia, Twentieth Century Fox, Disney, MCA-Universal, Paramount, and Warner Brothers. The studios are the backbone of the movie industry. In addition to shooting their own productions, they also lease their equipment and lot facilities (sound stages, for example) to independent production companies for television series, game shows, and various other projects.

Studios like MCA-Universal are diversified entertainment corporations with divisions ranging from music and television to motion pictures, book publishing, and home video. Since the studios are heavily involved in the business side of entertainment, they routinely have openings for accountants, financial analysts, systems analysts, and other administrative positions, said Janet Wood, vice president of human resources for MCA-Universal.

"So much of the business is not making motion pictures directly for our studio, but being part of some deal or distributing collateral materials," Wood said. "If people are interested in entertainment and they have a good business background, they'll be able to do whatever they're interested in. We'd love to see those people."

Like other employers in the motion picture industry, the studios look for experience, preferably in entertainment, and stellar backgrounds. A staff accountant for a "Big Six" accounting firm would have little difficulty finding an opening at one of the major studios. On the other hand, a recent college graduate, even from an Ivy League school, may have to start as an administrative assistant and work his or her way up from there.

"We hire some people right out of school, but generally speaking we look for applicants with three to five years' experience," said Leslee Pearlstein, vice president of human resources for the Twentieth Century Fox Film Corp. "I've seen recent college graduates take anything. But you're not going to start in personnel, for instance, and move over to creative development. It just doesn't work that way."

Once you're in, the opportunities do increase the longer you stay. But it's important to be realistic and up front. "We don't want someone who comes into an accounting job and then six weeks later says he or she wants to be in marketing," Pearlstein said. The studios have a strong promote-from-within policy, so keeping your career aspirations under wraps for the first year or so may work to your benefit in the long run.

"If you come into our marketing department, perhaps as a secretary, and pay your dues and do a good job and have an interest and a flair in marketing and maybe an advertising background through college, you may well at some point have the opportunity to become a junior publicist or publicist and move up through the ranks that way," Wood said.

Marketing, Pearlstein warns, "is our most requested area, but it also has the least opportunities." Both Twentieth Century Fox and MCA-Universal have job hotlines that you can call for a current list of openings.

The studios are one of the high-profile facets of the entertainment industry. But the majority of creative production jobs exist beyond the confines of the studio lots, at independent production companies or through one of Hollywood's numerous trade unions, or guilds.

Motion picture production is divided into above-the-line and below-the-line positions. Above-the-line staff include actors, directors, and producers; below-the-line people are responsible for all the technical aspects of moviemaking. They are the art directors, cinematographers, set designers, electricians, lighting specialists, editors, makeup artists, production assistants, sound technicians, prop managers, and various other craftspeople you'll find on a movie set.

Most big-budget feature films, television shows, and commercials are unionized. However, only about half of Hollywood's 44,400 film production workers belong to a guild, according to a California Film Commission report. Union membership is coveted and difficult to come by, mainly because it offers some semblance of security and guarantees a certain wage.

Below-the-line jobs can pay well, but the work isn't always steady. About half to three-quarters of Hollywood's tradespeople are not working on any given day. Eric Ward, a gaffer (lighting electrician) and key grip (camera tracker), said he was making about $400 a day as a union electrician during the shooting of "Wings of Apache" before the cinematographer, who was loyal to the director, quit the project halfway through filming over a creative dispute with the producer.

To join a union, you need to build up a certain number of hours on a union-sanctioned shoot (typically about 30), but union members have first bid at those jobs. It's the Catch-22 of the entertainment industry: you can't join a union unless you have experience, but you can't get experience unless you belong to a union. Occasionally, when union rosters are exhausted, there may be some nonunion hirings. Another route to membership is to be present when a union organizes a previously nonunion shoot.

Working on a set can be exciting and glamorous, but it also entails a lot of long hours and unrelenting demands. Productions are shot according to budget, and, even though these budgets are frequently overrun, there's a sense of urgency about the work, which can be very painstaking and detail-oriented. A two-minute scene may take 10 hours to shoot, with numerous takes in between.

"Mostly, it's calluses and sore backs," Ward said. "But it's also really fun. One day I'm working on a rock video with a heavy metal band and symphony orchestra, and the next day I'm on the set of 'Nightmare on Elm Street IV.' Most of the people I know, all they do is work. The money is good and, in a way, we're all our own bosses. It's not just a job, it's a lifestyle."

Above-the-line work is the hardest area to break into. A traditional background includes a film degree from a university known for its cinema department, such as USC or UCLA. But even with a film degree, you're still likely to start out as a production assistant, fetching snacks, dragging cables, and performing other menial tasks on location.

Tenacity and knowledge of the industry can carry you to the next step as a production coordinator or script person, recording each camera shot in the film log. From there, you might be able to become a second assistant director (AD), helping on the set with such logistical matters as crowd control and organizing the extras. Second ADs can eventually become first ADs, who act as the principal link between the director and the crew.

Following this route can ultimately lead to the position of unit production manager, a movie project's chief logistician. The unit production manager hires the crew and breaks down the script, or decides in what order the picture will be shot.

If you hold a college degree, one way to get a start in the direction of directing is through a postgraduate training program like those offered by the American Film Institute (AFI) or the Directors Guild of America (DGA).

The DGA Assistant Directors Training Program, open to college degree holders and production workers with at least two years of on-set experience, qualifies graduates to work as second assistant directors. During the two-year program, trainees are assigned to work on television episodes, movies of the week, pilots, miniseries, and feature films with studios and production companies. They also attend regular training seminars.

Becoming an assistant director does not put you in line to eventually call the shots as a director, however. Most directors have acting or screenwriting backgrounds. If you are creatively inclined, the surest way of breaking into directing is by writing a successful screenplay, follow it with a second script of sellable quality, and then negotiate with a producer to direct your next effort (no mean feat). For many writers, directing is a way of retaining some measure of creative control over their work.

The most widely used screenwriting text is *Screenplay* by Syd Field (New York: Dell, 1982). To date, the highest amount ever paid for a screenplay was $3 million for Joe Eszterhas's "Basic Instinct" in 1990. Name writers who consistently write hit movies typically garner $300,000 to $400,000 per screenplay. The median annual income for members of the Writers Guild of America West was approximately $50,000, said spokeswoman Cheryl Rhoden. But of WGA's 7,790 members in Southern California, half don't work in any given year, Rhoden added.

Directors who can put together a string of hits sometimes go into producing, hiring the lead creative staff—director, director of photography (cinematographer), editor—and arranging the financing for a production. Although some producers are very hands-on in their approach, others are involved strictly with money matters. Another way to become a producer is by owning the rights to a story or having a lot of money to spend.

If you're an aspiring actor and just want a taste of the movie business, you can respond to the calls for extras in such industry publications as *Drama Logue*, the *Hollywood Reporter*, or *Daily Variety*, or contact the various casting companies around town, such as Central Casting, Cenex Casting, or Disc Production Services, all in Burbank. As an extra, you can wait to be discovered, but that's not a very reliable way of making a living.

Acclaimed actor Edward James Olmos ("Stand and Deliver," "Miami Vice," "Zoot Suit") said the best place for aspiring actors to get training and experience is at a community college or university drama department. From there, get theater experience, gradually increase the importance of your roles, and go where your talents take you. But be prepared for rejection and intermittent employment. Olmos said he started his acting career in the drama department of East Los Angeles College in 1964.

"I went into it not so much to become an actor, but to find out who I was and how best to use what I had as a person. I went on to Cal State Los Angeles and then to do regional theater. Fourteen years after I started, I starred in 'Zoot Suit' on Broadway," Olmos said. "You can never tell how well you're doing at any given moment, so you have to keep trying to be the best you can be. You can't rest on your laurels."

KEY EMPLOYERS IN THE
MOTION PICTURE INDUSTRY

The Burbank Studios
4000 Warner Boulevard
Burbank, CA 91522
818/954-6000

Cannon Group Inc.
640 S. San Vicente Boulevard
Los Angeles, CA 90048
213/658-2100

Columbia Pictures/Sony
Columbia Plaza
Burbank, CA 91505
818/954-6000

De Laurentiis Entertainment
  Group Inc.
8670 Wilshire Boulevard
Beverly Hills, CA 90211
213/854-7000

Walt Disney Co.
500 S. Buena Vista Street
Burbank, CA 91521
818/840-1000

Sid and Marty Krofft Productions
1040 N. Las Palmas Avenue
Los Angeles, CA 90038
213/467-3125

Lorimar Film Entertainment
10202 W. Washington Boulevard
Culver City, CA 90230
213/202-2000

MCA Inc.
100 Universal City Plaza
Universal City, CA 91608
818/777-1000

Metro-Goldwyn-Mayer Pictures
  Inc. (MGM)
10000 Washington Boulevard
Culver City, CA 90232
213/280-6000

MGA/UA Communications Co.
450 N. Roxbury Drive
Beverly Hills, CA 90210
213/281-4000

New Horizons Picture Corp.
600 Main Street
Venice, CA 90291
213/399-9151

Orion Pictures Corp.
1888 Century Park East
Los Angeles, CA 90067
213/282-2500

Paramount Pictures
5555 Melrose Avenue
Los Angeles, CA 90038
213/468-5000

Aaron Spelling Productions Inc.
1041 N. Formosa Avenue
West Hollywood, CA 90046
213/850-2413

Touchstone Pictures
500 S. Buena Vista Street
Burbank, CA 91521
818/840-5045

Tri-Star Pictures
1875 Century Park East
Los Angeles, CA 90067
213/201-2300

Twentieth Century Fox Film Corp.
10201 W. Pico Boulevard
Los Angeles, CA 90035
213/277-2211

United Artist Pictures
450 Roxbury Drive
Beverly Hills, CA 90210
213/281-4000

Universal Pictures
100 Universal City Plaza
Universal City, CA 91608
818/777-1000

Warner Communications
4000 Warner Boulevard
Burbank, CA 91522
818/954-6000

PROFESSIONAL ORGANIZATIONS

**Academy of Motion Picture Arts
and Sciences**
8949 Wilshire Boulevard
Beverly Hills, CA 90211
213/278-8990

American Cinema Editors Inc.
4416½ Finley Avenue
Los Angeles, CA 90027
213/660-4425

American Film Institute
2021 N. Western Avenue
Los Angeles, CA 90027
213/856-7600

**American Society of
Cinematographers**
1782 Orange Drive
Los Angeles, CA 90028
213/876-5080

Directors Guild of America
7920 Sunset Boulevard
Los Angeles, CA 90046
213/289-2000

**Motion Picture Association of
America**
14144 Ventura Boulevard
Sherman Oaks, CA 91423
818/995-3600

Producers Guild of America
292 S. La Cienega Boulevard
Beverly Hills, CA 90211
213/557-0807

Screen Actors Guild
7065 Hollywood Boulevard
Los Angeles, CA 90028
213/465-4600

**Southern California Motion Pic-
ture Council**
1922 N. Western Avenue
Los Angeles, CA 90010
213/871-0551

**Stuntmen's Association of Motion
Pictures**
4810 Whitsett Avenue
North Hollywood, CA 91607
818/766-4334

Women in Film
6464 Sunset Boulevard
Los Angeles, CA 90028
213/463-6040

Writers Guild of America West
8955 Beverly Boulevard
Los Angeles, CA 90048
213/550-1000

PROFESSIONAL PUBLICATIONS

American Cinematographer (Los Angeles, CA)
American Film Magazine (Los Angeles, CA)
Back Stage (New York, NY)
Cashbox (New York, NY)
Drama Logue (Los Angeles, CA)
Film Comment (New York, NY)
Hollywood Reporter (Los Angeles, CA)
Premiere (New York, NY)
Variety (Los Angeles, CA)

DIRECTORIES

Annual Index of Motion Picture Credits (Academy of Motion Picture Arts and Sciences, Beverly Hills, CA)
Back Stage File/Tape/Syndication Directory (Back Stage Publications, New York, NY)
Blue Book (Hollywood Reporter, Los Angeles, CA)
Film Producers, Studios and Agents Guide (Packard Publishing, Beverly Hills, CA)
Pacific Coast Studio Directory (Pacific Coast Studio, Los Angeles, CA)
Who's Who in the Motion Picture Industry (Packard Publishing, Beverly Hills, CA)

CHAPTER 34

The Television Industry

*The explosion of independent
stations, cable, and home video
has created myriad opportunities.*

Television is a hectic, whirlwind business experiencing a heady
growth trend, but employment prospects are characteristically
spotty. The phenomenal rise of independent stations, cable, and
home video over the past decade has opened the field and created
opportunities in markets where literally none existed before, not
only in programming, news, and sports, but increasingly in original
productions.

"The television industry is doing very, very well," affirmed
Jack Kyser, chief economist for the Los Angeles Area Chamber
of Commerce, "and the prospects for the future are bright,
primarily due to the development of videocassettes and the
opening of foreign television markets."

For most people involved with the creative side of television,
the industry doesn't promise much security. TV executives are
constantly trying to please audiences and edge out competitors,
so even the most critically acclaimed shows are often axed at
mid-season. However, a popular series like "The Cosby Show"
may air for several years. Moreover, some shows canceled by
the networks, such as "Molly Dodd," are now being picked up
by cable channels like Lifetime.

"It's a very tough business," observed James Parriott, former
executive producer of the short-lived "Elvis" TV series who is
currently employed by New World Entertainment's television

division. Writing "probably is the strongest place to start," he said. "This business runs on scripts. There's always a need for good material." As a writer, Parriott said, the only way to get steady solid work is by writing outstanding material. "There are a ton of very bad writers who aren't working. But the writers who are good are all working."

Good material can pay well, too. The minimum fee for a one-hour network prime-time story and teleplay is $18,000, while a script for a two-hour movie of the week pays at least $37,000, said Cheryl Rhoden, public relations director for the Writers Guild of America West. (An original motion picture treatment and screenplay, by contrast, garners at least $60,000.)

"Once you get a staff assignment on TV, you basically give over your life to your work," Rhoden said. "Before and during the season, which runs from September to March, you work incredibly long hours with only a small hiatus. When you're successful, the rewards are great—people become wealthy. But the pressure is great and you work long, long hours."

There is no set formula for becoming a television writer. Most aspiring writers work at their screenplay or teleplay on the side, perhaps taking an occasional writing class through the Writers' Program at UCLA Extension. If you are serious about writing, your best bet is to enroll in a degree program in screenwriting or cinema-television at a film school, such as USC or UCLA.

Parriott, who also wrote and directed the movie "Heart Condition," said he was able to sign with an agent before he graduated with a master's degree from UCLA's motion picture/television department. "My agent submitted my work to the studios, they showed an interest, and that's how I got in. That's still the best way in the business. It's also one of the hardest and most competitive. You have to have completed scripts in hand. You can't even get an agent without a body of completed work."

Upon request, the Writers Guild for $1 will provide a list of recommended literary agents in the Los Angeles area. The guild also has a library open to the public filled with award-winning scripts of the past and videotape seminars that feature famous writers talking about various aspects of screenwriting, Rhoden said. In addition, the Writers Guild will register any written material for a $20 fee, documenting its date of origin.

The guild's library, located at 8955 Beverly Boulevard in West Hollywood, is open on Mondays, Wednesdays, and Fridays from 9:30 a.m. to 5:30 p.m. The main number is (213) 550-1000.

Writers with sellable scripts and marketable ideas for shows who attract the attention of network executives frequently become the directors and executive producers of prime-time television and, sometimes, network executives themselves.

Executive television producers are the counterparts of motion picture directors. They are the main creative force behind a show. As such, they usually come up with the original concept, and work closely with writers to develop scripted material for production. Very often they'll do a substantial portion of the rewriting themselves, Parriott said. Executive producers also hire the director, oversee the staff, and help cast the talent.

But the day-to-day running of a show is left to the line producer. Line producers work on location or in the studio—wherever the show is shot—ensuring that the production goes as planned.

Directors in television don't have the same creative-genius status as motion picture directors. Although they play an important creative role in a show's production, they have little input as to its direction. Directors work with the actors and executive producer on interpreting the script. They are heavily involved in the preproduction aspects of planning. During the filming, they orchestrate the production. Afterward, they may have a hand in the editing process for shows that are taped. Below the director are assistant directors who help the director with all the technical elements of a show. (For more on becoming an assistant director, see Chapter 33.)

In television, the pace is much faster than in the movie industry. Deals are made, scripts are written, and shows are produced in a fraction of the time allotted to a major motion picture production. A half-hour episode for a TV series typically takes a week to rehearse and shoot, a two-hour made-for-TV movie, two weeks. The filming of a major feature-length film, on the other hand, can consume six months or more. The main reason is money. A movie may be shot on a $60 million budget, while a TV series is lucky to receive $500,000 per half-hour episode.

Television is the primary source of employment for actors, said Mark Locher, national communications director for the Screen Actors Guild. "Other than your multimillion-dollar motion picture, the best way to make a really good living as an actor today is to work on a series. If it runs for more than three or four years, it may go into syndication. With residuals (payment for reruns), that can pay you for the rest of your life." SAG members earn a minimum of $414 daily, or $1,440 weekly for speaking parts.

Another source of steady income for actors is commercials, which pay a minimum of $366 a day. Some 40 to 45 percent of all SAG member earnings are from commercials, Locher said. "Doing commercials, you might make three to four times more in residuals than what you originally were paid. On just one national commercial, you can earn $10,000 to $20,000."

But, Locher warned, fewer than 3,500 of SAG's 73,000 members nationwide earned more than $50,000 in 1989. Average SAG earnings are about $10,500 a year. "For most actors, if they get six SAG jobs a year, that's a really good year," Locher said.

However, the Screen Actors Guild is not an employment service for actors, he stressed. To join, you need to have worked at least once in a principal, or speaking, role. Like the Writers Guild, SAG will provide a list of recommended talent agents and a compilation of available acting workshops upon request for $1.

"We get calls from people all the time who have no experience whatsoever," Locher said. "There's a lot of 'get-discovered' schemes in this business, but we generally advise people to get legitimate training. Put your money into practicing real skills—voice lessons, acting lessons, physical fitness.

"The more skills you have, the more employable you are. If you can only act, that limits your job prospects. But if you can act and sing and dance, that expands your employment possibilities significantly. The more versatile you are, the better chance you have of landing a role."

For college students, the Academy of Television Arts & Sciences in North Hollywood offers an eight-week internship program that exposes participants to such diverse areas of the television industry as business affairs, art direction, cinematography, directing, and network programming.

The TV Academy also has an extensive library with reference books, ratings information, trade publications, scripts, storyboards, set designs, animation and production stills, recordings, and oral history tapes, said Shirley Kennedy, library archivist.

KEY EMPLOYERS IN THE TELEVISION INDUSTRY

ABC Entertainment
2040 Avenue of the Stars
Los Angeles, CA 90067
213/557-7777

Barris Industries Inc.
1990 S. Bundy Drive
Beverly Hills, CA 90212
213/278-9550

CBS Entertainment
7800 Beverly Boulevard
Los Angeles, CA 90036
213/852-2345

Dick Clark Productions
3003 W. Olive Avenue
Burbank, CA 91505
818/841-3003

Columbia Pictures Television
Columbia Plaza
Burbank, CA 91505
818/954-6000

Walt Disney Co.
500 S. Buena Vista Street
Burbank, CA 91521
818/840-1000

Ralph Edwards Productions
1717 N. Highland Avenue
Los Angeles, CA 90028
213/462-2212

Fox Television
5746 Sunset Boulevard
Los Angeles, CA 90028
213/462-7111

**Gulf & Western Entertainment
  Division**
5555 Melrose Avenue
Los Angeles, CA 90038
213/466-4215

Hanna-Barbera Productions Inc.
3400 Cahuenga Boulevard
Los Angeles, CA 90028
213/851-5000

Landsburg Co.
11811 W. Olympic Boulevard
Los Angeles, CA 90064
213/478-7878

**MGM-UA Television Productions
  Inc.**
10000 Washington Boulevard
Culver City, CA 90232
213/280-6000

MTM Productions
4024 Radford Avenue
Studio City, CA 91604
818/760-5000

NBC Productions
4640 Lankershim Boulevard
North Hollywood, CA 91602
818/840-4623

New World Productions
1440 S. Sepulveda Boulevard
Los Angeles, CA 90025
213/444-8100

Orion Pictures Corp.
1888 Century Park East
Los Angeles, CA 90067
213/282-2500

United Television Inc.
8501 Wilshire Boulevard
Suite 340
Beverly Hills, CA 90211
213/854-0426

Warner Brothers Television
4000 Warner Boulevard
Burbank, CA 91522
818/954-6000

For a listing of television stations, see Chapter 43 on broadcasting.

PROFESSIONAL ORGANIZATIONS

Academy of Television Arts and Sciences
3500 W. Olive Avenue
Burbank, CA 91505
818/953-7575

Alliance of Motion Picture and Television Producers
14144 Ventura Boulevard
Sherman Oaks, CA 91423
818/995-3600

Association of Independent Television Stations
5455 Wilshire Boulevard
Suite 1209
Los Angeles, CA 90036
213/932-1200

Writers Guild of America West
8955 Beverly Boulevard
Los Angeles, CA 90048
213/550-1000

PROFESSIONAL PUBLICATIONS

Cable Television Business (Englewood, CO)
Drama Logue (Los Angeles, CA)
Emmy (Burbank, CA)
Hollywood Reporter (Los Angeles, CA)
Television International Magazine (Los Angeles, CA)
Television/Radio Age (New York, NY)
The TV Executive (New York, NY)
TV Executive Daily (New York, NY)
Variety (Los Angeles, CA)

DIRECTORIES

Blue Book (Hollywood Reporter, Los Angeles, CA)
International Television and Video Almanac (Quigley Publishing Co., New York, NY)
Who's Who in Television (Packard Publishing, Beverly Hills, CA)
The Working Actor's Guide, L.A. (Paul Flattery Productions, Los Angeles, CA)

The Lure of Hollywood

*Stargazers flock to the movie capital by the
thousands in pursuit of the elusive myth.*

You can tell who they are by that eager, self-assured look in their eyes. In conversation, they'll casually drop the name of every hot director in town and the movies they've directed. Before you finish talking, gossipy stories about Oliver Stone, Sylvester Stallone, Warren Beatty, and Madonna will roll off their tongues like trade secrets. No exchange would be complete without mention of the shows they've personally appeared in and the projects currently being shot.

Behold the stargazers—the aspiring actors, screenwriters, and moviemakers who have flocked to Hollywood by the thousands since the major studios set up shop in the 1920s. Many get on the set by working as extras. Others hold a "normal job," taking acting classes or writing scripts during their off-hours. Still others petition the studios or bus tables, hoping to intimate their talents in a chance encounter with the right producer or director.

"People come out here because they think they're going to be discovered," said Mitchell Fink, society columnist for *People* magazine and entertainment reporter for Fox Entertainment News. "There are so many stories that are legendary about Hollywood that people believe they can actually do that. People are attracted to the lifestyle."

For most, attending premieres, mingling with the stars, and leading a glamorous life are part of an elusive myth. Only a select few ever achieve actual stardom. Still, they come from far and near in a never-ending stream, all looking for their 15 minutes of fame. "We can just sit here and without any effort or outreach on our part get bombarded with phone calls and résumés," said Leslee Pearlstein, vice president of human resources for the Twentieth Century Fox Film Corp.

Employment opportunities in the screen trade vary wildly, depending on who you talk to—and who you know. "There's an impression out there that the entertainment industry is very closed and hard to break into. But that's mainly if you're looking at higher-level positions," said Michael Wittern, director of human resources for MCA-Universal City Studios. "If it is closed, it's only because the industry takes care of its own. The studios do promote from within. The way is to get your foot in the door, and don't despair."

People are drawn to the screen trade for reasons as diverse as the business itself.

"I went into it because I love film and I think I have something to say," said Bert Jayasekera, a production coordinator for Fox Broadcasting who took some film courses while attending UCLA. "Ever since high school, I've always loved movies, but I never thought it was possible to work in the movie business. Going to UCLA and checking out their film program reawakened that dream I had when I was younger. After reading up on it, I decided it's not that bad. You don't have to be a producer's son."

Like countless other Angelenos, Jayasekera is working on a screenplay. In the tradition of many now famous writer-directors (called "hyphenates" because of their dual responsibilities) before him, his ultimate aspiration is to write and direct a major feature-length film. Each year, the Writers Guild of America West registers 25,000 scripts. Only a fraction of those are ever sold. Even fewer go into production.

In Hollywood, "it seems like everybody's a writer," said Pearlstein of Twentieth Century Fox. "I know attorneys here who are writing scripts at night."

The promise of turning dreams into reality—both on the screen and in real life—is one of Hollywood's strongest drawing points. "Movies promise a dream," Fink said. "It's an unreal dream, but so are the movies. When you go to a show, the idea is the suspension of disbelief—to be swayed by the story. The movie industry is that. Coming here means to suspend disbelief."

The lure of Hollywood is so strong that even the remotest chances to break in are jumped at. A call put out over various L.A. radio stations for some 20,000 extras to appear in the 1990 shooting of Oliver Stone's movie "The Doors" (based on the life of rock legend Jim Morrison) was answered by more than enough late 1960s look-alikes. Fink said a facetious item he once wrote at the end of his *People* magazine column produced an enormous unexpected response.

"The item was about Michael J. Fox and James Woods starring in a movie together called 'The Hard Way.' When I wrote it, the woman's role was not yet cast. So I got on the phone with the producer and asked, 'Well, what are you looking for?' He told me an actress who was older than Fox but younger than Woods—not a drop-dead model type, but a more earthy, comedienne type.

"I wrote the item saying what they were looking for and I added one line that *People* magazine wasn't happy with. I said, 'Are there any takers out there?' We were just *besieged* with women calling from all over the U.S. saying they were between those ages, sending us pictures, résumés, asking how can they get in touch," said Fink, astounded. "The pull of Hollywood is constant. It's been this way for years."

The starry-eyed hopefuls who do land in Hollywood often find that the movie industry rarely measures up to their expectations. To lessen the impact and avoid being totally disillusioned, industry insiders advise celebrity seekers to take a few reality pills before arriving in Tinseltown and knocking on doors. In the immortal words of Shakespeare, all that glisters is not gold.

"Despite all the glamour, the jobs don't always pay very well," said Joe McBride, a reporter who covers the motion picture industry for *Daily Variety*. "You read about the Eddie Murphys, but there are very few around. For a $60 million movie, there's only one person directing it. A lot of the budget goes to a handful of people. Back in the 1920s and 1930s, they used to take out ads telling people not to come to Hollywood because there were very few openings. Sure, there's a glamour attraction to L.A., but there's a lot of heartbreak involved, too."

Nowhere in Hollywood will you find a more frustrated class of professionals than actors. Of the approximately 34,000 people who belong to the Screen Actors Guild (SAG) in Southern California—actors who have held principal, or speaking, roles— a whopping 80 percent earn less than $5,000 a year.

"On any given work day, about 10 percent of our members are working," said Mark Locher, SAG's national communications director. "That translates into a 90 percent unemployment rate. The reality is, the majority of our members are part-time actors. At least 85 percent have survival jobs to pay the bills.

"People shouldn't go into acting unless they have to, unless they have such strong drive and determination that they can't be talked out of it. It takes that kind of dedication, that kind of commitment. If you're lukewarm or not sure, you're probably not going to make it."

Some studio executives counsel people from out of the area *against* moving to Los Angeles for the express purpose of finding a job in the entertainment industry, particularly if they are under the assumption that fame and fortune will come easy.

"There's a misperception that money is just given out freely," said Janet Wood, vice president of human resources for MCA-Universal City Studios. "But there's nothing casual about it. I don't think anyone should come here *just* to work in the film business. If this is the place they want to live, then applying to the studios should be part of their job search. But to come out to be in the movies, hey, how many dreams are broken every day? This can be a pretty rugged place to be."

At the other end of the spectrum are those who dismiss the heartbreak warning as a flag habitually waved by people in the industry to keep outsiders from coming here, or an excuse employed by the insecure for never showing the world where their true talents lie, and therefore robbing themselves of potential success.

"Some succeed, some don't. But it's not the big heartbreak some people think it is," said Shirley Kennedy, library archivist for the Academy of Television Arts and Sciences. "Lives aren't destroyed. If anything, you're better off for having tried. Go for what you want. Settle later, but not when you begin. If you are successful in almost any area, you'll make all the money you'll ever need. That's the goal and that's the possibility."

Dreams can come true, as they did for *People* magazine's Fink when he moved to L.A. from New York in 1978 with little more than a background in the music industry.

"The odds are enormously against you, but how could I discourage anybody from trying to do what I did? I came out here really between careers and had absolutely nothing. I talked my way into a job covering rock and roll for the (now defunct) *Los Angeles Herald Examiner* and, ultimately, it changed my life. The thing you have to remember in this town is not to measure yourself in terms of other people's success. I don't care who you are, you're going to be disappointed."

Service
Industry
Careers

CHAPTER 35

The Hotel Industry

The doors of opportunity are open in this booming business.

The welcome mat is out at hotels, not only for travelers, but for workers as well. The fast-growing hospitality industry has created opportunity for job seekers who are good with people, service-oriented, or have management skills. You'd be hard-pressed to find any line of work in the Los Angeles area that is more accommodating, especially at the entry level.

Through the mid-1990s, a bevy of new hotels being built from Long Beach to Pasadena will need everything from skilled workers to sophisticated marketing executives to meet their staffing needs. "The industry's crying out for help so badly that if you have experience and knowledge, they're going to hire you," said Barbara Thomas, director of the American College of Hotel and Restaurant Management in North Hollywood. "It's absolutely a good time to be in the field."

There are 30 hotels with almost 12,000 rooms either planned or currently being built in Los Angeles County, according to the Los Angeles County Hotel and Motel Group. Over the next few years, these new ventures will add to the area's 65,000 existing hotel rooms by almost 20 percent. "The amount of growth is pretty staggering," remarked Lloyd Axelrod, vice president of public relations for the Southern California Visitors' and Convention Bureau.

From 1987 to 1992, the Employment Development Department projects that the number of job openings at hotels and motels in Los Angeles and Orange counties will increase 16.8 percent, from 55,600 to an estimated 64,925.

"One of the things you can be comfortable with in this industry is that it's a service industry, and the need to travel to conduct business and for leisure is always going to be there. The travel, tourism, and hotel industry is very vital to our regional economy," Axelrod said.

The hotel industry is divided into three basic employment areas that require vastly different skills: front of the house, back of the house, and sales/marketing positions. The first two are where most of the entry-level opportunities are clustered.

Front of the House

Front-of-the-house jobs, including bell attendant, front desk clerk, reservation clerk, and, in food service, waiter and busboy, are high profile and involve a considerable amount of contact with the public. Consequently, a premium is placed on maintaining a positive attitude and a well-kept appearance. Having good people skills is a must. Putting your best foot forward and seeing that guests are happy is equally important.

Applicants for entry-level jobs are often screened for attitude and appearance beginning with their first interaction with the front desk, said Anne Hanson, director of human resources for the Beverly Hilton Hotel. "You want someone who is cooperative and believes [he or she] can make a difference and who does everything for the guests. The most important thing is being friendly, being able to remain calm when there is pressure from someone who's upset. Just having that special touch."

"What really brings [guests] back to the property is not the amenities of the luxurious rooms, but the feeling they have when they leave the hotel," added Carl Cusato, vice president of Paul R. Ray & Co., an executive search firm that specializes in the leisure industry. "It really is an attitude that permeates the organization." The product, Cusato said to remember, is service.

Back of the House

People in back-of-the-house positions work behind the scenes in such jobs as room attendant, kitchen worker, cook, telephone operator, and parking valet. Room attendants are the biggest class of hotel employees, with a substantial number also working in food service, but there are also some entry-level office openings, including spots for bookkeepers and reservationists.

When contemplating a career move in the hospitality business, think of ways you can parlay your background and existing skills into different jobs. You may find that the grass is greener in another department. This is especially true at fine hotels with good reputations and low turnover rates.

"Say someone's a great secretary. That person can go into the catering department and become a secretary in catering and move up that way," Thomas said. Added Cusato: "Sometimes some situations are so static you have to move sideways before you move up and find the niche that is appropriate for you."

Hotels require continuous maintenance, so there are plenty of opportunities in the trades as well. Most front- and back-of-the-house jobs pay $6 to $10 an hour, plus tips where called for, to start. "Making $13 in the hotel or restaurant industry (in a back-of-the-house position) is not the reality," said Steve Dornbusch, business representative for the Hotel and Restaurant Employees Union Local 11, which represents about 12,000 hotel workers. "But it is possible to make over scale by being the best at whatever it is you do."

Sales/Marketing

People who work in sales and marketing, usually called hotel representatives, are responsible for making sure that hotel rooms are full as often as possible. Hotel reps either work on-site or as independent contractors, soliciting business from companies, travel agents, and tour operators.

Reps aren't reservationists. Their job is to generate enthusiasm about a particular locale or hotel. Reps frequently travel to trade shows to network and solicit new business. When they're not traveling, they're making sales calls, using the telephone as their primary business tool. "I've made 14 solicitation calls this morning and it's not even 11 o'clock yet," said Scott Feinerman, marketing and sales manager for the Singapore Carlton Hotel.

Independent reps may work on a commission or retainer basis, filling up rooms for hotels internationally. With many travelers and companies looking eastward, the Pacific Rim is a good place to develop a specialty. "The Orient has identified Southern California to be their No. 1 market," said Carmencita Galicia, western regional sales director for Mandarin Singapore International Hotels.

On-site reps, beginning as sales coordinators, may start at $24,000 a year working for a single hotel. Regional salespeople may make $35,000 to $45,000 a year, while someone selling the whole of North America may bring in $60,000 to $90,000 annually, Galicia said. Retainer fees for independent reps can reach upward of $1,000 a month or more, Feinerman said. Working for more than one hotel group increases reps' salaries.

What does it take to be a successful rep? "It's a game of being organized, persistent, and enthusiastic. You have to keep your exuberance and get people to listen to what you have to say," said Feinerman, who also represents seven hotels in the Sahid Group of Indonesia.

Sales rep positions usually require previous sales and marketing or hotel experience. "It's very hard to be a novice and go right into sales," said Thomas, a former general manager of the Royal Inn in Columbus, Ohio. "The industry is looking for good, qualified people. Hotel managers are tired of hiring actors who work for five days and then all of a sudden disappear."

In general, starting at a "fine house," or luxury hotel, provides the best all-around learning experience, Thomas said. But first-class hotels tend to attract the most qualified and highly trained workers, so it might not be possible to be hired without training or previous experience. Most cooks at fine houses, for example, have culinary arts degrees, Dornbusch said.

Is getting a formal education necessary? That depends on what your goals are. A bachelor's degree in hotel and restaurant administration can lead directly to an entry-level management position. Some schools that offer four-year degrees in hotel management include Cal Poly Pomona, Cornell University in New York, the University of Denver, the University of Nevada, Las Vegas, the University of Hawaii, and Washington State University.

In addition, many community colleges and vocational schools offer certificate and degree programs in hospitality.

In the American College of Hotel and Restaurant Management's 6- to 14-month program, professionals from the hospitality industry teach students "everything that is relevant to the business," Thomas said. Graduates from the school may start as a front desk clerk, concierge, housekeeping supervisor, or as an assistant restaurant manager, Thomas said. The cost for the program ranges from $2,390 to $7,190.

Formal education may enable you to bypass a lot of the front desk positions and result in a salaried job offer, but starting at an hourly position—where most of the openings are—does not preclude an eventual promotion to management.

Indeed, most large hotels offer their own training programs to promising employees. "Many of our senior people started at the entry level," Hanson said. "Say someone joins as a front desk clerk. (He or she) could be promoted to reception manager, assistant director, director, and, ultimately, general manager."

L.A. County's 10 Largest Hotels*

Hotel	Rooms & Suites	Employees
Westin Bonaventure	1,540	1,200
L.A. Airport Hilton & Towers	1,359	750
Century Plaza Hotel	1,148	1,250
Los Angeles Airport Marriott	1,031	1,700
Los Angeles Hilton & Towers	935	900
Sheraton Plaza La Reina Hotel	810	572
Airport Marina Hotel	757	250
Stouffer Concourse Hotel	750	685
Biltmore Hotel	724	600
Hacienda Hotel	640	300

*Ranked by number of rooms and suites.

SOURCE: Los Angeles Area Chamber of Commerce; hotels.

KEY EMPLOYERS IN THE HOTEL INDUSTRY

Beverly Hills Hotel
964 Sunset Boulevard
Beverly Hills, CA 90210
213/276-2251

Beverly Wilshire Hotel
9500 Wilshire Boulevard
Beverly Hills, CA 90212
213/275-4282

Biltmore Hotel
506 S. Grand Avenue
Los Angeles, CA 90071
213/624-1011

Century Plaza Towers
2049 Century Park East
Los Angeles, CA 90067
213/552-8100

Disneyland Hotel
1150 W. Cerritos Street
Anaheim, CA 92808
714/778-6600

Hollywood Roosevelt Hotel
7000 Hollywood Boulevard
Los Angeles, CA 90028
213/466-7000

Hotel Meridien
4500 MacArthur Boulevard
Newport Beach, CA 92660
714/476-2001

Hyatt Regency Los Angeles Hotel
711 S. Hope Street
Los Angeles, CA 90017
213/683-1234

Loew's Santa Monica Beach Hotel
1700 Ocean Park Boulevard
Santa Monica, CA 90405
213/458-6700

Los Angeles Hilton & Towers
930 Wilshire Boulevard
Los Angeles, CA 90017
213/629-4321

Ma Maison Sofitel
8555 Beverly Boulevard
Los Angeles, CA 90048
213/278-5444

The New Otani Hotel And Garden
120 S. Los Angeles Street
Los Angeles, CA 90012
213/629-1200

The Registry Hotel
555 Universal Terrace Parkway
Universal City, CA 91608
818/506-2500

Sheraton-Anaheim Hotel
1015 West Ball Road
Anaheim, CA 92802
714/778-1700

Torrance Marriott Hotel
3635 Fashion Way
Torrance, CA 90503
213/316-3636

Westin Bonaventure
404 S. Figueroa Street
Los Angeles, CA 90071
213/624-1000

PROFESSIONAL ORGANIZATIONS

**California Hotel & Motel
Association**
414 29th Street
Sacramento, CA 95816
916/444-5780

**Council on Hotel, Restaurant and
Institutional Education**
1200 17th Street, NW
Washington, DC 20036
202/331-5990

**Hospitality Lodging and Travel
Research Foundation**
c/o American Hotel and Motel
Association
1201 New York Avenue, NW
Washington, DC 20005
202/289-3117

**Hotel and Restaurant Employees
Union Local 11 AFL-CIO**
321 S. Bixel Street
Los Angeles, CA 90017
213/481-8530

**Hotel Sales Marketing Association
International**
1300 L Street, NW
Suite 800
Washington, DC 20005
202/789-0089

**Los Angeles County Hotel and
Motel Group**
c/o Southern California Businessmen's Association
727 W. Seventh Street
Suite 903
Los Angeles, CA 90017
213/624-7739

PROFESSIONAL PUBLICATIONS

The Cornell Hotel and Restaurant Administration Quarterly (Ithaca, NY)
Hotel & Motel Management (Cleveland, OH)
Hotel-Motel Professional (Denver, CO)
Hotel & Resort Industry (New York, NY)
Hotels & Restaurants International (Des Plaines, IL)
Meetings & Conventions (Secaucus, NJ)

DIRECTORIES

Directory of Hotel and Motel Systems (American Hotel & Motel Association, New York, NY)

Directory: Meetings and Conventions Magazine (Murdoch Magazines, New York, NY)

Guide to Hospitality and Tourism Education (Council on Restaurant and Institutional Education, Washington, DC)

Hotel & Motel Red Book (American Hotel & Motel Association, New York, NY)

Lodging Hospitality—400 Top Performers Issue (Penton Publishing Co., Cleveland, OH)

CHAPTER 36

The Restaurant Industry

From "California cuisine" to fine dining,
Los Angeles basically has it all.

Jobs are on the menu. The sprawling Southern California restaurant trade is serving up stacks and stacks of them. In Los Angeles and Orange counties, an estimated 358,225 people will work in eating and drinking establishments by 1992, up 17 percent from the 306,800 employed in 1987, according to the Employment Development Department (EDD).

"There are so many different types of positions available," said Stan Kyker, executive vice president of the Southern California Restaurant Association. "The opportunities are pretty widespread. The industry is unique in that there is almost every type of restaurant available—from fast-food and ethnic to 'California cuisine' and fine white linen restaurants. Los Angeles basically has it all."

In Los Angeles County, an area known for its culinary diversity, the industry breaks out into more than 19,000 separate bars, grills, bar *and* grills, restaurants, sushi bars, bistros, delis, steak houses, eateries, diners, and coffee shops (not counting restaurants in hotels) that do over $6 billion in annual sales, Kyker said.

The five-county greater Los Angeles area is home to seven major restaurant corporations as well, including the Restaurant Enterprises Group (owner of Baxter's, Charley Brown's, Coco's, Reuben's, and others), Denny's, Big Boy Restaurants of America,

Jack-in-the-Box, Collins Foods International (the Sizzler, Naugles, and Kentucky Fried Chicken), and Velvet Turtle Restaurants.

The corporate headquarters of these companies are a major source of opportunity and a good destination for job seekers interested in the restaurant industry, according to Kyker. "A lot of people overlook the fact that there are jobs at the headquarters of those companies—in management, food purchasing, marketing, accounting, payrolling, training and development—in just about every area you can imagine."

Food sales in Los Angeles County have grown about 5 percent a year over the past five years, said Bruce Baltin, partner in the management consulting firm Pannell Kerr Forster, which specializes in the restaurant industry. Since increased sales generally translate into more job opportunity, the field should remain an ample source of employment for some time to come.

If you're thinking about a career in the restaurant industry, whether as a waiter, hostess, store manager, maitre d', or regional supervisor, it's important to have good people skills and the ability to think on your feet. Formal hospitality training is another ingredient to success.

"You have to be able to communicate on all levels, with customers and fellow personnel," said Jay Mazor, catering coordinator of the Seventh Street Bistro in downtown Los Angeles. "You have to be prepared to make snap decisions and know how to present yourself to people. Education isn't really the main factor."

However, a specialized degree in, say, catering, culinary arts, or restaurant and hotel management, can open up a whole new range of career possibilities, namely, in supervision or management. As far as opportunities in food service management go, there's no time like the present, Baltin said.

"There really is a shortage of skilled management personnel at all levels of the restaurant industry because of the growth of the industry."

Most community colleges offer two-year programs in the above areas. Several universities, including Cal Poly Pomona, Cornell University, the University of Denver, the University of Nevada, Las Vegas, and Washington State University, offer four-year degrees in restaurant and hotel management.

Degree programs in restaurant and hotel administration like the one offered by Cal Poly Pomona typically have a core set of business courses in accounting, marketing, and finance, plus specialized classes in hotel and restaurant management and law.

Students must also accumulate 800 hours of hospitality-related work experience in order to graduate.

"Typically, students graduating with this degree go into training programs with major restaurant corporations," said Peggy Larson, industry relations and programs coordinator for the James A. Collins Center for Hospitality Management at Cal Poly Pomona. "Not only do they have the courses that are specific to the industry, they also have the work experience to back it up."

Tony Falls, director of management training and development for Coco's-California, said his company has a nine-week manager trainee program for recent college graduates that leads to an assistant manager position at one of the chain's 83 restaurants statewide.

From there, a promising employee might become an associate manager and then general manager of an individual store. The next step is to area supervisor in charge of six or seven stores. Area supervisors have the opportunity of becoming a regional director of operations and eventually moving on to vice president of operations for the entire corporation.

With the responsibilities of restaurant operators becoming more and more complex, Falls advises job seekers to get an education in restaurant and hotel administration. "Sometimes you can learn from the school of hard knocks. But if you have the opportunity, then I would say go to school. The business is a little harder than it was a few years ago. Managers have to be more knowledgeable."

Recent graduates can expect to make an annual salary in the low- to mid-$20,000 range, but with a few years' experience that figure can easily push $30,000, according to Baltin. For an experienced accountant or management consultant specializing in restaurants, the salary starts at around $40,000 a year, he said.

Though entering the restaurant industry right out of school may be desirable, it's not essential, Baltin said. "It's an easy entry field. You can enter the job market at all different levels depending on what level of education you have. You can enter at an early or later stage in life."

Moreover, the field has been very receptive to women. In today's restaurant industry, women are no longer confined to hostess or waitress positions, Kyker said. Rather, "we're seeing a lot of women becoming upward-oriented in both the kitchen and in management." Added Louise Lewis, controller and manager of the Seventh Street Bistro: "If you look into a restaurant today, you see a lot more women than you used to. We have a young, dynamic female pastry chef and a female bartender."

One area within the restaurant industry that could use more qualified people is the business side, Baltin observed. Accountants, chief controllers, and food and beverage cost controllers who oversee an operation's income and expenditures are in particularly short supply, as are restaurant managers and even maitre d's.

"There's a strong need for people who know the industry and who are attuned to the business end as well," Baltin said. "It's a growing field, but it's a precarious one as well. Fifty percent of the restaurants that open close in their first year."

While the opportunities are bountiful, especially for those with a college education, working in the restaurant industry has a few drawbacks. For instance, the hours aren't for everyone. "People working in this industry are working when other people are playing. Meal hours are what we're dealing with for the most part," Kyker said. "It takes a special kind of person to do that."

The Recipe for Success

Bruce Baltin, partner in the Los Angeles consulting firm Pannell Kerr Forster, knows the restaurant business like the back of his hand. And that's not just because his company specializes in the restaurant industry.

Since joining the workforce as a freshman in high school in the late 1950s, the 47-year-old numbers man has worked in virtually every phase of the restaurant and hotel business—from dishwasher at a coffee shop to national director of Pannell Kerr Forster's management services group.

Baltin's casual demeanor and friendly appearance belie his corporate status. Yet his restaurant experience reads like a list of industry opportunities: busboy, waiter, short-order cook, purchasing agent, food and beverage manager, operations analyst, and management consultant.

After four summers of restaurant experience in high school, Baltin realized he was hooked on hospitality and enrolled in Cornell University's School of Hotel Administration, one of the premier hotel and restaurant programs in the country. "I knew at that point in life I liked the industry," Baltin said during a recent interview from his windowed office on the 18th floor of the One Wilshire Building in downtown Los Angeles.

Throughout his college career, Baltin supplemented his classroom instruction with actual experience. During his first summer away from school, he landed a job as a pantry man and purchasing agent at a boys' camp in Massachusetts. Over the next two summers, he worked as the food and beverage manager of a country club in Philadelphia.

As a senior at Cornell, Baltin started his own catering company when he and a classmate were asked by a couple of professors to cater a faculty party. "We decided it was good business, so we did it," Baltin recalled.

Upon graduating with a degree in hotel and restaurant administration in 1966, he went to work as an analyst for the Sheraton Hotel Corp. in Boston. Only a month later, he was called by the Coast Guard Reserve for active duty.

"We were on hurricane patrol for a good part of that period," he said. "The seaman apprentices were up in the crow's nests doing watch duty and so on. I didn't like that, so I told my superior officers I was a cook. I wound up cooking on a Coast Guard cutter for about 75 people."

After the Coast Guard, he went back to the Sheraton Corp. as a corporate operations analyst. The job, he said, "was basically to try to improve the operating efficiency of the hotels by analyzing financial statements and designing management reports." Eventually, it evolved into a special projects position.

"It was a phenomenal learning experience. I was 22 when I started there. Everybody else I worked with was in their 40s and 50s. There basically were five vice presidents and me. We were kind of like the operating committee."

In 1968, at the age of 26, Baltin went to teach as a lecturer at the University of Nevada, Las Vegas, which was just then opening a hotel school.

During his two years at UNLV, Baltin met a partner at Pannell Kerr Forster, then named Harris, Kerr, Forster & Co., and started working as a part-time consultant for the firm in the booming Las Vegas hotel industry in the summer. He also helped write a two-volume textbook on food and beverage operations.

Wanting to stay current in the industry, Baltin began a full-time career with Pannell Kerr Forster as a senior consultant in 1970 at age 28. He was summarily promoted to supervisor, then to manager of the management consulting department, and became a partner in 1978.

Given his broad range of experience, Baltin said, it was natural for him to end up in consulting. "I like consulting because you're constantly changing from one project to another. You're not mired down in a lot of the details of the day-to-day operations of a restaurant or hotel. You're seeing the big picture and watching changing trends. It's problem solving."

HEADQUARTER LOCATIONS OF KEY RESTAURANT INDUSTRY EMPLOYERS

Acapulco Restaurants
Regional Headquarters
2690 E. Foothill Boulevard
Pasadena, CA 91107
818/449-5467

Bob's Big Boy Restaurants
A Division of the Marriott Corp.
Post Office Box 311
Glendale, CA 91209
818/507-7700

Charthouse, CHE Inc.
115 S. Acadia Avenue
Solana Beach, CA 92075
619/755-8281

Collins Foods International
Divisional Headquarters
12655 Jefferson Boulevard
Los Angeles, CA 90066
213/827-2300

Denny's Inc.
Corporate Headquarters
16700 Valley View Avenue
La Mirada, CA 90637
714/739-8100

El Torito Restaurants Inc.
2540 White Road
Irvine, CA 92714
714/863-6400

Foodmaker Inc./Jack-in-the-Box
9330 Balboa Avenue
San Diego, CA 92123
619/571-2121

Grace Restaurant Co.
Corporate Headquarters
2701 Alton Avenue
Irvine, CA 92714
714/863-6300

Host International
A Division of the Marriott Corp.
3402 Pico Boulevard
Santa Monica, CA 90406
213/450-7566

Howard Johnson
5901 Green Valley Circle
Culver City, CA 90230
213/338-0574

**International House of Pancakes
(IHOP) Corp.**
Corporate Headquarters
6837 Lankershim Boulevard
North Hollywood, CA 91605
818/982-2620

Lawry's Restaurants
2950 Los Feliz Boulevard
Los Angeles, CA 90039
213/660-2720

PROFESSIONAL ORGANIZATIONS

**Council on Hotel, Restaurant and
Institutional Education**
c/o National Restaurant
Association
1200 17th Street, NW
Washington, DC 20036
202/331-5990

**Hotel and Restaurant Employees
Union Local 11 AFL-CIO**
321 S. Bixel Street
Los Angeles, CA 90017
213/481-8530

**National Association of Restaurant
Managers**
5322 W. 78th Way
Scottsdale, AZ 85253
602/946-0180

**National Restaurant Association
(NRA)**
1200 17th Street, NW
Washington, DC 20036
202/331-5900

**Restaurant Association of
California**
3780 Wilshire Boulevard
Los Angeles, CA 90010
213/384-1200

**Restaurant Association of Southern
California**
448 S. Hill Street
Los Angeles, CA 90071
213/628-3371

Restaurant Research Association
202 Fashion Lane
Tustin, CA 92680
714/731-7991

PROFESSIONAL PUBLICATIONS

Independent Restaurants (Duluth, MN)
Nation's Restaurant News (New York, NY)

Restaurant Business (New York, NY)
Restaurant Hospitality (Cleveland, OH)
Restaurant Row Magazine (Long Beach, CA)
Restaurants & Institutions (Des Plaines, IL)
Restaurants USA (Washington, DC)
Restaurateur (McLean, VA)

DIRECTORIES

Directory of Chain Restaurant Operators (Chain Store Guide Information Services, New York, NY)

Membership Directory (Society for Foodservice Management, Louisville, KY)

Restaurant Hospitality—500 Issue and Restaurant Industry Almanac Issue (Penton Publishing, Cleveland, OH)

Restaurants & Institutions—400 Issue (Cahners Publishing, Des Plaines, IL)

CHAPTER 37

The Airline Industry

Air travel is on an upward swing, signaling increased demand for pilots, ground workers, and customer service reps.

Getting a career off the ground is easy in the airline industry. If you're willing to travel and relocate, then landing a job with an airline company—whether as a pilot, customer service representative, or mechanic—is as simple as acquiring the necessary training or experience and applying for a position.

"Anyone with the desire can find a career," said Tammy Bechard, placement director for the Travel & Trade Career Institute in Long Beach. "All it takes is desire, dedication, and determination. You have to have the 'three Ds' to succeed."

The climate of the early 1990s is especially conducive to pursuing an airline career. Due to increased travel and the retirement of older employees, opportunities in the airline industry are expanding at 10 to 12 times their normal rate, said Kit Darby, executive vice president of the Future Aviation Professionals of America (FAPA) in Atlanta, Georgia, a nationwide aviation career information service.

A national retirement rate of 500 pilots a year, coupled with a 10 to 15 percent growth rate in the airline industry, has created an unprecedented demand for commercial pilots and air transportation workers, especially in California, which employs twice the number of airline industry employees as any other state, Darby said. Statewide, 92,800 people were employed in air transportation in 1989, according to the state Department of Finance.

In Los Angeles and Orange counties, home to 13 airports including the massive Los Angeles International Airport, or LAX, the number of air transportation workers is expected to grow modestly, from 41,625 in 1987 to an estimated 43,500 in 1992, according to state Employment Development Department projections.

For every new pilot hired, two flight attendants and one airplane mechanic are required, so the number of jobs in these support positions will continue to expand, too. "We're looking at a 10-year (nationwide) forecast calling for 50,000 mechanics, 100,000 flight attendants, and 50,000 to 60,000 pilots," Darby said. Many of these openings will be created through widespread retirements at airline companies, he said.

Securely established carriers like United Airlines, US Air, Delta Airlines, American Airlines, and Northwest Airlines routinely have full-time openings for customer service and sales representatives, ticketing agents, and air cargo workers, Bechard said. These days, when applying to an airline, it doesn't hurt to inquire into its financial condition, for if it's the target of a takeover bid, or if it's rapidly losing its market share to competitors, it might not exist in its present form for very much longer.

The above-mentioned airlines, all of which have many new planes on order, "now clearly dominate the field," Louis Marckesano, airline analyst with the Philadelphia brokerage firm Janney Montgomery Scott, told the *Los Angeles Times*. The weak sisters of Pan Am, Continental, Eastern, and TWA will fall further behind just by standing still—a sign that there may be additional consolidation in the airline industry, Marckesano added.

Beginning as a customer service rep is as good an introduction to the industry as any. Customer service reps and reservationists are paid only $5.75 to $7 an hour to start. But their low entry-level pay is augmented by a flexible work schedule and "wonderful travel benefits," Bechard said. Flight privileges apply to all airline employees and, eventually, to their spouses and dependents.

"They're usually completely discounted fares," Bechard said. "As an employee at Continental, for example, you can travel from Long Beach to Hong Kong via Dallas for $38. That's why most people go into the airlines—within the first three months you can work three weeks and take off one week. If you want the opportunity to see the world, you can do that in the travel industry regardless of what avenue you take."

The qualifications for flight attendants have changed in recent years, opening the field up to more men and middle-aged women. Even the name has changed. Remember when they were called stewardesses? "You don't have to be 21 with dimples anymore," said Sherrie Lehman, a former flight attendant at Continental Airlines. "You can start at 45. Maturity is important. Most young people are too immature to be thrust into a job on an airplane."

In order to be competitive, flight attendants applying for their first job should have at least two years of college or some vocational training behind them, Bechard said. Flight attendants with seniority can eventually make between $30,000 and $45,000 a year.

Vocational programs in the airline and travel-related industries—for customer service reps and travel agents as well as for pilots—aren't cheap. A six-month, career-oriented program at the Travel & Trade Career Institute for customer service reps, reservationists, flight attendants, and travel agents, for instance, costs around $4,500.

Pilot training, especially for flight instructors and commercial pilots, is complex and demanding. Aztec Air offers an intensive, five-month professional pilot program at the Long Beach Airport for $14,995. A four-year or at least a two-year college degree is preferred, said Julian Ponce, a flight instructor at Aztec Air. Students in the program must have vision correctable to 20-20. They also must pass a series of written, oral, and practical tests before they receive their commercial license and professional ratings.

To qualify for a commercial pilot's license, a pilot must accumulate at least 190 hours of flight time at a Federal Aviation Administration (FAA)–approved school. As flight instructors, pilots can then work toward their multi-engine instructor rating, eventually logging the 1,500 hours of multi-engine time necessary to be considered as a possible pilot candidate by a commuter airline, Ponce said.

When applying to a vocational school, check to see whether it is accredited and offers financial aid. (For more information about vocational schools, see the article at the end of Section 13.) Less costly travel-related seminars are periodically offered by UCLA Extension. And certain community colleges offer certificate and even degree programs in travel.

Upon graduating, don't expect miracles to happen. Most top airline executives began their careers at the bottom, steadily working their way up through the ranks. With promote-from-within policies, the airline industry affords very few outsiders the opportunity to land high-level jobs without first paying their dues. This is especially true of pilots. "Everything in the airline industry, all promotions, are strictly by seniority," said John Mazor, spokesman for the Airline Pilots Association in Washington, D.C.

"The way you advance is by becoming a captain of a commuter plane and then get on, say, as a flight engineer with a major commercial airline," Ponce said.

Beginning flight engineers on a 727 aircraft, a standard-size commercial plane where many pilots "earn their wings," start at about $24,000 a year, Darby said. But the pay rises quickly. After five years on the job, flight engineers make an average salary of $42,000. They may then become a second officer on an L-1011 or larger plane, making somewhere around $50,000.

From there, a second officer might become the first officer or copilot of a smaller jetliner, such as an MB-80, earning up to $60,000 a year. Eight to 12 years after becoming a second officer, a pilot might make captain of a large aircraft, such as a 747 or 767, and earn over $100,000 a year. The top 5 percent of all pilots make upward of $165,000, according to the FAPA.

"For that amount of money, a pilot will fly 80 hours a month. Since you have to be at the airport in uniform about twice that, you have your 40-hour week," Darby said. "Basically, what you have is a good middle manager being away from home a lot."

To maximize your income and receive the best potential offer as a pilot, you must be willing to relocate. "If you want to fly the biggest, fastest airplane as soon as possible and make the most money, then you're mobile," Darby said. "If you grow roots and don't want to be budged for any reason, you'll move up slower and make less money. But you'll be home more often."

The well-compensated people who fly the planes are expected to be in strong demand for some time to come. "We are now in the process of hiring pilots," said Neil Monroe, manager of public relations for Delta Airlines in Atlanta. "We're graduating a class a month right now, anywhere from 30 to 40 pilots. There's no way to predict the future, but we see a continuing demand."

Opportunities for FAA-certified technicians and airplane mechanics with airframe and power plant licenses have never been stronger, Darby said, largely due to the scores of back orders by the major carriers for new planes and the aging of the world's existing airline fleet. "In the past, we had a requirement of three to five years' experience. Today, we're seeing mechanics coming right out of trade school with no experience and going to work directly for the major airlines."

What Jobs in the Airline Industry Pay

Average Salary for Pilots	
Top for senior captains on largest aircraft	$165,000
Average for senior captains on largest aircraft	$107,000
Overall average for all pilots	$82,500
Copilots	$65,000
Flight engineers on large aircraft	$42,000
Commuter pilots	$40,000–$65,000
Beginning flight engineer	$24,000

Airplane Mechanics	
Beginning mechanic	$10–$15/hr.
Experienced mechanic	$40,000
Lead supervisor or foreman	$50,000

Flight Attendants	
Beginning flight attendant	$20,000
Experienced flight attendant	$20,000–$30,000
Senior flight attendant	$30,000–$45,000

Customer Service	
Beginning representative or reservationist	$5.75–$7/hr.

SOURCE: U.S. Bureau of Labor Statistics; Future Aviation Professionals of America (FAPA).

KEY EMPLOYERS IN THE AIRLINE INDUSTRY

Air Canada
200 World Way
Los Angeles, CA 90045
213/646-8848

Air New Zealand
380 World Way
Los Angeles, CA 90045
213/642-7227

Alaska Airlines
400 World Way
Los Angeles, CA 90045
213/417-1634

American Airlines
6310 W. San Vicente Boulevard
Los Angeles, CA 90048
213/935-6045

British Airways
6167 Bristol Parkway
Culver City, CA 90230
213/337-0747

Continental Airlines, Texas Air
600 World Way
Los Angeles, CA 90045
213/568-3100

Delta Airlines, Western
3701 Wilshire Boulevard
Los Angeles, CA 90010
213/736-1231

Hawaiian Air
6033 W. Century Boulevard
Los Angeles, CA 90045
213/215-1866

Mexicana Airlines
5757 W. Century Boulevard
Los Angeles, CA 90045
213/646-0401

Northwest Airlines
200 World Way
Los Angeles, CA 90045
213/646-7705

Pan American Airlines
5959 W. Century Boulevard
Los Angeles, CA 90045
213/646-8381

Skywest Airlines
600 World Way
Los Angeles, CA 90045
213/646-0096

Southwest Airlines
100 World Way
Los Angeles, CA 90045
213/215-5810

Trans World Airlines (TWA)
1545 Wilshire Boulevard
Suite 411
Los Angeles, CA 90017
213/413-7200

United Airlines
5950 Avion Drive
Los Angeles, CA 90045
213/417-2663

US Air
100 World Way
Los Angeles, CA 90045
213/646-0093

PROFESSIONAL ORGANIZATIONS

**Airline Flight Attendants
  Association**
Post Office Box 158
Buellton, CA 93427
805/688-8909

**Future Aviation Professionals of
  America**
4291-J Memorial Drive
Atlanta, GA 30032
800/JET-JOBS

**International Airline Employees
  Association**
5600 S. Central Avenue
Chicago, IL 60638
312/767-3333

**International Airline Pilots
  Association**
1625 Massachusetts Avenue, NW
Washington, DC 20036
202/797-4181

National Air Transportation Association
4226 King Street
Alexandria, VA 22302
703/845-9000

Orange County Aviation Council
18103 Sky Park South
Irvine, CA 92714
714/261-5650

PROFESSIONAL PUBLICATIONS

AirLine Employee (Chicago, IL)
AirLine Executive (Atlanta, GA)
AirLine Pilot (Herndon, VA)
Business & Commercial Aviation (White Plains, NY)
National Travel Career Bulletin (Buellton, CA)
Piloting Careers (Atlanta, GA)
Professional Pilot (Alexandria, VA)

DIRECTORIES

Airline Companies Directory (American Business Information Inc., Omaha, NE)
Airline Handbook (AeroTravel Research, Cranston, RI)
Aviation Distributors & Manufacturers Membership Directory (ADMA, Philadelphia, PA)
Official Membership Directory (National Air Transportation Association, Alexandria, VA)

CHAPTER 38

Travel Agent and Tour Operator

The job offers a chance to travel, but it's no vacation.

Tahiti, Acapulco, Paris, Cairo... You've got the urge to travel. But you're not independently wealthy, and your current job gives you neither the time nor money to go far. Don't despair. Your horizons are wide open in the travel industry.

Careers in travel, whether they involve leading groups through exotic lands, organizing tours from the home office, hosting guests aboard cruise lines, or selling travel packages at trade shows, all guarantee one thing: the opportunity to see the world.

"One of the biggest assets of the travel industry is that you don't have to sit at a desk all day," said Suzanne Graven-Smith, an L.A.-based independent travel director and consultant. "It's a marvelous industry to get into, but it's tough. You can't be afraid of a lot of hard work and long hours."

Deregulation in the airline industry, which practically doubled the number of passenger flights in the past decade, has intensified the already competitive travel business, causing the industry to fragment and become highly specialized, said Linda Frushon, promotions coordinator for United Vacations, a subsidiary of United Airlines, in Culver City.

From 1987 to 1992, the number of travel agents and clerks in Los Angeles and Orange counties is expected to grow 16.5 percent, from 8,600 in 1987 to an estimated 10,020 by 1992, according to state Employment Development Department projections. By mid-decade, the number of travel agents and clerks statewide should reach an estimated 24,350, up 38.7 percent from 1985, when 17,560 people were employed in the travel agent profession.

The broader category of passenger transportation arrangement companies, including travel agencies, tour operators, motorcoach operators, cruise ship lines, and the airlines, is growing at a slightly slower pace, said Jack Kyser, chief economist for the Los Angeles Area Chamber of Commerce. The focus here is on tour operators and travel agencies.

Tour Operators

Tour operators specialize in the planning and operation of pre-paid tours, acting as the wholesale packager and supplier to travel agents, who in turn act as the retailer to the consumer. As with the industry overall, the greatest opportunity is in sales. But that's not necessarily the best place to start, especially since most sales positions require previous experience.

Frequently, it's possible to find entry-level employment at a tour operator in the operations department. Entry-level operations jobs don't pay that well, typically from $900 to $1,500 a month, but they are a way to get your foot in the door and get experience.

Operations jobs are mostly clerical in nature, particularly at large tour operators. They may involve finalizing itineraries, making sure a client's paperwork is in order, and taking care of any necessary documentation. "The person has to be organized to the max, detailed to the point of perfection," said Viviane Tondeur, operations manager of Professional Travel Service in Los Angeles. "Unfortunately, they are often the lowest paid."

After gaining some experience, it may be possible to advance into sales. Sales reps typically make $1,800 to $2,500 base salary a month plus expenses. If they're selling outside the office, they might receive commissions of up to 25 percent on top of that. Independent reps working on their own for more than one company typically make around $25,000 a year, Tondeur said.

Being a sales rep for a tour operator means long hours on the road, either traveling, attending trade shows, or calling on travel agencies to pitch your company's packages and attract new clients. Smaller operators tend to combine the operations and sales functions, said Steve Goldsmith, co-owner of Odyssey

Tours in Santa Monica. The same person may be responsible for fielding inquiries, working out itineraries, and making the sale.

"They go to bat for the client. They also need to try to clinch the deal," Goldsmith said. "We need someone who really knows what they're talking about. We're selling the idea that when you call us, you'll talk to an expert."

Other travel opportunities with tour operators include the positions of tour director and tour guide or leader. Tour directors usually deal with large groups and arrive at destinations ahead of time to take care of logistical matters concerning their planned activities in advance.

Tour guides or leaders accompany tour groups from start to finish. They are responsible for the success or failure of the tour and for contending with problems as they arise. Good tour guides can make $125 to $175 a day, depending on their expertise, familiarity with the destination country, and size of their group. Fluency in one or more foreign languages also enhances their marketability.

"You have to think on your feet and be flexible," said Sherrie Lehman, an independent tour guide who worked for 21 years as a flight attendant for Continental Airlines. "No matter how much you plan ahead, there are 47,000 variables coming down at the last minute."

Good tour guides don't always have to be experts on the country they're visiting. Familiarity is often secondary to having the right combination of patience, personality, and experience. "No one expects you to know everything or have seen every single sight," Goldsmith said. "Many times you'll pick up a local guide who's an expert. But you still need to know the basic facts of the country, such as when the Taj Mahal was built."

Travel Agencies

Travel agencies sell tour packages, transportation arrangements, and hotel accommodations on a retail basis to the consumer. Travel agents do not receive a fee for their services, but make a commission off the wholesale cost of the package.

Opportunities at travel agencies are almost all sales-oriented. Agencies employ inside and outside agents to sell travel packages and make reservations. Perhaps the most important quality for a travel agent to have is the ability to generate excitement and enthusiasm about a particular trip or location, said Scott Feinerman, professor of tourism and travel at West Los Angeles College.

Short of owning your own travel agency, agents with corporate accounts are among the highest paid. An ongoing relationship with a company that travels a lot may even develop into a full-time, in-house corporate travel planner position. Corporate travel planners spend most of their time out of the office conducting site inspections at potential locations and can earn an annual salary of up to $100,000, Graven-Smith said.

At the other end of the spectrum, travel agents at small independent agencies who are new to the field may make as little as $18,500 a year—or less.

Most of an agent's time in the office is spent conferring with clients, completing paperwork, contacting airlines and hotels to make reservations, and promoting group tours. Once established, agents can usually travel at substantially reduced rates. Travel agents typically receive four free flight passes a year, Lehman said. Occasionally, hotels and resorts will offer free vacations to travel agents in order to provide them with firsthand knowledge of a new locale, which the company hopes the agent will then promote.

Sometimes the only way to get your foot in the door at an agency is by starting out as a receptionist or clerk. Another way to develop a background in travel is by working for a convention center or tourism organization, such as the Greater Los Angeles Visitors' and Convention Bureau, or by enrolling in a certificate or degree program in travel.

Several private and public schools offer travel programs, some with better reputations than others. The most affordable programs can be found at public community colleges, such as West Los Angeles College and Pasadena City College. There's also the Los Angeles Airport Center College in Los Angeles, which is considerably cheaper than most private schools.

When applying to a travel program, it's important to have realistic expectations, Lehman said. "Travel schools tend to promise more than they're ever going to deliver." But Feinerman added: "A person with *some* kind of background will get chosen over a person with no background."

If you're thinking about enrolling in a travel program, make sure it is comprehensive and up to date. The industry is evolving continuously. Travel agents and reservationists, for example, must be computer literate and know how to use such airline computer systems as Apollo (United Airlines), Pars (TWA), Sabre (American Airlines), and System One (Eastern Airlines).

For specific travel-related opportunities, look in the Sunday travel sections of newspapers. An even bigger selection of job listings can be found in two key travel industry trade magazines, *Travel Age West* and *Travel Weekly*, said Frushon of United Vacations. Another way to find work is through a temporary service that specializes in the travel industry, such as Travel Temps in North Hollywood, which serves the Los Angeles and San Fernando Valley areas.

KEY EMPLOYERS OF TRAVEL AGENTS AND TOUR OPERATORS

American Express Travel Related Management Services
9920 S. La Cienega Boulevard
Suite 1101
Inglewood, CA 90017
213/338-2236

Ask Mr. Foster Travel Services
7833 Haskell Avenue
Van Nuys, CA 91406
818/988-0181

Automobile Club of Southern California
World Travel Agency Service
2601 S. Figueroa Street
Los Angeles, CA 90007
213/741-4030

Corporate Travel Services
515 S. Flower Street
Suite 325
Los Angeles, CA 90071
213/486-6500

Freight Boat Travel Inc.
246 S. Robertson Boulevard
Beverly Hills, CA 91211
213/854-8500

Hoffman Travel Service
9601 Wilshire Boulevard
Suite GLA
Beverly Hills, CA 90210
213/278-9850

Inter Pacific Tours International
233 S. Barrington Avenue
Los Angeles, CA 90049
213/471-8897

Maritz Travel Co.
3638 Motor Avenue
Los Angeles, CA 90034
213/204-4490

May Co. Travel
425 E. Colorado Boulevard
Suite 500
Glendale, CA 91205
818/241-6776

McDonnell Douglas Travel Co.
5432 Bolsa Avenue
Huntington Beach, CA 92647
714/896-6382

Pleasant Hawaiian Holidays
2404 Townsgate Road
Westlake Village, CA 91361
818/991-3390

The Plot Thickens Mystery Trains & Tours
5333 Russell Avenue
Los Angeles, CA 90027
213/465-6371

Travel Temps Inc.
Post Office Box 15984
North Hollywood, CA 91615
213/730-8987

United Vacations
100 Corporate Pointe
Suite 200
Culver City, CA 90230
213/410-0246

Unitours
425 E. Colorado Boulevard
Suite 500
Glendale, CA 91205
818/241-6776

PROFESSIONAL ORGANIZATIONS

American Society of Travel Agents (ASTA)
Southern California Chapter
7080 Hollywood Boulevard
Los Angeles, CA 90028
213/466-7717

Association of Retail Travel Agents
Western Region
4941 Lincoln Avenue
Cypress, CA 90630
714/828-7170

Institute of Certified Travel Agents (ICTA)
148 Linden Street
Wellesley, MA 02181
617/237-0280

National Association of Business Travel Agents
3255 Wilshire Boulevard
Suite 1514
Los Angeles, CA 90010
213/382-3335

U.S. Tour Operators Association
211 E. 51st Street
Suite 12-B
New York, NY 10022
212/944-5727

PROFESSIONAL PUBLICATIONS

ASTA Travel News (Greensboro, NC)
Business Traveler Management (New York, NY)
Business Travel News (Manhasset, NY)
Meetings & Incentive Travel (Toronto, Can.)
Tour & Travel News (Manhasset, NY)
TravelAge West (San Francisco)
Travel Agent Magazine (New York, NY)
Travel Weekly (Secaucus, NJ)

DIRECTORIES

Membership Directory (American Society of Travel Agents, Alexandria, VA)

Membership Directory (Institute of Certified Travel Agents, Wellesley, MA)

Tours—Operators and Promoters (American Business Information Inc., Omaha, NE)

Travel Industry Personnel Directory (American Traveler, New York, NY)

....

CHAPTER 39

The Tourism
Industry

Work just for the fun of it in one of
L.A.'s largest industries: tourism.

L.A.'s the Place

Come to L.A. and lose your blues
The water's fine, the sun's out
The sand's warm, and
Who knows if it's January or June?
And who cares?

——Greater Los Angeles
Visitors' and Convention Bureau

People from around the world dream of visiting "the
Californias"—the diverse, rich, lush, wine-producing, rugged,
mountainous, cosmopolitan, fun-loving, sunny, beachy, and star-
struck regions that make up one of the most resplendent and
dynamic places anywhere. Now that those dreams are being
realized (in ever increasing numbers, too), the tourism and
convention business has emerged as the Golden State's top
industry, according to the California Office of Tourism.

In Los Angeles County, host to the lion's share of the state's
visitors each year, tourism is now the third-largest source of
employment, just behind business services and aerospace/high
tech, according to the Los Angeles Area Chamber of Commerce.
And while the number of people who flock to Southern
California's famous beaches, amusement parks, and shopping
destinations is holding steady at just under 50 million visitors
yearly, the thriving tourism industry has a growing need for
workers.

In 1988, 327,800 people were employed in tourism-related occupations, an increase of 8,000 jobs over the year before, said Jack Kyser, the chamber's chief economist. "We have a good infrastructure in tourism and a growing number of people coming here," Kyser said. "You talk to people in the industry and they still have a tremendous need for people at the entry level."

The planned $1 billion expansion of Disneyland in either Anaheim or Long Beach is sure to draw even more visitors to the Southland's world-renowned tourist attractions, including the television and movie studios, Santa Monica and Malibu beaches, Knott's Berry Farm, Magic Mountain, the *Queen Mary*, and shopping meccas like Rodeo Drive and Melrose Avenue.

The 10-year project—Disney's most aggressive expansion in its 35-year history—promises to boost the local tax base, provide an estimated 10,000 new jobs, and bring tourists swarming.

"This is the '90s—the decade we reinvent the Disney experience, not just in California, but worldwide," Michael D. Eisner, Disney's chairman and chief executive, said at a press conference unveiling his company's plans. The expansion calls for the addition of rides based on the hit movies "The Little Mermaid," "Dick Tracy," and the "Indiana Jones" series. Two new theme areas also will be added: Mickey's Starland and Hollywoodland, a fantasy re-creation of Hollywood Boulevard.

In addition to Disneyland's massive remodeling, the 2.5-million-square-foot expansion of the Los Angeles convention center, planned for 1992, and the completion of the World Trade Center in Long Beach are likely to bring an increased flow of business and leisure travelers to Los Angeles, Kyser said.

"The recent Disney announcement about the expansion of Disneyland—the possibility of a second gate—plus the expansion of the Convention Center, plus the boom in international tourism means that the (local) tourist industry is going to be serious business in the 1990s," Kyser said.

Ensuring a steady flow of visitors is the strength of certain foreign currencies compared to the dollar, and the relative affordability of Los Angeles compared to other international destination points, such as London, Paris, and Tokyo. "America still remains a bargain on a world scale," said Carl Cusato, vice president of the L.A.-based search firm Paul R. Ray & Co. "Taking a vacation in the U.S., in international terms, certainly is a deal."

The tourism industry is broken into four general job categories: retailing, amusement and recreation services, hospitality, and transportation. (For information about careers in hospitality, see Chapter 35 on the hotel industry.)

Though the demand for retail workers is highest during the winter months, and the need for hotel employees is fairly constant year-round, both amusement parks and transportation services do most of their hiring in the spring for their busy summer season. Literally thousands of seasonal employees are needed to keep the wheels of tourism rolling each year.

"During spring we really push. We look for dozens of drivers," said Phil Boucher, executive vice president and general manager of Gray Line Tours Co. in Los Angeles. "We've been having big seasons lately."

Bus drivers at Gray Line must possess a Class B driver's license (formerly Class 2) and a California tour bus driver's certificate, for which the tour company provides a month of training. Beginning drivers start out performing hotel pickups and gradually take on the larger responsibility of a guided tour around the city and to amusement parks. Van drivers at Gray Line, who only need to have a standard, Class C automobile license (formerly Class 3), also conduct tours of movie stars' homes.

With experience, tips, and overtime, bus drivers can make up to $40,000 a year, Boucher said. The hours are irregular, however. Drivers typically start work at 6 a.m. and work a 13-hour day that includes picking up and dropping off travelers at their hotels, and taking them on a guided tour in between. Not all of that time is spent driving, however. Some is spent waiting.

In addition to drivers, Gray Line hires bilingual "step-on" tour guides to accompany foreign tourist groups. Step-on guides, who make $80 a day plus tips, must be fluent in one of the following high-demand foreign languages: Japanese, German, French, Italian, or Korean, Boucher said.

The region's numerous amusement parks also hire in the spring. Six Flags Magic Mountain, for example, hires over 1,500 part-time seasonal staff, for positions ranging from hostess to to vendor to ride operator to stage tech, said Gary Vien, personnel manager for Magic Mountain. Universal Studios, which staffs its tour division with about 2,300 employees, hires some 1,000 tour guides and park employees for its summer season, said Karin Trzepacz, employment representative for the studio.

In general, careers in the service-intensive tourism industry require an upbeat attitude, a well-groomed appearance, a healthy work ethic, and the ability to interact with the public with a smile under demanding work conditions.

"At Disneyland, even an engineer or accountant has got to be the type of person who can speak to the public," said Mark Neynaber, senior professional staffing representative at Disneyland, which currently employs about 10,000 people during the summer months. "Everybody's got to have that Disney image."

A career in tourism also means working when other people are relaxing or on vacation: during evenings, weekends, and holidays.

At the entry level, training is provided, but it never hurts to have basic computer skills and cash-handling experience. Knowing a trade is a sure way to find work, since amusement parks are in constant need of maintenance and repair, especially when they're expanding like Disneyland. "There's work to be done and money to hire new people," Neynaber said. "Our company's just booming in all areas."

A college education is not essential to work at a theme park. But having a bachelor's degree in business, marketing, or hotel and restaurant administration can be important to career advancement. At Disneyland, degree holders may apply for management trainee openings. But the competition is keen. Of the 20 to 30 trainee slots that open up yearly, only a handful are filled by outside applicants. "Most of the people who are here in management started as seasonal employees," Neynaber stressed.

Disneyland has scores of salaried job opportunities at any given time, including openings for accountants, engineers, and construction project managers. Most of these positions require 3 to 10 years of previous work experience, Neynaber said.

In the amusement park business, dedication and longevity are rewarded. "The president of Universal Studios, Ron Bension, started out 16 years ago as a parking attendant," Trzepacz said. "Now he's our CEO."

Tourism-related jobs carry many perks, such as discount travel and entertainment packages. Some theme parks also give their employees free park passes and discounts on merchandise. At Universal Studios, tour guides are privileged with a unique benefit: access to the lot and anyone thereabouts, including movie stars who are on location. (Consequently, many tour guides are aspiring actors and actresses.)

People who work in tourism and leisure-related fields often find that what they do is a labor of love. Vien of Magic Mountain said his first job was with Six Flags. He has worked for the company ever since, transferring to several locations and receiving far more than a paycheck from his experience.

"I met my wife at Six Flags. We worked together in St. Louis when we were both in high school. I was working at an ice cream stand called the Big Dipper and she used to work across the street at the shooting gallery. She used to come up and get ice cream from me. She was my favorite customer."

L.A.'S MOST POPULAR TOURIST ATTRACTIONS

1. Beverly Hills/Rodeo Drive

2. Hollywood

3. Disneyland

4. Universal Studios

5. *Queen Mary*

6. Knott's Berry Farm

7. Griffith Park Observatory

8. Magic Mountain

9. Hollywood Wax Museum

10. NBC Studios Tour

SOURCE: CIC Research Inc. (commissioned by the Los Angeles Visitors and Convention Bureau).

A Breakdown of the Tourism Industry in Los Angeles County

Job Category	Workers
Retailing	216,300
Hotels and motels	39,200
Amusement and recreation services	38,000
Transportation services	34,300
Total	327,800

SOURCE: Los Angeles Area Chamber of Commerce.

KEY EMPLOYERS IN THE TOURISM INDUSTRY

Selected Attractions and Amusement Parks

Catalina Cruises
320 Golden Shore Boulevard
Long Beach, CA 90802
213/547-1162

Disneyland
1313 Harbor Boulevard
Anaheim, CA 92802
714/999-4000

Gray Line Sightseeing Tours
6541 Hollywood Boulevard
Hollywood, CA 90028
213/481-2121

Knott's Berry Farm
8039 Beach Boulevard
Buena Park, CA 90620
714/827-1776

Lion Country Safari
8800 Irvine Center Drive
Laguna Hills, CA 92653
714/837-1200

Los Angeles County Museum of Art (LACMA)
5905 Wilshire Boulevard
Los Angeles, CA 90036
213/937-2590

Los Angeles Zoo
5333 Zoo Drive
Los Angeles, CA 90027
213/485-2468

Movieland Wax Museum
7711 Beach Boulevard
Buena Park, CA 90620
714/522-1154

Museum of Natural History
900 Exposition Boulevard
Los Angeles, CA 90007
213/744-3411

Princess Cruises
1404 W. Vacation Road
San Diego, CA 92109
619/274-4630

Queen Mary & Spruce Goose
Pier J
Long Beach, CA 90802
213/435-3511

Sea World
1720 S. Shore Road
San Diego, CA 92109
619/222-6363

Six Flags Magic Mountain
26101 Magic Mountain Parkway
Valencia, CA 91355
805/255-4111

Universal Studios
100 Universal City Plaza
Universal City, CA 91608
818/777-2264

Selected Visitors' Bureaus and Convention Centers

Anaheim Area Visitors' & Convention Center
800 W. Katella Avenue
Anaheim, CA 92802
714/999-8999

Catalina Island Chamber of Commerce & Visitors' Bureau
No. 1 Green Pier
Post Office Box 217
Avalon, CA 90704
213/510-1520

**Greater Los Angeles Visitors' &
Convention Bureau**
ManuLife Plaza
11th Floor
515 S. Figueroa Street
Los Angeles, CA 90071
213/624-7300

**Long Beach Convention & Visitors'
Council**
One World Trade Center
Suite 300
Long Beach, CA 90831
213/436-3631

**Santa Monica Convention &
Visitors' Bureau**
2219 Main Street
Santa Monica, CA 90405
213/392-9631

PROFESSIONAL ORGANIZATIONS

**Greater Los Angeles Zoo
Association**
5333 Zoo Drive
Los Angeles, CA 90027
213/664-1100

**National Recreation & Parks
Association (NRPA)**
3101 Park Center Drive
12th Floor
Alexandria, VA 22302
703/820-4940

**Travel & Tourism Research
Association**
Post Office Box 8066
Foothill Station
Salt Lake City, UT 84108
801/581-3351

PROFESSIONAL PUBLICATIONS

California Parks & Recreation (Sacramento, CA)
Dateline: NRPA (Alexandria, VA)
Meetings and Conventions (Secaucus, NJ)
Parks and Recreation Magazine (Alexandria, VA)
Tour & Travel News (Manhasset, NY)

DIRECTORIES

Guide to Hospitality and Tourism Education (Council on Restaurant and In-
stitutional Education, Washington, DC)
Meetings and Conventions Magazine Directory (Murdoch Magazines, New
York, NY)
Research Supplier Directory (Travel and Tourism Research Association,
Salt Lake City, UT)

Relocation

Been offered a transfer? Contemplating a move? There is more assistance available than you might think.

The United States is the most mobile society in the world. More than 20 percent of the population moves each year. In 1989, an estimated 540,000 people moved due to job transfers, according to the Employee Relocation Council (ERC) in Washington, D.C. Relocation doesn't necessarily entail a cross-country journey; it can mean an intrastate move as well, perhaps from Los Angeles to San Diego, or from San Francisco to Los Angeles.

Relocations occur for a variety of reasons. But whether the decision to move is a planned part of a company's policy to broaden the experience of its employees or a personal decision to change careers, you don't have to go it alone. Several programs and forms of assistance are available.

Starting at the professional to middle management level, most large companies now offer substantial relocation assistance to their employees—veterans and new hires alike—and in many instances extend some benefits to their spouses. On average, employers spend between $35,000 and $40,000 on moving and related expenses for each currently employed worker they transfer, and between $25,000 and $30,000 for new hires, said Anita Brienza, the ERC's director of communications.

For homeowners, such relocation programs typically include the following types of assistance:

- Reimbursement for one or more house-hunting trips to the new location.
- Temporary living expenses for up to 30 days.
- Real estate assistance, usually in the form of a home purchase plan where the company guarantees the sale of the employee's home at its appraised price.

- Packing and moving fees.
- Closing costs associated with the purchase of a new home.
- A mortgage differential to ease the burden of a higher interest payment.
- A miscellaneous expense allowance, usually equal to one month's salary for costs incidental to the move.

For renters, relocation costs drop dramatically. But many employers will still pay a finder's fee for the employee's new apartment and penalties, if there are any, for breaking the old lease. Moving and temporary housing expenses are covered as well. On average, companies spend about $11,000 to relocate current employees who are renters, and close to $7,000 for new-hire renters, ERC data shows.

If the relocation involves a move to an area with a higher cost of living, some companies will also grant cost-of-living allowances above and beyond the raise associated with the promotion, although this frequently has to be negotiated. Employers place a premium on a successful relocation, so they are often open to making fair concessions in their own self-interest.

In addition to these aid packages, many firms also offer spousal or partner relocation assistance. This is especially important for two-earner households where the incomes of both wage earners are equally vital. Some programs are also extended to nonworking spouses to help involve them in social, volunteer, or charitable activities.

"Companies are offering spousal relocation because they want their employees to feel satisfied and be productive as soon as possible after a move," said Susan Miller, a career counselor in Los Angeles who specializes in spousal relocation. "If the spouse is not happy, then the employee is not going to be happy, or very productive, either. They're looking at bottom-line issues."

Indeed, according to Catalyst, a nonprofit career development organization in New York, it takes transferees four to six months to achieve even 50 to 75 percent efficiency in a job at a new location, and a full year to work at top efficiency. Relocating can be especially rough, if not more trying, on the spouse, said Brad Taft, vice president of the Los Angeles office of Lee Hecht Harrison, an outplacement consulting firm. (In today's job market, that can mean the woman *or* the man.)

"The person being transferred has made the commitment to the opportunity and for him or her that's a real positive step,"

Taft said. "But with the proliferation of the two-career family, the spouse really has to make some tough decisions about giving up *his or her* job and making the move, on top of other family issues, such as schools, housing, and friends."

Spousal relocation programs typically consist of referral to a certified career counselor or outplacement agency. The professional acts as the spouse's initial contact to the job market, providing information about the opportunities in their specific field, linking them to professional organizations, making recommendations for other possible career choices, and arming them with the skills and knowledge to plan, develop, and implement an effective job search in the new locale.

They also provide personal referrals. "The counselor should be willing to make the initial phone call and open doors for them," Miller said.

Once a transfer is confirmed, there are several things the "trailing spouses" can do before they leave their current place of employment to facilitate their job search once they reach their destination. Among these: Ask for kudos letters and letters of recommendation for future employers—and get them before you leave; contact any friends or colleagues you know in the new location; and join the local chapter of your profession's national association and find out when it meets.

Just because a company offers spousal relocation assistance, don't become complacent. Investigate the quality of the program. The focus should be heavily weighted toward job search and placement strategies rather than self-assessment, Miller said. Look for a counselor who is nationally certified and state licensed, preferably someone with at least a master's degree in the field and who is well connected.

Career counselors typically charge from $300 to $500 for job placement services, while outplacement firms, which often allow clients to use their offices and equipment, are more expensive, billing up to $2,000.

Fortunately, if you're searching for employment in the Los Angeles area, you won't have to look very far. The California Employment Development Department projects that between 1987 and 1992, Los Angeles and Orange counties alone will generate 694,375 new jobs, bringing the total employment figure to around 5.8 million. Miller said her office, Vocational Training Consulting Services, has a 100 percent spousal relocation placement rate.

"We're blessed in the Southern California area with tens of thousands of employers," said Taft of Lee Hecht Harrison. "That translates into a lot of opportunities. Moreover, the employee population in L.A. is very mobile and that creates even more openings. But it can be mind-boggling to anyone moving to the area. There's no one place you can go that's going to be a cure-all. It takes a lot of knocking on doors, information sources, and referrals."

One of the best places to get oriented and start a job search is a local chamber of commerce, of which there are close to 200 in the five-county greater Los Angeles area. Most have relocation kits for new arrivals. The Los Angeles Area Chamber of Commerce, 404 S. Bixel Street in Los Angeles, sells various publications about the job market, including the *Southern California Business Directory and Buyer's Guide*, and a relocation guidebook called *California Bound*, which describes and illustrates the area's myriad communities, school systems, and services.

"In terms of lifestyle, L.A.'s a smorgasbord," said Jack Kyser, chief economist for the Los Angeles Area Chamber of Commerce. "You can find almost any type of lifestyle you want here. You can lead a big-city life in a high-rise apartment building, or you can have beachfront casual along the coast. If you want to go out far enough, you can even live in a pastoral landscape amongst animals and trees."

At what stage in the moving process should you seek career assistance? That usually depends on your financial needs. "For the most part, people will come out to see me during their house-hunting trip," Miller said. "They're anxious to get going because they need the job to qualify for the loan."

Chances are, if you're being transferred by a company, it's for a positive reason. An Employee Relocation Council study found that 67 percent of the moves its nearly 1,000 member companies asked employees to make were accompanied by a promotion. On the other hand, turning down a transfer can have damaging effects on your future promotability.

"When managers say no to a transfer, they are sending a negative message to their employer," said James E. Challenger, president of the Chicago-based outplacement firm Challenger, Gray & Christmas. "The impression the company gets is that the employee does not want to accept more responsibility. At that point, the rejecting manager has reached a career dead end with that company. It may be better to look for another job."

Not all firms actively publicize their relocation policies, so you should take it upon yourself to learn about your company's benefits for transferees. If there is a formal, written relocation policy, ask to obtain a copy. Getting the best package often depends on knowing your full range of options.

RECOMMENDED READING

Bastress, Frances. *The Relocating Spouse's Guide to Employment.* Chevy Chase, MD: Woodley Publications, 1989.

Benson, Gail G., and Holston, Jane E. *Smart Moves for the Relocating Family.* Houston, TX: River Forest Publishing, 1987.

Catalyst Staff. *Human Factors in Relocation: Corporate & Employee Points of View.* New York: Catalyst, 1983.

Catalyst Staff. *Moving People: Relocation Policies That Pay Off.* New York: Catalyst, 1984.

Catalyst Staff. *No False Moves: How to Make a Relocation Work for You.* New York: Catalyst, 1985.

Dickinson, Jan. *Complete Guide to Family Relocation.* Lake Oswego, OR: Wheatherstone Press, 1983.

Employee Relocation Council Staff. *A Guide to Employee Relocation & Relocation Policy Development.* Washington, DC: Employee Relocation Council, 1987.

Pike, Jody P., and Singer, Pamela M. *On the Move: What to Do After the Moving Van Leaves.* Perrysburg, OH: Three Meadows Press, 1982.

For a selected list of career and outplacement counselors, see the Career Trends article on career counseling at the end of Section 3 and the article on job loss at the end of Section 14.

SECTION
12

Careers in Advertising and Media

Advertising

*If you're looking for tough creative
challenges, consider the ad business.*

New York's Madison Avenue is still king when it comes to opportunities in advertising. But the competitive West Coast market is rapidly gaining ground, with California ad agencies producing 7 of the "10 Best Ads of the 1980s" and innovative firms like Chiat/Day/Mojo recently being named advertising agency of the year by both *Advertising Age* and *Adweek.*

L.A.'s prestige in the advertising world is established, no question. But the opportunities are sparse. Usually, the only way to get your foot in the door of an advertising agency is to start at the bottom, either in the mailroom or as a receptionist. This news should hardly come as a surprise. Advertising professionals note that there always have been more job seekers than openings, partly because of the industry's glamorous reputation.

"It has always been an excruciatingly difficult business to get into," said Leonard Pearlstein, president and CEO of keye/donna/pearlstein. "It's as hard as ever."

Los Angeles–based advertising agencies got a shot in the arm in the mid-1980s when several major Japanese car manufacturers, as well as the Korean giant Hyundai, located their U.S. headquarters in Southern California, said Jack Kyser, chief economist for the Los Angeles Area Chamber of Commerce. Since this "foreign invasion," growth in the local advertising industry has leveled off. The L.A. ad industry currently employs over 12,000 people—5,000 more than in 1980, Kyser said.

At a highly-rated advertising agency like Chiat/Day/Mojo in Venice a beginner can expect to work for six months to a year in the mailroom or as a receptionist—and that's *with* a college degree, said Barbara Stolar, Chiat/Day/Mojo's personnel manager. "Advertising is very popular right now, so the field is very tough. We can afford to be very selective. Most (new graduates) didn't go to college to type. I get that a lot. But it's probably been like this for the past three years."

Though the Los Angeles ad industry is admittedly tough to break into, there are several ways to make inroads and better your chances for employment.

First, as Tom Hanks in the role of a successful advertising executive tells a group of students in the movie "Something in Common," you have to really want a career in advertising—not as a writer, artist, reporter, filmmaker, or some other related creative pursuit—to really get anywhere in the business. Being committed is a prerequisite.

Second, realize that almost all jobs in advertising require a bachelor's degree, preferably in marketing, business administration, or advertising itself. Agencies are open to applicants with degrees in fields like sociology, public relations, or journalism, but an understanding of business is essential.

"A good background is a business degree or MBA, (but) advertising is a career that rewards people who have broad interests," said Tim McPartlin, senior vice president and group management director of Foote, Cone & Belding, one of the three largest Los Angeles-based ad agencies.

Several public and private universities in the Los Angeles area offer four-year degrees in advertising, including Cal State Fullerton, Cal State Northridge, San Diego State, Mount St. Mary's College, and Pepperdine University.

A third way to make yourself a hot prospect is to learn the industry from the inside out—*before* you apply for your first job. How? By holding a full-time summer internship while still in school. Internships allow you to understand the business from an insider's point of view and get a taste of what the work is like. They also enable you to compile a portfolio of work to show to prospective employers. The Advertising Club of Los Angeles sponsors a summer internship program for college juniors and seniors at 29 universities throughout Southern California.

Advertising agencies are broken into three general divisions: creative production, administration, and account management.

Creative Production

The most common creative production jobs are for copywriters and art directors. Copywriters create the witty phrases and compelling captions that grab your attention on billboards, in magazines, and on radio and television. Art directors develop the visual designs to complement or enhance the message of an ad.

Both of these positions require considerable originality and talent. "From the creative standpoint, if you can't write or draw, you're in trouble," said Sharon Benoit, editor of *Ad L.A.*, a publication of the Advertising Club. "It's not something that anybody can do."

The creative function also includes print and broadcast production, with jobs ranging from pasteup artist, copy reader, and print production manager on the print side to producer on the broadcast side.

Producers primarily act as coordinators between in-house account teams and outside production companies. They are responsible for bidding out the conceptual work of the account team and for finding the film director best suited for a particular commercial. "Producers might spend days looking at reels of film for the right director," Benoit said.

Once an ad is finished being produced, it then goes to the advertising agency's media department for "trafficking"— placement in whatever form of media (newspapers, magazines, radio, televison) it is scheduled to appear.

A media planner then suggests appropriate media outlets for a given client's advertising campaign. After the best vehicles for getting a company's message across are determined, a media buyer contacts the different media organizations to solicit bids and make a recommendation to the client.

The average advertising salary is about $36,000 a year, Kyser said. But earnings can rise much higher than that.

Overseeing the creative operation is the creative director, who, if good, can make an annual salary between $180,000 and $225,000, depending on the agency's income. Most agencies receive a flat rate of 15 percent of the total cost of the ad campaign, including television time and newspaper and magazine rates.

In the middle of a campaign, the hours can be long, the deadline pressure intense, and the work never-ending. What, then, are the rewards? "I personally like the business because it compels earnestness and promptly penalizes mistakes, shiftlessness, and inefficiency, while rewarding those who give the best they have in them," Dick Macedo, president of Wells, Rich, Greene/West, said in a recent commentary. "Each day is a fresh adventure."

Administration/Account Management

At Chiat/Day/Mojo, clerical and administrative-type jobs can eventually lead to creative or account management positions. Diligence as a receptionist may result in a promotion to secretary. From there, an account coordinator or traffic position might open up, Stolar said. One way to avoid strictly clerical work at large agencies is to start as an assistant media planner, she added. But these opportunities are somewhat scarce.

The average starting salary for entry-level jobs above the secretarial level is $18,000 a year, according to the Advertising Club. During your first few years, you might make less. If you are on a management track, the next move would be to assistant (or junior) account executive, then account executive. Account executives, who typically start at $22,000 a year base salary, require a certain modicum of salesmanship, and an even greater understanding of marketing strategies and market research.

"You're more of a marketing consultant than a salesman per se," McPartlin said. "You're building a long-term relationship with the client." Sunkist, a case in point, has been Foote, Cone & Belding's client for over 80 years, he added.

Account executives act as a conduit between the client and the agency, conveying the client's needs to the account team and then relaying the creative approach of the account team back to the client for input and approval. "If you're the supreme competitive individualist, then this is not a field for you," McPartlin said. "It's a team process."

Successful account executives may be promoted to account supervisors and managers. Account managers act as group leaders. They form account teams made up of copywriters, art directors, media planners, buyers, and account executives to serve each client.

Besides orchestrating campaigns, account managers should have the management skills to motivate people within the agency and provide them with the support they need to do their best work, even if that means making room for an occasional lemon of an idea, McPartlin said. "People have to feel free to take chances. Not every idea is going to be a winner."

Since talent is being recruited *away* from such outlying areas as San Diego and Orange County, it may be advantageous to seek employment outside of Los Angeles right out of school. As Stolar of Chiat/Day/Mojo remarked about her agency's practice of hiring college graduates for clerical positions: "They might show up at another agency at the right place at the right time and be offered a (better) position."

KEY EMPLOYERS IN ADVERTISING

AC&R/CCL
5750 Wilshire Boulevard
Los Angeles, CA 90036
213/938-1888

Admarketing
1801 Century Park East
Los Angeles, CA 90067
213/203-8400

BBDO Worldwide
10960 Wilshire Boulevard
Los Angeles, CA 90025
213/444-4500

Bozell, Jacobs, Kenyon & Eckhardt
12121 Wilshire Boulevard
Los Angeles, CA 90025
213/442-2400

Chiat/Day/Mojo
320 Hampton Drive
Venice, CA 90291
213/314-5000

Dailey & Associates
3055 Wilshire Boulevard
Los Angeles, CA 90010
213/386-7823

Davis, Ball & Colombatto Inc.
818 W. Seventh Street
Los Angeles, CA 90017
213/688-7000

DDB Needham Worldwide Inc.
5900 Wilshire Boulevard
Los Angeles, CA 90036
213/930-5400

Foote, Cone & Belding
11601 Wilshire Boulevard
Los Angeles, CA 90025
213/312-7000

Grey Advertising
6100 Wilshire Boulevard
Los Angeles, CA 90048
213/936-6060

HDM Los Angeles
4751 Wilshire Boulevard
Los Angeles, CA 90010
213/930-5086

keye/donna/pearlstein
11080 Olympic Boulevard
Los Angeles, CA 90064
213/477-0061

McCann-Erickson Los Angeles
6420 Wilshire Boulevard
Los Angeles, CA 90048
213/655-9420

Ogilvy & Mather
5757 Wilshire Boulevard
Los Angeles, CA 90036
213/937-7900

Rubin Postaer and Associates
11601 Wilshire Boulevard
Los Angeles, CA 90025
213/208-5000

Saatchi & Saatchi DFS/Pacific
3501 Sepulveda Boulevard
Torrance, CA 90505
213/214-6000

J. Walter Thompson West
10100 Santa Monica Boulevard
Los Angeles, CA 90067
213/553-8383

PROFESSIONAL ORGANIZATIONS

Advertising Club of Los Angeles
514 Shatto Place
Suite 328
Los Angeles, CA 90020
213/382-1228

The Advertising Council
825 Third Avenue
New York, NY 10022
212/758-0400

American Advertising Federation
1400 K Street, NW
Suite 1000
Washington, DC 20005
202/898-0089

**American Association of
  Advertising Agencies Inc.**
8500 Wilshire Boulevard
Suite 502
Beverly Hills, CA 90211
213/657-3711

**Western States Advertising
  Agencies Association**
2410 Beverly Boulevard
Suite 1
Los Angeles, CA 90057
213/387-7432

PROFESSIONAL PUBLICATIONS

Ad L.A. (Los Angeles, CA)
Advertising Age (New York, NY)
Adweek/West (Los Angeles, CA)
American Advertising (Washington, DC)
Journal of Advertising Research (New York, NY)
Journal of Marketing Research (Chicago, IL)
Madison Avenue (New York, NY)
Marketing & Media Decisions (New York, NY)

DIRECTORIES

Adweek Agency Directory (A/S/M Communications, New York, NY)
Roster and Organization (American Association of Advertising Agencies,
    New York, NY)
Standard Directory of Advertising Agencies (National Register Publishing
    Co., Skokie, IL)

CHAPTER 41

Printing/ Lithography

The majority of opportunities are clustered in Orange County.

Printing has come a long way since the days of Benjamin Franklin, America's most famous printer. Computer technology and offset printing techniques introduced in the 1970s have revolutionized the business, leaving little room for workers who aren't computer literate.

"It's not the wave of the future, it's here," said Ted DeWitt, vice president of manufacturing for Lithographix in El Segundo. "All of our pre-press jobs are done electronically now. What used to be handcrafts are done by computer. Pretty soon, just about every aspect of production will be computerized."

The printing industry works on two labor bases: production workers and management/sales staff. Increasingly, the manu-facturing side of the business requires some vocational training and work experience to reach journey-level status. For managerial openings, most large employers look for a college degree in printing management. However, the majority of shops are small and will hire nondegreed applicants.

Whatever your skill level, opportunities are fairly abundant and training is readily available. With statewide revenues exceeding $6.5 billion yearly, California is the largest printing state in the country. The Los Angeles area, the biggest player in the state, has over 2,700 printing establishments (including commercial printers, newspapers, periodicals, book publishers, and greeting card companies), which employ some 24,900 printing-related workers, mostly in Orange County.

"There are many opportunities for all phases of background," said Nancy Maser, personnel manager for the Printing Industries Association of Southern California, which offers an employment referral service for its 2,000 member companies. "The hands-on people are just as in demand as the desk job. We've placed people in every job title imaginable, from entry-level minimum-wage openings to executive positions paying $94,000 a year."

Lithography basically means color printing. The sophisticated technical process involves separating a drawing or piece of art to be printed into four or six colors and then re-creating it with just the right mixture of ink on a roll, or web, of special printing paper. Four- and six-color offset web presses are now the norm. Like the old mechanical presses that preceded them, they are anything but easy to operate.

"The ability to judge color and reproduce it is highly valued in this industry," said Bill Jacot, vice president of production services for California Offset Printing in Glendale. "Employees who can, rise to the top very quickly. It's a fiercely competitive business, so those who perform are going to do well for the company and get rewarded for it."

In today's job market, even natural talent needs to be complemented with training, Jacot said. Color lithography represents a quantum leap over basic black and white printing in terms of the knowledge and expertise required.

"The key jobs in our plant are for the people who run the equipment, the press operators. It takes 7 to 10 years' experience before we would even consider putting someone on as a lead operator. Lead operators supervise five people on a $6 million piece of equipment. That's not something you can take a chance with," Jacot said.

In production, training is available at selected community colleges and vocational schools. Local community colleges that offer associate degrees in printing include Los Angeles Trade-Tech, Pasadena City College, and Riverside City College. Printing programs are also offered at institutes like the East Los Angeles Occupational Center and Whittier Institute of Technology.

Private programs are generally costlier than public instructional courses. But they're quicker. The six-month commercial printing program at the Whittier Institute, for example, prepares graduates for press operator slots in smaller print shops or for entry-level paste-up, camera operator, and platemaker positions at large commercial printers. It costs $5,200.

Community colleges offer the same basic training for $50 a semester, but it takes two years to complete. Besides a lower tuition rate, an advantage to the community college route is that courses taken there are generally transferable to four-year colleges and universities.

The production phase of printing is broken into two stages: preparation and printing. Preparation entails several different processes. If a particular job requires typesetting or original artwork, typesetters and graphic artists are employed. Typesetters arrange text that has been input into the computer system in the proper format and insert the necessary codes. Graphic artists draw original art and design whatever illustrations are required.

Camera operators then shoot the art or typeset copy and reproduce it on film. The film then goes to the stripping department, where strippers assemble the artwork and/or printed pages in the correct order and put the border colors together. Platemakers expose the film onto metal printing plates and deliver the plates to the press operator.

The printing phase is coordinated by the lead press operator, who oversees the roll tender who feeds the paper into the machine, two or three press operators who work to achieve the right color balance, and a jogger who unloads the printed product off the end of the press.

The uncut signatures (printed sheets) are then taken to the bindery department, where they are stitched into complete publications and trimmed to the right dimensions. In bindery, there are feeders who load the signatures into the bindery pockets, collators who insert tabs, punch holes, and affix spiral or adhesive bindings, managers who oversee the operation of the machine, and takeoff people who unload the finished product.

Entry-level production workers with some vocational training usually start in takeoff or jogger positions, essentially performing go-fer jobs on the plant floor but learning the trade along the way. Typically, the first promotion, which comes in six months to a year, is to feeder, Jacot said. Production workers make anywhere from $6 an hour to over $40,000 a year.

Lead operators in large shops may be promoted to supervisor positions, overseeing two to five presses. With a four-year degree in printing management, the promotion could come in as little as two years.

Over time and with consistent performance, mid-level printing managers can make $60,000 to $70,000, said Elliott Levin, director of personnel for Continental Graphics. With 1,600 employees, Continental is the largest printing company in L.A. As senior executives continue climbing, so do their salaries, Levin added. "We've had people hit $90,000 and $100,000."

Printing is one of the few industries left in which a high school diploma can carry you into an eventual managerial position. Most printing companies have a strong promote-from-within policy, said Marge Porter, director of marketing for National Printing Converters in Van Nuys.

"The growth potential in our company is extraordinary. If you are willing to be trained, you can start anywhere," Porter said. "Once you get your foot in the door, familiarize yourself with the business and create your own value. Our national sales manager began with a data processing background, but was very successful in creating a niche for himself."

Working your way up through the production ranks into management takes about 5 to 10 years and requires "cross training, knowledge of the manufacturing process, and the ability to motivate and coordinate the actions of people," said Levin of Continental Graphics.

The most direct path into management is a four-year degree in printing management. The graphic communications department at Cal Poly San Luis Obispo some 200 miles north of Los Angeles offers one of the only printing management programs on the West Coast. It teaches management techniques and offers practical experience through the student-run on-campus printing company, University Graphics Systems.

Printing management majors can also learn the nuts and bolts of the business by helping print the student newspaper. Cal Poly is currently the only university in the country that prints its paper on campus, said Henry "Red" Heesch, an assistant professor in the graphic communications department.

"Our graduates are in high demand. They get all the practical experience plus the management experience. Just about every student who graduates from our program has a job either before they graduate or shortly after they leave," said Heesch, who also acts as the department's placement coordinator. "Knowing the technology is one thing, but being able to manage that capability is where the demand is."

The Cal Poly program consists of courses in personnel and printing management, estimating, labor negotiations, plant layout, and general business practices, Heesch said. Graduates are qualified to hold a variety of positions depending on their interests, including management trainee, customer service representative, sales rep, estimator, and quality control supervisor. Salaries for beginning management and sales staff average around $2,300 a month, Heesch said.

Local printing industry executives say they routinely hire graduates of the Cal Poly program. "If I'm a college graduate and majored in the field, my résumé would knock at the door of every major printing company in town," Levin said. "We just hired somebody that way as an estimator."

Estimators determine the price of a given job, taking into account various overhead costs associated with the business, the cost of materials and labor, price-quantity discounts for high-volume orders, and the going market rate. Estimators then pass this information on to sales reps, who present it in the form of bids to customers. Experienced estimators' salaries are in the $35,000 range, Levin said.

Customer service is another good place to start because it affords regular client contact and offers broad exposure to the administrative side of the business, said Porter of National Printing Converters. "It's an information-critical position. From there you can go just about anywhere in the company."

KEY EMPLOYERS OF PRINTERS AND LITHOGRAPHERS

Alan Lithograph Inc.
550 N. Oak Street
Inglewood, CA 90302
213/671-8808

American Offset Printers
3600 S. Hill Street
Los Angeles, CA 90007
213/231-4133

Anderson Lithograph Co.
3217 S. Garfield Avenue
Los Angeles, CA 90040
213/727-7767

Bert-Co Graphics
1855 Glendale Boulevard
Los Angeles, CA 90026
213/669-5700

Bowne of Los Angeles
1706 Maple Avenue
Los Angeles, CA 90015
213/742-6600

California Offset Printers
620 W. Elk Avenue
Glendale, CA 91204
213/245-6446

ColorGraphics
150 N. Myers Street
Los Angeles, CA 90033
213/261-7171

Continental Graphics Corp.
101 S. La Brea Avenue
Los Angeles, CA 90036
213/938-2511

Pandick Los Angeles
1900 S. Figueroa Street
Los Angeles, CA 90007
213/747-4321

Penn Lithographics Inc.
16221 Arthur Street
Cerritos, CA 90701
213/926-0455

George Rice & Sons
2001 N. Soto Street
Los Angeles, CA 90021
213/223-2020

Sinclair Printing Co.
4005 Whiteside Street
Los Angeles, CA 90063
213/264-4808

Treasure Chest Advertising
511 W. Citrus Edge Street
Glendora, CA 91740
818/914-3981

Welsh Graphics
2181 E. Foothill Boulevard
Pasadena, CA 91107
213/684-1700

Wolfer Printing Co.
6670 Flotilla Street
Los Angeles, CA 90040
213/721-5411

Charles P. Young/Jeffries Co.
1330 W. Pico Boulevard
Los Angeles, CA 90015
213/742-8888

PROFESSIONAL ORGANIZATIONS

Graphic Artists Guild
Los Angeles Chapter
1258 N. Highland Avenue
Los Angeles, CA 90038
213/469-9409

Graphic Communications
Association
1730 N. Lynn Street
Suite 604
Arlington, VA 22209
703/841-8160

Graphic Communications Union
District Council No. 2
1201 S. Beach Boulevard
La Habra, CA 90631
213/947-0361

National Association of Printers
and Lithographers
780 Palisade Avenue
Teaneck, NJ 07666
201/342-0700

Printing Industries Association of
Southern California
5800 S. Eastern Avenue
Los Angeles, CA 90015
213/728-9500

Technical Association of the
Graphic Arts
Post Office Box 9887
T and E Center
Rochester, NY 14623
716/272-0557

PROFESSIONAL PUBLICATIONS

American Printer (Chicago, IL)
Graphic Arts Monthly (New York, NY)
Printing Journal (Pasadena, CA)

Printing Manager (Teaneck, NJ)
Printing News (New York, NY)

DIRECTORIES

Graphic Arts Directory: Los Angeles and Orange County (PEN Publications, Glendale, CA)

Graphic Arts Monthly Buyer's Guide/Directory Issue (Cahners Publishing, New York, NY)

Printers Directory (American Business Directories, Omaha, NE)

Printing Trades Blue Book (A. F. Lewis & Co., New York, NY)

CHAPTER 42

Public Relations

A profession growing in size and stature needs good writers.

A public image is a fragile thing. It can make or break a company just as credibility, or lack of it, can assure the success or failure of a political candidate. An organization or political campaign that has worked for months or years on developing a positive image can be sent into a tailspin with just one well-publicized gaffe.

As awareness of the power of the press to shape public opinion has grown, demand has increased for image makers and protectors—namely, public relations professionals. "Businesses have recognized that an article in the press can have a significant impact on their sales or image," affirmed Sue Bohle, president of the Los Angeles chapter of the Public Relations Society of America (PRSA).

Public relations specialists field calls from the news media and create publicity campaigns that place their client in the most favorable light, typically by pitching story ideas to TV stations, newspapers, and trade magazines. A PR person may also be asked to handle fundraising activities, write speeches, or advise executives on how to present themselves, and by extension the company, positively on television.

Though public relations involves more than just writing, PR specialists first and foremost must be able to translate their original ideas into a coherent press release, a convincing pitch letter, or an intelligent speech.

368 L.A. JOB MARKET HANDBOOK

"If you want to be in PR, you had better be able to write," said Gregory Elliott, public relations administrator for Toyota Motor Sales USA. "When putting out a release, we rely on the inverted pyramid style, just like a journalist would. If you can't write, don't even bother."

The trick to putting together a successful news release is knowing what's newsworthy, writing it in an accurate and seductive style, and having contacts in the media to follow up on your idea.

Pitching a story usually involves suggesting an idea about a company, person, or event that is of interest to the public or a specific publication. PR professionals need to stay abreast of the news. Often, a client will be involved in an activity similar to an issue occurring on a national level. A PR person would then have a tie-in for the client's story. Providing a local angle to a national issue makes an idea eminently marketable.

People skills invariably are a plus, but they can't stand on their own. "I get sick and tired of people asking me for a job because they're 'good with people,'" said Richard Taylor, president and CEO of Rogers & Cowan, the largest public relations agency in Los Angeles. "They need skills, too. I want to know if they can write a press release, if they can sell something over the phone, if they can create an idea and implement a marketing plan."

The field of public relations has expanded in scope in recent years and now encompasses information campaigning, survey research, special event planning, and crisis management preparation. "Companies that didn't place an emphasis on public relations in the past are doing so now," said Greg LaBrache, vice president of media relations for Hill and Knowlton. "The public relations function is becoming an integral part of many companies' marketing strategies."

That public relations is becoming more accepted and more utilized is reflected by the field's growth rate. In Los Angeles, the management and public relations consulting industry grew roughly 78 percent from 1980 to 1987, said Jack Kyser, chief economist for the Los Angeles Area Chamber of Commerce. In 1987, there were 3,497 management and public relations firms in Los Angeles County employing some 37,623 people, compared to 1,716 firms with 21,127 employees in 1980.

"There has been a good growth trend in this area," Kyser said. "It mirrors the diversity of our economy. All of those businesses out there need people to tell their story and to help them when they run into problems. You have new firms coming into the market all the time."

Yet despite this growth, the field remains supremely competitive. Similar to advertising, there are more public relations graduates emerging from the Southland's numerous colleges and universities than the industry can absorb, Bohle said. A bachelor's degree *with* experience, usually in the form of an internship, is virtually essential.

"Public relations is very competitive; it's even more competitive coming right out of school," affirmed Smooch Reynolds, vice president of the communications search division of Mitchell, Larsen & Zilliacus, an executive search firm in Los Angeles.

Positive internship experiences in many cases can lead to permanent employment. "Some people who do a good job stay on with us," said Susan Romeo, media director for Cerrell Associates, an L.A. public relations agency that specializes in business and political consulting.

Another way to enter the field is through journalism. Former journalists make good public relations professionals because of their inside take on the newspaper or broadcast industry. They have contacts. They know how to work effectively under pressure and on a tight deadline. And they are familiar with what's newsworthy and what's not.

An entry-level position at an agency, such as account coordinator or assistant account executive, generally pays from $18,000 to $22,000 a year. At a large corporation, beginning public relations assistants may start in the mid-$20,000 range.

Showing initiative, especially at an agency, can result in rapid advancement. "People who come in and right away prove that they can handle things are the people who move rapidly up in the ranks," said LaBrache of Hill and Knowlton. "Everything is judged by performance. If a junior member of my staff brainstorms and comes up with a good idea, then that idea would rule."

With three to four years of experience, public relations professionals can earn upward of $30,000. Moving up the ladder at an agency leads to the position of account executive and then senior account executive, which pays from $30,000 to $40,000 a year. With additional experience, senior account executives can be promoted to account supervisor and, eventually, to group supervisor, making an annual salary upward of $60,000.

On the corporate side, public relations jobs can vary widely. In media relations, PR specialists are responsible for developing and maintaining press contacts and for publicizing events, while in corporate communications the responsibilities may be more in-house, such as writing company newsletters and helping executives develop better communications skills.

The key difference between corporate and agency work is that agencies tend to be more proactive (generating ideas, coming up with new angles, writing pitch letters, etc.), while PR specialists for corporations tend to be more reactive (fielding calls from the media, writing speeches and briefing executives before they give speeches or appear on television, etc.). Another difference is the number of clients you work for.

"You're serving far more masters at an agency than at a company," said Elliott of Toyota, who has worked in both agency and corporate settings. "When I was at an agency, I had half a dozen clients, so my day was very regimented."

"The average agency represents much more of a pressure cooker environment than a corporation," added Bohle. "I wouldn't advise public relations for someone who wants a cushy job. The kind of people who are successful are those who enjoy the challenge of keeping several things in the hopper at once."

Besides agency and corporate work, there is the political side of public relations, including government relations and campaign management. Cerrell Associates is one of the largest public relations firms in the Los Angeles area to specialize in political consulting. "We have an ongoing need for staff," Romeo said. "There's always a campaign going on somewhere."

High technology promises to be an up-and-coming area of PR in the decade ahead. "There will be a high demand for PR in high tech, but not enough qualified applicants," said Ester Ramirez, director of career advisement for USC's School of Journalism. "So someone who is interested in this area will be able to write [his or her] own ticket as far as a job and a salary are concerned."

Finding an entry-level position in public relations may not be easy, but it's not impossible either. Timing may improve your chances. Agencies tend to have more openings in the summer, Reynolds said. If the opportunities are scarce in the private sector, don't despair. Try a nonprofit, government, or community organization instead.

The City and County of Los Angeles have regular openings for public relations specialists in their various departments. In the long run, these jobs may not pay as well as the private sector, but they can provide valuable experience as well as business and career contacts. The City of Los Angeles starts beginning public relations specialists out at $1,989 a month.

SELECTED PUBLIC RELATIONS FIRMS

Berkhemer, Kline, Golin, Harris, Inc.
261 S. Figueroa Street
Suite 250
Los Angeles, CA 90012
213/620-5711

Braun & Co.
3580 Wilshire Boulevard
Suite 1520
Los Angeles, CA 90010
213/385-3481

Burson-Marsteller
3333 Wilshire Boulevard
Suite 400
Los Angeles, CA 90010
213/386-8776

Cerrell Associates Inc.
12400 Wilshire Boulevard
Suite 200
Los Angeles, CA 90004
213/466-3445

Doremus Porter Novelli
11755 Wilshire Boulevard
Suite 1600
Los Angeles, CA 90025
213/444-7000

Fleishman-Hillard Inc.
515 S. Flower Street
Seventh Floor
Los Angeles, CA 90071
213/629-4974

Hill and Knowlton
5900 Wilshire Boulevard
Los Angeles, CA 90036
213/937-7460

Ketchum Public Relations
11755 Wilshire Boulevard
Suite 1900
Los Angeles, CA 90025
213/444-5000

The Lippin Group Inc.
6100 Wilshire Boulevard
Suite 400
Los Angeles, CA 90048
213/965-1990

Manning, Selvage & Lee
10 Universal City Plaza
Suite 2600
Universal City, CA 91608
818/509-1840

Rifkind Pondel & Parsons
11601 Wilshire Boulevard
Los Angeles, CA 90025
213/478-3523

Rogers & Associates
2029 Century Park East
Suite 1010
Los Angeles, CA 90067
213/552-6922

Rogers & Cowan Inc.
10000 Santa Monica Boulevard
Fourth Floor
Los Angeles, CA 90067
213/201-8800

Rowland Grody Tellem
11150 W. Olympic Boulevard
Suite 840
Los Angeles, CA 90064
213/479-3363

Carl Terzian Associates
12400 Wilshire Boulevard
Suite 200
Los Angeles, CA 90025
213/207-3361

PROFESSIONAL ORGANIZATIONS

**International Association of
  Business Communicators**
2500 Wilshire Boulevard
Los Angeles, CA 90057
213/384-1602

Publicity Club of Los Angeles
5000 Van Nuys Boulevard
Sherman Oaks, CA 91403
818/872-0525

**Public Relations Society of
  America**
Los Angeles Chapter
7080 Hollywood Boulevard
Los Angeles, CA 90028
213/461-4595

**Women Executives in Public
  Relations**
Post Office Box 781
Murray Hill Station
New York, NY 10156
212/683-5438

Women in Communications Inc.
1539½ Westwood Boulevard
Los Angeles, CA 90024
213/477-6388

PROFESSIONAL PUBLICATIONS

Jack O'Dwyer's Newsletter (New York, NY)
PR Reporter (Exeter, NH)
PRSA News (New York, NY)
PR Week (New York, NY)
Public Relations Journal (New York, NY)
Public Relations Review (Silver Spring, MD)

DIRECTORIES

O'Dwyer's Directory of Corporate Communications (J. R. O'Dwyer Co.,
  New York, NY)
O'Dwyer's Directory of Public Relations Firms (J. R. O'Dwyer Co., New
  York, NY)
Public Relations Journal, Directory Issue (Public Relations Society of Amer-
  ica, New York, NY)
Where to Study Public Relations (International Association of Business
  Communicators, San Francisco, CA)

CHAPTER 43

News Reporter, Photographer, and Broadcaster

Competition is stiff in the nation's second-largest media market.

Let's not kid ourselves. The hours are long, the pay is low, the work is demanding, an opening is almost impossible to find, and the egos you encounter are enormous. But covering the news offers reporters, broadcasters, and photojournalists a window on the world of events, whether they happen across the street or halfway around the globe, and a chance to record and interpret the unfolding of history.

"You've got to do it because you love it," said King Harris, news director of KEYT-TV in Santa Barbara, whose station recently sent a team of reporters to the Soviet Union. "Good reporters are curious about life and other people. They dig for information and have an ability to learn and be flexible. If you're in it for glamour and money, you're a fool."

Southern California is considered by many in the industry to be one of the best places in the country to pursue a career in journalism, primarily because of the climate, the relaxed atmosphere, the profusion of college and university degree programs in journalism, and the fact that Los Angeles is the second-largest media market in the nation.

"New York considers itself the center of the communications industry. But that's changing," said Jim Foy, executive director of the Greater Los Angeles Press Club. "There will be great growth here in the publication of Asian newspapers."

One of the things that make finding a full-time position difficult is that talented journalists from all over the country have their sights set on working here. "This town is awash in people trying to get into the business," said Robert Sims, director of news for KNX-AM. "I certainly know radio is that way ... television's even worse. In Los Angeles, you have to have that competitive instinct."

There are some 214 newspaper operations, 185 magazines and trade journals, 82 radio stations, 67 television stations, and 21 cable companies in Los Angeles County, together employing about 27,000 people, said Jack Kyser, chief economist for the Los Angeles Area Chamber of Commerce.

Yet for the aspiring journalist, the number of media outlets is deceptive; there are so many competing with each other that none of the big newspapers, wire services, or radio or TV news departments can afford to take a chance on inexperienced help. Indeed, rarely does a major publication or broadcast company need to advertise its editorial job openings.

"Unfortunately, the standards you try to maintain work against the people who are trying to break into the business, because they have to go somewhere else to develop that competence level," Sims said.

Reporters are part investigators, part writers. While it helps to be a good storyteller, reporters must be able to get their facts straight and do a thorough job of gathering information. The assignments they receive vary from breaking stories, such as fires and plane crashes, to features about people or trends, to specific beats, like city hall, the police station, or the courts.

The job of reporter can be stressful but exhilarating. In all three areas of reporting—print, radio, and TV—most stories are covered under heavy deadline pressure that leaves little room for mistakes and missed opportunities. And reporting the news frequently does not conform to a 9-to-5 daily routine. The hours are often long and irregular, especially when an unexpected major story breaks.

Most of the above holds true for photojournalists, who show the news rather than tell it. Even for photographers, emphasis is placed on attracting—and holding—the reader's attention. "You're trying to come back with a picture that draws the reader into the story," said Dean Musgrove, photography editor for the *Los Angeles Daily News*. "It's important that a photographer know what approaches are appropriate for a given assignment."

Entry-level photographers should have a well-rounded portfolio consisting of 12 to 40 pictures that show expertise in all areas of news, including hard news, features, sports, fashion, and photo essays, Musgrove said. They should also know how to develop their own film and shoot in both black-and-white and in color, since many newspapers are now printing color.

"Applicants need to tailor their portfolio to a certain publication," Musgrove said. "Smaller, community papers might be more interested in someone who is strong on features. Here, I need to see a little more news. A portfolio is only as strong as its weakest photo."

For those just entering the field, a college degree is essential, although a journalism major is not required. "As far as I'm concerned, a broad-based education in liberal arts or a major in political science or history may be even more valuable than a journalism degree," said Mark Nelson, Los Angeles bureau chief for ABC Network News.

Local schools that offer degrees in journalism include USC and Cal State Long Beach, Cal State Northridge, and Cal State Fullerton. Having a degree doesn't guarantee employment, however. Most major daily newspapers, wire services, and television and radio stations in Los Angeles won't even consider hiring someone straight out of college for a staff writing or on-air position.

Large newspapers like the *Los Angeles Times* require five to seven years' experience for staff writers, who are usually hired for a suburban section (not Metro). Local and network news teams require their correspondents to have previous on-air experience in a smaller market. At the larger papers, experienced reporters can make $40,000 to $60,000 a year or more.

Mid-size papers such as the *Los Angeles Daily News* and the *Orange County Register*, the biggest paper in Orange County, normally require their staff writers to have three to five years' previous daily experience. At smaller papers, which can serve as jumping-off points to larger publications, the hiring requirements are slightly more relaxed.

When hiring, editors generally assign more weight to news clips than to an applicant's grade point average. "I've hired people [straight] out of college, but I'm going to want to see some internship experience and clips from their college paper," said Terry Greenberg, managing editor of the Pasadena *Star News*. "I'm worried about the quality of clips and a reference who can tell me how much editing was done."

To bolster your career prospects, accumulate as many internships and job contacts as possible while still in school. A standout performance as an intern could lead to a job offer after graduation—or extra consideration in the future. This is true in both print and broadcasting.

"Somebody who comes here and demonstrates through an internship that, No. 1, he or she has the desire and, No. 2, he has the qualities we would be looking for has a better chance," said Steve Shusman, Los Angeles bureau chief for Cable News Network (CNN). "Lots of times, because interns are known to us, they will get first refusal to the jobs that open up."

In both TV and radio news, one way to start is as a desk assistant, production assistant, or researcher for a particular show. If you're still in school, the job of courier is even considered a starting point. "Anything can lead to anything," said Nelson of ABC.

Sometimes it is possible for beginning correspondents and news desk assistants to become stringers for smaller television stations or work at a network on an as-needed (per diem) basis.

Desk assistants monitor the wire services for important breaking stories, answer the phones, and, at network news affiliates, coordinate stories with the home office. Production assistants are for the most part technicians who assist in filming, recording, and preparing tapes for playback. At more advanced levels, they help edit the tape or footage to be aired.

A production assistant, or even a camera operator who demonstrates an understanding of the entire news operation, may move up to the associate producer rank, Shusman said. Desk assistants may be promoted to the posts of assignment editor, field producer, or newswriter. Newswriters report on stories from the home office, writing copy for the anchors to announce later.

At the major networks, most news jobs are unionized, so there is little crossover between correspondents, who appear in front of the camera, and newswriters, who work behind the scenes. At smaller stations and nonunion broadcast companies, such as CNN, correspondents are allowed much greater latitude.

In radio, a desk assistant job might lead into a newswriting position and, eventually, a shot at reading your own work on the air. But broadcast openings are rare, especially at the city's two all-news radio stations, KNX-AM and KFWB-AM. "If you can't get on the air here, then you need to go someplace where you can," said Sims of KNX. "You have to go to a place that will let you do your stuff."

Largest Newspapers in the Los Angeles Area

Newspaper	Daily Circulation
Los Angeles Times	1,137,000
Orange County Register	334,000
Los Angeles Daily News	195,000
Riverside Press Enterprise	153,000
Long Beach Press-Telegram	132,000
LA Opinion	98,000
The Daily Breeze	93,000
San Gabriel Valley Tribune	60,000
Antelope Valley Press	56,000
Korea Times	50,000

SOURCE: Newspapers. 1989 figures.

KEY EMPLOYERS OF NEWS REPORTERS, PHOTOGRAPHERS, AND BROADCASTERS

Daily Newspapers

Antelope Valley Press
37404 Sierra Highway
Palmdale, CA 93550
805/273-2700
Circulation: 56,000

Copley Los Angeles Newspapers
The Daily Breeze/Outlook/News
 Pilot
5215 Torrance Boulevard
Torrance, CA 90509
213/540-5511
Combined circulation: 135,500

LA Opinion
(Spanish Language)
1436 S. Main Street
Los Angeles, CA 90015
213/748-1191
Circulation: 98,000

Long Beach Press-Telegram
604 Pine Avenue
Long Beach, CA 90844
213/499-1340
Circulation: 132,000

Los Angeles Daily Journal
210 S. Spring Street
Los Angeles, CA 90054
213/625-2141
Circulation: 15,000

Los Angeles Daily News
21221 Oxnard Street
Woodland Hills, CA 91365
818/713-3030
Circulation: 195,000

Los Angeles Times
Times Mirror Square
Los Angeles, CA 90053
213/237-4463
Circulation: 1,137,000

*Circulation as of November 1989.

Orange County Register
625 N. Grand Avenue
Santa Ana, CA 92711
714/835-1234
Circulation: 334,000

Pasadena Star-News
525 E. Colorado Boulevard
Pasadena, CA 91109
818/578-6510
Circulation: 38,000

Riverside Press Enterprise
3512 14th Street
Riverside, CA 92501
714/684-1200
Circulation: 152,697

San Bernardino Sun
399 N. D Street
San Bernardino, CA 92401
714/889-9666
Circulation: 90,000

Wire Services

Associated Press (AP)
1111 S. Hill Street
Los Angeles, CA 90015
213/746-1200

City News Service (CNS)
6255 W. Sunset Boulevard
Los Angeles, CA 90028
213/461-6397

United Press International (UPI)
316 W. Second Street
Los Angeles, CA 90012
213/620-1230

News Radio Stations

KFWB-AM (980)
6230 Yucca Street
Los Angeles, CA 90028
213/871-4612

KNX-AM (1070)
6121 Sunset Boulevard
Los Angeles, CA 90028
213/460-3321

Television Stations

ABC Network News (Ch. 7)
4151 Prospect Avenue
Los Angeles, CA 90027
213/557-6193

Cable News Network (CNN)
6340 W. Sunset Boulevard
Los Angeles, CA 90028
213/460-5000

CBS Network News (Ch. 2)
Television City
7800 Beverly Boulevard
Los Angeles, CA 90036
213/852-2345

KABC-TV (Ch. 7)
4151 Prospect Avenue
Los Angeles, CA 90027
213/557-7777

KCAL-TV (Ch. 9)
5515 Melrose Avenue
Los Angeles, CA 90038
213/467-5459

KCBS-TV (Ch. 2)
6121 Sunset Boulevard
Los Angeles, CA 90028
213/460-4000

KCOP-TV (Ch. 13)
915 N. La Brea Avenue
Los Angeles, CA 90038
213/850-2252

KNBC-TV (Ch. 4)
3000 W. Alameda Avenue
Burbank, CA 91523
818/840-3425

KTLA-TV (Ch. 5)
5800 Sunset Boulevard
Los Angeles, CA 90028
213/460-5751

KTTV-TV (Ch. 11)
5746 Sunset Boulevard
Los Angeles, CA 90028
213/856-1000

NBC Network News (Ch. 4)
3000 W. Alameda Avenue
Burbank, CA 91523
818/840-3418

PROFESSIONAL ORGANIZATIONS

American Society of Journalists and Authors
Southern California Chapter
Post Office Box 35282
Los Angeles, CA 90035
213/934-2305

Asian American Journalists Association (AAJA)
1765 Sutter Street
San Francisco, CA 94115
415/346-2051

California Chicano News Media Association (CCNMA)
USC School of Journalism
University Park
Los Angeles, CA 90089-1695
213/743-7158

Greater Los Angeles Press Club
600 N. Vermont Avenue
Los Angeles, CA 90004
213/665-1141

Investigative Reporters & Editors (IRE)
Post Office Box 838
Columbia, MO 65205
314/882-2042

National Association of Black Journalists
Post Office Box 17212
Washington, DC 20041
703/648-1270

Radio & Television News Association of Southern California
14755 Ventura Boulevard
Sherman Oaks, CA 91403
818/986-8168

Society of Professional Journalists
53 W. Jackson Street
Chicago, IL 60604
312/922-7424

PROFESSIONAL PUBLICATIONS

Broadcaster (Nashua, NH)
Broadcasting (Washington, DC)
Columbia Journalism Review (New York, NY)
Editor & Publisher (New York, NY)
IRE Journal (Columbia, MO)
Journal of Broadcasting and Electronic Media (Amherst, MA)
The Quill (Chicago, IL)

Radio Week (Washington, DC)
Washington Journalism Review (Washington, DC)

DIRECTORIES

Bacon's Radio/TV Directory (Bacon's Publishing Co., Chicago, IL)
Broadcasting Cable Sourcebook (Broadcasting Publishing Co., Washington, DC)
Broadcasting Yearbook (Broadcasting Publishing Co., Washington, DC)
Editor & Publisher's International Yearbook (Editor & Publisher, New York, NY)

Telecommuting

*Working at home is becoming an option for
more and more office-oriented employees.*

In the 1990s, a combination of factors ranging from air pollution and traffic congestion to high housing costs and a changing labor market is prompting changes in the way people work. Telecommuting, or working at home via computer, telephone, modem, and fax machine, is rapidly emerging as one the most effective and flexible ways of getting work done while helping to reduce the amount of smog and number of cars on the road.

"People are discovering it more and more out of necessity, whether it's due to air quality or an earthquake," observed Lisa Zanville, who telecommutes part-time in her job as director of media relations for Pacific Bell in Los Angeles. "It's an electronic bridge. Through my modem, I have access to all my files at work. I can also call in and hear my voice mail. This is quite effective in working emergency situations. If an earthquake hits, I have everything at home. I don't need to come in."

Natural disasters notwithstanding, business theorists like Peter F. Drucker argue that with the arrival of the Information Age, commuting to an office has become obsolete. In many instances, it is now easier, cheaper, and faster to move work rather than people, using communications technology. Even President George Bush, in a March 1990 address to the California Chamber of Commerce, touted telecommuting as a new business "frontier."

Formerly the domain of a select group of freelance writers, consultants, computer programmers, and small-business owners, telecommuting has opened up to a broad range of professionals who were traditionally office-oriented—from architects to insurance adjusters to public relations specialists.

"The easiest telecommuters are relatively high-tech already," said Jack Nilles, a Santa Monica–based consultant who coined the term *telecommuting* in 1973 while director of USC's

Information Technology Program. "They're used to dealing with computers and have fairly autonomous jobs. Even accountants and attorneys, though they clearly have to be in the office some of the time, are finding they can do a lot of their work at home."

Most corporate telecommuters work at home rather than the office once or twice a week, although many telecommute more frequently. Some companies have also set up satellite offices and neighborhood work centers for telecommuting. In a typical telecommuting arrangement, employees borrow their high-tech equipment from work. Others purchase it outright, converting their residences into "electronic cottages."

Not every employee is cut out for telecommuting. Ideal candidates, says Elham Shiriza of Commuter Transportation Services in Los Angeles, require minimum supervision, are moderately people-oriented, and have a high level of job skill and job knowledge. Moreover, they must be well organized, self-motivated, have good time management skills, and be able to work independently and productively.

Employees identified as potential telecommuters usually aren't new hires, Shiriza added. They are seasoned veterans who have developed a positive reputation in their department and have built up a solid relationship with their supervisor. "Trust is the key word. I think it takes a while to build that trust."

Who telecommutes? According to a 1987 survey by the Link Resources Corp., a New York market research firm, the typical telecommuter is usually married, between the ages of 35 and 40 years old, and earns an average income of $40,000 a year. As a group, telecommuters are split almost down the line between men and women. Roughly three-fourths are married and a little more than half have some college education.

An estimated 3 million people in the United States currently telecommute. By the mid-1990s, that number is expected to grow to 4 or 5 million. Nilles, who estimates there are between 100,000 and 200,000 telecommuters in California, says that most large corporations already have a reasonable number of telecommuters—up to 5 percent or so—but haven't identified them as such.

The vast majority of telecommuters work in service and information industries like sales, public relations, personnel, advertising, financial services, consulting, and publishing. All told, information workers constitute about 60 percent of the California workforce, Nilles said. Manufacturing, construction, and agriculture provide only about 25 percent of all home office workers.

Telecommuting in Southern California is likely to rise dramatically in the next few years. Recently adopted air quality guidelines have prompted many local firms to initiate pilot telecommuting projects, along with other commuting options such as ride sharing and four-day work weeks, as a way of reducing overall work trips and vehicle emissions in the Los Angeles basin.

Zanville of Pacific Bell offers the following basic guidelines for becoming an effective telecommuter:

- Make sure you have the right match of job, employee, supervisor, home working environment, and telecommuting arrangement. Consider your personality type. Are you a self-motivated person who enjoys solitude, or do you crave structure and thrive on the bustling social milieu of a busy office?

  "For some people, it doesn't work out because they get too lonely," Shiriza said. "Some people need the discipline and social support of the office."

  Zanville stresses the importance of making regular visits to the office to keep abreast of ongoing business at the company. "I recommend that they don't telecommute full-time. It's more effective to have a combination, especially for the socialization. A lot of times, information is passed around at the water cooler."

- Set aside a specific area at home, preferably an entire room if one is available, and dedicate it exclusively to work-related activities. Equip your work area with all the office furniture, supplies, and business machines you need to perform your job. If practical, install an additional phone line for business calls. Don't let work intrude too much on your home life.

- Take the kids to a day care center. Parenting and working don't mix. Telecommuting promises a more flexible work schedule, not an all-expense-paid babysitting arrangement. "Telecommuting is not a substitute for child care," Zanville said. "And it's not a women's issue. It's really an environmental and quality-of-life issue."

- Budget your time and map out a work plan so you don't fritter your time away. Take a professional approach. Act like it's a normal business day. "When I work at home, I try to do things that are conducive to working at home, like working on a database, learning a new software program, writing speeches, or putting together a press kit," Zanville said.

The payoffs to employers are manifold, advocates claim: Telecommuting can increase productivity 20 to 50 percent while reducing overhead costs. Proponents like Shiriza contend it can also decrease absenteeism and turnover, enable employees to make more efficient use of time, and boost morale by giving telecommuters more control over their work styles.

"Telecommuting is a very real way of attracting talented employees," agreed Ken Croley, telecommuting manager for AT&T in Los Angeles. "It gives companies leverage in hiring quality people." Of AT&T's 160 managerial employees who currently telecommute one or two days a week, most say they are "working harder and faster and were happier doing it," Croley said.

Following the success of its pilot project, Pacific Bell has expanded its staff of telecommuters to 1,500 people statewide, said Carol Nolan, Pac Bell's sales support manager in Los Angeles.

On the downside, there can be a stigma attached to working out of your home. "People think that if you work at home, you're not working," Zanville said. There's even the potential of abuse, of working yourself too hard without overtime pay and turning your home into what in essence is an electronic sweatshop.

Telecommuters also face the very real prospect of landing on a career plateau. Critics of telecommuting contend that telecommuters are frequently left out of the decision-making loop and overlooked at promotion time. Due to these and other gray employment issues that are still left to resolve, most telecommuters are nonunion.

Even with the pitfalls, employees have shown resounding interest in telecommuting. When the South Coast Air Quality Management District (AQMD) distributed 600 surveys to employees soliciting volunteers for a pilot telecommuting project, 594 respondents indicated they wanted to participate in the program, said Gracie Tucker, an AQMD air quality specialist.

Besides yielding environmental and quality-of-life dividends, telecommuting saves time. Why waste two hours a day (or more), five days a week, sitting in traffic when you could be at home getting work done? "It's much easier to work on certain projects without all the distractions, without people walking into your office all of the time," said Claudia Keith, also of the AQMD. "A lot of people are looking for alternatives to the rigid scheduling that existed before."

*KEY EMPLOYERS OF TELECOMMUTERS

ARCO
515 S. Flower Street
Los Angeles, CA 90071
213/486-2692

AT&T
611 W. Sixth Street
Suite 1200
Los Angeles, CA 90017
213/239-7594

City of Los Angeles
City Hall
200 N. Spring Street
Los Angeles, CA 90012
213/485-6142

Control Data Corp.
18730 Crenshaw Boulevard
Torrance, CA 90504
213/719-7400

Coopers & Lybrand
Accounting and Mangement
  Consulting
1000 W. Sixth Street
Los Angeles, CA 90017
213/481-1000

County of Los Angeles
Chief Administrative Office
Policy Support Division
222 N. Grand Avenue
Room 585
Los Angeles, CA 90012
213/974-2632

Daniel Freeman Memorial Hospital
333 N. Prairie Avenue
Inglewood, CA 90301
213/674-7050

GTE
Telephone Operations–West Area
One GTE Place
Thousand Oaks, CA 91362
805/372-6000

Hartford Insurance Group
15350 Sherman Way
Van Nuys, CA 91406
818/902-1305

Hughes Communications Inc.
1990 E. Grand Avenue
El Segundo, CA 90245
213/607-4000

IBM
355 S. Grand Avenue
Los Angeles, CA 90071
213/621-7391

Orange County Transit District
Commuter Network
11222 Acacia Parkway
Garden Grove, CA 92642
714/638-9000

Pacific Bell
1010 Wilshire Boulevard
Suite 1300
Los Angeles, CA 90017
213/975-7495

**Riverside County Transportation
  Commission**
3560 University Avenue
Suite 100
Riverside, CA 92501
714/787-7141

**South Coast Air Quality
  Management District (AQMD)**
9150 Flair Drive
El Monte, CA 91731
818/571-5160

Travelers Insurance
3600 Wilshire Boulevard
Suite 1602
Los Angeles, CA 90010
213/381-0600

Xerox Corp.
Post Office Box 25075
2200 E. McFadden Avenue
Santa Ana, CA 92799
213/562-3550

* Please note that the above employers rarely, if ever, directly hire "telecommuters" as such. They do, however, give senior employees whose jobs lend themselves to telecommuting the option of working from their homes or a satellite office once or twice weekly. Employer names were provided by the Telecommuting Advisory Council.

PROFESSIONAL ORGANIZATIONS AND CONSULTANTS

Commuter Transportation Services Inc.
Commuter Computer
3550 Wilshire Boulevard
Suite 300
Los Angeles, CA 90010
213/380-7750

Fleming Ltd.
Management Consultants
1107 Halifax Avenue
Davis, CA 95616
916/756-6430

Ghaffari Associates
Management Consultants
2807 Highland Avenue
Suite 3
Santa Monica, CA 90405
213/392-3909

JALA Associates
Management Consultants
971 Stonehill Lane
Los Angeles, CA 90049
213/476-3703

National Association for the Cottage Industry
Post Office Box 14460
Chicago, IL 60614
312/472-8116

Telecommuting Advisory Council
c/o Carol Nolan
Pacific Bell
1010 Wilshire Boulevard
Room 1300
Los Angeles, CA 90017
213/975-7495

PROFESSIONAL PUBLICATIONS

Home Office Computing (New York, NY)
SCAG Telecommunity (Los Angeles, CA)
Telephone News (Potomac, MD)

RECOMMENDED READING

Fleming, Lis. *The One-Minute Commuter: How to Keep Your Job and Stay at Home Telecommuting.* Davis, CA: Acacia Books, 1989.

Creating a Flexible Workplace. New York: AMACOM, 1989.

Gordon, Gil. *Telecommuting Review: The Gordon Report.* Monmouth Junction, NJ: Gil Gordon Associates, 1987.

Telecommuting: A Review of Literature and Programs. Garden Grove, CA: Orange County Transit District, 1989.

SECTION
13

Mass Transit, Manufacturing, and Construction Jobs

CHAPTER **44**

Transportation

*Unprecedented demand is putting
qualified workers in the driver's seat.*

Local officials enjoy talking about the strength of the Southern California economy. They like to point out the region's phenomenal growth pattern, as Los Angeles and Orange counties continue to attract new business and residents, generating close to 140,000 new jobs each year.

With this economic expansion has come an increased demand for the "grease" that keeps the engine of the greater Los Angeles area's broad-based regional economy humming: the drivers, dispatchers, and transportation managers who move passengers and goods around L.A.'s vast urban and suburban sprawl.

Opportunities in transportation are so plentiful, especially for drivers, that job seekers have their choice of industry. Provided an applicant has a good driving record and some knowledge of the highways and byways that traverse the Southland, employers from grocery chains and soft drink bottlers to parcel delivery services and freight carriers are eager to do the hiring.

"I don't know of any company in the trucking industry that isn't doing everything they can possibly do to get drivers," said Brad Proctor, terminal manager for JB Hunt Transportation in South Gate. "It's one of the most open industries I know of."

JB Hunt, one of the largest trucking companies in Los Angeles (Viking Freight System in Whittier is another), is an example of the growth potential in transportation. Over the next few years, the company plans to double its number of local drivers from 100 to 200, Proctor said.

The industry overall is growing at a healthy rate. From 1987 to 1992, the number of truck drivers in Los Angeles and Orange counties is expected to increase about 13 percent, from 81,640 in 1987 to an estimated 92,050 by 1992, according to the state Employment Development Department. The broader category of motor vehicle operators should grow at about the same rate, from 118,740 drivers in 1987 to an estimated 133,680 by 1992.

The transportation industry has its own geography in the Los Angeles area. Driving jobs are divided regionally. Most of the messenger or delivery services are congregated in the Wilshire and downtown districts, while the booming airport shuttle service industry is based near Los Angeles International Airport (LAX). Opportunities in conventional, big-rig truck driving can be found in such industry-oriented communities as Commerce, South Gate, Vernon, Carson, and Wilmington.

Truck driving positions require training for a Class A commercial driving license (formerly Class 1), which can be obtained by attending one of the Southland's numerous professional trucking schools. Superior Training Service, one of the more highly regarded schools according to people in the trucking industry, has campuses in Rialto and Long Beach. Superior offers a Class A training program that lasts from four to eight weeks and costs about $3,000.

A new driver with a Class A license at JB Hunt makes $450 a week after undergoing a 90-day probationary period at a lower pay scale. Driver trainers with at least six months' driving experience and a clean record—no more than three moving violations in three years—can bring home about $1,200 per week, Proctor said.

There are two types of truck driving: line and local. Line drivers embark on long-distance trips that take days or even weeks to complete. They may haul their cargo across state lines or even cross-country. Local drivers, on the other hand, deliver loads to nearby destinations and return to their home base on the same day. Local drivers generally load and unload the cargo they are carrying themselves; long-distance line drivers hire others to do that work for them.

Truck drivers are required to pass a rigorous physical examination in accordance with U.S. Department of Transportation (DOT) regulations. The DOT also regulates the amount of time long-distance drivers can spend on the road—no more than 60 hours in any seven-day period, and no more than 10 hours at any one stretch without being off-duty at least 8 hours.

Interestingly, husband-wife teams make up about 20 percent

of all truckers on the road, Proctor said. The requirements are the same for men and women truck drivers. Although two drivers on the road might be better than one, husband-wife teams who work together split their pay rather than earning two incomes.

Finding a job in transportation doesn't necessarily mean getting behind the wheel of a big rig. With an estimated 9,000 employees, the Southern California Rapid Transit District ranks as one of the 50 largest employers in Southern California. Even so, the RTD has a backlog of applicants for the position of bus operator (driver), said RTD spokesman Rick Jagger.

With the RTD, an applicant's best shot is to apply for a part-time driving position in hope of eventually getting full-time work, Jagger said. Bus drivers, who are required to have a Class B license (formerly Class 2), can advance to the positions of road supervisor and dispatcher, two jobs that are typically filled internally.

Many other areas, such as Torrance, Santa Monica, and Orange County, have mass transit districts as well.

In the bustling transportation services industry, the duties of a dispatcher can resemble those of an air traffic controller. On a busy day at United Independent Taxi in downtown Los Angeles, a dispatcher with 100 to 150 cabs in the field may handle up to 200 calls per hour, or 3.3 per minute, said Nathaniel Howard, the taxi company's vice president. Dispatchers in high-volume transportation companies are in a hot seat. Their position calls for lightning-quick reaction time and a levelheaded personality.

"The job entails the patience of a saint, a doctorate in psychology, and the ability to do five or six things at once," said Marian Smith, United Independent Taxi's dispatch supervisor. "It's a real high-speed, high-tension, high-anxiety kind of job. If you crave excitement and a fast pace, then this job's for you. It's rewarding when things are going well. There's a lot of satisfaction to it. When there isn't, it's a challenge."

At United, beginning dispatchers, usually former taxi drivers, start at around $10 an hour, Smith said. Cab drivers, on the other hand, operate as independent contractors, earning $100 or more a day after paying for their own gas and the cost of leasing the cab (about $40 for 12 hours), Howard said. "A guy could make a pretty good living working as a cab driver."

Because of the risk factor involved in hiring inexperienced drivers to successfully navigate L.A.'s busy city streets, United requires all its drivers to have at least nine months' previous taxi driving experience in the Los Angeles area. The company also requires its drivers to attend a school in defensive driving. Some areas of the transportation industry are seasonal. Parcel delivery companies such as United Parcel Service (UPS) and Federal Express mainly hire drivers during the autumn and late spring months. At UPS, temporary drivers are paid $11 or $12 an hour. UPS also hires early-morning loaders and unloaders on a temporary basis for $8 to $9 an hour, said Harley Johnson, Los Angeles district personnel manager for UPS.

In two years, drivers hired at UPS on a permanent basis can make up to $17 an hour, Johnson said. "Beyond that, they'll make incentive pay based on doing more work. If the balance sheet shows that nine hours of work was done in eight, they'll get one hour of overtime pay."

UPS, which has about 8,000 employees in Los Angeles, 2,500 of whom are drivers, hires about 1,000 new drivers each year, Johnson said. (Federal Express has about 1,200 employees in the greater Los Angeles area.) The UPS motto—"We run the tightest ship in the shipping business"—especially applies to the delivery end, as drivers make an average of 225 individual stops each day and probably handle 500 or 600 packages per shift.

"It's a demanding job. You can't make mistakes. It takes some-one who has a good ability to concentrate," Johnson said. "It's a very difficult job to learn. You have to keep track of 225 different stops and which one comes next. Service commitments are important to us. You can get fired for late deliveries. Some people just don't make it."

On top of possessing keen organizational skills, UPS drivers must be physically strong and be able to lift packages weighing up to 70 pounds. "It's a painful job the first couple of weeks," Johnson admits. "The average package weighs 30 pounds. But once you do it for a month or so, it's just exercise."

Johnson said UPS has a low turnover rate among its dedicated staff of permanent drivers, 11 percent of whom are female. "Some of our best drivers are the old hands. You give them an address and they can tell you the color of the house. Drivers don't leave us. They make good money. Our highest-paid driver makes close to $60,000 a year."

One of the fastest-growing areas in transportation is the airport shuttle service industry. Increased airplane and automobile traffic, a headache to most, has been a boon to ground passenger carriers. Super Shuttle, which recently bought out 24-Hour Airport

Shuttle Express in order to service Orange County, employs about 700 drivers in Los Angeles alone. Super Shuttle consistently has openings, especially during the early fall, when students who worked as summer drivers return to school, and the holiday season, when the airports become the most crowded, said Joe Frilot, reservation supervisor for Super Shuttle in Los Angeles. "Naturally, when the airlines are busy, it makes us busy."

Frilot, a former driver trainer, said Super Shuttle looks for personable, reliable, and motivated drivers who learn fast, know how to read a Thomas Brothers map book, and love to drive. Drivers must be 21 years old, possess a valid Class C (formerly Class 3) California driver's license, and have had no more than two accidents in the past five years, he said. As with all the other driving jobs, be warned: A drunk-driving notation on a Department of Motor Vehicles (DMV) printout is the kiss of death.

Super Shuttle drivers typically work four days a week, earning a 27 percent commission on the cost of their runs, which averages about $7 per hour. They also receive medical and dental benefits, Frilot said.

As long as there are cars and trucks on the road, the need for drivers and dispatchers will continue. An experienced driver with a Class A license is virtually guaranteed a job, industry experts say. "A good truck driver can always find a job," said Ben Akins, safety supervisor for JB Hunt. "I'll hire him. Send him on down. I have 14 drivers in orientation right now."

KEY EMPLOYERS IN THE
TRANSPORTATION INDUSTRY

Atlas Motor Freight Lines Inc.
12133 Greenstone Avenue
Santa Fe Springs, CA 90670
213/944-9721

Bulk Transportation
415 Lemon Avenue
Walnut, CA 91789
714/594-2855

Consolidated Freightways
21300 S. Wilmington Avenue
Carson, CA 90810
213/549-2660

Container Freight Corp.
110 W. Ocean Boulevard
Long Beach, CA 90802
213/432-8099

Federal Express
3333 S. Grand Avenue
Los Angeles, CA 90007
213/687-9767

General Carrier Corp.
1512 Gage Road
Montebello, CA 90640
213/726-8845

G.I. Trucking Co.
14727 Alondra Boulevard
La Mirada, CA 90638
818/845-8883

Heavy Transport Inc.
6242 N. Paramount Boulevard
Long Beach, CA 90805
213/422-1237

JB Hunt Transportation
5650 Southern Avenue
South Gate, CA 90280
213/928-9446

Industrial Freight System Inc.
Post Office Box 15060
9120 San Fernando Road
Sun Valley, CA 91352
818/767-8568

L.A. Xpress
5256 W. 111th Street
Los Angeles, CA 90045
213/827-8000

Orange County Transit District
11222 Acacia Parkway
Garden Grove, CA 92640
714/636-7433

**Southern California Rapid Transit
   District (RTD)**
425 S. Main Street
Los Angeles, CA 90013
213/972-6712

Super Shuttle
7001 W. Imperial Highway
Los Angeles, CA 90045
213/338-1111

Taxicab Systems Inc.
2129 W. Rosecrans Avenue
Gardena, CA 90249
213/627-7000

United Independent Taxi
6435 W. Sunset Boulevard
Los Angeles, CA 90028
213/653-5050

United Parcel Service (UPS)
1200 W. Ninth Street
Los Angeles, CA 90015
213/626-1551

Viking Freight System Inc.
3200 Workman Mill Road
Whittier, CA 90601
213/692-7076

Yellow Cab Co.
1680 Vine Street
Los Angeles, CA 90028
213/469-2227

PROFESSIONAL ORGANIZATIONS

**Air and Expedited Motor Carriers
   Conference**
2200 Mill Road
Alexandria, VA 22314
703/838-1887

**American Public Transit
   Association**
1201 New York Avenue, NW
Suite 400
Washington, DC 20005
202/898-4000

American Trucking Associations
2200 Mill Road
Alexandria, VA 22314
703/838-1700

California Trucking Association
1251 Beacon Boulevard
Sacramento, CA 95691
916/373-3500

PROFESSIONAL PUBLICATIONS

Caltrux (Sacramento, CA)
Go West Magazine (Sacramento, CA)
Intermodal Age International (New York, NY)
Passenger Transport (Washington, DC)
Transport Topics (Alexandria, VA)
Transport 2000 and Intermodal World (San Francisco, CA)

DIRECTORIES

Directory of Transportation Services (Cahners Publishing Co., Newton, MA)
Moody's Transportation Manual (Moody's Investors Service, New York, NY)
Specialized Transportation Services Guide (J. J. Keller and Associates, Neenah, WI)

CHAPTER 45

Messenger and Delivery Services

The job isn't glamorous, but it delivers money and freedom.

Delivery jobs are not known for their glamour; however, they do deliver money and freedom. Drivers who work for messenger and delivery services can make from $5 an hour to $40,000 a year or more if they are reliable, hardworking, and don't mind driving a few hundred miles a day. They may work either on an on-call basis, waiting to be dispatched from destination to destination, or drive along a prescribed route, adhering to a schedule.

Delivering everything from flowers to luggage to business documents to subpoenas, drivers are well compensated for their seemingly endless hours on the road battling traffic. "I'm making more as a messenger than I was as a manager for a drugstore," said Chris Cagle, a driver for CIF Messenger in Paramount. "And I'm in a virtually stress-free situation, other than just getting my delivery there."

Another advantage to working in the delivery field is that you can set your own pace, choosing to either hustle all day and make extra money, or roll along at a nice, even tempo. "It gives you a feeling of being in control of your own destiny," observed Chuck Fuentes, director of courier operations for Now Courier in Los Angeles.

"It's a five-day work week, you're operating during normal

398 L.A. JOB MARKET HANDBOOK

business hours, you have weekends off, holidays off, you get time-and-a-half if you choose to work overtime and, if you choose to work on Sunday, you get double time," Cagle added.

For delivery hustlers who are willing to work 15-hour shifts driving hundreds of miles a day, six days a week, a healthy income is yours for the asking. Dave Moreno, a dispatcher at Minute Man Delivery in Lawndale, said his company's top drivers earn upward of $50,000 a year. Minute Man's roughly 40 drivers make between 200 and 300 deliveries a day, receiving a 45 percent commission on each run, Moreno said. Commissions vary from 45 to 60 percent company to company.

"The name of the game is volume. The more volume you have, the more money you're going to make," said Fuentes, adding that he made $1,000 a week during his peak years as a driver.

A high turnover rate among part-time drivers and a solid growth trend in the industry ensure a steady supply of openings. Delivery and route jobs in Los Angeles County grew by about 16 percent over the past decade, from 33,280 in 1980 to an estimated 38,530 in 1990, according to the state Employment Development Department (EDD).

Increased opportunities for drivers has meant more openings for dispatchers. In Los Angeles and Orange counties, the number of vehicle dispatching jobs (excluding police, fire, and ambulance dispatchers) will increase from 7,240 in 1987 to an estimated 8,160 by 1992, EDD statistics show. Dispatchers, typically former drivers or office workers who learn their trade on the job, organize incoming orders for pickups and deliveries, assign calls on a priority basis, and coordinate the activities of drivers using a two-way radio from the home office.

Within the messenger and delivery service fields, there are three basic types of drivers: contract couriers, owner/operators, and independent contractors. The way these drivers work varies slightly, but they all must have the same minimum qualifications. In general, drivers must be at least 18 years old, have a valid Class C (formerly Class 3) California driver's license, and, if they use their own car, carry automobile insurance. Drivers also should be clean-cut, punctual, reliable, have a sense of direction, and know how to read a Thomas Brothers map book.

Familiarity with the Southland's elaborate freeway system also helps (there are 21 freeways in Southern California, stretching some 562 miles in all directions), and having a good driving record (usually no more than three moving violations in three years) with no felony convictions is essential, since most employers ask for a Department of Motor Vehicles printout.

"Hopefully, they'll have prior knowledge of Los Angeles and Orange counties, even down to San Diego—I've had to dispatch drivers down to San Diego on more than one occasion," said Robert Goldenson, manager of Coastal Courier in Santa Monica. "Our drivers are all courteous. They have to come across with a good presentation. They can't have too many points against them."

Contract couriers normally drive their delivery company's cars, vans, or trucks for an hourly wage that can start as low as $5 an hour and go up to a $9 hourly rate. These drivers usually follow a fairly rigid schedule and perform pickups and drop-offs along their prescribed route, much like postal carriers.

"This is steady, reliable, everyday work," said Don MacAdam, owner of MacAdam International, a private mail delivery service with offices in Los Angeles and the City of Industry. "You're not going to get rich on it, but you can count on it every day. It's a solid business."

MacAdam, who tries to hire drivers who are 25 and over for insurance reasons, said his employees are required to make deliveries within a 15-minute time period to stay on schedule. Contract couriers at MacAdam, most of whom are part-time, may start work in the predawn hours to make their first deliveries. "With our business, it's rushed in the morning and rushed in the evening," MacAdam remarked.

At Courier Express, the second-largest contract courier in Los Angeles (United Courier is the largest), about 60 to 70 percent of its 600 drivers are part-time, said Mark Carson, a corporate account executive. Part-time shifts at Courier Express, where drivers might make between 20 and 60 scheduled stops a day, vary from early morning (6 a.m. to noon) to late at night (8 p.m. to 2 a.m.), affording drivers flexibility.

"We want to cater to the retiree and college student. We have people coming in and working their way through school," Carson said. While driving for a contract courier isn't necessarily a career job, experienced drivers might become dispatchers or sorters and from there go on to supervision, he added. "The person who is running our company started as a driver. You move up fast."

Owner/operators drive their own cars or trucks and are paid on a commission, usually 45 to 50 percent of the billed cost of each delivery. They are required to pay for their own gas, supply their own liability insurance, and possess a vehicle in good running order. These drivers work on an on-call basis, waiting in the field at a "holding spot" to be dispatched via two-way radio to their next stop.

Owner/operators and independent contractors must file their own paperwork, which consists of keeping a detailed record of the destinations visited, the number of miles traveled during each run, and the amount billed, and then calculating a commission based on the overall cost to the customer. Because drivers calculate their own commission, they usually know exactly how much they make each day and at the end of the week.

Fuentes said he usually looks for drivers who have a 1982 or newer economy pickup truck or hatchback, since they can be registered as commercial vehicles, which are allowed to park in loading zones. Pickup trucks, flatbeds, and vans are good delivery vehicles because they can carry more freight than a car. Usually, the larger the load, the higher the billing and commission.

Independent contractors make more money than other drivers, garnering a 60 percent commission with each delivery. Like owner/operators, they too are paid on a piecework basis. Although independent contractors work for a messenger company, they are equipped with their own Public Utilities Commission license and are required to carry a full-coverage insurance policy—extra expenses that can add up to $3,500 a year.

With their higher commission rate, independent contractors can earn from $5,000 to $10,000 a year more than owner/operators, but they usually aren't given medical and dental benefits by the company as owner/operators are. Independent contractors must also file their own taxes on a quarterly basis with the state Board of Equalization just like any small-business owner.

Perhaps the main drawbacks to working as a driver are the Southland's notorious traffic congestion and parking problems. The job is not for the fainthearted or impatient. But with a little practice and street savvy, drivers can familiarize themselves with special delivery parking areas and become desensitized to traffic jams and freeway snarls.

"After the first month, driving in traffic is just a part of the job," said Cagle of CIF. "You're getting paid to sit in traffic. If it's rush hour, the company knows it's going to take you longer, so there's not added pressure to get there."

Prospective drivers should check that the company they're applying at has both auto insurance for company-owned cars and worker's compensation insurance to cover costs in the event a driver is involved in an accident while on duty, said Jim Myers, office manager for Executive Express in Los Angeles. In addition, make sure the company doesn't pay its employees under the table. "I would make sure they're taking taxes out of your paycheck so they're classifying you as an employee," Myers said.

KEY EMPLOYERS OF MESSENGERS AND DELIVERY DRIVERS

Airborne Express
5651 W. 96th Street
Los Angeles, CA 90045
213/642-0195

Best Delivery Service Inc.
Post Office Box 1348
1045 S. Greenwood Avenue
Montebello, CA 90640
213/724-6350

Brake Delivery Service Etc.
2626 E. 26th Street
Los Angeles, CA 90058
213/583-9901

CIF Messenger
6803 Somerset Boulevard
Paramount, CA 90723
213/979-8221

Courier Express Inc.
1533 Echo Park Avenue
Los Angeles, CA 90026
213/250-4041

Dart Transportation Service
4343 E. Washington Boulevard
Los Angeles, CA 90040
213/264-1011

DHL Worldwide Express
4882 W. 145th Street
Hawthorne, CA 90250
213/973-7300

Direct Delivery Service Inc.
900 W. Florence Avenue
Inglewood, CA 90301
213/776-2670

Executive Express
2005 Quail Street
Newport Beach, CA 92660
714/852-0600

Fast Run Delivery Service
4880 Fountain Avenue
Los Angeles, CA 90029
213/662-7595

MacAdam International Inc.
4218 Whiteside Street
Los Angeles, CA 90063
213/264-2480

Minute Man Messenger Service Inc.
3379 S. Robertson Boulevard
Los Angeles, CA 90034
213/559-7390

Now Courier Service
1543 W. Olympic Boulevard
Los Angeles, CA 90015
213/252-5000

Pro Express Inc.
1220 E. Washington Boulevard
Montebello, CA 90640
213/726-2147

Ready Express Inc.
4880 Fountain Avenue
Los Angeles, CA 90029
213/662-7595

Santa Monica Express
506 Santa Monica Boulevard
Santa Monica, CA 90401
213/458-6000

Sonic Messenger & Air Courier
Service
333 S. Hindry Avenue
Inglewood, CA 90301
213/215-4230

Space Age Delivery Service Inc.
7300 Peterson Lane
Paramount, CA 90723
213/633-8395

U.S. Courier Corp.
1848 Echo Park Avenue
Los Angeles, CA 90026
213/628-3333

United Couriers Inc.
3220 Winona Avenue
Burbank, CA 91504
818/845-8883

Universal Mail Delivery Service
950 E. Dovlen Place
Carson, CA 90746
213/532-2900

For other employers of drivers, see Chapter 44 on transportation.

PROFESSIONAL ORGANIZATIONS

American Package Express
Carriers Association
2200 Mill Road
Alexandria, VA 22314
703/838-1887

Messenger Courier Association of
America
2200 Mill Road
Alexandria, VA 22314
703/838-1987

National Association of Special De-
livery Messengers
c/o American Postal Workers
Union
1300 L Street, NW
Washington, DC 20005
202/842-4200

DIRECTORIES

Delivery Service Directory (American Business Directories, Omaha, NE)
Messenger Service Directory (American Business Directories, Omaha, NE)
Service Directory (American Package Express Carriers Association, Alexandria, VA)

CHAPTER 46

Metro Rail Openings

*L.A.'s new mass transit system offers
lots of jobs in the fast lane.*

All aahhboooaard! The first phases of the long-awaited, much-
anticipated, roundly debated, and greatly needed Metro Rail
system are beginning to operate, carrying Los Angeles into the
21st century, streamlining travel into and out of the downtown
area, helping to reduce smog and congestion, and creating
hundreds of jobs in the process.

The Los Angeles area has been without an urban mass transit
rail system since 1961, when the Pacific Electric Red Car system
was junked in favor of the web of freeways that exists today.
Since then, freeway traffic has slowed to an average speed of
32 mph and air quality has gradually deteriorated. Indeed, for
more than half the year, air quality in the L.A. basin fails to
meet federal health standards, studies have shown.

"If nothing else, the environment calls for a new rail system,"
said Richard Flores, rail transportation operations supervisor for
the Southern California Rapid Transit District (RTD), the agency
responsible for operating and staffing Metro Rail.

Regarded by local traffic experts as a linchpin to improving
the traffic flow, Metro Rail is gathering steam as an employment
source. As the various lines are put into operation, scores of
operations, engineering, security, and maintenance workers will
be needed to run the country's newest—and some say most
advanced—electric rail transit line, which is designed to carry
an estimated 300,000 passengers a day by the year 2000.

"We need everything from the basic starting positions of unskilled car cleaners all the way up to superintendents," said Joel Sandberg, director of systems design and analysis for the RTD. "In between, we need quality assurance people, maintenance analysts, electro-mechanical repair people, and instructors."

For their expertise, Metro Rail employees will be well compensated. Fare inspectors start at $11.44 an hour, while train operators, police officers, and track workers earn in the $13 to $14 range. Supervisors begin at $17.15 an hour and, advancing to higher management levels, senior supervisors, division managers, and superintendents make from $20.95 to $24.32 an hour, according to an RTD Metro Rail Project cost estimate report.

There are three basic components to the first phase of the Metro Rail system: the Blue Line, the Red Line, and the Green Line. A segment of the 21.5-mile Long Beach-to-Los Angeles light rail Blue Line was to begin operation in July 1990. When it is fully completed, the Blue Line will run from First Street in Long Beach to Seventh and Flower streets in Los Angeles, dipping underground at 12th Street going into downtown.

The opening of the entire light rail Blue Line is scheduled to coincide with the opening of phase one of the heavy rail Red Line in 1993, said Erica Goebel of the Los Angeles County Transportation Commission (LACTC). The LACTC is responsible for obtaining the financing for the $3.5 billion Metro Rail project.

Ultimately, the Red Line will stretch 18 miles from downtown Los Angeles to North Hollywood in the San Fernando Valley, Goebel said. The initial 4.4-mile underground subway segment of the heavy rail Red Line will run west from Union Station, the main train depot, to the intersection of Wilshire Boulevard and Alvarado Street.

In order to get both lines up and running, hundreds of operations and maintenance workers will have to be hired. "We're creating a whole operating section for Metro Rail," said William Rhine, the RTD's assistant general manager of transit systems development. "We're talking about a couple of hundred positions for the first four-mile section alone."

Behind-the-scenes operations that ensure the safety and reliability of Metro Rail trips will be directed from the Metro Rail system's brain center, officially known as the Rail Control Center (RCC), which is located a half mile southeast of Union

Station. RCC employees will oversee and coordinate train operations, power systems, safety and security, communications, scheduling, and system maintenance. Typical positions include closed-circuit TV operator ($11.71/hr.), line supervisor ($17.15), and operations supervisor ($19.90).

Maintenance personnel are responsible for the smooth day-to-day operation of Metro Rail by maintaining the condition of the cars and track as well as the communications and electrical systems. They inspect, service, and repair the numerous components of the urban mass transit system. They also are needed to keep up the physical appearance of the cars and Metro Rail facilities. (The exteriors of the stainless steel cars are being specially treated to make them graffiti-proof.) Common maintenance positions include car cleaner ($11.12/hr.), track worker ($14.18), and electro mechanic ($15.69).

A substantial number of Metro Rail employees will be hired from within the RTD, said Barbara Hanson, director of rail activation for the RTD, adding that 9 out of 10 of the first group of supervisors were culled from the RTD's own ranks of 9,000 employees. However, Metro Rail's top brass—a troika of superintendents, one for operations, facilities maintenance, and equipment maintenance—were all hired from transit authorities in other cities, Hanson said.

The RTD is mainly looking for applicants who have either a mass transit or rail line background, or who have worked in jobs comparable to what they would be doing at Metro Rail. Current bus drivers, for instance, are in the strongest position to be considered for train operator openings ($13.07/hr.). In fact, the Los Angeles bus drivers' union contract has a stipulation that allows them to bid for the available train operator slots.

Sandberg said the RTD has had difficulty recruiting enough engineers who are experienced in rail transit construction and design, adding that the RTD has had to hire some 400 engineers from around the country to work on the first phase of the project. "Some of our electronics engineers have come from aerospace and communications industries and that corresponds very well, but when you get into something like the design of a rail transit car, that's fairly unique," he said.

Security, an element considered by many to be vitally important to the long-term success of Metro Rail, is another employment area with ample opportunity. A self-service, barrier-free ticketing system based on the honor system will provide free access to virtually anyone who wants to board the train—troublemakers included. While fare inspectors will perform spot checks of ticket holders, a high level of security nevertheless will be needed to guarantee the ultimate safety of patrons and overall success of the system, said Jack Kyser, chief economist for the Los Angeles Area Chamber of Commerce.

According to RTD spokesman Greg Davy, crime prevention programs will involve a coordinated effort between the RTD Transit Police, the Los Angeles County Sheriff's Department, and the Los Angeles Police Department. Metro Rail's surveillance system is patterned after similar systems in San Francisco, Washington, D.C., and Atlanta, where subways are virtually crime-free, Sandberg said.

Metro Rail's third component is the Green Line, which will run east-west along the median divider of the Century Freeway (I-105), from Norwalk to El Segundo, within close proximity of the Los Angeles International Airport. When the Green Line opens in 1994, it will be possible to transfer to and from the Blue Line, which runs north-south, at the intersection of Wilmington Avenue and Imperial Highway in Watts, Goebel said.

When the entire Metro Rail system is completed sometime after the year 2000, it will form a 150-mile network of light and heavy semi-automated rail cars driven by electricity at speeds of up to 70 mph both above and below ground.

"It's a good system with great potential," said Rail Operations Superintendent Paul O'Brien, who previously worked as an assistant superintendent for the Niagara Frontier Transportation Authority in Buffalo, New York. "That's what attracted me to it. Both the light rail line and heavy rail line have a good combination of modern technology and proven techniques."

If you're thinking about a career in mass transit, don't wait until the system is fully operational. Getting in on the ground floor, even before the doors first open and the trains start rolling, is a good way to assure yourself of a timely promotion, since those employees with most seniority usually wind up with the best jobs. "In some cases, it may be easier to transfer from the RTD to Metro Rail (than being hired directly)," Hanson said. "Once you get in the Rapid Transit District and get to know it, you'll find there are lots of transfer opportunities among departments."

Applicants interested in Metro Rail openings can contact the RTD personnel office at (213) 972-7153 for more information, or may apply in person at 425 S. Main Street in downtown Los Angeles. The RTD also has a jobs hotline number, (213) 972-6217, which announces professional and managerial positions currently available throughout the district.

Metro Rail Job Opportunities: The Red Line

Position	Staffing Needs 1993/2000	Hourly Salary
Car cleaner	7/11	$11.12
Fare inspector	7/11	$11.44
Closed-circuit TV operator	7/8	$11.71
Train operator	17/28	$13.07
Police officer/investigator	8/13	$13.92
Track worker	2/3	$14.18
Electro mechanic	14/18	$15.69
Line supervisor	5/7	$17.15
Yard dispatcher	3/5	$17.15
Operations supervisor/ communications control	5/5	$19.90
Equipment maintenance supervisor	3/5	$19.90

The Red Line, or MOS-1, is the initial 4.4-mile underground segment of the Metro scheduled to begin operation by 1993. It will run from Union Station in downtown Los Angeles to the intersection of Wilshire Boulevard and Alvarado Street.

SOURCE: Southern California Rapid Transit District.

CHAPTER 47

Manufacturing

*L.A. has jobs producing everything
from aircraft to zippers.*

It may seem like the Southern California economy runs on surf
and sun, but it's not just Hollywood and Disneyland that have
taken the Southland so far. Los Angeles County is the
manufacturing capital of the United States, ahead of the Windy
City of Chicago, the Motor City of Detroit, and, yes, even the
Big Apple—New York City.

Over 900,000 workers countywide are employed under the
manufacturing umbrella, which encompasses such myriad industries as electronics, aircraft building, and defense contracting,
garment and furniture making, printing, publishing, and petroleum
refining. Including Orange County, there are over 1.2 million
manufacturing workers, according to Jack Kyser, chief economist
for the Los Angeles Area Chamber of Commerce.

"We're in a watershed period," Kyser said. "Manufacturing
is back because people overseas are realizing that we don't make
shoddy products. There also has been some lessening of foreign
competition because the dollar has declined in value."

The L.A. area has an edge in some areas of manufacturing,
especially when it comes to products associated with the
California image. "There is this mystique about something being
made in Southern California," Kyser said. Such locally made
garment lines as L.A. Gear, Body Glove, and Ocean Pacific have
achieved success partially by exploiting that fun-in-the-sun
mystique.

While other industrialized nations like Japan are just now being
forced to downsize in order to remain competitive in areas like
steel making, American manufacturing has already undergone

a period of major restructuring and has faced hard decisions on where to cut back and how to improve efficiency, Kyser said. "As a result, we're pretty lean and mean in the manufacturing industries. Most people expect continued modest growth. The main increase will be in small- to medium-size firms."

Southern California exemplifies the tough and ready nature of American manufacturing. During the eight-year shrinkage period from 1979 to 1987, when Chicago lost over 300,000 manufacturing jobs and Detroit lost over 100,000, Los Angeles County held fairly steady, with only 18,000 jobs lost. Meanwhile, Orange County actually added some 30,000 manufacturing jobs, Kyser said.

The Los Angeles economy is so resilient, in part, because it consists mainly of small and highly adaptable businesses that are responsive to changing conditions, said Jerry Hawbaker, labor market analyst with the state Employment Development Department. Of an estimated 216,000 companies in L.A. County, roughly 170,000 have 9 employees or fewer, Hawbaker said. Of the 19,342 companies in the manufacturing industry, more than half have 19 or fewer workers, he added.

Rather than restrict the number of job openings, the small size of most L.A.-area companies actually works to the advantage of first-time job hunters in the manufacturing trades, since smaller shops require less experience than larger operations, said Daniel Hernandez, a machine shop instructor at Los Angeles Trade-Technical College.

Beginning machine operators with little or no experience start at $5 an hour and can easily make up to $12 an hour with a few years' experience, Hernandez said. From machine operator, the next promotion is to machinist, then toolmaker, fixture maker, diemaker, and mold maker. "There's not enough tool and die makers to go around right now," Hernandez said. First-rate mold makers, also in great demand, earn upward of $60,000 a year, he added.

Mold makers with several years' experience can either open their own shop or move into a supervisory position. Indeed, the best journeypeople often find themselves in management positions at larger companies if they stick around long enough and are committed to ongoing education.

"There's plenty of jobs here for skilled people as long as they are willing to learn," said Chuck Michael, business representative for the International Association of Machinists & Aerospace

Workers. "Management comes up through the ranks. If you're working in the trades, you're continuously going to school. You have to keep up with the times. The old jobs where the guy could do the same thing for 40 years aren't here anymore."

Increasingly, a solid educational background, such as a two-year A.S. degree from a technical college, is becoming essential to securing a good manufacturing job. Even the job of machinist requires basic mathematical skills and the ability to read blueprints at most companies.

Machinists make precision metal or plastic parts for industrial machinery, instruments, aircraft, automobiles, and countless other goods. They are skilled at using a variety of tools, including lathes, milling machines, grinders, and drill presses. From a set of blueprints, they select the proper tools and materials and produce the part or fitting that meets the desired specifications.

"There used to be low-, medium-, and highly skilled workers," Hernandez said. "Now, there's no need for low- or medium-skilled people. Companies aren't making 'standard' machinery anymore. It's all computerized. And since the industry is becoming more sophisticated, workers must be more sophisticated. Twenty years ago you would pick up machining from a master machinist. Now many of the apprentice programs are gone. You have to attend college."

Indeed, the industry is changing and advancing so rapidly that many colleges, such as L.A. Trade-Tech, have been forced to revise their manufacturing curricula, adding numerical control and computer science courses, in order to graduate students with employable skills. "The blue collar worker was never considered to be a professional," Hernandez said, "but you've got to be a professional to operate this new, high-tech machinery."

A manufacturing education not only provides job training, it also can produce immediate career results. L.A. Trade-Tech graduates are frequently hired by such aerospace companies as Rockwell and Hughes. Recently, 33 L.A. Trade-Tech machine shop graduates were hired by the Japanese firm U.S. Sonoike in Buena Park, Hernandez said. According to Sonoike's vice president, Oichi Yonebayashi, the company needed entry-level workers who possessed current mechanical knowledge. The college delivered.

In manufacturing, the higher the skill level, the fatter the paycheck. Skilled workers who start working in their early 20s or sooner can, by the time they reach age 30, make an annual salary of $40,000 to $45,000, Michael said. On the mechanical side, maintenance mechanics who repair and maintain industrial machinery, including trucks, make as much as $16 to $17 an hour. Production line workers for breweries and soft drink bottlers make $13 to $15 hourly, he added.

Studies have shown that manufacturing employees earn more than service sector employees. In 1987, the average manufacturing position paid $14.79 an hour, compared to $12.08 an hour for the average nonmanufacturing job, according to the U.S. Bureau of Labor Statistics.

Michael, a former truck mechanic who oversees the truck mechanic apprentice programs at L.A. Trade-Tech and Rio Hondo College, advises workers entering the industry to "get an associate of arts degree in anything" before entering the job market. "If you want to make decent money, get an education and then get into any trade you're good at and you'll be able to buy a home in a reasonable amount of time."

Given an industry that is undergoing radical transformation with the introduction of new technology, assuring job security has become a matter of choosing a field with ample opportunity and then getting an education in it. In manufacturing, the surest way of doing this is by plugging into the electronics sector. That's where the jobs are more prevalent and diverse.

Electrical equipment and supplies is the largest segment of the manufacturing industry in Los Angeles and Orange counties. In 1987, there were 219,175 electronics workers making everything from toasters to satellite dishes. By 1992, the local electronics field is expected to be the source of nearly 256,000 jobs.

While the electronics field is large, there is no room for complacency. In the 1990s, job security will hinge on the ability to adapt to continually evolving technology, including computerized machinery and robotics, Kyser said. "A lot of the skills are changing. You can't drop out of high school and expect to be employed. It's a lot more complicated than that. It's getting to the point where you've got to have at least some kind of basic computer literacy."

Technical expertise can be harnessed in many ways. For instance, former technicians sometimes turn to selling the sophisticated electronic equipment they used to build, test, and repair. Selling requires yet another skill, however. "You've got to have the gift of the gab," said Bob Feldman, sales manager of Calrad Electronics in Hollywood.

412 *L.A. JOB MARKET HANDBOOK*

Whether in sales or production, the greatest opportunities depend on training and knowledge. "The only future is for the highly skilled worker," affirmed Michael of the International Association of Machinists & Aerospace Workers.

Made in L.A.*

Type of Manufacturing	Employees 1987	1992	Percent Change
Electrical equipment	155,400	195,000	25.5%
Aircraft & parts	129,000	150,800	16.9%
Apparel	92,300	108,200	17.2%
Fabricated metal products	67,900	73,400	8.1%
Nonelectrical machinery	65,300	75,200	15.2%
Printing & publishing	59,800	67,300	12.5%
Food products	48,700	54,400	11.7%
Transportation equipment	43,100	47,200	9.5%
Furniture & fixtures	37,600	44,700	15.5%
Rubber & plastic	33,100	35,000	5.7%
Instruments	28,300	34,400	21.6%
Chemical products	28,100	31,100	10.7%
Primary metal industries	20,800	24,600	18.3%
Paper products	18,800	21,300	13.3%
Stone, clay, & glass products	17,700	20,800	17.5%
Misc. industries	13,700	15,200	10.9%
Lumber & wood products	12,800	15,200	18.8%
Textile mill products	10,600	12,200	15.1%
Petroleum refining	10,600	12,200	15.1%
Toys & sporting goods	6,600	7,500	13.6%
Leather products	5,200	5,500	5.8%
Total:	906,500	1,051,300	16.0%

* Los Angeles County figures only.
SOURCE: Employment Development Department.

SELECTED EMPLOYERS IN THE
MANUFACTURING INDUSTRY

Anthony Industries
(Pools, recreational and industrial products)
4900 S. Eastern Avenue
Suite 200
Los Angeles, CA 90040
213/724-2800

Bell Industries
(Electronic and computer components)
11812 San Vicente Boulevard
Suite 300
Los Angeles, CA 90049
213/826-6778

Cal Mat
(Cement, concrete, asphalt)
3200 San Fernando Road
Los Angeles, CA 90065
213/258-2777

Daiwa Corp.
(Fishing rods and reels)
7421 Chapman Avenue
Garden Grove, CA 92641
714/895-6662

Douglas Furniture of California Inc.
(Cabinets)
4000 Freeman Boulevard
Redondo Beach, CA 90278
213/643-7200

Eastman Kodak Co.
(Photography equipment and chemical supplies)
12100 Rivera Road
Whittier, CA 90606
213/945-1255

Fender Musical Instruments
(Guitars, synthesizers, drums)
1130 Columbia Street
Brea, CA 92621
714/990-0909

Firestone Tire and Rubber Co.
(Tires and rubber products)
17842 Skypark Boulevard
Irvine, CA 92714
714/250-8855

JBL Inc.
(Audio loudspeaker systems)
8500 Balboa Boulevard
Northridge, CA 91329
818/893-8411

Kerr Glass
(Glass, plastic, metal containers)
1840 Century Park East
Los Angeles, CA 90067
213/556-2200

Los Angeles Die Mold
(Diemakers)
1942 N. Rosemead Boulevard
South El Monte, CA 91733
213/283-5184

Mattel Inc.
(Toys)
5150 Rosecrans Avenue
Hawthorne, CA 90250
213/978-5150

McCulloch Corp.
(Outdoor power equipment)
5433 Beethoven Street
Los Angeles, CA 90066
213/827-7111

Sony Manufacturing Co. of America
(Television sets)
16540 W. Bernardo Drive
San Diego, CA 92127
619/271-9333

Standard Brands Paint Co. Inc.
(Paint and home decorating products)
4300 W. 190th Street
Torrance, CA 90509
213/214-2411

U.S. Divers
(Oceanography and diving equipment)
3323 W. Warner Avenue
Santa Ana, CA 92702
714/540-8010

Also see Chapter 6 for apparel manufacturers, Chapter 19 for aerospace and defense firms, and Chapter 21 for computer makers.

PROFESSIONAL ORGANIZATIONS

California Manufacturers Association
1121 K Street
Suite 900
Sacramento, CA 95806
916/441-5420

Manufacturers Industrial Council
255 N. Hacienda Boulevard
Suite 100
Industry, CA 91744
818/968-3737

National Association of Manufacturers
1331 Pennsylvania Avenue
Suite 1500-N
Washington, DC 20004
202/637-3000

National Tooling and Machining Association
9300 Livingston Road
Fort Washington, MD 20744
301/248-6200

PROFESSIONAL PUBLICATIONS

California Manufacturer (Sacramento, CA)

DIRECTORIES

California Manufacturers Register (Times Mirror Publishing, Newport Beach, CA)

Register of Corporations, Directors and Executives (Standard and Poor's Publishing Co., New York, NY)

Southern California Business Directory & Buyer's Guide (Times Mirror Publishing, Newport Beach, CA)

Thomas Register of American Manufacturers (Thomas Publishing Co., New York, NY)

CHAPTER 48

Construction

*Building activity is on an upward swing,
providing good job opportunities.*

The sky's the limit for Southern California's booming construction industry. As long as building projects are on the rise, so are opportunities for workers. "Right now we're at the zenith of a big upswing in construction cycles," said Jeffrey Rock, a construction manager for Maguire-Thomas Partners. "Everybody's worried because we're experiencing a big up, but there aren't any signs that it's going down. We're having a renaissance."

The construction industry provides jobs for an estimated 155,000 workers at projects ranging from residential tracts in the swelling suburbs to skyscrapers in the bustling downtown central business district, said Jack Kyser, chief economist for the Los Angeles Area Chamber of Commerce. In Los Angeles and Orange counties, the number of people employed in construction activity is expected to reach 245,250 by 1992, according to the Employment Development Department (EDD).

Opportunities in construction vary according to location. For union work, downtown L.A.'s the place. In fact, there are few, if any, nonunion jobs in the central business district, said Maguire-Thomas's Rock. Once you're in a union—the Los Angeles County Building and Trades Council represents some 120,000 workers belonging to 85 unions—there's plenty of work to be had, especially with the numerous high-rise industrial and residential projects that are continuously under way.

And with the population of the Los Angeles basin forecast to swell from 13.8 million to 19 million by the year 2010, a vast array of new housing and office projects will have to be built. With land values soaring, it has become both desirable and practical for current building and home owners to remodel or rebuild from the ground up.

Among the projects recently or soon to be completed are the massive, 73-story First Interstate World Center and 54-story Central Library sister tower; the 52-story Mitsui Fudosan building at Wilshire Boulevard and Figueroa Street; the 50-story second phase of Citicorp Plaza located at 777 S. Figueroa Street; and the 35-story ManuLife building at Ninth and Figueroa streets.

"The news you hear about construction is all sort of downbeat," Kyser said. "In California, and especially in Southern California, we're running counter to the trend. Our construction employment picture has been moving up strongly. What other major downtown area has five high rises in construction and probably two more ready to get under way by year's end?"

In addition to the above-mentioned projects, the state is building a 1-million-square-foot Ronald Reagan office building on Spring Street, and another 1 million square feet of space is being added to the already monolithic California Mart. Other projects contributing to L.A.'s renaissance are the new Fashion Institute of Design and Merchandising building on Grand Avenue and the $390 million downtown Convention Center expansion, which will more than double the center, to 4 million square feet.

While each of these projects will cost millions of dollars and employ hundreds of workers, there are even bigger state and federal projects under way, namely, in mass transit. "These buildings pale in comparison to the Metro Rail projects," said Walter Beaumont of the Los Angeles Community Redevelopment Agency. "They'll probably put more people to work than all of these projects combined."

As construction of the multibillion-dollar Metro Rail project continues, the number of jobs will swell to a peak of about 2,000 in the early to mid-1990s, said Erica Goebel of the Los Angeles County Transportation Commission. The majority of construction jobs in mass transit, including the Century Freeway (I-105) project, are union, said Ron Kennedy, business agent for the Los Angeles County Building and Trades Council.

The big money involved in big projects translates into high wages for construction workers. Journeymen who belong to a union in L.A. County make $23 an hour, while foremen are paid $24 an hour and general foremen $25 an hour, Kennedy said. What's more, competent workers are urgently needed. "There is a high demand for good construction labor," affirmed Ben

Bartolotto, research director for the Construction Industry Research Board in Burbank.

There are basically two ways to become a construction worker: either learn on your own under the wing of a private contractor or join a union and apprentice in a trade. The only way to become an apprentice is to join a union, Kennedy said.

Champions of the union system tout its long-term advantages, such as a guaranteed pay scale, negotiated benefits, union pension plan, and the availability of consistent work. Apprentices receive extensive on-the-job training that raises them to journeyman status in four to six years.

"When they come out as journeymen, they're fully qualified in every area," said Martin Hunt, director of the county Electrical Training Trust apprenticeship program. "A journeyman (electrician) can wire a house, a factory, or a high-rise building." Journey-level construction workers can also study for their state contractor's license and start working for themselves.

Applicants for the apprenticeship programs must be at least 18 years old, have a high school diploma or equivalent, and one year of high school algebra or a semester of college algebra, Hunt said. "Math is fundamental to the construction business," said Rock. "Plans, money, time—they're all math-oriented."

Once accepted, apprentices are required to work with a contractor 40 hours a week while taking classes in their area of specialty two nights a week. Beginning apprentices earn $8.05 an hour, or 35 percent of what a journeyman makes.

If they keep their grades up and regularly attend classes, they can receive 5 percent pay increases every six months for the first two years, and 10 percent increases thereafter, eventually earning 80 percent of journey-level wages. Union members must attend regular meetings and receive work assignments from their local chapters. They are also barred from nonunion projects.

When it comes to nonunion work, opportunities are perhaps the most abundant in home building. Outside of Los Angeles, particularly in the Antelope and Moreno valleys, Palmdale, and south Riverside County, there is a great demand for residential construction workers and subcontractors, said Frank Scardina, northwest division president of Kaufman & Broad, a major Los Angeles contractor.

"There are significant shortages in the areas of painting, drywall, carpentry, and framing. We have a greater backlog of orders than we've ever had. Our subcontractors are literally hiring walk-ons," Scardina said.

The Employment Development Department projects continuing growth in construction jobs in the Riverside–San Bernardino area, which along with Long Beach–Los Angeles is ranked among the top five regions in the country for single-family home building, according to the National Association of Home Builders. In just one year, the number of construction jobs in Riverside–San Bernardino increased 10 percent, from 57,000 in 1988 to 62,700 in 1989, said Edward Kulp, an EDD labor market analyst.

Is there security in nonunion work? That depends on how well established the employer is, and whether the individual worker is competent and dependable. "We treat our employees as full-time, long-term employees. We don't hire and fire them for a particular job. If you do a good job and keep your nose clean, you could be hired by Kaufman & Broad for the rest of your life," Scardina said.

Though construction traditionally has been dominated by men, opportunities for women are increasing. "At the last company I was with, a secretary who knew nothing about construction when she started became an assistant project manager, then project manager," Rock said. "She now has my old job."

Big construction companies like Kaufman & Broad often hire workers with four or five years of construction experience as assistant superintendents. Central to this job is an understanding of construction management. Advises Scardina: "Go to trade school or occupational school and learn the whole trade. You won't be hunting for very long in today's job market."

If you have an eye for bidding projects, another way to emerge from the labor ranks is to become an estimator. Estimators can make anywhere from $35,000 to $55,000 a year, depending on their expertise, said Rock.

After working as an estimator or assistant superintendent for 5 to 10 years, it's then possible to become a project superintendent or project manager, making $45,000 to $65,000 a year, eventually rising to the position of a construction manager, bringing in between $55,000 and $75,000.

"There's an awful lot of opportunity for people who want to apply themselves," said Rock. "And you don't have to be a genius either. I started in masonry at $3.25 an hour 13 years ago. All I have done is continued to work. Just persevere; the door's open."

KEY EMPLOYERS IN THE CONSTRUCTION INDUSTRY

Bechtel Group Inc.
12440 E. Imperial Highway
Norwalk, CA 90650
213/807-2300

C. F. Braun Inc.
1000 S. Fremont Avenue
Alhambra, CA 91802
818/300-1000

CRSS Constructors Inc.
5858 W. Century Boulevard
Suite 1406
Los Angeles, CA 90045
213/216-5602

Dillingham Construction N.A. Inc.
135 W. Victoria Street
Long Beach, CA 90805
213/603-9633

Dinwiddie Construction Co.
1145 Wilshire Boulevard
Suite 100
Los Angeles, CA 90017
213/482-1900

Kaufman & Broad Home Corp.
11601 Wilshire Boulevard
Los Angeles, CA 90025
213/312-5000

Macco Constructors
14409 Paramount Boulevard
Paramount, CA 90723
213/630-5801

Maguire-Thomas Partners
1299 Ocean Avenue
Suite 1000
Santa Monica, CA 90401
213/680-1782

Ohbayashi America Corp.
2975 Wilshire Boulevard
Suite 619
Los Angeles, CA 90010
213/385-8361

Overton, Moore & Associates Inc.
1125 W. 190th Street
Suite 200
Los Angeles, CA 90048
213/321-5100

Thomas Pankow Builders Ltd.
2476 N. Lake Avenue
Altadena, CA 91001
213/684-2320

C. L. Peck/Jones Brothers Construction Corp.
10866 Wilshire Boulevard
Los Angeles, CA 90024
213/470-1885

Stolte Inc.
11300 W. Olympic Boulevard
Suite 900
Los Angeles, CA 90064
213/479-8066

Tishman Realty & Construction Co. Inc.
10960 Wilshire Boulevard
Los Angeles, CA 90024
213/477-7033

Turner Construction Co.
445 S. Figueroa Street
Los Angeles, CA 90071
213/683-1430

Tutor-Saliba Corp.
15901 Olden Street
Sylmar, CA 91342
818/362-8391

PROFESSIONAL ORGANIZATIONS

Building Industry Association of California
14411 Hamlin Street
Van Nuys, CA 94101
213/782-2762

Electrical Training Trust
515 S. Avenue 19
Los Angeles, CA 90031
213/221-5881

International Conference of Building Officials
5360 S. Workman Mill Road
Whittier, CA 90601
213/699-0541

Los Angeles County Building and Construction Trades Council
1626 Beverly Boulevard
Los Angeles, CA 90026
213/483-4222

National Association of Women in Construction
327 S. Adams Street
Fort Worth, TX 76104
817/877-5551

National Construction Industry Council
2100 M Street, NW
Washington, DC 20037
202/638-2121

PROFESSIONAL PUBLICATIONS

Builder (Washington, DC)
Building Design and Construction (Des Plaines, IL)
California Builder (San Francisco, CA)
The Carpenter (Washington, DC)
Construction Review (Washington, DC)
Nation's Building News (Washington, DC)

DIRECTORIES

Blue Book of Major Homebuilders (LSI Systems, Crofton, MD)
Building Contractors Directory (American Business Directories, Omaha, NE)
ENR—Top 400 Construction Contractors Issue (McGraw-Hill, New York, NY)
Southern California Building Industry Guide (Building Industry Association, Los Angeles, CA)

How to Choose a Vocational School

Vocational programs can put you to work, but deciding between a public and private school is important.

Preparing for a career doesn't always mean getting a college education. Vocational training can provide a shortcut into the job market—or give you the boost necessary to get into a new job. The greater Los Angeles area has a plethora of technical institutes, private schools, and college trade programs that offer training in almost every conceivable field.

Certificate and degree programs ranging from computer operator to truck driver can be completed in four weeks to two years, depending on the school and course of study. Many specialized vocational schools are placement-oriented. Some programs boast a job placement rate of 90 percent or higher.

"We try to place every single graduate of our program as soon as they are finished," said Fred Freedman, vice president of marketing for ATI, a computer training school in Van Nuys which offers six-month certificate programs in computer repair and word processing for $5,025. "The people who come out of our program are very marketable."

Despite sincere-sounding promises, not all schools have students' best interests in mind. The state Student Aid Commission periodically audits, and sometimes suspends, the financial aid programs of California training schools to guard against faulty recordkeeping and improper administering of student loans.

Contact the Student Aid Commission in Sacramento at (916) 445-0880, the Better Business Bureau of the Southland in Cypress at (714) 527-0680, or the named accrediting agency if you are unsure about the financial condition or educational reputation of a particular school. Another source of information about vocational schools is the Private Post-Secondary Education Division of the state Department of Education, (213) 620-4257.

According to Freedman, there are several factors to consider when shopping for a potential school:

- What are the quality and quantity of equipment available for students to learn on? This is especially important in industries such as manufacturing and electronics in which workers must master the very latest technology in order to be employable. If the learning facility's equipment is old and outdated, it might be an indication that the school places more emphasis on its sales and enrollment figures than it does on education.

- What is the average size of a class? A key indicator of the quality of education offered by a particular school or program is its student-to-teacher ratio. Class sizes should be relatively small, usually no more than 10 to 15 students per instructor for hands-on courses.

- Is the school accredited by a reputable agency, such as the Western Association of Schools and Colleges, the Accrediting Commission of Continuing Education and Training (ACCET), or the National Association of Trade and Technical Schools (NATTS)? "Make sure they're fully accredited so that the full range of scholarship, financial aid, and loan programs is available," Freedman said.

  While searching for the right school, watch out for those that are simply student mills, set up to pull in student loan money rather than provide training. There are substantial differences between public and private schools: namely, public schools are regulated by the state, while private institutions very often determine their own quality standards.

  "With a private school, you're dependent on the quality of the people running the school," said Leon Wood, associate dean of Long Beach City College's trade and industrial division. "Some of these schools are outstanding and some are not so good." James Russell, an instructor at Los Angeles Trade-Technical College, agreed: "One generally has to be cautious when dealing with private schools."

- Does the school have a high placement rate, and, if so, does it make available a list of recent placements? "Ask about the attrition rate," Freedman recommended. "If it's high, there's a reason why people are dropping out. Placement is everything. Part of a school's responsibility is to place students in jobs after graduation."

When enrolling in a vocational program, it is important to know exactly what job you will be qualified for upon receiving the certificate, diploma, or degree and how your training will translate into a paid position. Be sure that you are learning something useful, a skill that can be directly applied to the job market. At the Nick Harris Detective Academy in Van Nuys, graduates of the private investigator courses are eligible for lifelong free job placement assistance.

A well-established technical school such as Northrop University's Institute of Technology, which offers programs in avionics and airframe, power plant, and helicopter maintenance, encourages students to work in their field while studying to better their chances of employment after graduation, said Catherine Graham, a Northrop University admissions counselor.

- Ask whether the school has minimum entrance requirements besides the ability to fill out loan applications and/or registration materials. "Basically, 50 percent of the people who apply don't pass our entrance test," said Freedman, adding that ATI's exam is written on an 11th-grade level, as are most good vocational school tests. "You can't make everybody a computer technician. You have to have the aptitude for it."

  While some technical programs require incoming students to have a high school diploma or GED certificate, most vocational schools simply ask that students be a minimum of 18 years old and able to pass the entrance exam. At certain technically oriented schools, preparatory classes may be available for students who don't feel they're ready for a particular course of study.

- Does the school have an assessment or counseling office, or, at the very least, an obligation-free information session in which prospective students can determine whether their interests and career goals are accommodated by the school? "I would recommend that a prospective student ask to sit in on a class to get a real feel for the program," Freedman said.

  If you're not decided on a program but would like to

learn a new skill, most community colleges have a placement center or career office where potential students—virtually anyone who is interested—can have their abilities and aptitudes assessed.

"Prospective students are going to walk out with an appraisal of their skills and a possible career suggestion," said Irving Weinstein, vice president of academic affairs for Los Angeles Southwest College. "If they at least have a general idea of what they're interested in, they can explore different career options."

- Lastly, don't be too easily wowed by a school with elaborate training facilities and outrageous tuition fees. The money could be spent in the wrong places. "Some schools are better than others. Price is not everything," Freedman said. Since it's a buyer's market, be discriminating. There are many different schools to choose from.

Unfortunately, the test of whether one's money was well spent is not determined until after graduation. "A lot of people new to a field will take a school's pitch at face value and they'll get lousy training and feel they've been had," said John Stevenson, president of John Stevenson & Associates, a career consulting service in Los Angeles. "The quality of education is something you almost have to find out the hard way."

Champions of public education contend that the scope and affordability of community colleges, which offer up to 200 vocational programs in everything from welding and auto shop to horticulture and nursing, are more desirable than private institutions. The same basic education, they argue, can be obtained for a fraction of the price of a private education—a maximum of $50 per semester. What's more, much of the coursework can be applied toward a four-year degree.

Private schools, on the other hand, tout their more personal learning environment, which they say is tailored to the needs of individual students and often takes less than half the time. Individualized attention does have its price, however. Private schools such as Flavio Beauty College in Torrance charge around $4,400 for a 10-month course in cosmetology. The Nick Harris Detective Academy charges $3,940 for its full-time, seven-week masters investigation course.

Whether a better education can be obtained from a public or private school ultimately depends on the goals and interests of the individual student. Many job seekers don't have the time or inclination to learn in a college-like atmosphere where their vocational courses must be supplemented by general education classes, and so go the private route.

"A person who goes to a private school is mostly self-motivated," said Russell, who teaches courses in the extended opportunity program at L.A. Trade-Tech. "We'll provide 1,600 hours of instruction in two years. They'll do 1,600 hours in one year. Most students at private schools are not high school students just coming out. They might have a family. They might need to take the quick approach."

SELECTED COMMUNITY COLLEGES AND UNIVERSITY EXTENSION PROGRAMS

Community Colleges

Cerritos Community College
11110 E. Alondra Boulevard
Norwalk, CA 90650
213/860-2451

Cypress College
9200 Valley View Street
Cypress, CA 90630
714/826-9999

East Los Angeles College
1301 Brooklyn Avenue
Monterey Park, CA 91754
213/265-8650

El Camino College
16007 Crenshaw Boulevard
Torrance, CA 90506
213/532-3670

Fullerton College
321 E. Chapman Avenue
Fullerton, CA 92634
714/992-7000

Long Beach City College
4901 E. Carson Street
Long Beach, CA 90808
213/420-4206

Los Angeles City College
855 N. Vermont Avenue
Los Angeles, CA 90029
213/669-4000

Los Angeles Harbor College
1111 Figueroa Place
Wilmington, CA 90744
213/518-1000

Los Angeles Pierce College
6201 Winnetka Avenue
Woodland Hills, CA 91371
818/347-0551

Los Angeles Southwest College
1600 W. Imperial Highway
Los Angeles, CA 90047
213/777-2225

Los Angeles Trade-Technical College
400 W. Washington Boulevard
Los Angeles, CA 90015
213/744-9019

Los Angeles Valley College
5800 Fulton Avenue
Van Nuys, CA 91401
818/781-1200

Mount San Antonio College
1100 N. Grand Avenue
Walnut, CA 91789
714/594-5611

Pasadena City College
1570 E. Colorado Boulevard
Pasadena, CA 91106
818/578-7123

Orange Coast College
2701 Fairview Road
Costa Mesa, CA 92628
714/432-0202

Rio Hondo College
3600 S. Workman Mill Road
Whittier, CA 90608
213/692-0921

Saddleback College
28000 Marguerite Parkway
Mission Viejo, CA 92692
714/582-4500

Santa Monica College
1900 Pico Boulevard
Santa Monica, CA 90405
213/450-5150

West Los Angeles College
4800 Freshman Drive
Culver City, CA 90230
213/836-7110

University Extension Programs

UC Irvine Extension
Post Office Box AZ
Pereira Drive
Irvine, CA 92716
714/856-5414

UCLA Extension
10995 Le Conte Avenue
Los Angeles, CA 90024
213/825-9971

UC Riverside Extension
3637 Canyon Crest Drive
Riverside, CA 92521
714/787-3806

University Extension
Cal State Dominguez Hills
1000 E. Victoria Street
Carson, CA 90747
213/516-3741

University Extension
Cal State Los Angeles
5151 State University Drive
Los Angeles, CA 90032
213/343-4900

Also see Chapter 28 for a listing of specialized colleges and educational institutions.

PROFESSIONAL ORGANIZATIONS

Accrediting Council of Continuing Education and Training (ACCET)
530 E. Main Street
Suite 501
Richmond, VA 23219
804/648-6742

Association of Independent Colleges and Schools
One Dupont Circle, NW
Suite 350
Washington, DC 20036
202/659-2460

Better Business Bureau of the Southland
6101 Ball Road
Cypress, CA 90630
714/527-0680

California Association of Private Post-Secondary Schools
9570 W. Pico Boulevard
Los Angeles, CA 90035
213/553-8626

California Department of Education
Private Post-Secondary Education Division (PPED)
601 W. Fifth Street
Los Angeles, CA 90071
213/620-4257

National Association of Trade and Technical Schools (NATTS)
2251 Wisconsin Avenue, NW
Washington, DC 20007
202/333-1021

California Department of Education
Student Aid Commission
Post Office Box 944272
721 Capitol Mall
Sacramento, CA 94244
916/445-0880

Western Association of Schools and Colleges
Post Office Box 9990
Mills College
Oakland, CA 94613
415/632-5000

DIRECTORIES

Accredited Institutions of Postsecondary Education (American Council on Education, Washington, DC)

Directory of Vocational-Technical Schools (Media Marketing Group, De-Kalb, IL)

Guide to Community, Technical and Junior Colleges (American Association of Community and Junior Colleges, Washington, DC)

Handbook of Trade and Technical Careers and Training (NATTS, Washington, DC)

SECTION
14

Careers in
Law Enforcement
and Public Safety

CHAPTER 49
. . . .

City, County, and State Law Enforcement

The sheriff, police chief, and Highway Patrol are in a continuous hiring mode.

Put out an all-points bulletin! The sheriff needs a few good men and women to enforce and uphold the law. The chief of police wants some more hired guns as well. Law enforcement agencies at the city, county, and state level—from local police departments to the California Highway Patrol—are expanding and hiring.

Though they're not economic indicators in a traditional sense, L.A.'s problems have turned the field of local law enforcement into a growth industry that has an urgent need for labor.

In Los Angeles and Orange counties, there were a total of 26,840 sheriffs, deputy sheriffs, police detectives, patrol officers, police and detective supervisors, correction officers, and parking enforcement officers in 1987, according to the Employment Development Department (EDD). By 1992, their ranks are expected to increase to an estimated 28,090, EDD statistics show.

The LAPD has authorization to add more than 300 officers to increase its strength to 8,414, and Mayor Tom Bradley recently announced that he will seek to hire 400 more officers on top of that. The CHP employs some 4,700 traffic officers statewide and graduates around 150 cadets from the CHP Academy every five months.

"Is the Highway Patrol hiring? Are you kidding? We have

continuous hiring at this time," said Sgt. Mike Brey, local recruitment coordinator for the CHP. Even the smaller Marshal's Department, with 710 sworn deputies, regularly has openings.

As the motto of the Los Angeles Police Department, "To Protect and Serve," suggests, police officers both prevent and investigate crimes as well as perform various public services for the local citizenry, such as directing traffic, providing first aid to accident victims, and keeping order at large events.

Increasingly, they are becoming more involved in community relations programs, such as D.A.R.E. (Drug Abuse Resistance Education), sponsored by the LAPD, and S.A.N.E. (Substance Abuse Narcotics Education), sponsored by the Los Angeles County Sheriff's Department, as part of an outreach effort to raise awareness of the drug problem, enhance public confidence in law enforcement, and help the community help itself.

"We're the third-largest city in the country and we have a horrible problem right now with the cocaine and gangs in South Central L.A. We need officers with a lot of confidence in themselves, but we also have to realize that the police cannot solve this problem alone," said Sgt. Joe Peyton, officer in charge of the LAPD's development division.

At large agencies, law enforcement officers are often assigned to specific details, such as narcotics and gang units, special weapons and tactics (SWAT) teams, bomb squads, or air patrols. "The diversity of the department and the range of assignments is one of the reasons the LAPD is considered over other law enforcement agencies," Peyton said. "We are a professional choice and offer good benefits."

Many specialized assignments require expertise, seniority, and a good work performance record. Motorcycle officers at the CHP, for example, must score high on a difficult riding test that is passed by only about half of the candidates who take it. "It's very unlikely that anyone without experience will be able to pass the test, although it has happened before," Brey said. "Riding a motorcycle is considered hazardous duty. It requires a whole different set of driving skills. You have to be one of the best riders to be a motorcycle officer."

In the short term, the most jobs in local law enforcement will be available with the Sheriff's Department, which plans to expand from 7,000 to 9,000 deputies by 1993.

"We're looking for a lot of deputies," said Deputy Tim Murakami of the sheriff's recruitment unit. "We're pushing hard right now." In addition to patrolling unincorporated areas of the county, sheriff's deputies maintain county jails, act as baliffs in Superior Court, and provide inmate transportation.

While a career in law enforcement may not be at the top of everyone's list, there are numerous reasons to consider it as a career possibility, Peyton said: the exciting nature of the work; the personal satisfaction in performing a valuable service to the community; the ready availability of jobs; and the wide array of work assignments, just to name a few.

"A career in law enforcement is a career in public service, so if you're a person who feels as though you'd be motivated to help other people, it's for you," Brey said. "In the Highway Patrol, we render many services to the public. For as many enforcement contacts that are made, just as many are for motorist service. You really get a feeling of satisfaction."

Next to the community service aspect, perhaps the most compelling reason for entering law enforcement is the money factor. Entry-level positions at the four agencies mentioned pay more than $30,000 a year. The minimum education requirement is a high school diploma or GED certificate. Applicants with a bachelor's degree can make over $35,000. And that's just to start.

"We're talking about a pretty healthy salary for someone with a minimum of a high school diploma or GED coming on the department," Peyton said.

A few exceptional years on the job can lead to a promotion to the sergeant rank, where some officers with seniority make over $50,000 annually. Moving up to lieutenant and then captain results in an even higher salary. Captains, who typically have 15 years of experience, command $70,000 to $80,000 a year.

At the LAPD, officers can earn bonus pay for marksmanship skills, bilingual ability, longevity, hazardous duty, and additional education. During an officer's years on the force, the department will reimburse tuition expenses for approved degree programs at rates equal to current Cal State University fees. The LAPD also offers scholarship and professional training programs to officers who wish to continue their education.

Despite the stereotypical macho image of law enforcement, you don't have to be a man to be effective or to make rank. "We would like to see as many women as possible. Right now we have five female captains," said Murakami. "A lot of the job is not so much physical force as it is your ability to communicate. There's a lot more to police work than physical size."

Although law enforcement officers are well compensated once they are hired, getting the job is by no means easy. Applicants must undergo a series of intensive screenings, evaluations, and tests that can last four to six months before they are given the green light. "This year we'll probably hire approximately 750 officers, but in doing so we'll probably have to look at 12,000 to 13,000 people to end up with those 750," Peyton said.

Most candidates fall down during the first step of the LAPD's seven-part screening process: the pass/fail written exam that tests for reading comprehension, spelling, and vocabulary, Peyton said. Writing skills are important because a lot of police work involves writing reports. The next hurdle for would-be officers is an interview, followed by a physical abilities test, medical exam, and psychological evaluation.

Next, LAPD applicants are subject to a thorough background investigation that includes a review and assessment of their work history, prior involvement with law enforcement, driving record, use of drugs, arrests, and moral character. An officer candidate can have no felony convictions. Even "high-grade" misdemeanors, such as driving under the influence or burglary charges reduced to trespassing, can be grounds for disqualification, Peyton said.

The minimum age requirement for most law enforcement officers is 20 or 21. The maximum age for applying is 35 (31 for the CHP). Once officers and deputies are approved as candidates, they enter an academy and begin drawing a salary while in training.

The screening at smaller suburban departments can be just as intense as at larger agencies. "If you don't give us a complete, honest answer on your background, we'll confront you with it," said Lt. Gregg Henderson of the 221-officer Pasadena Police Department. "In terms of stress, working in an agency our size is just as stressful as working for something the size of the LAPD. Anything can happen at any time, no matter where or what size you are. You can always come into an extremely volatile situation."

Upon graduating from the police academy, new officers with the LAPD must work in the field on patrol for at least a year and are subject to a year-and-a-half probationary period. "We allow the officer to develop into the position," Peyton said. After probation, officers may request a transfer. At the Sheriff's Department, beginning deputies are assigned to the downtown Hall of Justice jail for a year before they may go out on patrol and submit a transfer request. After probation, however, their job prospects are wide open.

"Whatever specialized interest or skill you have, you can find it on this job, whether you're an engineer or an artist," said Murakami of the sheriff's recruitment unit. "We have about 250 assignments in all."

KEY EMPLOYERS OF LAW ENFORCEMENT OFFICERS

California Highway Patrol
4016 Rosewood Avenue
Los Angeles, CA 90004
213/736-3468

City of Anaheim
Police Department
425 S. Harbor Boulevard
Anaheim, CA 92805
714/999-1910

City of Beverly Hills
Police Department
450 N. Crescent Drive
Beverly Hills, CA 90210
213/285-2128

Culver City
Police Department
4040 Duquesne Avenue
Culver City, CA 90232
213/837-1221

City of Hawthorne
Police Department
4460 W. 126th Street
Hawthorne, CA 90250
213/970-7975

City of Huntington Beach
Police Department
200 Main Street
Huntington Beach, CA 92648
714/536-5936

City of Inglewood
Police Department
One Manchester Boulevard
Inglewood, CA 90301
213/412-5200

City of Los Angeles
Police Department
Parker Center
150 N. Los Angeles Street
Los Angeles, CA 90012
213/386-LAPD

City of Pasadena
Police Department
142 N. Arroyo Parkway
Pasadena, CA 91103
818/405-4505

City of Santa Ana
Police Department
24 Civic Center Plaza
Santa Ana, CA 92701
714/647-5030

City of Santa Monica
Police Department
1685 Main Street
Santa Monica, CA 90401
213/458-8491

Los Angeles County Marshal's
Department
210 W. Temple Street
Los Angeles, CA 90012
213/974-6324

Los Angeles County Sheriff's
Department
211 W. Temple Street
Los Angeles, CA 90012
213/974-4248

Orange County Marshal's
Department
700 Civic Center Drive W.
Santa Ana, CA 92701
714/834-3500

Orange County Sheriff's
Department
550 N. Flower Street
Santa Ana, CA 92703
714/647-1870

PROFESSIONAL ORGANIZATIONS

International Association of
Women Police
11 W. Monument Avenue
Suite 510
Dayton, OH 45401
513/223-2625

Los Angeles County Professional
Peace Officers Association
1910 W. Sunset Boulevard
Los Angeles, CA 90026
213/413-3650

Los Angeles Police Protective
League
600 E. Eighth Street
Los Angeles, CA 90014
213/626-5341

National Police Officers
Association of America
1316 Gardiner Lane
Suite 204
Louisville, KY 40213
502/451-7550

National Sheriffs' Association
1450 Duke Street
Alexandria, VA 22314
703/836-7827

PROFESSIONAL PUBLICATIONS

The California Highway Patrolman (Sacramento, CA)
California Peace Officer (Sacramento, CA)
The National Sheriff (Alexandria, VA)
Police Times Magazine (Washington, DC)
Sheriff and Police Reporter (Seattle, WA)

Today's Policeman (Los Angeles, CA)
WomenPolice Magazine (Dayton, OH)

DIRECTORIES

Directory (National Sheriff's Association, Alexandria, VA)
Law Enforcement Careers (Lawman Press, Tarzana, CA)
Law Enforcement Employment Guide (Lawman Press, Tarzana, CA)

CHAPTER 50

Federal Agent

The work is diverse and challenging, and usually top secret.

Contrary to its thrilling image, work as a federal agent isn't always exciting and action-packed. Nevertheless, the job does have a certain mystique. "There's not the type of glamour that you see in the movies," said Special Agent Jim Neilson of the FBI's Los Angeles office. "It involves a lot of paperwork, but it's also very rewarding when you've been working hard on a case and reach a successful conclusion."

Law enforcement jobs at the federal level generally offer lower starting salaries than those at local law enforcement agencies, but the work is considered more interesting and momentous because of the complex, sometimes national or international, nature of the assignments. Key employers of special agents include the Central Intelligence Agency (CIA), U.S. Customs Service, Drug Enforcement Administration (DEA), Federal Bureau of Investigation (FBI), the criminal investigation division of the Internal Revenue Service (IRS), and the U.S. Secret Service.

A special agent's primary responsibility is to investigate violations of federal laws and matters involving national security. Beginning agents are required to have a four-year college degree with at least a B average and be at least 21 years old (23 at the FBI). Because of the demanding nature of the work, special agents have a mandatory retirement age of 55. The maximum age for applying as a special agent is 35.

Including overtime, first-year Secret Service agents start at $20,381 a year, while DEA agents make $25,244. Top-of-their-class FBI agents earn $34,007—which is comparable to what the Los Angeles Police Department and Los Angeles County

Sheriff's Department pay their rookie officers with only a high school diploma or equivalent.

However, at the mid- to senior-level management ranks, the pay scales start to even out. Journey-level drug agents, for instance, earn about $41,000. At the IRS, top managers in the criminal investigations division make upward of $60,000, eventually topping out at $83,930.

While patrol officers for local police departments spend much of their time tracking down street criminals, preventing crimes, and offering public assistance, FBI and IRS agents may be involved in a sting operation that exposes payola scandals in the state legislature or white collar corruption in the stock market. They may also investigate bank fraud, money-laundering schemes, securities violations, extortion, racketeering, or embezzlement.

FBI agents may employ clandestine surveillance techniques, including physical observation, room bugging, and wiretapping, to gather information vital to a case in which the U.S. government is or may be an interested party. They also use computer databases to compile information about suspects and organizations. "If you're working on white collar crime, there's a good amount of work done in the office," Neilson said.

The U.S. Secret Service originally was founded as a bureau of the Treasury Department at the close of the Civil War to guard against counterfeiting. Secret Service agents rotate between protecting the president, vice president, and visiting foreign dignitaries and investigating counterfeit currency and documents as well as stolen and forged U.S. government checks and bonds. They also investigate major credit card and bank fraud.

One special agent stereotype consistent with the image is undercover work. It's alive and well, especially at the FBI, DEA, and CIA. **CIA operations officers** collect information on secret organizations, protect classified activities and institutions from foreign interests, and carry out covert operations to support policy goals of the United States government. Their true CIA relationship is hidden from all but discreet immediate family members and selected associates who have a "need to know."

Many federal agent positions offer the opportunity to travel. At the CIA, about half an operations officer's career is spent abroad on tours of duty lasting two to four years. Operations officers gather intelligence about foreign countries and recruit informants to supply the U.S. government with useful information about hostile governments, terrorism and drug trafficking, potential military coups, and other unadvertised international developments.

"Not all of our positions are overseas, but there is an opportunity to travel," said CIA spokesman Mark Mansfield in McLean, Virginia. "Some of our people spend their whole careers in Washington, D.C. We are an enjoyable place to work. It's a very challenging environment."

Special agents at the IRS defy another stereotype, that of bespectacled auditors buried beneath mounds of paperwork. In the IRS's criminal investigation division, the bulk of a special agent's work is in the field—interviewing sources, meeting with informants, accompanying the U.S. attorney during trials, and conducting surveillances and raids—as opposed to just analyzing financial documents in an office. "Just poring through records is a very small portion of the job," said C. Philip Xanthos, branch chief with the IRS's criminal investigation division in Los Angeles.

"Most of our people conduct a wide variety of investigations. One day they might be interviewing a world-famous actress, another day a bank president, and the next day a pimp on the street. The real attraction of this job is diversity, which you can't compare in dollars and cents."

Since IRS agents must be able to identify bogus bookkeeping techniques found in financial fronts, they must have an extensive accounting background, including 15 semester hours of college accounting courses and 9 hours of business-related subjects. "There's not a lot of auditing, but you have to know how to read books and records to be able to follow the paper trail," said William Gilligan, also of the IRS's L.A. office.

The IRS gives applicants with degrees in the humanities equal consideration, Gilligan said. More than book knowledge is required for the job, however. "Someone with a high grade point average will certainly catch our eye, but how he or she performs during the interview is equally important. We look for people with good judgment who can think on their feet and have a sense of independence," he said.

DEA agents are charged with enforcing the drug laws of the United States. Their duties include infiltrating illicit drug rings on an undercover basis and arresting drug traffickers, an assignment that proves to be highly dangerous at times.

Significantly, the drug laws have received new attention under the Bush administration to the point of involving the military in the "war on drugs." When former Panama strongman Manuel Noriega turned himself in after being rousted by U.S. troops in 1989, he was placed in the custody of drug agents and indicted on drug-trafficking and money-laundering charges.

Enforcing the drug laws also means regulating legitimate drug companies, so there are a certain number of nonhazardous positions available to applicants who aren't willing to put their life on the line for their job, according to Special Agent June Miller of the DEA's Los Angeles office.

With relatively low pay and frequent exposure to large amounts of drugs and cash, DEA agents, like all federal agents, must have a high degree of professional ethics and personal integrity. Agents who have skimmed money from illegal cash reserves they helped confiscate during raids have not only lost their jobs but also faced criminal prosecution.

Customs agents, like DEA and IRS special agents whom they assist on big, multi-agency operations, are on the lookout for large-scale fraud, the illegal shipment of narcotics across international borders, money-laundering schemes, and the like. Although they are not recognized as peace officers in California, customs agents are law enforcement officers and most carry a gun.

The job of customs agent requires a watchful eye and the ability to smell a rat. "When you're trying to detect a smuggler, you have to be aware. You have to be observant as to what they're really saying as opposed to what they seem to be saying," said Maryanne Noonan, public affairs officer for the U.S. Customs office in Los Angeles.

Becoming a special agent entails a series of written and physical examinations, an extensive background investigation, a panel interview, a security check, a review of an applicant's credit history, and, at the IRS, an income tax audit before selection. Upon receiving an appointment, DEA and FBI agents are required to attend a 14-week training academy in Quantico, Virginia. All other special agents are required to enroll in a 15- to 18-week training program in Glynco, Georgia. "Our agents are cops, so it's similar to police training," said Noonan of U.S. Customs.

Applications for special agent positions are routed through the federal Office of Personnel Management in Washington, D.C., and newly trained special agents are usually assigned where they are most needed, not where they would prefer to work.

Working as an agent translates into a career of continuous education. CIA operations officers typically must learn one or more foreign languages and study other cultures to enhance their effectiveness in strange lands. IRS agents need to stay abreast of changes in the tax laws. Sting operations at the FBI may require in-depth knowledge of stock markets or commodities exchanges. "It's a professional career and we're looking for people who are educated" and willing to learn, Neilson said.

The 1990s will be a good time to enter the special agent field, particularly in Southern California, as the local branches of many federal agencies are facing a staffing crisis due to attrition and transfers caused by the high cost of living and relatively low starting salaries, according to a recent Federal Executive Board proposal for salary reform. Yet starting in Los Angeles can be beneficial to an agent's career.

"Our people are very strong in practical field experience, which is what you're looking for in a front-line manager," Xanthos said. "Los Angeles is the seedbed of every fraud and every illegal activity known to mankind. But this is valuable experience. You have so much to sell when you go competing for jobs in other areas. The experience you get here helps you career-wise for a long time to come."

What Law Enforcement and Federal Agent Jobs Pay

Agency	*Starting Salaries	Minimum Education
LAPD	$32,500–$38,000	high school diploma
Marshal's Dept.	$31,944–$39,564	high school diploma
Sheriff's Dept.	$31,824–$35,544	high school diploma
CHP	$30,252–$36,132	high school diploma
Federal Agencies		
FBI	$34,007–$42,601	bachelor's degree
DEA	$25,244–$35,825	bachelor's degree
Secret Service	$20,381–$25,244	bachelor's degree
U.S. Customs	$20,381–$25,244	bachelor's degree
IRS	$20,381–$25,244	bachelor's degree

* Entry-level salaries at the upper end reflect additional education, experience, or expertise. Federal agent salaries include 25 percent overtime, which is automatically factored into an agent's salary.

SOURCE: Law enforcement agencies.

The Staff Size of Selected Federal Agencies in L.A. County

Agency	Positions
Internal Revenue Service (IRS)	4,074
U.S. Customs Service	696
Federal Bureau of Investigation (FBI)	671
Drug Enforcement Administration (DEA)	132
U.S. Secret Service	110

SOURCE: Federal Executive Board. October 1988.

KEY EMPLOYERS OF FEDERAL AGENTS

**Bureau of Alcohol, Tobacco &
Firearms**
United States Treasury Department
Criminal Enforcement Division
300 N. Los Angeles Street
Los Angeles, CA 90012
213/894-4812

Central Intelligence Agency (CIA)
Post Office Box 3127
South El Monte, CA 91733
818/442-4845

**Drug Enforcement Administration
(DEA)**
United States Department of Justice
350 S. Figueroa Street
Suite 800
Los Angeles, CA 90071
213/894-4258

**Federal Bureau of Investigation
(FBI)**
United States Department of Justice
11000 Wilshire Boulevard
Los Angeles, CA 90024
213/477-6565

Internal Revenue Service
Criminal Investigation Division
300 N. Los Angeles Street
Los Angeles, CA 90012
213/894-4151

Secret Service
United States Treasury Department
300 N. Los Angeles Street
Los Angeles, CA 90012
213/894-4830

United States Customs Service
Office of Investigations
300 S. Ferry Street
Terminal Island, CA 90731
213/514-6231

**United States Department of
Agriculture**
Criminal Investigation Division
300 N. Los Angeles Street
Los Angeles, CA 90012
213/894-7268

**United States Department of
Justice**
Organized Crime & Racketeering
Section
300 N. Los Angeles Street
Los Angeles, CA 90012
213/894-5812

PROFESSIONAL ORGANIZATIONS

Association of Federal Investigators
1612 K Street, NW
Suite 506
Washington, DC 20006
202/466-7288

Association of Former Agents of the U.S. Secret Service
Post Office Box 11681
Alexandria, VA 22312
703/256-0188

Association of Former Intelligence Officers
6723 Whittier Avenue
Suite 303-A
McLean, VA 22101
703/790-0320

Federal Law Enforcement Officers Association
106 Cedarhurst Avenue
Selden, NY 11784
516/698-0179

Friends of the FBI
1001 Connecticut Avenue, NW
Room 1135
Washington, DC 20036
202/223-5110

Society of Former Special Agents of the FBI
2416 Queens Plaza S.
Room 312
Long Island City, NY 11101
718/361-0051

RECOMMENDED READING

Phillips, David A. *Night Watch.* New York: Atheneum, 1977.

DIRECTORIES

Directory (Association of Federal Investigators, Washington, DC)
Directory (Federal Criminal Investigators Association, Chicago, IL)
Handbook of Federal Police and Investigative Agencies (Greenwood Press, Wesport, CT)

FOR FURTHER INFORMATION ON FEDERAL AGENTS

Federal Job Information Center
Office of Personnel Management
Third Floor
845 S. Figueroa Street
Los Angeles, CA 90017
213/894-3360

Government Printing Office
Los Angeles Branch Bookstore
ARCO Plaza, Level C
505 S. Flower Street
Los Angeles, CA 90071
213/894-5841

Library of Congress
Photoduplication Service
Washington, DC 20540
202/707-5650

National Technical Information Service
U.S. Department of Commerce
5285 Port Royal Road
Springfield, VA 22161
703/487-4650

CHAPTER 51

Private Investigator

The job is more akin to investigative reporting than undercover crime fighting.

Give up your melodramatic notions. Private investigators don't do in real life what they do on TV. They don't get into shoot-outs or high-speed chases, and they rarely spy on unfaithful spouses anymore. But the job still entails a certain amount of intrigue, excitement, and, of course, sleuthing. There's money to be made, too.

"There isn't a private eye show I've seen that ever resembled the real private investigation profession," said John T. Lynch, president of John T. Lynch Inc., one of the largest investigation firms in Los Angeles. "We don't beat people up. We don't break down any doors. We don't harass people. We do one thing: find the truth, deliver the facts, and keep it confidential."

Despite its dangerous image, the job really is more akin to investigative reporting or auditing than it is to undercover crime fighting. Modern-day investigators spend much of their time conducting extensive background checks and searches for missing persons, witnesses, and assets—often without ever leaving the office. Although they are all licensed to carry a concealed police-size tear-gas weapon, most do not carry firearms.

Modern-day gumshoes wait for their computer search to hit a stumbling block before they take their work into the field. But when they do, watch out. "There's no one who can escape a real private investigator," said Lynch, 70, a tenacious former FBI agent.

Computer databases that allow investigators to cross-reference magazine subscription lists, voter registration records, *Who's Who* directories, and consumer buying surveys have revolutionized the industry. But traditional interviewing is still important.

"The investigative business has become a lot more sophisticated than it used to be," observed Ralph Thomas, director of the National Association of Investigative Specialists in Austin, Texas. "The field is booming. The PI's day has come. There's a lot of areas that are wide open right now."

Specific growth areas include missing persons, business intelligence, pre-employment background investigations, and bank fraud, Thomas said. In years past, the mainstay of private eye work was in divorce—determining whether one spouse was cheating on the other. However, with the adoption of no-fault divorce laws, the investigations field has changed dramatically.

But it continues to flourish. Suspicions about white collar crime, industrial espionage, employee drug use, and embezzlement, as well as security concerns over copyrighted products have helped keep investigators' hands full, said Jack Kyser, chief economist for the Los Angeles Area Chamber of Commerce.

In addition, the banning of polygraph, or lie-detector, tests to verify an employee's honesty has forced employers to obtain accurate information by other means—frequently through direct observation by an undercover investigator. "If things don't look quite right, it's easy to call in an investigator, because he or she knows what to look for," Kyser said.

The growth in the investigations field parallels the growth of the California economy. In Los Angeles County, the number of licensed private investigators virtually doubled in the 1980s, from 874 in 1980 to 1,639 in 1989, according to the California Department of Consumer Affairs.

Statewide, the number of licensed PIs rose from 2,647 to 5,832 during this period. Nationwide, the number of investigators is increasing by about 10 to 15 percent annually, Thomas said. By 1992, there will be an estimated 2,140 private detectives in Los Angeles and Orange counties, according to the Employment Development Department.

"It's a growing field, but it's a sleeper field because most people don't know about it," said Milo Speriglio, chief of the Nick Harris Detective Bureau in Van Nuys. "It's one of the few fields you can go into with just a high school education and within three years start earning a lot of money."

There are several ways to enter the profession. If you're looking to moonlight or start a new career, one way is to attend a school for private investigators, such as the Nick Harris Detective Academy in Van Nuys, selected as the nation's top nontraditional school in a survey by Gannett News Service. The academy offers two programs, a full-time, seven-week masters investigation course for $3,940, or a part-time, 22-week advanced course for $2,660.

Entry-level investigators mainly work undercover, either in surveillance or as "shoppers." Undercover investigators in a business setting primarily look for evidence of theft or drug use among employees. Going undercover entails working long hours and frequently reporting to the home agency. The job requires a sharp eye, good writing skills for the drafting of detailed reports, and the ability to stay mum when the situation calls for it.

Undercover investigators are often hired for a particular specialty, such as having an accounting background or knowing their way around a manufacturing plant, to infiltrate the business at the level where the crime or problem is occurring. On occasion, PIs are also hired to investigate the questionable activity of public officials. "We've had powerful people in public life face the music or resign," Lynch said. "And you know what happens every time? They resign."

Private investigators who work undercover and perform a second job at the client's place of business, say at an office or industrial plant, garner two salaries—one from the investigation firm and one from the company under investigation, Lynch said. "We've had undercover agents working in plants for years and years. When they came up for promotion (at their undercover place of employment), they've had to turn it down because they couldn't leave their immediate work area."

In surveillance, much of an investigator's work involves verifying insurance claims—seeing whether the person who claims to be sick or hurt really is. Proving yourself at this level can often lead to more advanced assignments. Entry-level investigators can make anywhere from $17,680 to $29,120 a year plus expenses, according to Speriglio.

Another way to enter the field is as a shopper. Shoppers make purchases, which they later return, to determine whether store employees are embezzling money at the point of purchase and whether they have friendly attitudes. Shoppers may go into a hotel, restaurant, or bar to observe the help and watch for any thefts or pocketing of cash that management may be too busy to notice.

In general, applicants for most investigative jobs need to be at least 21, have a clean criminal record, and be able to pass a drug test. Bigger agencies prefer applicants to have previous business experience or some area of expertise.

Most people in the field did not set out to become private investigators. PIs come from all walks of life—from housewives seeking diversion to retired doctors. "Ninety percent of the PIs out there came from other fields," Thomas said. "A lot have news-reporting or insurance-claims-related backgrounds, or come from the paralegal field."

Some investigators get their start by first working at a collections agency or in auto repossessions (a potentially dangerous area, since car owners who are delinquent in their payments may think you're a thief trying to steal their vehicle). A collector who develops a knack for locating people may become a skip tracer and specialize in tracking down people on the run.

From there, the next step up is to become a staff investigator and then, with experience, chief investigator for an agency, making anywhere from $17 to $22 an hour. A veteran investigator at a firm like John T. Lynch can make an annual salary of $40,000 to $50,000. Master private detectives such as Speriglio charge as much as $250 an hour for their services, including testifying as an expert witness in court.

With either three years (6,000 hours) of investigative experience or two years plus a law degree or a bachelor's in police science, criminal justice, or criminal law, private investigators are eligible to take the state licensing exam and open their own office. Licensed private investigators bill their time at around $55 an hour plus expenses, Speriglio said.

While the television show "Moonlighting" glamorized the life of private investigators, the owner of the detective agency in the series, Maddie Hayes (Cybill Shepard), *is* typical of today's real-life private eye in some respects: smart, resourceful, and female. Currently, about 40 percent of all PIs are women, said Speriglio, noting that the majority of investigators at Nick Harris are women. There is a great need for bilingual investigators, he added.

If you're the type who enjoys a structured lifestyle, a 9 to 5 workday, and the same two-week vacation every year, working as a private investigator may not be for you. "Not everybody is cut out for this sort of thing. It's good for people who like being out and about, who like being part of a solution to a crime, who can observe and report and keep their mouth shut," Lynch said.

KEY EMPLOYERS OF PRIVATE INVESTIGATORS

American Research Bureau
846 W. Sunset Boulevard
Los Angeles, CA 90012
213/628-7221

Barnes & Mitchell Inc.
3345 Wilshire Boulevard
Los Angeles, CA 90010
213/384-1800

Philip J. Burruel and Associates
879 S. Figueroa Street
Los Angeles, CA 90017
213/972-0188

Chavez & Associates Institute
7668 Telegraph Road
Los Angeles, CA 90040
213/726-2372

CPP Pinkerton
3440 Wilshire Boulevard
Los Angeles, CA 90010
213/385-4522

Foresight Investigative Group
5410 Wilshire Boulevard
Los Angeles, CA 90036
213/937-2166

Nick Harris Detectives
16917 Enadia Way
Van Nuys, CA 91406
818/981-9911

Intercept Inc.
6043 Hollywood Boulevard
Los Angeles, CA 90028
213/461-4174

J.H.R.I. Inc.
3777 N. Harbor Boulevard
Fullerton, CA 92635
714/526-7300

Kamer Investigations
13249 Sherman Way
North Hollywood, CA 91605
213/931-7768

L.A. Private Detectives & Attorney Service
106 W. Fourth Street
Suite 207
Santa Ana, CA 92702
213/628-2077

John T. Lynch Inc.
727 W. Seventh Street
Los Angeles, CA 90017
213/624-4301

Searchers Investigative Co. Inc.
3600 Wilshire Boulevard
Suite 1200
Los Angeles, CA 90010
213/383-7875

West Coast Detectives
5113 Lankershim Boulevard
North Hollywood, CA 91601
818/980-7393

PROFESSIONAL ORGANIZATIONS

**California Association of Licensed
Investigators (CALI)**
1408 Claremont Way
Sacramento, CA 95822
916/456-9908

**National Association of
Investigative Specialists (NAIS)**
Post Office Box 33244
Austin, TX 78764
512/832-0355

**National Association of Legal
Investigators**
c/o James Mazour Investigations
2507 62nd Street
Des Moines, IA 50322
313/279-8383

**Society of Professional
Investigators**
Post Office Box 3032
Church Street Station
New York, NY 10008
212/889-1656

**United States Private Security and
Detective Association**
Post Office Box 6303
Corpus Christi, TX 78411
512/888-6164

World Association of Detectives
Post Office Box 1308
Belmont, CA 94002
415/348-5895

PROFESSIONAL PUBLICATIONS

CALI Newsletter (Sacramento, CA)
Inside Detective (New York, NY)
Legal Investigator (Des Moines, IA)
Master Detective (New York, NY)
Official Detective (New York, NY)
True Detective (New York, NY)

DIRECTORIES

Investigations International All-in-One Directory (Thomas Publications, Austin, TX)
Investigators (National Business Information Inc., Omaha, NE)
NAIS Directory (National Association of Investigative Specialists, Austin, TX)
P.I. Catalog (Thomas Publications, Austin, TX)

CHAPTER 52

Firefighter and Paramedic

If you can take the heat and enjoy time off, look into firefighting.

There are few professions whose image hasn't been sullied in one way or another. But firefighters are accorded the same respect they received decades ago. Putting out blazes and coming to people's rescue has always been an honorable thing to do.

"Heroes are a vanishing breed in America. We're the last of the good guys," observed Don Forrest, president of United Firefighters of Los Angeles City Local 112. "It's a career that you stay with. Everybody in the community respects you, from little children to the elderly."

Although fire departments don't expand very often, new firefighters are continually needed to replace those who retire, are promoted, or transferred. Opportunities are routinely available at most cities and county jurisdictions. The total number of firefighters, inspectors, supervisors, and paramedics in Los Angeles and Orange counties is expected to increase from 12,860 in 1987 to an estimated 13,770 by 1992, according to the Employment Development Department.

Before they are admitted into a training program, firefighter candidates must pass a series of intensive screenings, tests, and evaluations similar to those that prospective police officers undergo. Specific guidelines about the multi-step testing process and how to prepare for it are available at fire department recruitment offices.

The Los Angeles City Fire Department (LAFD) hires between

150 and 200 new recruits a year. For this relatively small number of openings, however, there are literally thousands of applicants. "We hire constantly," said Captain Craig Hurst of the LAFD's recruitment guidance office. "The only problem is, we have so many applicants."

At the Los Angeles County Fire Department, which has 2,803 personnel compared to the LAFD's 2,485, there may be 20 to 30 openings a month, said Inspector John Tabak. The county fire department attracts anywhere from 5,000 to 7,000 applicants during each open enrollment period, which usually occurs once a year depending on staffing needs, Tabak said.

Why all the surplus of available labor? Because the City and County of Los Angeles fire departments generally pay more and offer more promotional opportunities and mobility than smaller, suburban departments, recruiters say.

Firefighters for both the city and county start at around $2,400 a month and can earn upward of $3,600 monthly. Because of the volume of applicants, the city and county fire departments can afford to be highly selective. At the county, the screening process includes a check of an applicant's credit report, citizenship, motor vehicle driving record, and criminal history, Tabak said. Applicants must be at least 18 years old, have a high school diploma or equivalent, and possess a driver's license.

At the LAFD, there's currently an 18- to 24-month waiting period for white males to start testing. For minority groups it's a year. For women, there's virtually no waiting period (see page 456). "We don't have nearly enough female firefighters," Hurst said.

The healthy salary and high level of respect firefighters command should be weighed against the unusual hours and the fact that firefighters have the highest death and injury rate of all workers in North America, Forrest said.

"One of the things that's always been an issue is someone coming into the department who is married and used to a 'normal,' 9 to 5 lifestyle," Forrest said. "In addition, statistics show that you stand a good chance of being injured."

Firefighters, who remain on call around the clock while on duty, typically work ten 24-hour shifts a month, alternating every other day. In between work stints, they get four days off. Most of the time, firefighters have to work holidays and at least one weekend day. "What a normal person does in three days, we do in one," Hurst said.

While on active duty, firefighters spend most of their time at their assigned fire station, attending ongoing classroom training, cleaning and maintaining equipment, and conducting practice drills and fire inspections. In their off-hours, they may speak before school, community, and civic groups and hold open houses to answer any questions the public may have.

During their first year, LAFD firefighters are transferred among three active battalions that receive a high volume of calls so they can gain experience as quickly as possible and be evaluated by three different captains, Hurst said.

Regardless of the time, firefighters must be ready to respond at a moment's notice when an alarm comes into the station and handle any emergency that arises. Sometimes they spend hours on end in inclement weather under adverse conditions. Fighting fires is not for the fainthearted or weak-spirited. When the situation demands, firefighters must work overtime and with ample amounts of courage, alertness, and endurance.

"Almost every night, something crazy like the First Interstate fire happens. It's a terrible thrill, but it's a real test of staying power," Hurst said.

One way to accelerate the testing process is to apply for a high-demand position. The city and county fire departments, for example, have an ongoing special need for paramedics and firefighter-paramedics, who work double-duty and are paid extra for it. At the county, firefighter specialists who are also trained as paramedics earn between $4,157 and $4,633 a month.

Unlike the position of firefighter, there rarely is a waiting period for applicants who want to test for paramedic positions at the LAFD, Hurst said. "Once they get through testing, they're put on a list and, as we need paramedics, the people at the top of the list get hired." The LAFD currently employs about 350 paramedics, he said.

In addition to two months of regular firefighter training, LAFD paramedics undergo six months of intensive medical training at either Daniel Freeman or Harbor General hospital. They then ride along with two other paramedics as an intern-trainee for 20 shifts before being assigned to an ambulance, assisting at the scene of automobile accidents, shooting incidents, heart attacks and other major medical crises.

Once hired, "uniformed, firefighting, water-squirting fire-fighters" at the county must work at least three years before being eligible to take the test to become an engineer, Tabak said. Engineers drive the trucks and pump the fire apparatus, while firefighters are on the front line during a fire, holding the hoses and entering any buildings where people may be trapped. Engineers, called firefighter specialists at the county, earn from $3,834 to $4,271 a month.

Engineers are eligible to make the rank of captain within a year, bringing in $4,500 to $5,000 a month, Tabak said. Each promotion is usually accompanied by a transfer, he added. To continue promoting upward into an even higher-paying income bracket, say from captain to battalion chief, "takes maybe 15 years depending on dedication, sacrifices, involvement, and a whole lot of luck," Tabak said. "Timing's real important."

With such long odds of gaining employment, why do so many people want to become firefighters? "Maybe it's the enjoyment of having a job where you come home feeling good," Hurst ventured. "When you go to a fire or are called to an accident, you see right away that your training and ability saved a person's life. That's gratifying and that's something we experience almost every day."

What It Pays to Fight Fires and Be a Paramedic for L.A. County

Position	Salary
Fire suppression aide	$66.05/day
Firefighter	$2,421–$3,590/mo.
Paramedic	$2,865–$3,891/mo.
Firefighter specialist (engineer)	$3,835–$4,271/mo.
Firefighter specialist with paramedic training	$4,157–$4,634/mo.
Captain	$4,532–$5,051/mo.
Battalion chief	$5,014–$6,229/mo.
Asst. fire chief	$66,795–$100,193/yr.
Deputy fire chief	$71,805–$107,707/yr.
Chief deputy	$77,190–$115,786/yr.
Chief engineer	$82,979–$124,469/yr.

SOURCE: Los Angeles County Fire Department Personnel Office. 1989 figures.

SELECTED EMPLOYERS OF FIREFIGHTERS AND PARAMEDICS

City of Anaheim
Fire Department
500 E. Broadway
Anaheim, CA 92805
714/999-1800

City of Beverly Hills
Fire Department
445 N. Rexford Drive
Beverly Hills, CA 90210
213/281-2701

City of Burbank
Fire Department
353 E. Olive Avenue
Burbank, CA 91502
818/953-8771

Culver City
Fire Department
4010 Duquesne Avenue
Culver City, CA 90232
213/202-5800

City of Gardena
Fire Department
1650 W. 162nd Street
Gardena, CA 90247
213/217-9643

City of Glendale
Fire Department
633 E. Broadway
Glendale, CA 91206
818/956-4814

City of Huntington Beach
Fire Department Training Center
18301 Gothard Street
Huntington Beach, CA 92648
714/536-5413

City of Inglewood
Fire Department
One Manchester Boulevard
Inglewood, CA 90301
213/412-5350

City of Long Beach
Fire Department
400 W. Broadway
Long Beach, CA 90802
213/436-2219

City of Los Angeles
Fire Department
200 N. Main Street
Los Angeles, CA 90012
213/485-5982

City of Monterey Park
Fire Department
320 W. Newmark Avenue
Monterey Park, CA 91754
818/307-1262

City of Orange
Fire Department
176 S. Grand Street
Orange, CA 92666
714/532-0377

City of Pasadena
Fire Department
175 N. Marengo Avenue
Pasadena, CA 91101
818/405-4655

City of Santa Ana
Fire Department
1439 S. Broadway
Santa Ana, CA 92707
714/647-5700

City of Santa Monica
Fire Department
1444 Seventh Street
Santa Monica, CA 90401
213/458-8651

City of Torrance
Fire Department
1701 Crenshaw Boulevard
Torrance, CA 90501
213/618-2920

Los Angeles County Fire Department
1320 N. Eastern Avenue
Los Angeles, CA 90063
213/267-2433

Orange County Fire Department
180 S. Water Street
Orange, CA 92666
714/744-0400

PROFESSIONAL ORGANIZATIONS

International Association of Fire Chiefs (IAFC)
1329 18th Street, NW
Washington, DC 20036
202/833-3420

International Association of Fire Fighters
1750 New York Avenue, NW
Washington, DC 20006
202/737-8484

National Association of Emergency Medical Technicians
9140 Ward Park
Kansas City, MO 64114
816/444-3500

United Firefighters of Los Angeles City
1539 Beverly Boulevard
Los Angeles, CA 90026
213/250-8904

PROFESSIONAL PUBLICATIONS

American Fire Journal (Bellflower, CA)
The California Fireman (Sacramento, CA)
Fire Command (Quincy, MA)
Fire Engineering (New York, NY)
Fire Journal (Quincy, MA)
International Fire Fighter (Washington, DC)
Journal of Fire Sciences (Lancaster, PA)

· ·

Fighting Fires Isn't Just a Man's Job

Fighting fires has traditionally been a man's job. But more and more women are now donning yellow hats and finding that the work, though physically demanding, suits them just fine. "You have to get down and dirty and smoky," said Jennifer Boscoe, a firefighter with the Los Angeles Fire Department. "The majority of people don't want to do that."

A former public relations specialist, Boscoe said she abandoned the routine of her office job because she didn't like knowing what to expect every day. With firefighting, she said, every moment is different. "I gave up a very good job for one that pushes me to the limits," Boscoe commented. "I have no regrets. Going to work is exciting. It's also fun, because you work with such a great group of people."

When asked why they want to pursue a career in firefighting, women provide answers that are no different from men: It's a respectable job that pays well; promotion opportunities are ample; and it's a line of work in which you see immediate results. "The job appealed to me because I enjoy getting out and helping people," said Linda Eddie, a senior paramedic for the LAFD who used to work as an emergency medical technician for a private ambulance company.

The LAFD, which holds quarterly orientation sessions for interested female applicants, actively encourages women to join its mostly male ranks. Currently, only 35 firefighters and 70 paramedics out of some 2,485 fire department personnel are women, said Captain Craig Hurst of the LAFD's recruitment guidance office.

"We don't have nearly enough female firefighters," said Hurst. "Women can get into the department very rapidly. In three to four months, they can be in training." For male applicants, the waiting period from the time they file an interest card to the time they are able to start training is much longer—a year for minorities and 18 to 24 months for white males, Hurst said.

After attending orientation, female applicants may take a physical evaluation test to determine whether they are strong enough to pass the rigorous training exercises necessary to become a firefighter. At the end of a month, they take this test again, Hurst said.

If they pass, they may enroll in a tutorial program to enhance their physical strength and improve their delivery for the oral interview, which they must pass to be placed on the department's active training list. With a few more months training (also paid), a strong female candidate can be out fighting fires.

"This is a career women can get into and excel at, especially if they are looking for a job that pays well and has promotion opportunities," Hurst said.

A paramedic with the LAFD for over five years, Eddie said she recently received her second promotion to senior paramedic. Getting started wasn't so easy, she said. It took her two tries to pass the department's physical agility test before she was able to start training.

"I'm at the gym almost every day off," Eddie said. "You have to be determined and you have to have the strength. They're not going to push you through just because you're female." The department shows little favoritism genderwise when it comes to physical fitness, she said.

As an example of the physical agility required of firefighters, Los Angeles County Fire Department recruits must be able to drag 150 feet of fire hose a total distance of 310 feet in 39 seconds. They also are required, among other things, to raise and lower a 60-pound section of rolled hose to the top of a 35-foot tower four times in 54 seconds. Physical requirements for the city fire department aren't much different.

While Eddie and Boscoe say they are treated as equals by their male colleagues when they are on the job, one drawback for women who work as firefighters is that their mandatory 24-hour shifts may put a strain on traditional family life. Required to clock in on holidays and at least one weekend day, firefighters typically work ten 24-hour shifts a month, alternating every other day and getting four days off between work stints.

Yet for all the nontraditional aspects associated with the job, women who have chosen firefighting as a career couldn't imagine anything they'd like better. "Women who work for the fire department tend to love the job," Boscoe said. "I don't know why more women out there aren't doing it."

Coping with Job Loss

*An unexpected termination doesn't
have to be the end of the world.*

The issue may be as simple as a personality conflict with your immediate supervisor, or as sweeping as mass layoffs implemented as part of a cost-cutting scheme. Many times, the announcement comes without warning. Whatever form it takes, job loss is nothing to take lightly. Psychologists have identified sudden unemployment as one of the three most traumatic crises in life, behind divorce and death of a loved one.

As with any major transition period, a certain amount of anxiety and uncertainty about the future is only natural. But there are steps you can take to get your career back on track, according to veteran career counselors and outplacement consultants.

"I don't care what age you are, you still have options and choices in front of you. There are a variety of directions you can go," said Camille Caiozzo, a licensed psychologist and outplacement counselor with Anthony Kane Associates in Los Angeles. "The worst thing to do is make a decision in panic."

An important first step is to not deny what just happened or start placing blame, said Brad Taft, vice president of the Los Angeles office of Lee Hecht Harrison, an outplacement consulting firm.

"Realize a decision has been made. You may not like it, you may not agree with it, but you also don't have any control over it," Taft said. "Now is the time to take control. Anybody can take away a job, but they can't take away the skills, knowledge, and experience that you have gained. Now is the time to go out there and utilize those talents for an even better opportunity."

While some time may be necessary to deal with the initial shock of a job loss, career counselors stress that it is counterproductive to dwell on any particular stage of the process, especially if you harbor resentment toward your former employer or are entertaining thoughts of filing a wrongful-termination lawsuit.

"I would recommend not suing. Bringing a suit keeps you in the same position for months or even years. You have the same emotions you did on the day you were fired," said Elaine Kaback, a career counselor who specializes in outplacement counseling. "I would recommend some kind of counseling or career help, unless it's a clear case of discrimination or bias and other people feel the same way. The whole idea is to acknowledge what happened and admit it doesn't feel good. But move on.

"The best way to start taking action is to sit down with a professional, talking through what has happened, and get ready for the next steps in planning ahead. You want someone who is objective, who can guide and coach you, not Uncle Joe or Aunt Mary or your best friend, because they can be very emotional with you. Your mind has to be clear from the clutter of the fallout."

Most firms that implement wholesale layoffs offer career counseling or outplacement assistance, in addition to federally mandated severance packages that typically include 60 days' worth of pay and benefits.

Outplacement services provide displaced employees with office space and a structured working environment which allow them to continue their established routines of getting up early, going to an office, and feeling like a productive member of the workforce.

Even if you have the resources to begin job hunting—a telephone and typewriter, maybe even a personal computer, photocopier, or fax machine—the distractions at home can become limitless if no one is encouraging you to concentrate on the matter at hand.

"A lot of people have grown into the habit of getting up and going to an office. This is what we enable them to do," said Gerry Corrigan, partner in the Los Angeles outplacement firm McCarthy Resource Associates. "The advantage to this setup is that this is a business office where the business is to find a job."

In addition to providing standard equipment in an office setting, many outplacement firms have installed in-house computer databases that connect job seekers with career exploration programs like Discover and directories like the *California*

Manufacturers Guide. Using mail merge programs, clients can also send out mass mailings broadcasting their interest in various openings.

A constructive way to deal with the hostility that being fired arouses is to pamper yourself for a few weeks—within your means, of course—and to remain physically active through an exercise program, Kaback said. "Indulge yourself, go to the beach, do something physical. Exhaustion releases a lot of the pent-up emotional blockage that comes from being so upset. Jog, walk, do aerobics. 'Just do it.' "

In general, the weeks immediately following a job loss are not the time to take a long vacation or worry about paying off all your bills. Make your minimum payments and save a little for yourself to enjoy some of life's simple pleasures, such as dining out or going to a movie.

"It's not going to be a good vacation sitting on the beach worrying about, 'Once I charge this, how am I going to pay for it?' " said Lee Hecht Harrison's Taft. "You should be shifting your job search into high gear. There's usually a period of time, a week or two, once you're hired but before you start a new job. That's the time to take a vacation."

Taft advises displaced workers to use the cooling-off period immediately following a job loss as an opportunity to take stock of their interests and abilities, and perhaps explore other career alternatives. "I've had people come back and say that this is the best thing that could have ever happened to them," he said. "Job loss allows you to put on that explorer's cap and see what is going to be a better match."

Eileen Brabender, a career counselor in private practice who also teaches career exploration strategies through UCLA Extension, has discharged clients write down a list of their "professional competencies," or marketable skills, with an explanation of how they've used them in the past. She then has them think of ways their current abilities might apply toward future endeavors or a slightly different line of work.

Take the example of an experienced computer operator who, upon being laid off, finds there is a glut of people with similar talents on the market.

"They might consider going to a company that provides sales training and then selling computers, or taking some management classes and move into managing people involved in computers. If they have some writing ability, they might think about doing some technical writing about the use of computers. Or they could get educational training and teach other people how to learn computer skills," Brabender said.

If you need to get into a new job as soon as possible, don't overlook the possibility of temporary employment. It's a viable way of making ends meet and it affords some flexibility in the search for a new career. Sometimes, temping itself can lead to a full-time job.

"It's not going to be great pay, but you will be working," said Jack Kyser, chief economist of the Los Angeles Area Chamber of Commerce. "Moreover, if you're out on a temporary assignment and you're good, you're going to be snapped up. Forget the reputation. Temping is a very viable option. You can earn enough to make ends meet and come up with some interesting job situations."

Some people take longer to get over a job loss than others. The limbo period of relative inactivity immediately following a termination may last two days or two months. But the sooner you get into a job hunt and start putting out your feelers, the sooner you will see that the sun is still shining.

A key factor in becoming gainfully employed during a career transition is attitude. Even in the opportunity-laden Southland, it's important to be aggressive and diligent in your job search. "As much as Los Angeles is where everybody says the action is, you don't just walk out, take a deep breath, and find yourself a job," said Philip W. Hauhuth, president of Forty Plus of Southern California, a nonprofit career guidance service for people age 40 and over.

Prolonging the search may only wilt your self-confidence and cause employers to start questioning the length of your hiatus. If you are involved in a plant closing, you should work fast to capitalize on your former company's good name. Start talking, work your network, and let other employers know that you're available.

"Even though the stigma of being out of a job is less than in the past, it still exists and biases some employers," Taft remarked. "They want to know why they let you go. Hunting for a new job six days after you lose your old one is a lot easier than waiting six months."

In today's unpredictable economic climate, some industry experts recommend keeping an up-to-date copy of your résumé on hand at all times, especially if there are signs that the company isn't healthy, that a wave of layoffs is imminent, or if some tension exists between you and your employer. Employers tend to make decisions for employees when there isn't a match.

"It behooves anyone to have a current résumé, so if something happens unexpectedly, it doesn't take you a week to draft a new one," Kyser said. "You can start shooting it out there in a day or two."

Finally, realize that it takes the average person, even with career guidance, three to seven months to find a new job. If you've been looking for a couple of months already, don't despair. Be patient and remember: You still have your whole life in front of you.

"I will get clients in for the first visit and they may be distressed because of a lack of focus," Brabender said. "They've wasted time, they don't know what they want to do with their life. The situation they're in might be very untenable. However, once they start planning for their future, although nothing outside has changed, their attitude shifts.

"Instead of viewing themselves as trapped, they see themselves in control and in a position of having the means to achieve a long-term goal. That is very exciting and empowering."

*SELECTED OUTPLACEMENT CONSULTANTS AND FIRMS

Camille M. Caiozzo, PhD
15235 Burbank Boulevard
Suite B-5
Van Nuys, CA 91411
818/904-3391

**Career Counseling and Assessment
  Associates**
9229 W. Sunset Boulevard
Los Angeles, CA 90069
213/274-3423

Career Planning Center
1623 S. La Cienega Boulevard
Los Angeles, CA 90035
213/276-3008

Career Transition Group
12100 Wilshire Boulevard
Los Angeles, CA 90025
213/820-4992

Challenger Gray & Christmas Inc.
11661 San Vicente Boulevard
Suite 615
Los Angeles, CA 90049
213/640-1322

Drake Beam Morin Inc.
333 S. Grand Avenue
Los Angeles, CA 90012
213/680-1661

The Ellermeyer Co.
17802 Sky Park Circle
Suite 200
Irvine, CA 92714
714/250-9541

Experience Unlimited Job Club
Employment Development
  Department
233 E. Commonwealth Avenue
Fullerton, CA 92632
714/680-7800

Experience Unlimited Job Club
Employment Development
  Department
933 S. Glendora Avenue
West Covina, CA 91790
818/962-7011

Forty Plus of Southern California
3450 Wilshire Boulevard
Los Angeles, CA 90010
213/388-2301

Forty Plus of Southern California
23141 Verdugo Drive
Laguna Hills, CA 92653
714/581-7990

Jannotta/Bray, deRecat, Gallagher
  & Parker Associates
500 S. Grand Avenue
Suite 2050
Los Angeles, CA 90071
213/895-7500

Anthony Kane Associates Inc.
2170 Century Park East
Suite 1908
Los Angeles, CA 90067
213/552-6969

Outplacement Advisory Services
10990 Wilshire Boulevard
Los Angeles, CA 90024
213/312-9000

Univance Outplacement
  Consultants
2049 Century Park East
Suite 2290
Los Angeles, CA 90067
213/552-6969

Vocational Training Consulting
  Services
6363 Wilshire Boulevard
Suite 210
Los Angeles, CA 90048
213/651-5102

* Inclusion in this list in no way implies endorsement.

PROFESSIONAL ORGANIZATIONS

Association of Outplacement
  Consulting Firms
c/o O'Donnell Associates
364 Parsippany Road
Parsippany, NJ 07054
201/887-6667

International Society of Pre-
  Retirement Planners
c/o L. Malcolm Rodman
11312 Old Club Road
Rockville, MD 20852
301/881-4113

National Association of Career Development Consultants
145 Oak Hill Plaza
King of Prussia, PA 19406
215/265-6266

National Career Development Association
5999 Stevenson Avenue
Alexandria, VA 22304
703/823-9800

RECOMMENDED READING

Allen, Jeffrey. *Finding the Right Job at Midlife*. New York: Simon & Schuster, 1985.

Breidenbach, Monica E. *Career Development: Taking Charge of Your Career*. Englewood Cliffs, NJ: Prentice-Hall, 1988.

Dolan, Richard C. *Fresh Starts: Charting a New Career* Chicago: Pluribus Press, 1984.

Falvey, Jack. *What's Next? Career Strategies After 35*. Charlotteville, VT: Williamson Publishing Co., 1987.

Hecklinger, Fred J., and Curtin, Bernadette M. *Training for Life: A Practical Guide to Career and Life Planning*. Dubuque, IA: Kendall-Hunt, 1984.

Nicholson, Nigel. *Managerial Job Change: Men and Women in Transition*. New York: Cambridge University Press, 1988.

Robbins, Paula. *Successful Midlife Career Change: Self-Understanding and Strategies for Action*. New York: AMACOM, 1980.

Weinstein, Bob. *How to Switch Careers*. New York: Simon & Schuster, 1985.

Wolfer, Karen S., and Wong, Richard G. *The Outplacement Solution: Getting the Right Job After Mergers, Takeovers, Layoffs & Other Corporate Chaos*. New York: John Wiley, 1988.

Conducting the Job Search

CHAPTER 53

Résumé Writing

A winning résumé can serve as your "sales brochure."

In this, the age of desktop publishing, a résumé should be as visually attractive as it is functional. It should have a simple, clean design with understandable organization that makes your experience and accomplishments easy to identify. Keep in mind that its primary purpose is to obtain an interview. Therefore, you should save a lot of verbiage for the interview itself.

There are two basic types of résumés: reverse chronological and functional. A reverse chronological résumé organizes your experience by date, beginning with your most recent position and working back 10 to 15 years, or however far seems appropriate and relevant. This format is used mostly by recent graduates with limited job experience and job seekers with a stable, progressive work history relating to their career goal.

A functional résumé affords the opportunity to showcase your qualifications in terms of work categories, irrespective of time or place. This approach also allows you to group your experience according to areas of expertise. It is used mostly by experienced professionals who wish to stress their accomplishments rather than workplaces, employment dates, and job titles.

As a starting point, your résumé should contain your name, address, and telephone number centered at the top of the page. On a typical résumé, the objective usually comes next. Leave it out. A more appropriate place to mention your career intentions is in the cover letter.

In lieu of an objective, you may want to include a short summary of skills or a two- to three-line background statement describing your experience. In this statement, present a global yet succinct picture of the qualifications you are offering an employer in 25 words or less. This provides a quick look at what you've been doing. The body of the résumé then fills in the details. A statement for a senior manager of a software company, for example, might read:

> Twenty-two years' experience in all aspects of software development, management, and business acquisition, including strategic planning and marketing support in the aerospace industry.

In a reverse chronological résumé, education comes either next (for recent graduates) or last (for experienced professionals). List in reverse order all degrees conferred and unversities attended, along with dates of graduation, or dates attended. State major and minor fields of study. Include academic honors if awarded (such as summa cum laude). Following your education should be a few lines devoted to other honors, activities, or professional affiliations, if relevant.

Education isn't limited to college coursework. It also can mean vocational training, military experience, or other professional designations, including teaching certificates and even security clearances. If you have two or more years of college or work experience, leave out your high school education. In a functional résumé, save education for the second to last item, followed by professional affiliations.

Next comes your work experience. The aim here is to be concise and factual while highlighting your primary skills and accomplishments. Be sure to also list any experience that demonstrates problem-solving abilities. Spend two to three lines at the most describing your responsibilities. For proper format, refer to the example at the end of this chapter.

Elaborate on how you contributed to past employers. Did you increase sales, streamline operations, head a task force, reduce costs, implement a new program? Were you promoted? "Where most job seekers fall short is they don't talk about what the results of their activities were," noted Brad Taft, vice president of the Los Angeles office of Lee Hecht Harrison, an outplacement firm.

If you recently graduated or are about to, you may want to

add a category on "other experience," including any unrelated jobs, study projects, or internships that help present a truer picture of your background.

Actually drafting the résumé is really the fourth step in the job search process, Taft said. The first three are writing a career history about yourself, analyzing it in terms of your priorities and interests, and then setting a new objective.

"The key thing is not to let anybody ever put your résumé together for you," said Elaine Kaback, a career counselor and coordinator for UCLA Extension's Career Transition Program. "Part of the struggle is for you to pull up all the highlights and put together all the things you've done. It's a real confidence builder. You get a whole new perspective on yourself."

A résumé is a summary of your experience and qualifications, not a life history. Keep it brief and to the point, but include enough about yourself to convey a sense of uniqueness Try to limit your résumé to one page, unless significant experience warrants two. Avoid long sentences and large blocks of type. It is more likely to be scanned than read. Even so, make sure there are no typographical errors, or "typos," as your résumé is as much a reflection of your basic grammatical skills, communication abilities, and attention to detail as it is your work experience.

The language used in a résumé should be upbeat and positive. You want to create curiosity and interest in a prospective employer. Outplacement consultant Camille Caiozzo calls a résumé a sales brochure. As such, it should virtually read like ad copy about yourself. All sentences should begin with action verbs like: *implemented, planned, developed,* or *managed.* Use short phrases and omit subjects and personal pronouns. Do not mention yourself in the body of the résumé. Write in the third person.

In addition, do *not* include any of the following personal information in a résumé: salary history, age, weight, height, race, sex, marital status, state of health, high school graduation date, names of supervisors, or reason for leaving past employers. Moreover, avoid technical jargon, obscure acronyms (DOD, LACTC, etc.), abbreviations, personal opinions, and unnecessary wordiness.

"References available upon request" is a standard but meaningless phrase that appears at the bottom of almost every résumé. It has no use. List an additional skill or accomplishment instead. References naturally will be furnished upon request and you should have at least three to five dependable people who know your work, either as a student or as a professional, to call on. Print your references on a separate piece of paper. Be sure to request permission before using anyone as a reference.

A line about hobbies and interests is optional, but may spark some ice-breaking small talk with an interviewer who shares similar interests.

When sending résumés out by mail, be selective. Know who you're sending your résumé to and whether they're even interested. "Don't send out 1,000 at a time and sit back and wait for people to call you," Caiozzo said. "All you're doing is wallpapering the city with your résumé. Most unsolicited résumés are put in the back file anyway. Mail maybe 50 copies and place them strategically."

For a professional look, use white, light gray, or cream-colored bond with matching envelopes. Either typeset or laser print about 100 copies of your résumé and obtain an additional 200 sheets of blank paper to use for reference lists and cover letters.

Whenever you send a résumé, it should be accompanied by a cover letter, which is the appropriate place to mention your career objective. In three to four paragraphs, a cover letter should: express in a businesslike manner your interest in a position; highlight one or two skills and accomplishments the employer can use; make reference to your knowledge about the firm; and request an interview appointment. Always type or print your cover letters individually (no photocopies), and sign them with a pen.

Unless you're responding to a blind ad that lists only a post office box number, always address the cover letter to the person in charge of hiring. Get his or her exact title and department name. Find this out by calling the company. Effectiveness comes with getting to the decision maker. As a rule, at the professional and managerial levels, you never want to deal with the human resources or personnel department.

At the end of the letter, ask for the employer to contact you to set up a mutually convenient time for an interview, or suggest that you will call in a few days to set up an appointment. Again, maintain a positive tone. *Expect* an appointment. "If you say you're going to call, then call," said Kaback of UCLA Extension. "So many opportunities are missed by people who never follow up it's amazing."

Examples of a sample cover letter and a two-page reverse chronological résumé follow.

SAMPLE COVER LETTER

4617 Ocean Boulevard
Long Beach, CA 90815

April 7, 1990

Person in Charge of Hiring, Title
Department
Company
Address

Dear Mr. (Ms.) _____:

  In a businesslike manner, immediately express your interest in the position. Name the specific opening for which you are applying. Mention anyone who might have referred you to the company. Make reference to your enclosed résumé.

  Highlight one or two skills and accomplishments in your résumé and suggest ways you can contribute to this department. Demonstrate how your qualifications will benefit the employer. Explain why your background makes you the best candidate for the position.

  Describe your interest in the company, emphasizing your knowledge about this firm in particular and your familiarity with the industry in general. Show that you have researched your subject thoroughly. Keep the tone of the letter positive and upbeat. Project a sense of confidence and eagerness.

  In the closing paragraph, request an interview. State that you would appreciate the opportunity to meet with the employer personally to discuss your qualifications and career prospects further. Announce your intention to follow up with a phone call in the next few days.

Sincerely,

[signature]

Your Full Name

Encl.

SAMPLE RÉSUMÉ

JAY THOMPSON
4617 Ocean Boulevard
Long Beach, CA 90815
(213) 555-3344

BACKGROUND

Fifteen years' experience in product management, development, and promotion, including progressively senior positions in sales, marketing, and national customer service management.

EXPERIENCE

British Petroleum   **1988–1990**
Filon Division
Hawthorne, California
Marketing Services Manager

Managed customer service, advertising, public relations, and marketing research departments. Oversaw annual budget of $1.5 million. Supervised 3 managers and 8 support staff. Reduced marketing expenses by $250,000 while increasing effectiveness of the division's programs. Streamlined order entry, quoting, and pricing systems, improving processing time by 40 percent.

Avery International   **1985–1988**
Business Systems Division
Azusa, California
Product Manager

Implemented marketing and sales support programs for data processing label product lines. Launched a new laser label line, exceeding sales plan by 20 percent. Revitalized the semi-custom label line, increasing sales 50 percent.

Masco Corporation
Weiser/Falcon Lock Division   **1984–1985**
Huntington Beach, California
Marketing Manager

Initiated all marketing activities, including advertising and public relations campaigns. Created dynamic sales promotions. Conducted market research and planning. More than doubled orders and sales leads.

American Metal Products Division   **1982–1984**
Los Angeles, California
Sales & Market Development Manager

Responsible for new market development, price administration, sales forecasting, and market research. Designed and implemented a sales forecasting system that increased service levels and reduced inventories. Ensured that sales quotas were met. Enhanced sales 15 percent.

American Metal Products Division   **1980–1982**
Los Angeles, California
Product Specialist

Engaged in new product development, sales support, market research, and marketing campaigns. Augmented sales 65 percent, moving the division from a net loss position to profitability status.

Corporate Headquarters   **1975–1978**
Taylor, Michigan
Marketing Analyst

Conducted market research projects and acquisition analyses for residential and commercial markets. Reports and presentations to top management were instrumental in the success of several acquisitions and new product additions.

EDUCATION

University of Southern California   **1978–1980**
Graduate School of Business Administration
M.B.A. Marketing Management

University of Michigan, Ann Arbor   **1971–1975**
B.S. Economics and Psychology (magna cum laude)

AFFILIATIONS

Member of the American Marketing Association, Los Angeles chapter.

RECOMMENDED READING

Bolles, Richard N. *Tea Leaves: A New Look at Resumes.* Berkeley, CA: Ten Speed Press.
Bostwick, Burdette E. *Resume Writing.* New York: John Wiley, 1990.

Brennan, Lawrence D. *Resumes for Better Jobs.* New York: ARCO, 1990.

Foxman, Loretta D. *Resumes That Work.* New York: John Wiley, 1984.

Parker, Yana. *The Resume Catalog: 200 Damn Good Examples.* Berkeley, CA: Ten Speed Press, 1988.

Rosenberg, Arthur D., and Hizer, David V. *The Resume Handbook.* Holbrook, MA: Bob Adams, 1990.

Schuman, Nancy, and Lewis, William. *Revising Your Resume.* New York: ARCO.

Also see the Career Trends article at the end of Section 3 for a list of career counselors in the Los Angeles area.

CHAPTER 54

Networking

The "secret" of finding the "hidden" job market.

With your résumé and cover letter in hand, the next step is to commence the job search itself. There are several ways to obtain job leads: scour the classified sections of newspapers; visit your college or university placement center; read the trade magazines of your particular field of interest; broadcast your résumé to specific companies; and, if you are experienced, introduce yourself to executive search firms.

But the most effective method of finding employment, according to many career experts, is by networking.

Networking is regarded as an indispensable part of the job search because the majority of jobs that are available—an estimated 70 to 80 percent—*aren't* advertised, creating a situation where the preponderance of job seekers are vying for 20 to 30 percent of the opportunities, said Philip W. Hauhuth, president of Forty Plus of Southern California, a nonprofit career guidance service for people age 40 and over.

"There are jobs out there that you will never see," Hauhuth said. "It's important to let people know the person that you are, to be on the offensive rather than the defensive." Added Elaine Kaback, a career counselor and coordinator for UCLA Extension's Career Transition Program: "The people who succeed are the ones who are going to work to find work."

The term *networking* connotes a "secret" process of finding a "hidden" job market. But there's really nothing mysterious about it at all. Networking basically involves writing the head of a department or company in your field of interest, announcing your experience and career plans, and asking for 10 to 15 minutes of his or her time to discusss possible opportunities at *other* companies.

"You're never looking for a job from the people you want to talk to," Hauhuth advises. "You ask them for a few minutes of their time, and you're very careful not to overstep your bounds." Eventually, networking can lead to referrals that can lead to job interviews that can lead to a job offer. "It's nothing more than learning how to market yourself," Hauhuth said.

Proper form is important during a job search, particularly in a networking campaign. "If you go into an information interview but in reality your intent is to get a job, that can generate mistrust. You have to be careful. I've had employers tell me they've been very angry because they felt misled," said Judith Sommerstein, a career counselor with offices in Torrance and Santa Monica. Announce what your true plans are, Sommerstein said.

Working your network entails making a list of every person you know, which becomes your network contact list, and then calling or writing each name on that list for suggestions, references, and introductions to people currently employed in your field of interest with the goal of obtaining a series of information interviews and, eventually, a job offer.

With some employers, an official opening doesn't have to exist for you to have a successful meeting. If you can convince them that you would make a good addition to their staff, they may create a job for you where none existed before.

During a networking campaign, there are certain basic guidelines you should follow:

- Before starting, compile a list of companies you want to work for, and have a specific career goal in mind. Don't go at it blindly without a set objective. (For a compendium of business directories, see the reference list at the end of this chapter.)
- When putting together your network contact list, include anyone you associate with: friends, relatives, acquaintances, neighbors, business associates, old school buddies, even your dentist, doctor, accountant, or insurance agent.
- If you don't belong to a professional or college alumni association, join one. If you already do, attend all the meetings, seminars, and receptions you can. Serving on committees and volunteering with various community organizations is another great way of establishing contacts.

- Call the various visitors' bureaus and ask about upcoming conventions and job fairs. (For a list of those in the Los Angeles area, see Chapter 39 on tourism.) Take advantage of all the opportunities to network that are available.

- Another source of potential contacts is annual reports, which list the various business services (law firms, accounting firms, banks, etc.) a particular company uses. Contacts from these firms can act as a bridge to the target industry or company.

- Don't leave out anybody, because you never know who someone might know. Your 85-year-old neighbor may have a 55-year-old daughter who is the creative director of an advertising agency who has a son who works in the entertainment industry who knows someone in your field of interest, etc., etc.

- Provide a copy of your résumé and preferred company list to whomever you have a personal rapport with. Even if the people you give them to have no immediate leads, they may in the future. Use your network to its widest potential. You never know who can cut through some red tape on your behalf. Don't exclude even the remotest possibilities.

  "I counseled a gentleman who was a branch manager of a bank who found his next job through a janitor who happened to know the president of a bank down the street because he cleans his office," said Camille Caiozzo, an outplacement consultant with Anthony Kane Associates in Los Angeles. "I have a slew of these examples."

- Realize that the art of networking, according to Caiozzo, is getting beyond the first level of contacts. Eighty-five percent of the jobs found through networking are discovered at the third and fourth levels, Caiozzo said. "The key to networking is getting from one tier to the next."

- Keep track of who you've called, and don't forget to return phone calls. Get an answering machine and leave a straightforward, professional-sounding message.

Inasmuch as networking is a marketing game, it might take 10 phone calls or contacts to arrange even two appointments for information interviews. But you don't have to start with a network contact list of 100 people. If you are new to the area, it can start with your real estate agent or bank loan officer.

Information interviews serve three basic purposes: as a forum for learning about a given industry, as a source of referrals for job interviews, and as practice interviewing sessions. The tone of your conversation should be friendly, not formal, but you should dress as if you were going on a job interview. Since people in general love to give advice, frame your discussion around advice-oriented questions. And bring your résumé—just in case. On rare occasions, an information interview may turn into a job interview.

After an information interview, be sure to thank your contact and follow up with a thank-you note. It demonstrates your interest and shows employers that you are thorough. In essence, it makes a good impression and may result in a return call. It also leaves the door open for you to call back in a few weeks to ask about possible job leads or openings at that company. Before you know it, you could be sitting across from your ideal job in the next step of the job search, the interview.

RECOMMENDED READING

Bolles, Richard N. *The Quick Job-Hunting Map—Advanced Version.* Berkeley, CA: Ten Speed Press, 1990.

Bowman, David, and Kweskin, Ronald. *How Do I Find the Right Job?* New York: John Wiley, 1990.

Figler, Howard. *The Complete Job Search Handbook.* New York: Henry Holt, 1988.

Krannich, Ronald L. *Network Your Way to Job and Career Success.* Manassas, VA: Impact Publications, 1989.

Levine, Michael. *The Corporate Address Book.* New York: G. P. Putnam's Sons, 1987.

Noble, John. *The Job Search Handbook.* Holbrook, MA: Bob Adams, 1988.

Petras, Kathryn and Ross. *The Only Job Hunting Guide You'll Ever Need.* New York: Poseidon Press, 1989.

Taggart, Judith et al. *The Job Hunter's Workbook.* Princeton, NJ: Peterson's Guides, 1989.

DIRECTORIES

California Manufacturers Register (Times Mirror Publishing, Newport Beach, CA)

Career Employment Opportunities Directory (Ready Reference Press, Santa Monica, CA)

The Career Guide: Dun's Employment Opportunities Directory (Dun's Marketing Services, Mountain Lakes, NY)

Career Opportunity Index of Western Employers (Career Research Systems, Fountain Valley, CA)

Directories in Print (Gale Research, Detroit, MI)

The Directory of Corporate Affiliations (National Register Publishing Co., Wilmette, IL)

Dun & Bradstreet's Reference Book of Corporate Managements (Dun & Bradstreet, New York, NY)

Dun's Top 50,000 Companies (Dun & Bradstreet, New York, NY)

Los Angeles Business Journal Book of Lists (Los Angeles Business Journal, Los Angeles, CA)

Orange County Business and Industrial Directory (Orange County Chamber of Commerce, Orange, CA)

Southern California Business Directory & Buyer's Guide (Times Mirror Publishing, Newport Beach, CA)

Standard & Poor's Register of Corporations, Directors and Executives (Standard & Poor Corp., New York, NY)

Ward's Directory of 49,000 Private U.S. Companies (Baldwin H. Ward Publications, North Petaluma, CA)

CHAPTER 55

The Interview

To get the most out of an interview, practice, prepare, and don't let anything get in the way.

The interview is your passkey to a job opportunity. If you have gotten as far as an interview, your chances are good for turning it into a concrete offer, or at least an invitation back for a second look, so long as you take the appropriate steps beforehand. As with the other components of an effective job search, the key to coming out ahead is preparation.

Once you are invited for an interview, you need to do some homework. Namely, find out as much about the company as possible: its players, its various divisions and holdings, its range of products and services, its financial health. The first and most logical place to start is the library.

There are three directories in particular you should ask the reference librarian for: Standard & Poor's *Register of Corporations, Directors, and Executives*, Dun & Bradstreet's *Million Dollar Directory*, and Moody's manuals. Use Moody's *Complete Corporate Index* to find the specific manual your company is in. Two regional directories you may want to consult are the *California Manufacturers Register* and the *Southern California Business Directory and Buyers Guide*.

These references will tell you everything you need to know about a company on paper going into the interview. Another good source of information, at least for publicly held companies, is its most recent annual report. Trade magazines, also stocked by libraries, can provide valuable insight into current industry-wide issues as well as up-close analyses of individual companies. The higher the position, the more valuable your research becomes.

For a qualitative assessment, talk to anyone you know who works at the firm or in the industry. And if time permits and decorum allows, observe employees and watch for their attitudes as they leave for lunch or go home in the evening. The other main element of preparation involves you. Before waltzing into an interview, you need to develop a clear understanding of how your education and experience can benefit an employer. Identify your skills and interests and assess them in terms of personal qualities, then be prepared to cite examples that bring these qualities to light.

Do you work well under pressure? Are you good at finding creative solutions to problems? Are you an organizer, motivator, or team builder? Are you good at making presentations? Have you measurably improved your company's position in relation to competitors'? Have you saved your present company money? Have these, and other, examples ready to fire off.

During the interview, focus on your strengths rather than dwelling on your weaknesses, but be prepared to answer both parts of this infamous question honestly. It *will* come up. So will the interrogatory: Tell me about yourself. Ideally, at this stage in the interview, you should be able to launch into a 90-second "commercial" or synopsis about yourself.

According to Camille Caiozzo, an outplacement consultant with Anthony Kane Associates in Los Angeles, your personal synopsis should provide a thumbnail sketch of your background and touch on the following elements: early family history, educational background, early career, mid to late career, current position, goals, and personal traits. After waxing rhapsodic for a minute or two, get off yourself.

"An interviewer doesn't want to know your life history, he or she wants to know what skills you have and how they are applicable to a particular position," said Judith Sommerstein, a career counselor with offices in Torrance and Santa Monica. Don't be your own worst enemy, she went on, by saying things that aren't relevant.

Write down your synopsis ahead of time and practice going over it so you are able to talk comfortably and knowledgeably about your background. But don't have it completely memorized. You want it to sound natural, not mechanical. Another area that might benefit from some rehearsal is demeanor. Identify any nervous mannerisms, embarrassing habits, off-putting gestures, repetitive utterings, or strange vocal qualities *before* they have the opportunity to make a negative impression on a prospective employer.

"Research shows that most decisions in interviews are made in the first 5 to 10 minutes," said Caiozzo, also a licensed clinical psychologist. "Some decisions are even made in the first 30 seconds."

Entire books have been written about different interviewing strategies. Indeed, some are listed at the end of this chapter. But you don't have to "major" in interviewing to have a successful meeting with a hiring authority. Sommerstein and Caiozzo offer the following advice:

- Arrive early, no matter what it takes. Bring a magazine with you in case you have to wait. If you're offered coffee, politely decline to avoid the chance of spilling it on yourself, the table, or the interviewer. Don't let anything get in the way.

- Dress according to the work environment. For almost any type of office situation, men should wear a coat and tie. In a conservative setting, a pin-striped suit. Women should wear a skirt no higher than the knee and blazer, or business outfit. Acceptable colors are blue and gray. Carry an attaché or professional-looking portfolio to show that you are serious and organized. Bring a pad of paper and a pen for taking notes.

- Proper body language and a firm handshake are crucial. Slouching can be deadly, whether sitting or standing. Positioning yourself on the front of your chair, on the other hand, shows enthusiasm and interest. Eye contact is extremely important and projects a sense of confidence. Avoiding direct eye contact is a sign of insecurity and lack of trustworthiness. Stay relaxed and self-assured.

- Be assertive but not overbearing. You don't want to dominate the discussion; rather, part of your mission is to extract information from the interviewer by participating in a dialogue and asking questions. Find out what the company's needs, problems, and plans are—and how you can fit in. The sooner you accomplish this, the better. As a goal, strive to talk 25 percent of the time. Let the interviewer do the rest.

- Try to avoid the subject of salary until the end of the second interview. The money improves the more obvious your benefit to the company becomes. Find out what they're willing to pay, then ask for your ideal salary. Avoid stating what you earned in your last job. If the dollar figure in the company's counteroffer is still too low, ask for perquisites like a car allowance or hiring bonus if you are in a position to do so.

* Never accept a job offer on the spot. Ask for a few days to think it over. You don't want to create an impression that you're overly grateful or eager, thereby precluding opportunities for additional hiring benefits. Leave the interview on good terms and call back in a day or so to inform the employer of your decision.

If you are a serious contender for a professional position, you won't have just one interview, but three or more. The entire process from the point of initial contact to the time you receive a final answer may take six weeks. As a minimum, you should leave the first interview having met the person you would be working for and with a clear understanding of what the job entails.

After the first interview, write the employer a courtesy letter thanking them for their time and reiterating your interest in the position (if you're still interested). If you haven't heard back in a week's time, call to stress your continuing interest and to request a second interview. In the meantime, work on other leads and keep your options open. The search isn't over until you decide to accept an offer and actually start a new job. There doubtless will be many rejections along the way, but the more active you remain, the more likely you are to eventually find the right match.

RECOMMENDED READING

Allen, Jeffrey G. *How to Turn an Interview Into a Job Offer*. New York: Simon & Schuster, 1988.

Allen, Jeffrey G. *Complete Q&A Job Interview Book*. New York: John Wiley, 1988.

Biegelein, J. I. *Make Your Job Interview a Success*. New York: ARCO, 1984.

Block, Deborah Perlmutter. *How to Have a Winning Job Interview*. Lincolnwood, IL: VGM Career Horizons, 1987.

Burroughs, William S. *Job Interviews with William S. Burroughs*. New York: Penguin, 1989.

Danna, Jo. *Winning the Job Interview Game: Tips for the High-Tech Era*. Briarwood, NY: Palomino Press, 1986.

Marcus, John J. *The Complete Job Interview Handbook*. 2nd ed. New York: Harper & Row, 1988.

Pell, Arthur R. *How to Sell Yourself in an Interview*. New York: Monarch Press, 1982.

Yate, Martin John. *Knock 'Em Dead with Great Answers to Tough Interview Questions*. Holbrook, MA: Bob Adams, 1990.

CHAPTER 56

Becoming Happily Employed

Do what you love, and pick a field in which you enjoy the unavoidable day-to-day tasks. Money should be one of the last considerations.

Consider for a moment:

- The 36-year-old CPA who abandons the stuffiness of his corporate office to become a mail carrier because he enjoys the outdoors.
- The senior management consultant who tosses everything to open an ice cream store.
- The Harvard-educated real estate attorney who junks the power and prestige of a high-paying law career in favor of the Salvation Army.

These are true stories. What's going on here?

"For a lot of people, work equals drudgery—throwing the rock up the hill and then killing the identity," said Sue Moore, partner in the life management firm Stephan/Moore Associates in Santa Monica. "But we're no longer living in the Industrial Age. People have options. There's a great deal of room for individuality, especially in Los Angeles."

More than ever, the pursuit of happiness is being defined in terms of a career. People are spending so much time working that it has begun to supersede other ways of expressing themselves. A recent Priority Management Systems survey of 1,344 American and foreign business executives found that almost 60 percent worked 6 to 20 hours beyond a 40-hour work week—20 percent longer on average than a decade ago.

Career development specialists note that if you are doing something you enjoy, your identity becomes closely linked to your career. On the other hand, merely tolerating a job that demands your time and energy can be a terrible burden. A recent Gallup Poll found a majority of people, 57 percent, derive a sense of identity from their job, while 40 percent saw it merely as something they do for a living.

The happiest, it seems, lead careers that are an example of who they are.

"Anything you're doing 40 to 60 to 80 hours a week is bound to really impact on your personality. It becomes the core of your existence," Moore said. "It's important to view work as more than a paycheck. Joy and fulfillment *can* have some relevance to the job market. We're better wage earners when we pursue careers that we support emotionally because the motivation is there."

The critical first step in finding the right career involves a careful assessment of your skills, interests, and values, and determining what forms of work match these characteristics and abilities. In the final analysis, one of the last reasons you should pursue a career is money. Do what you love, and pick a field in which you enjoy the unavoidable day-to-day tasks.

After you have thought through some of these issues, and perhaps solicited the advice and services of a professional career counselor, you may decide you want to change careers. (The average person entering the workforce today will change careers three times, according to the U.S. Department of Labor.)

According to Susan Miller, a Los Angeles career counselor, three conditions must exist for someone to undergo a career transition. First, you have to be unhappy with your current situation. Next, you need a concept of what might be better. And third, you have to believe in yourself and have confidence that there's a way for you to get where you want to be.

"The question I pose is, 'If you could wake up Monday morning and go to the job of your choice, how would you define it?'" said Brad Taft, vice president of the Los Angeles office of Lee Hecht Harrison, an outplacement consulting firm. "That forces people to think, 'If I was in control and could develop my own job description, here's what it would be.' Where do you want to be in five years? That's a very important question."

Indeed, career experts say that work becomes part of your sense of self only if it has a long-term orientation. Will a standout performance lead to opportunities for advancement or promotion? Does it offer you the chance to learn new skills and grow as a person? Have other people used it as a catalyst for further development?

"Career planning and career exploration is not one time only. It's an ongoing process that should take into account developmental experiences at different stages in a lifetime," said Gladys De Necochea, counseling psychologist and assistant director of UC Irvine's Career Planning and Placement Center.

"Some people get caught in a trap that prevents them from making a career change because they're afraid of income loss, or they would stay miserable in a position knowing that it guarantees them a certain salary. But if you continue to develop your skills and look to lateral promotions in addition to advancement opportunities in the linear sense, you can avoid getting stuck. It takes a constant assessment of skills and a survey of what opportunities apply to those skills."

When does the breaking point occur for the unhappy minions? Usually at middle age, when the so-called mid-life crisis hits, Moore said. "For the people who are detoured, it hits them hard. They no longer have the emotional energy to sustain incorrect emotional patterns. Intimations of mortality start to bear down on them. They realize they have unfulfilled goals and unfulfilled desires."

Righting this imbalance, Moore says, doesn't always necessitate a major life overhaul, but simply envisioning creative ways to put the skills you already possess to another, more meaningful use. She gave the example of a client who had always dreamt of being an athlete who was studying to become a social worker. After some self-assessment, the man realized he could reconcile his two interests by becoming a sports counselor, teaching motivational skills, and dealing with the psychology of losing teams.

Identifying desirable qualities in role models is a good way of identifying characteristics we would like to develop in ourselves, Moore said. Most people are already well along the way to finding their true passion, but have somehow or other become stumped in the middle of the process, she added.

"Some folks are just at sea with what they could do. But in California, especially now, it's not always a matter of looking for an existing new job. We're living in a very creative market for jobs and businesses. A lot of people need to invent their own specialty and become entrepreneurs," she said.

An important consideration when looking for a new career within a corporate context is how well your personality fits with that of the potential company, said Jack Kyser, chief economist for the Los Angeles Area Chamber of Commerce. "You have to look at the corporate culture," Kyser said. "If you're a bright, lively type of individual, you need to make sure the company is outgoing."

Think of the long term as well, and don't be swayed too easily by the rosy descriptions of corporate recruiters. During the interview, you see only the best side of the company. Try to envision what going to work every day would be like at a certain company after the initial honeymoon phase passes. "It's just like getting married," Kyser said.

Added Taft of Lee Hecht Harrison: "Interviewing is a two-way street. You're also analyzing them. You should ask yourself, 'Is this company going to be supportive? Is this job really going to be challenging? Besides the office and the salary, what am I going to get out of it?'"

For further guidance in identifying your true passion and turning it into a career, Moore recommends reading *Finding Your Life Mission* by her partner, Naomi Stephan (Stillpoint Press, 1989).

RECOMMENDED READING

Bullock, R. J. *Improving Job Satisfaction.* New York: Pergamon Press, 1984.

Connellan, Thomas K. *How to Grow People into Self-Starters.* Ann Arbor: Achievement Institute, 1980.

Garfield, Charles. *Peak Performers: The New Heroes of American Business.* New York: Avon, 1987.

Harvard Business School. *Designing and Managing Your Career.* Boston: Harvard Business School Press, 1989.

Levering, Robert, Moskowitz, Milton, and Katz, Michael. *The 100 Best Companies to Work For in America.* New York: Signet, 1987.

Mackay, Harvey. *Swim with the Sharks, Without Being Eaten Alive.* New York: William Morrow, 1988.

Mazzei, George. *Moving Up: Digging In, Taking Charge, Playing the Power Game and Learning to Like It.* New York: Poseidon Press, 1984

Morrow, Jodie B. *Not Just a Secretary: Using the Job to Get Ahead.* New York: John Wiley, 1984.

Pines, Ayala, and Aronson, Elliot. *Career Burnout: Causes & Cures.* New York: Free Press, 1989.

Roth, William F. *Work and Rewards: Redefining Our Work-Life Reality.* New York: Praeger, 1989.

Sinetar, Marsha. *Do What You Love, The Money Will Follow.* New York: Dell, 1987.

Taylor, Harold L. *Making Time Work for You: A Guidebook to Effective and Productive Time Management.* New York: Beaufort, 1982.

Waitley, Dennis, and Witt, Reni. *The Joy of Working: The 30-Day System to Success, Wealth and Happiness on the Job.* New York: Ballantine, 1986.

Zeitz, Baila, and Dusky, Lorraine. *The Best Companies for Women.* New York: Simon & Schuster, 1988.

INDEX

A

ABC Network News, 375–376, 378
AQMD. *See* South Coast Air
    Quality Management District
A&R representative, 281
ARCO, 133, 177, 385
AT&T, 182, 184, 217–218, 384–385
Academy of Television Arts &
    Sciences, 303, 305
Account executive,
    advertising, 357
    computer, 182
    public relations, 369
Accountant, 11, 293, 382
Accountants On Call, 12–13
Accountants Overload Group, 13
Accounting, 10–16; career path, 14;
    directories, 16; key employers, 15;
    occupations, 11–14; organizations
    and publications, 16; outlook for
    jobs, 10–13; salaries, 11–14
Accrediting agencies, educational
    422, 426–427
Actor, 296–297, 302–303, 308
Actuary, 18
Ad L.A., Advertising Age, Adweek,
    354, 356, 359
Administrative Management Society,
    185, 191–192, 197
Advertising, 354–359, 382; directo-
    ries, 359; key employers, 358–359;
    occupations, 356–357; organiza-
    tions and publications, 359; out-
    look for jobs, 354–355, 358;
    salaries, 356–357
Advertising Club of Los Angeles,
    355–357, 359
Aerospace/high-tech, xviii, 97, 159,
    165–166, 168. *See also* Defense
    industry; Space, careers in
Affirmative action polices, 202
Agents,
    federal, 437–441
    insurance, 18
    literary, 274–276, 301
    real estate, 51–52
    talent, 274–279

    travel, 329, 334–338
Air Quality Management Plan, xx,
    89. *See also* South Coast Air
    Quality Management District
Airline industry, 327–333; directo-
    ries, 333; key employers, 331–332;
    occupations, 327–331; organiza-
    tions and publications, 332–333;
    outlook for jobs, 327–328, 330;
    salaries, 328–331
Airline Pilots Association, 330, 332
Airport, Los Angeles International,
    23, 406
Airport Center College, Los
    Angeles, 337
American
    Academy of Physician Assis-
        tants, 117
    Bar Association, 128, 131
    College of Hotel and Restau-
        rant Management, 312, 315
    Film Institute (AFI), 295, 298
    Hospital Association, 113,
        115–116
    Institute of Stress, 71
    Society of Interior Designers,
        83, 87
    Technical Institute (ATI),
        191–192, 421, 423
    Translators Association, 144, 149
Analyst,
    business and financial, 161, 293
    computer, 180–181, 185
    systems, 160, 185, 293
Anthony Kane Associates, 459, 464,
    478, 482
Anthony Schools, 53. *See also* Real
    estate
Apparel. *See* Fashion design
Architect, 74–77, 85, 381
Architecture, 74–79; big vs. small
    firms, 76–77; directories, 79;
    innovative examples, 74–75; key
    employers, 78; occupations,
    75–77; organizations and publica-
    tions, 79; outlook for jobs,
    74–75; salaries, 77

491

Another essential resource for your California job search!

CALIFORNIA:
WHERE TO WORK, WHERE TO LIVE

In any one year, an estimated 350,000 newcomers arrive in California. Another 500,000 move within the state. The reason for migration is simple: the desire for the better life that California offers.

In this much-needed work, employment expert Helena Barreto offers a detailed examination of 40 California communities. Among the topics covered are:

- Employment opportunities including major employers
- Housing costs and commuting conditions
- Schools and colleges
- Weather conditions
- Cultural activities
- Much, much more!

Communities covered include: Anaheim, Fresno, Huntington Beach, Monterey, Oakland, Pasadena, Redding, Sacramento, San Jose, San Luis Obispo and 30 more!

FILL IN AND MAIL...TODAY

Prima Publishing & Communications
P.O. Box 1260EB
Rocklin, CA 95677

Use Your Visa/MC and Order by Phone
(916) 624-5718
Mon.–Fri. 9–4 PST (12–7 EST)

Dear People at Prima,
I'd like to order copies of the following titles:

_____ copies of California: Where to Work, Where
to Live at $9.95 each for a total of . . . . _____

_____ copies of L.A. Job Market Handbook
at $15.95 each for a total of . . . . _____

Subtotal	_____
Postage & Handling	**$3.00**
Sales Tax	_____
TOTAL (U.S. funds only)	_____

☐ Check enclosed for _____, payable to Prima Publishing
    Charge my ☐ MasterCard ☐ VISA

Account No. _____ Exp. Date _____

Signature _____

Your Name _____

Address _____

City/State/Zip _____

Daytime Telephone _____

GUARANTEE
YOU MUST BE SATISFIED!
You get a 30-day, 100% money-back guarantee on all books.

Thank you for your order.